All the pages in this book were created—and are printed here—in Japanese RIGHT-to-LEFT format. No artwork has been reversed or altered, so you can read the stories the way the creators meant for them to be read.

P9-BYB-783

FLIP IT!

RIGHT TO LEFT?!

Traditional Japanese manga starts at the upper right-hand corner, and moves right-to-left as it goes down the page. Follow this guide for an easy understanding.

For more information and sneak previews, visit cmxmanga.com. Call 1-888-COMIC BOOK for the nearest comics shop or head to your local book store.

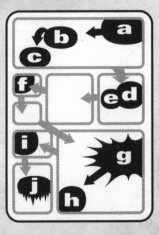

OMUKAEDESU. Volume 5 © 2001 Meca Tanaka. All Rights
Reserved. First published in Japan in 2002 by HAKUSEN-
SHA, INC., Tokyo.

OMUKAE DESU. Volume 5, published by WildStorm
Productions, an imprint of DC Comics, 888 Prospect St.
#240, La Jolla, CA 92037. English Translation © 2007. All
Rights Reserved. English language translation rights in the
United States of America and Canada arranged with
HAKUSENSHA, INC., Tokyo, through Tuttle-Mori Agency,
Inc., Tokyo. CMX is a trademark of DC Comics. The stories,
characters, and incidents mentioned in this magazine are
entirely fictional. Printed on recyclable paper. WildStorm
does not read or accept unsolicited submissions of ideas,
stories or artwork. Printed in Canada.

DC Comics, a Warner Bros. Entertainment Company.

Sheldon Drzka – Translation and Adaptation
Wilson Ramos – Lettering
Larry Berry – Design
Jim Chadwick – Editor

ISBN:1-4012-1120-8
ISBN-13: 978-1-4012-1120-2

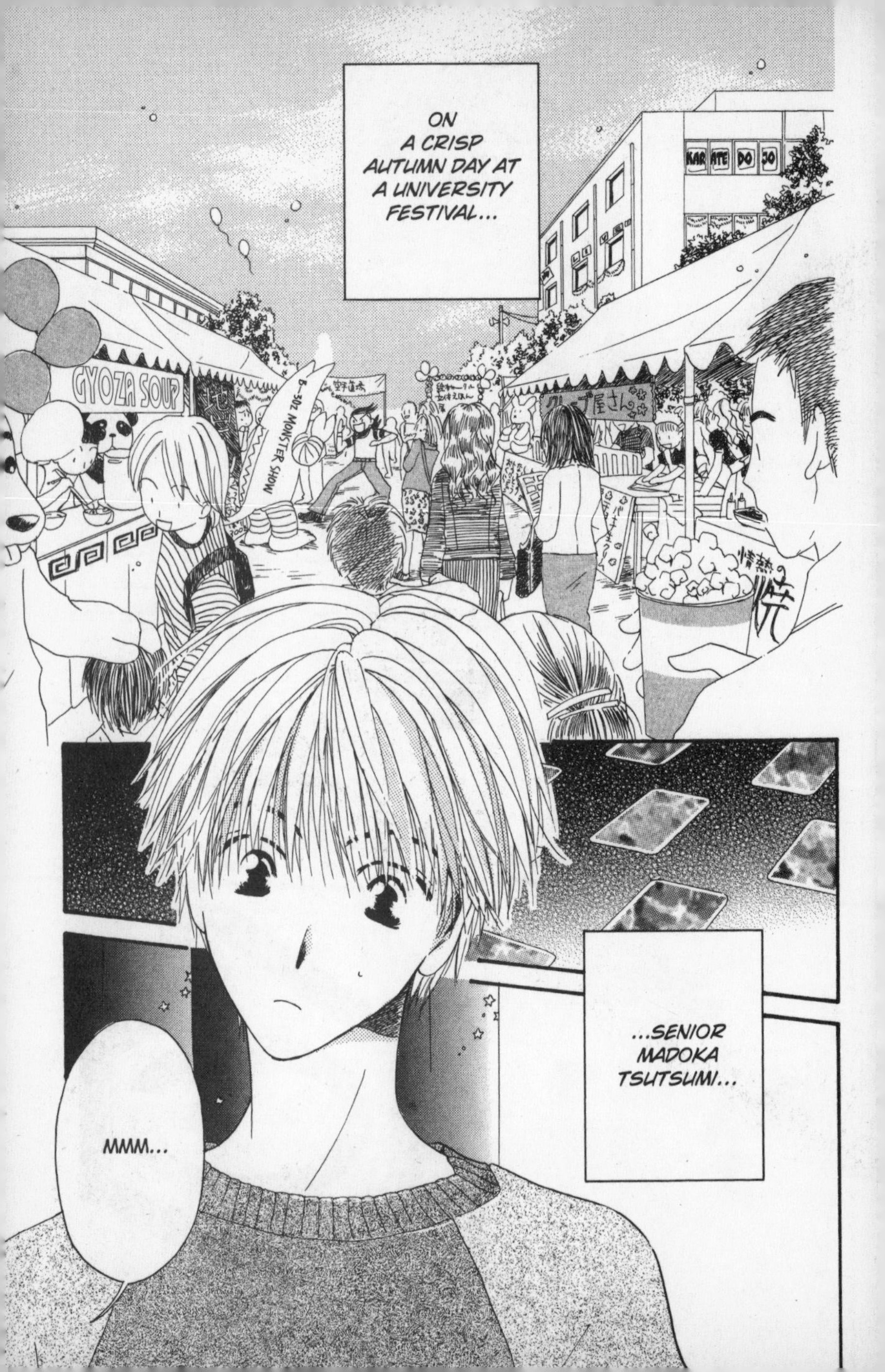
ON A CRISP AUTUMN DAY AT A UNIVERSITY FESTIVAL...
KARATE DOJO
B-302 MONSTER SHOW!
GYOZA SOUP
...SENIOR MADOKA TSUTSUMI...
MMM...

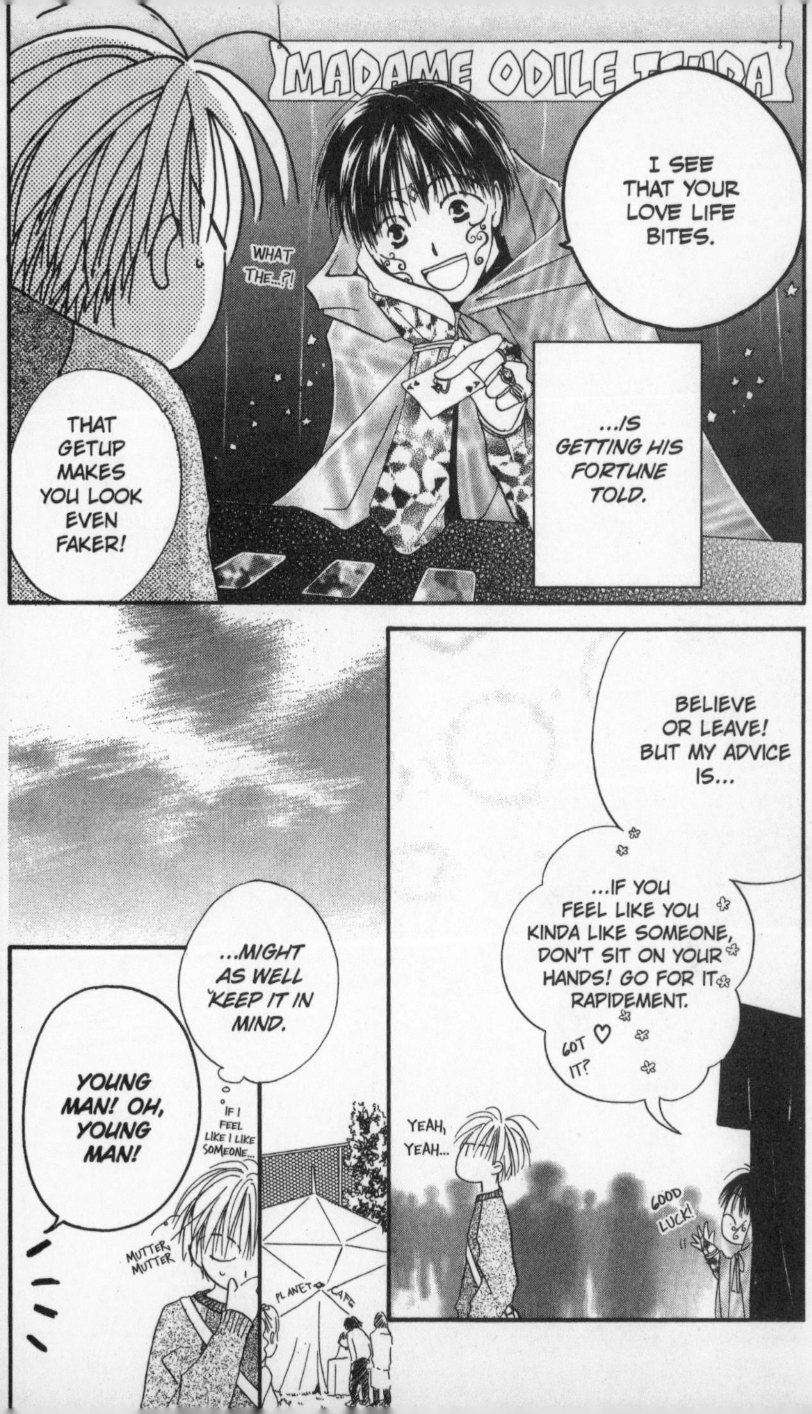
MADAME ODILE
I SEE THAT YOUR LOVE LIFE BITES.
WHAT THE...?!
...IS GETTING HIS FORTUNE TOLD.
THAT GETUP MAKES YOU LOOK EVEN FAKER!
BELIEVE OR LEAVE! BUT MY ADVICE IS...
...IF YOU FEEL LIKE YOU KINDA LIKE SOMEONE, DON'T SIT ON YOUR HANDS! GO FOR IT RAPIDEMENT.
GOT ♡ IT?
YEAH, YEAH...
GOOD LUCK!
...MIGHT AS WELL "KEEP IT IN MIND.
IF I FEEL LIKE I LIKE SOMEONE...
YOUNG MAN! OH, YOUNG MAN!
MUTTER MUTTER
PLANET CAFE

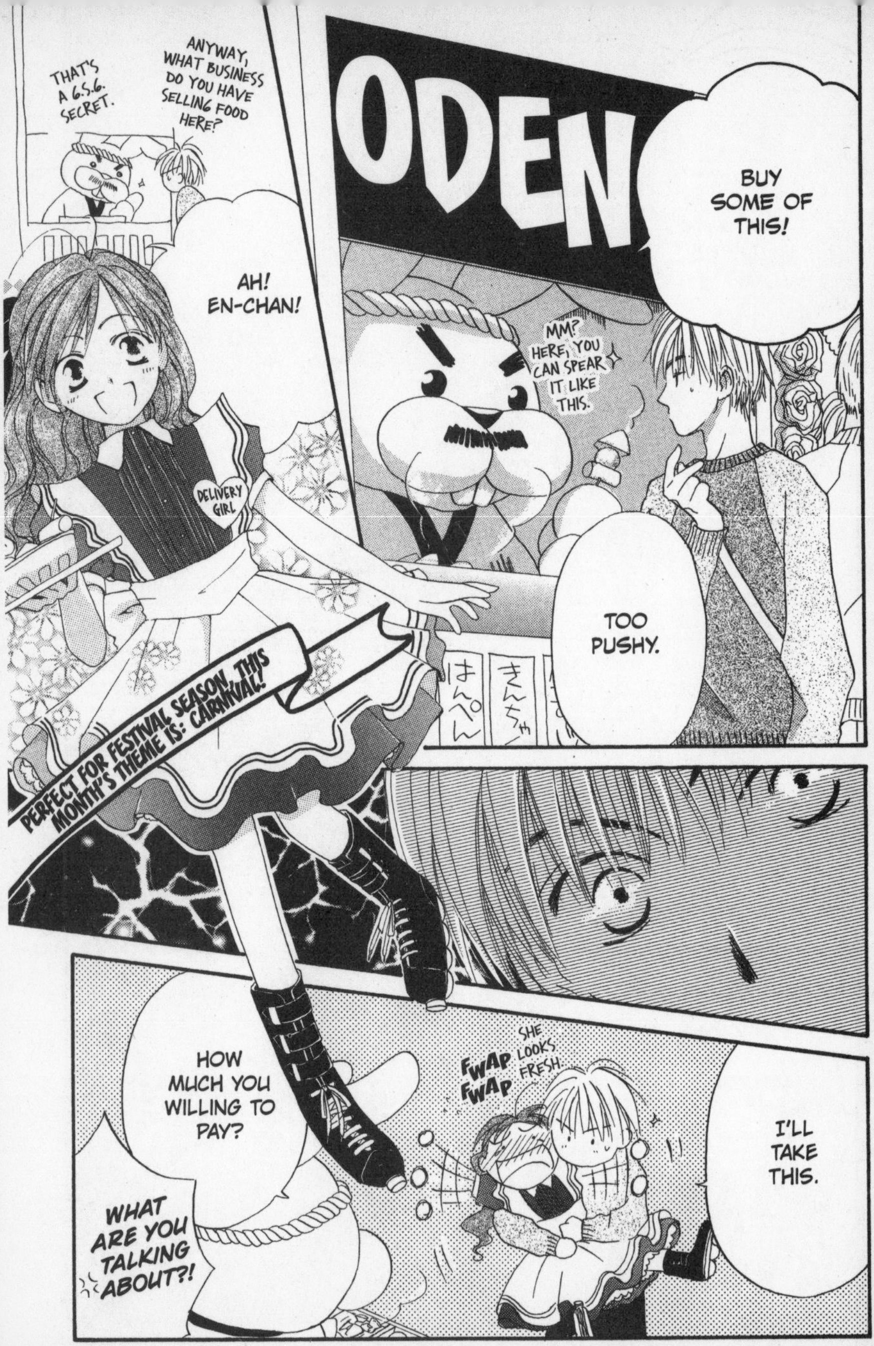
ODEN
BUY SOME OF THIS!
MM? HERE, YOU CAN SPEAR IT LIKE THIS.
TOO PUSHY.
はんぺん
ANYWAY, WHAT BUSINESS DO YOU HAVE SELLING FOOD HERE?
THAT'S A G.S.G. SECRET.
AH! EN-CHAN!
DELIVERY GIRL
PERFECT FOR FESTIVAL SEASON, THIS MONTH'S THEME IS: CARNIVAL!
I'LL TAKE THIS.
SHE LOOKS FRESH.
FWAP FWAP
HOW MUCH YOU WILLING TO PAY?
WHAT ARE YOU TALKING ABOUT?!

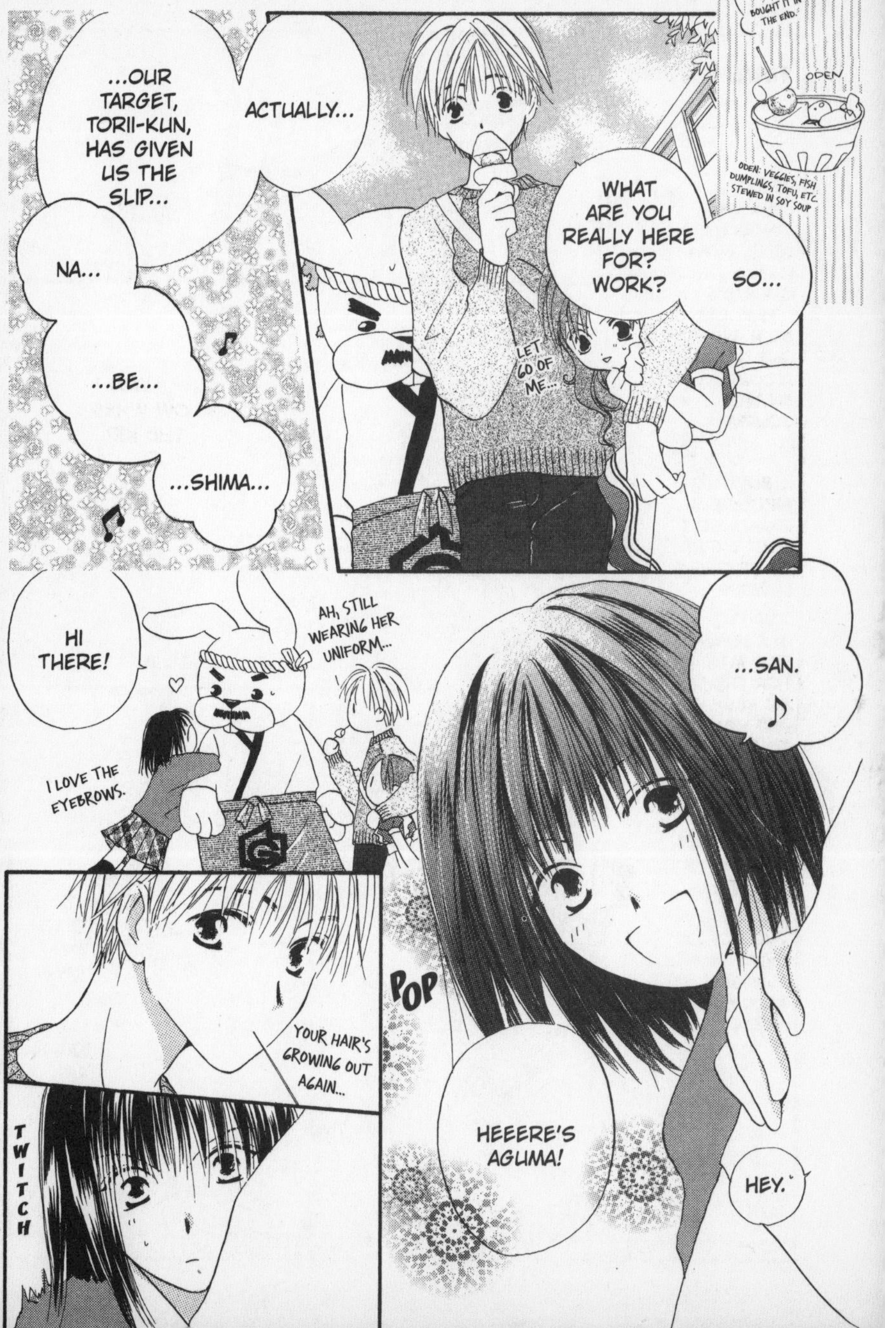
BOUGHT IT IN THE END.
ODEN
ODEN: VEGGIES, FISH DUMPLINGS, TOFU, ETC. STEWED IN SOY SOUP
SO...
WHAT ARE YOU REALLY HERE FOR? WORK?
LET GO OF ME...
ACTUALLY...
...OUR TARGET, TORII-KUN, HAS GIVEN US THE SLIP...
NA...
...BE...
...SHIMA...
...SAN.
POP
HEEERE'S AGUMA!
HEY.
HI THERE!
AH, STILL WEARING HER UNIFORM...
I LOVE THE EYEBROWS.
YOUR HAIR'S GROWING OUT AGAIN...
TWITCH

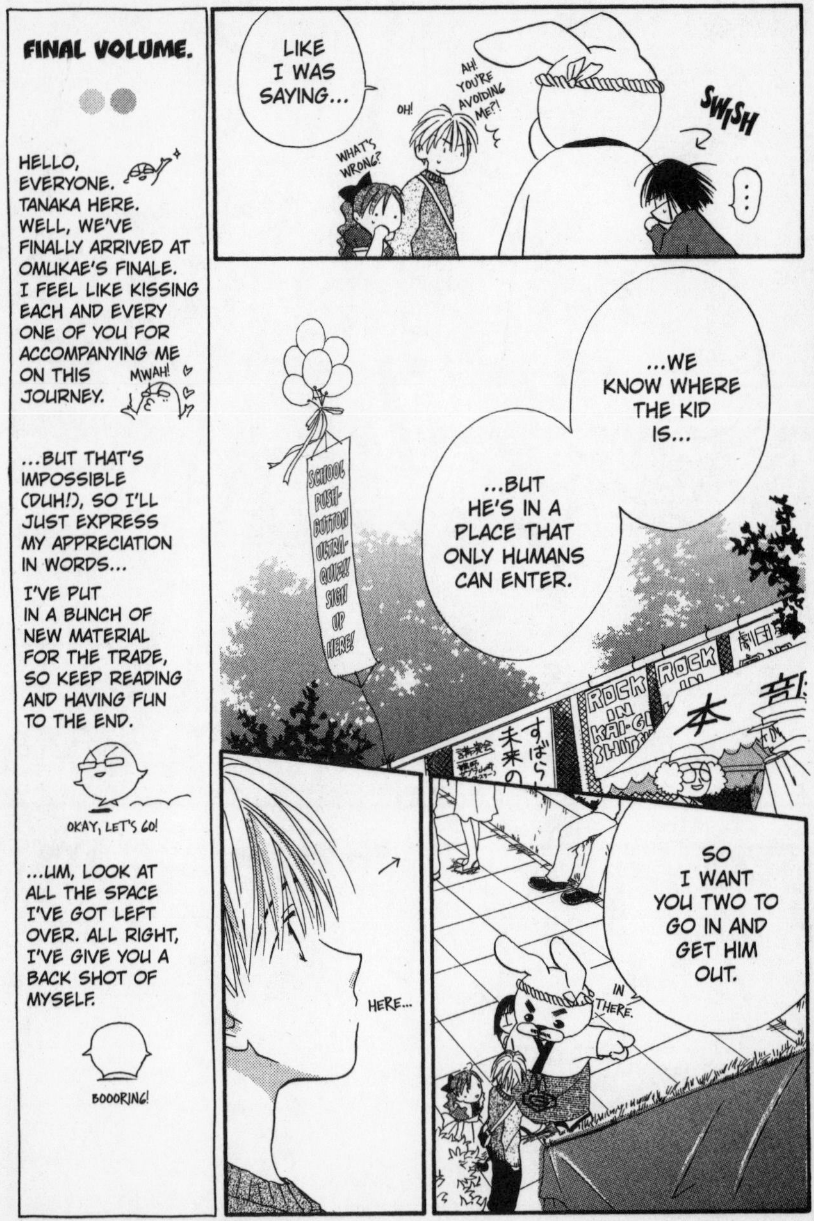
SWISH
...
AH! YOU'RE AVOIDING ME?!
LIKE I WAS SAYING...
OH!
WHAT'S WRONG?
...WE KNOW WHERE THE KID IS...
...BUT HE'S IN A PLACE THAT ONLY HUMANS CAN ENTER.
SCHOOL PUSH-BUTTON ULTRA-QUIZ!! SIGN UP HERE!
ROCK IN
ROCK IN KAI-GI SHITSU
SO I WANT YOU TWO TO GO IN AND GET HIM OUT.
IN THERE.
HERE...

FINAL VOLUME.

HELLO, EVERYONE. TANAKA HERE. WELL, WE'VE FINALLY ARRIVED AT OMUKAE'S FINALE. I FEEL LIKE KISSING EACH AND EVERY ONE OF YOU FOR ACCOMPANYING ME ON THIS JOURNEY. MWAH!

...BUT THAT'S IMPOSSIBLE (DUH!), SO I'LL JUST EXPRESS MY APPRECIATION IN WORDS...

I'VE PUT IN A BUNCH OF NEW MATERIAL FOR THE TRADE, SO KEEP READING AND HAVING FUN TO THE END.

OKAY, LET'S GO!

...UM, LOOK AT ALL THE SPACE I'VE GOT LEFT OVER. ALL RIGHT, I'VE GIVE YOU A BACK SHOT OF MYSELF.

BOOORING!

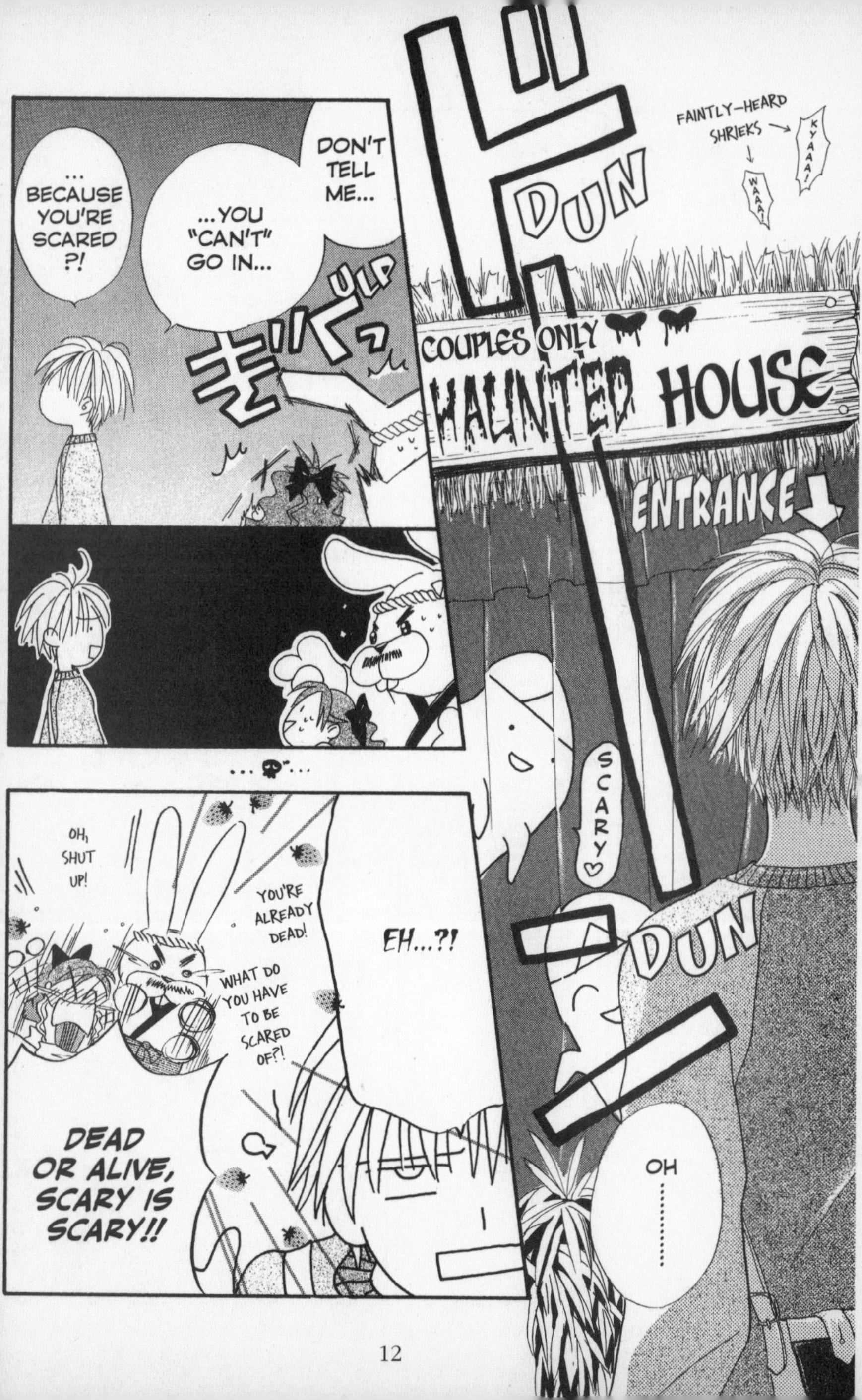
DUN
FAINTLY-HEARD SHRIEKS
KYAAA!
WAAA!
COUPLES ONLY
HAUNTED HOUSE
ENTRANCE
SCARY♡
DUN
OH ....
DON'T TELL ME...
...YOU "CAN'T" GO IN...
...BECAUSE YOU'RE SCARED?!
ULP
...
EH...?!
YOU'RE ALREADY DEAD!
OH, SHUT UP!
WHAT DO YOU HAVE TO BE SCARED OF?!
DEAD OR ALIVE, SCARY IS SCARY!!

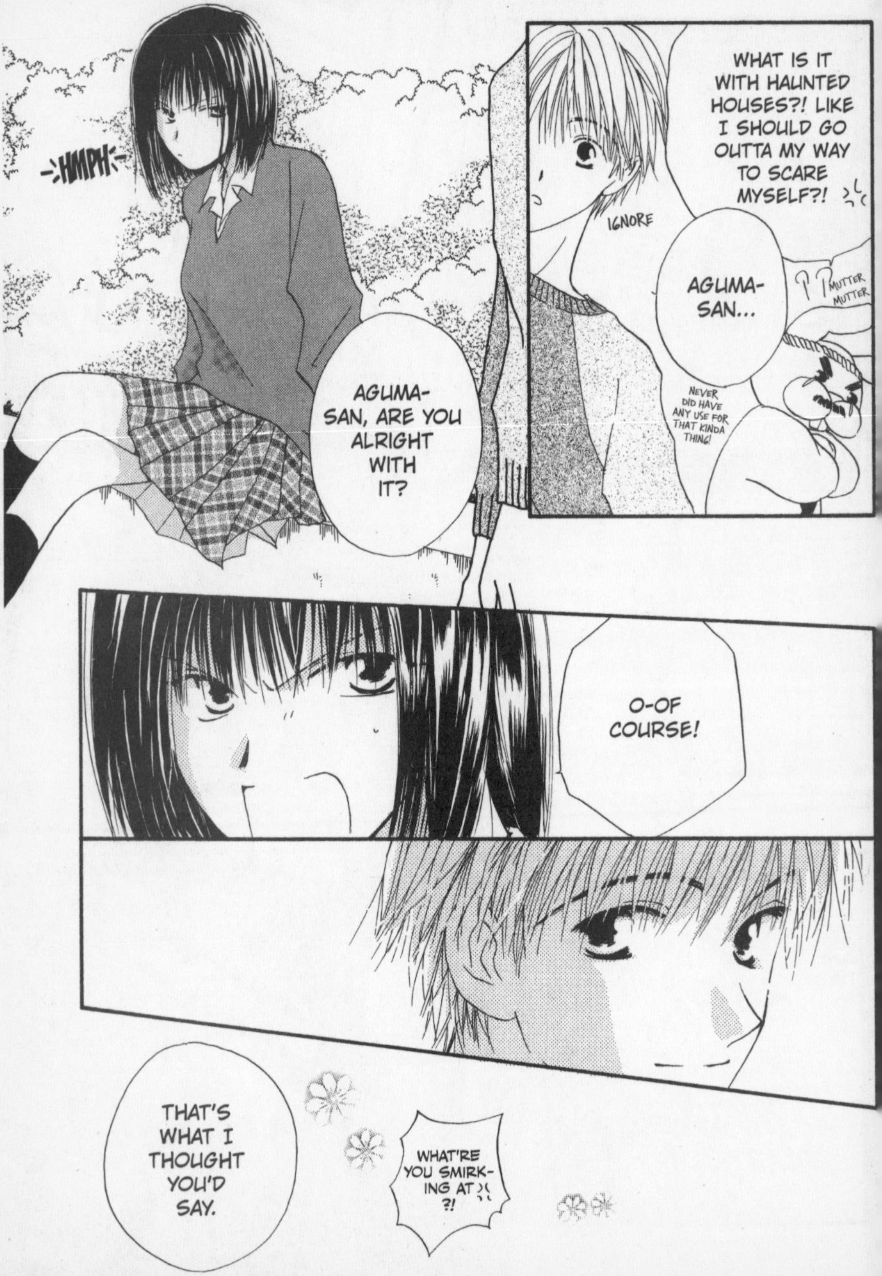
WHAT IS IT WITH HAUNTED HOUSES?! LIKE I SHOULD GO OUTTA MY WAY TO SCARE MYSELF?!
IGNORE
MUTTER MUTTER
AGUMA-SAN...
NEVER DID HAVE ANY USE FOR THAT KINDA THING!
HMPH
AGUMA-SAN, ARE YOU ALRIGHT WITH IT?
O-OF COURSE!
WHAT'RE YOU SMIRKING AT?!
THAT'S WHAT I THOUGHT YOU'D SAY.

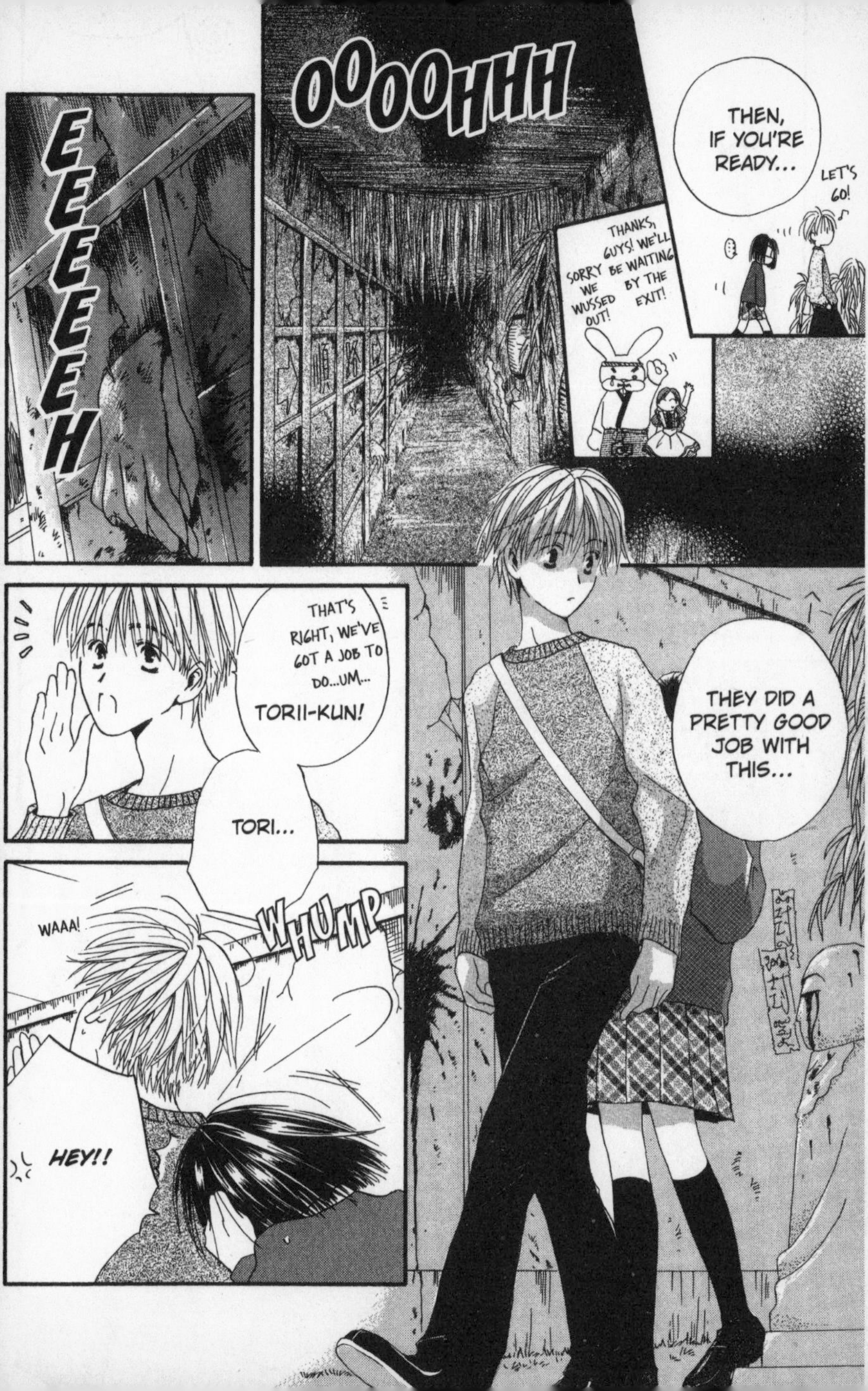
THEN, IF YOU'RE READY...
LET'S GO!
THANKS, GUYS! WE'LL BE WAITING BY THE EXIT!
SORRY WE WUSSED OUT!
OOOOHHH
EEEEEEH
THEY DID A PRETTY GOOD JOB WITH THIS...
THAT'S RIGHT, WE'VE GOT A JOB TO DO...UM...
TORII-KUN!
TORI...
WAAA!
WHUMP
HEY!!

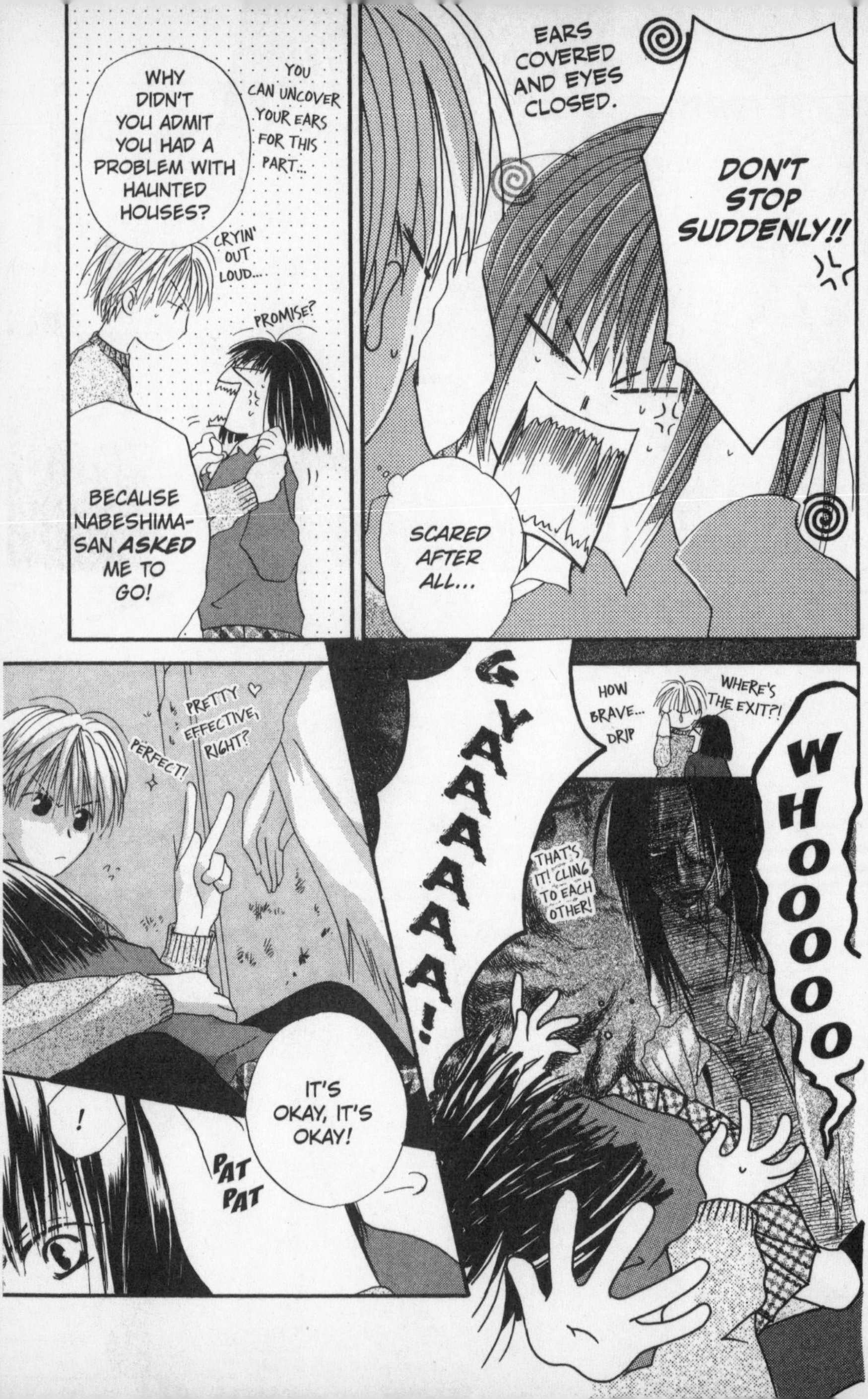
EARS COVERED AND EYES CLOSED.
DON'T STOP SUDDENLY!!
SCARED AFTER ALL...
WHY DIDN'T YOU ADMIT YOU HAD A PROBLEM WITH HAUNTED HOUSES?
YOU CAN UNCOVER YOUR EARS FOR THIS PART...
CRYIN' OUT LOUD...
PROMISE?
BECAUSE NABESHIMA-SAN ASKED ME TO GO!
WHERE'S THE EXIT?!
HOW BRAVE... DRIP
WHOOOOOO
GYAAAAAAA!
THAT'S IT! CLING TO EACH OTHER!
PRETTY EFFECTIVE, RIGHT?
PERFECT!
IT'S OKAY, IT'S OKAY!
PAT PAT
!

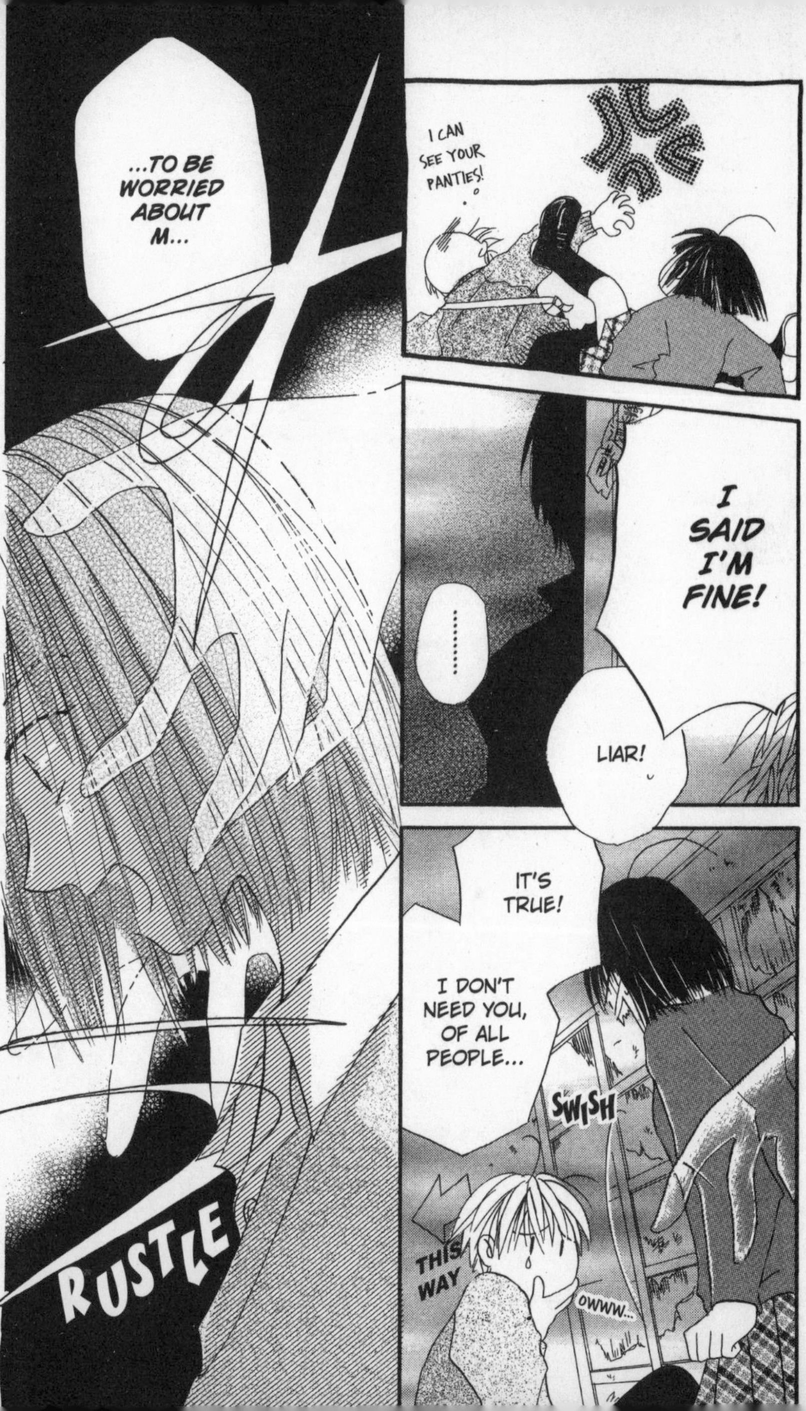
I CAN SEE YOUR PANTIES!
I SAID I'M FINE!
......
LIAR!
IT'S TRUE!
I DON'T NEED YOU, OF ALL PEOPLE...
SWISH
THIS WAY
OWWW...
...TO BE WORRIED ABOUT M...
RUSTLE

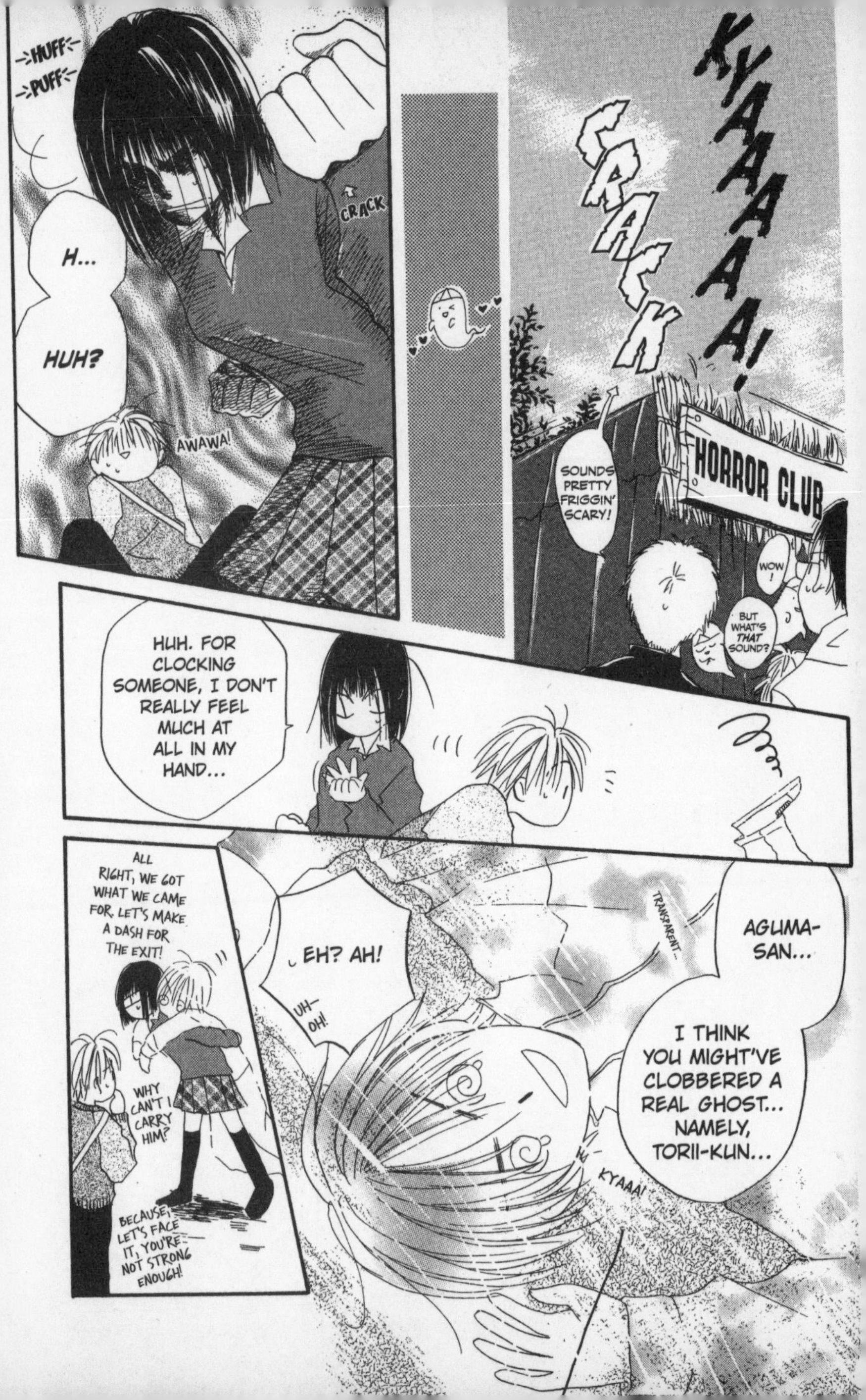
KYAAAAA!
CRACK
HORROR CLUB
SOUNDS PRETTY FRIGGIN' SCARY!
WOW!
BUT WHAT'S *THAT* SOUND?
HUFF
PUFF
CRACK
H...
HUH?
AWAWA!
HUH. FOR CLOCKING SOMEONE, I DON'T REALLY FEEL MUCH AT ALL IN MY HAND...
AGUMA-SAN...
I THINK YOU MIGHT'VE CLOBBERED A REAL GHOST... NAMELY, TORII-KUN...
TRANSPARENT...
EH? AH!
UH-OH!
KYAAA!
ALL RIGHT, WE GOT WHAT WE CAME FOR. LET'S MAKE A DASH FOR THE EXIT!
WHY CAN'T I CARRY HIM?
BECAUSE, LET'S FACE IT, YOU'RE NOT STRONG ENOUGH!

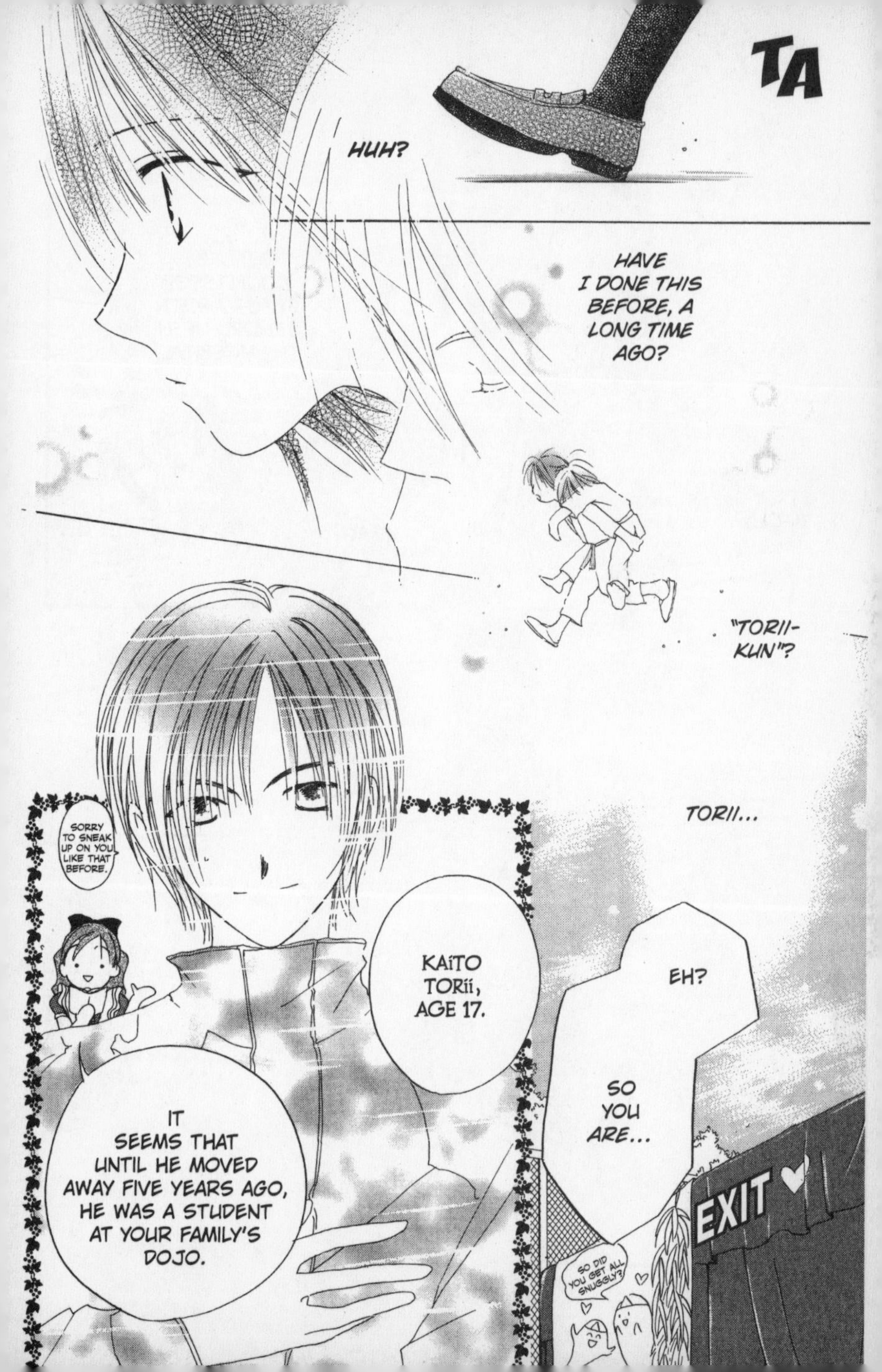
TA
HUH?
HAVE I DONE THIS BEFORE, A LONG TIME AGO?
"TORII-KUN"?
TORII...
EH?
SO YOU ARE...
EXIT
SO DID YOU GET ALL SNUGGLY?
KAiTO TORii, AGE 17.
IT SEEMS THAT UNTIL HE MOVED AWAY FIVE YEARS AGO, HE WAS A STUDENT AT YOUR FAMILY'S DOJO.
SORRY TO SNEAK UP ON YOU LIKE THAT BEFORE.

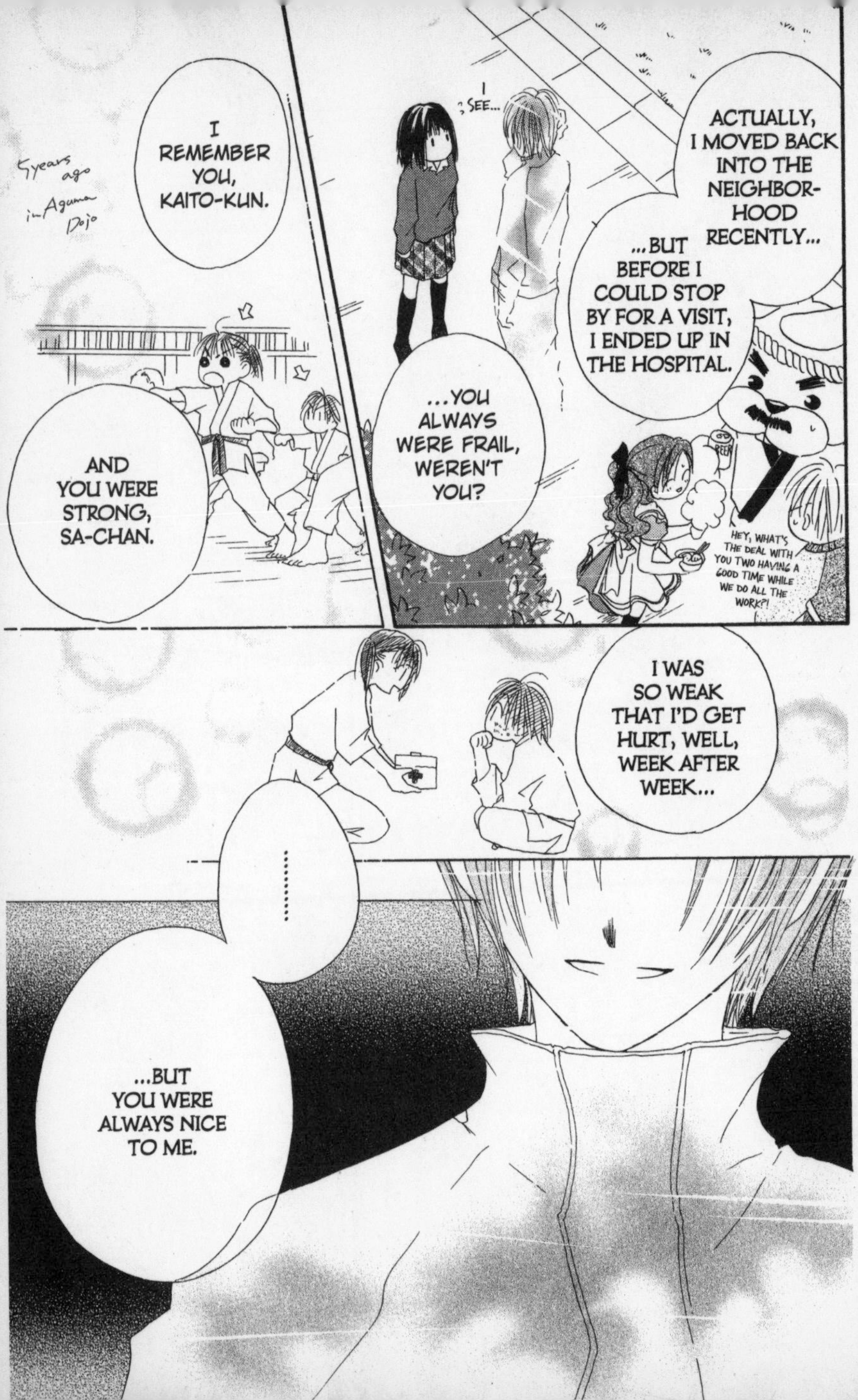
ACTUALLY, I MOVED BACK INTO THE NEIGHBOR-HOOD RECENTLY...
...BUT BEFORE I COULD STOP BY FOR A VISIT, I ENDED UP IN THE HOSPITAL.
I SEE...
...YOU ALWAYS WERE FRAIL, WEREN'T YOU?
HEY, WHAT'S THE DEAL WITH YOU TWO HAVING A GOOD TIME WHILE WE DO ALL THE WORK?!
BEER
I REMEMBER YOU, KAITO-KUN.
5 years ago in Aguma Dojo
AND YOU WERE STRONG, SA-CHAN.
I WAS SO WEAK THAT I'D GET HURT, WELL, WEEK AFTER WEEK...
....
...BUT YOU WERE ALWAYS NICE TO ME.

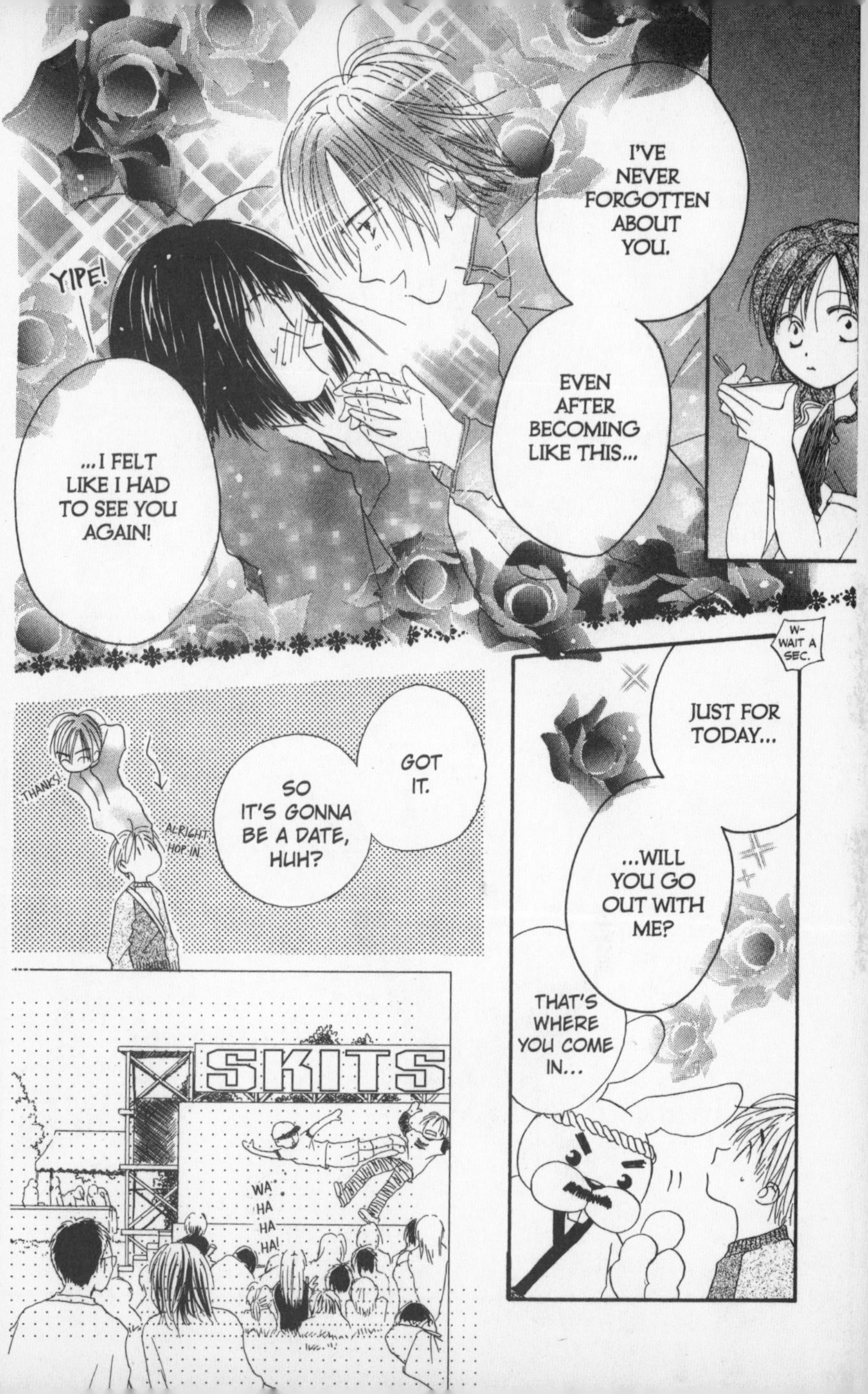
I'VE NEVER FORGOTTEN ABOUT YOU.
EVEN AFTER BECOMING LIKE THIS...
...I FELT LIKE I HAD TO SEE YOU AGAIN!
YIPE!
W-WAIT A SEC.
JUST FOR TODAY...
...WILL YOU GO OUT WITH ME?
THAT'S WHERE YOU COME IN...
GOT IT.
SO IT'S GONNA BE A DATE, HUH?
THANKS.
ALRIGHT. HOP IN.
SKITS
WA HA HA HA!

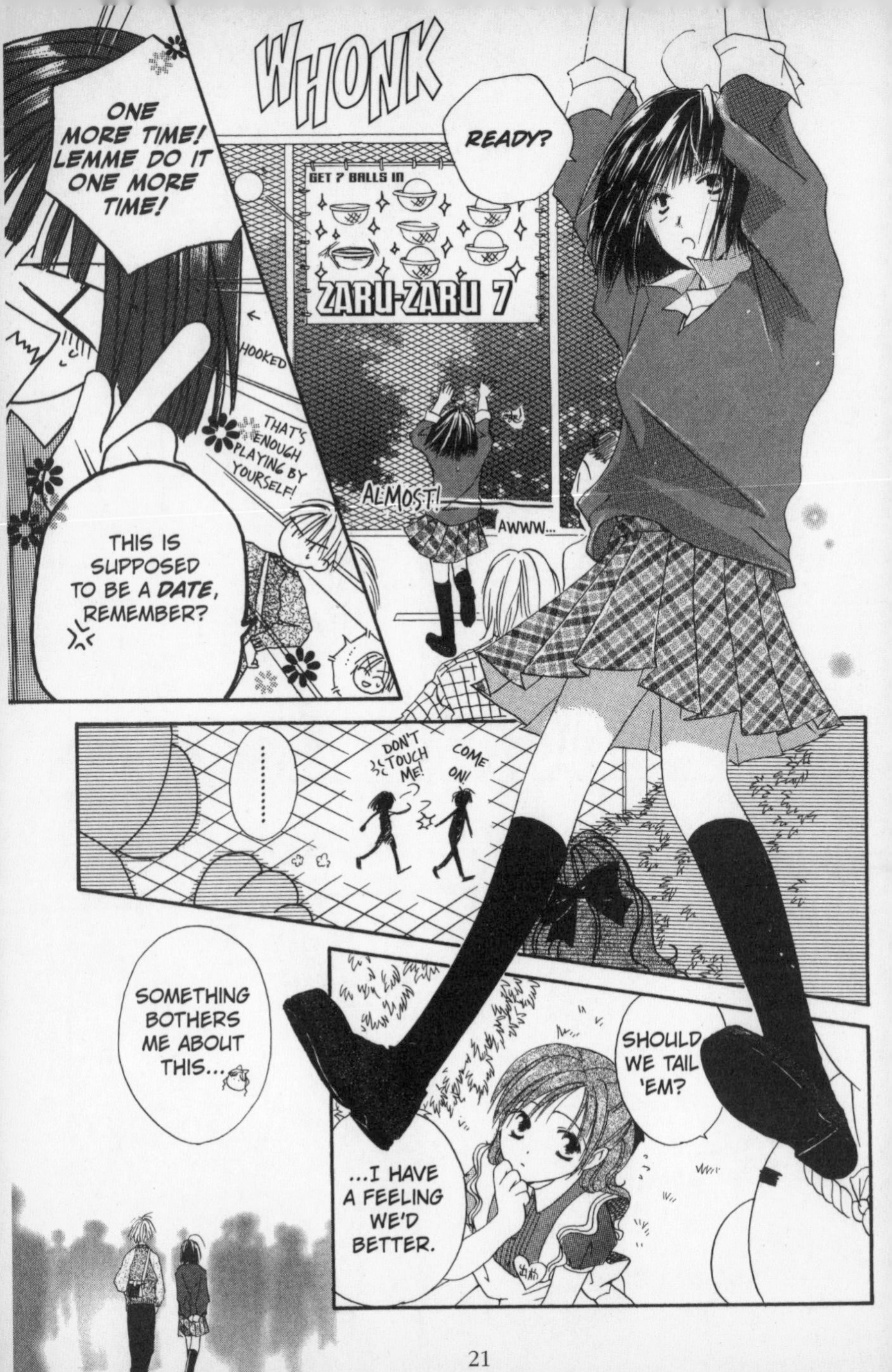
WHONK
READY?
GET 7 BALLS IN
ZARU-ZARU 7
ALMOST!
AWWW...
ONE MORE TIME! LEMME DO IT ONE MORE TIME!
HOOKED
THAT'S ENOUGH PLAYING BY YOURSELF!
THIS IS SUPPOSED TO BE A DATE, REMEMBER?
COME ON!
DON'T TOUCH ME!
......
SHOULD WE TAIL 'EM?
SOMETHING BOTHERS ME ABOUT THIS...
...I HAVE A FEELING WE'D BETTER.

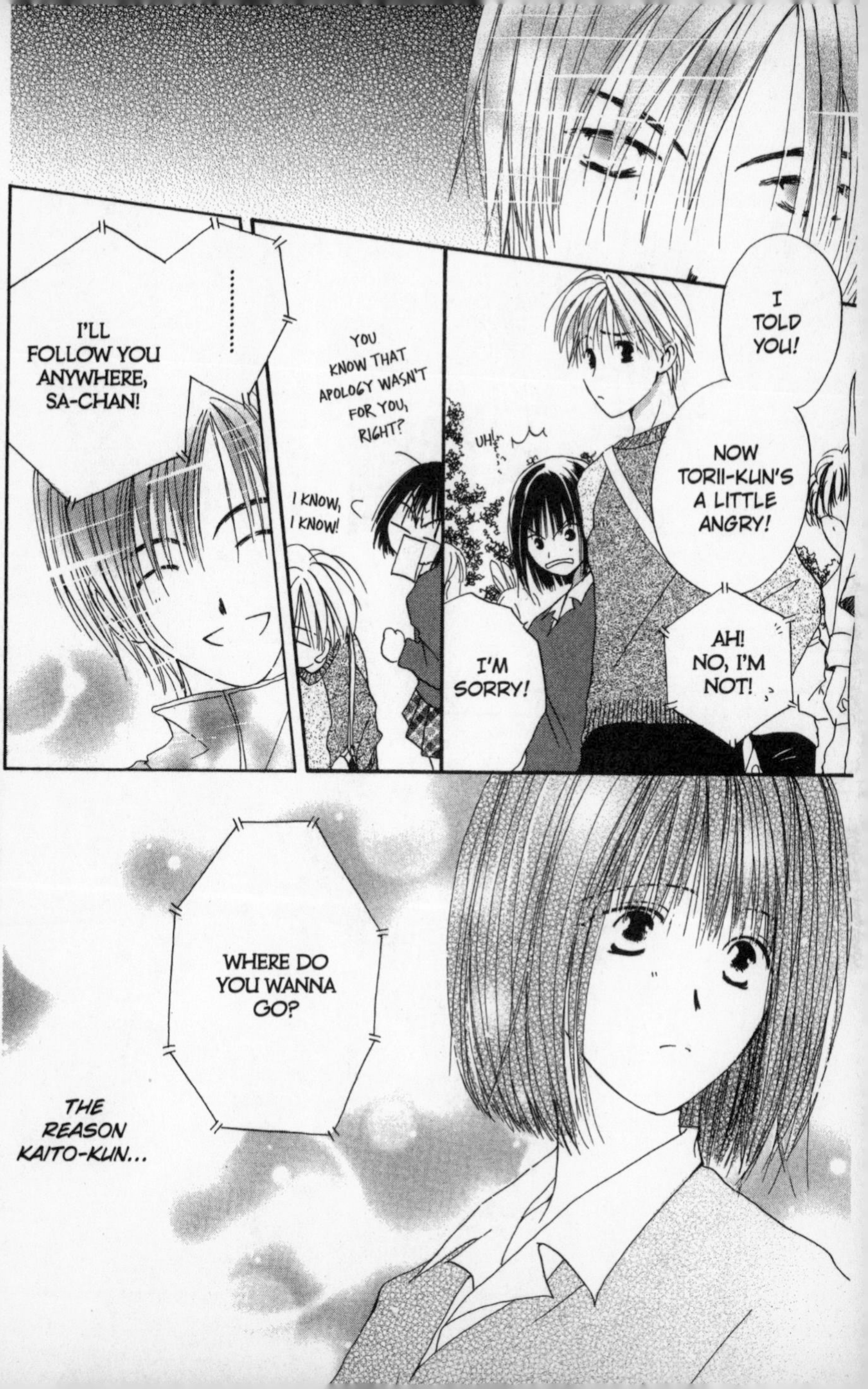
I TOLD YOU!
NOW TORII-KUN'S A LITTLE ANGRY!
AH! NO, I'M NOT!
UH!
I'M SORRY!
YOU KNOW THAT APOLOGY WASN'T FOR YOU, RIGHT?
I KNOW, I KNOW!
......
I'LL FOLLOW YOU ANYWHERE, SA-CHAN!
WHERE DO YOU WANNA GO?
THE REASON KAITO-KUN...

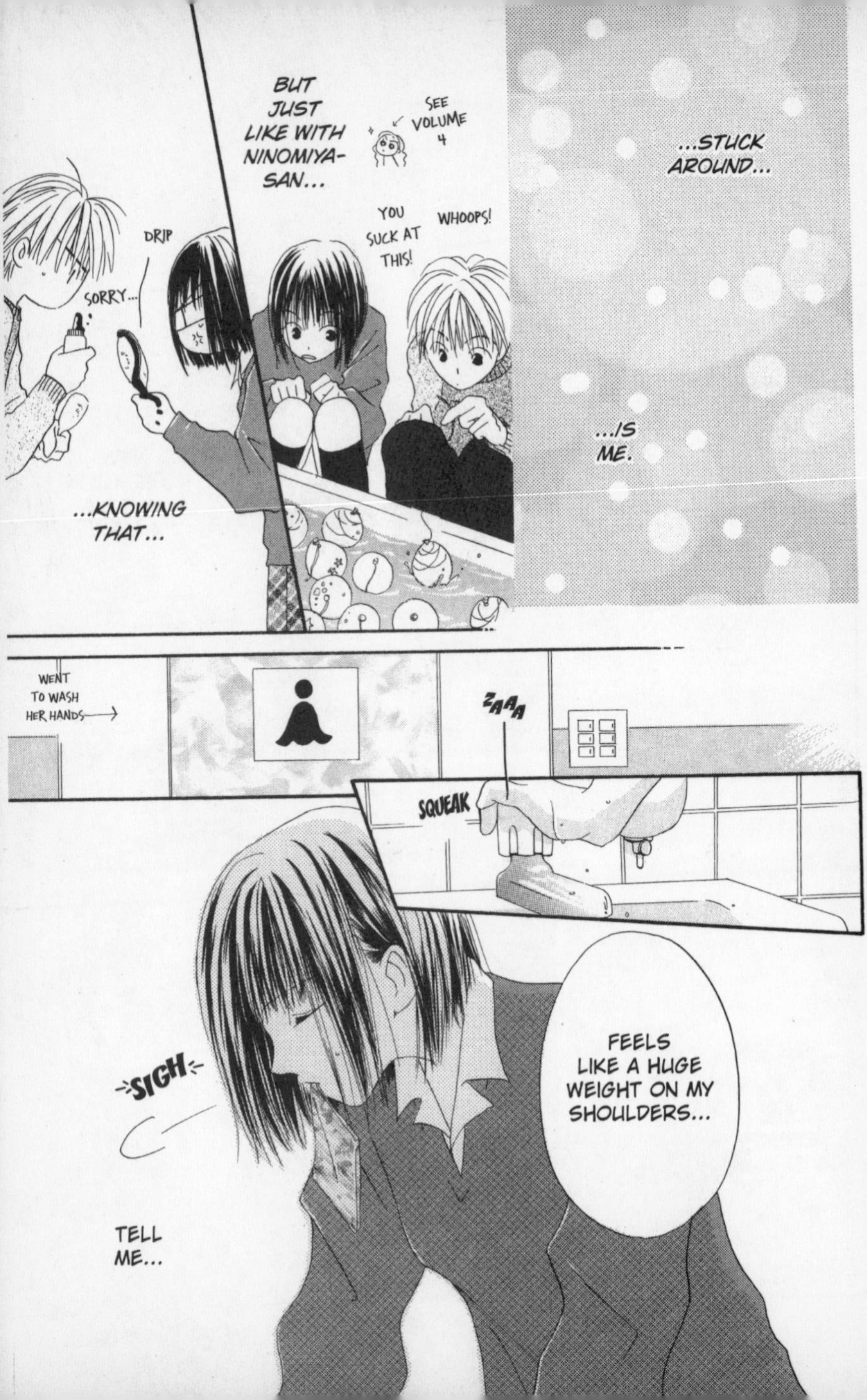
...STUCK AROUND...
...IS ME.
BUT JUST LIKE WITH NINOMIYA-SAN...
SEE VOLUME 4
WHOOPS!
YOU SUCK AT THIS!
DRIP
SORRY...
...KNOWING THAT...
WENT TO WASH HER HANDS
ZAAA
SQUEAK
FEELS LIKE A HUGE WEIGHT ON MY SHOULDERS...
SIGH
TELL ME...

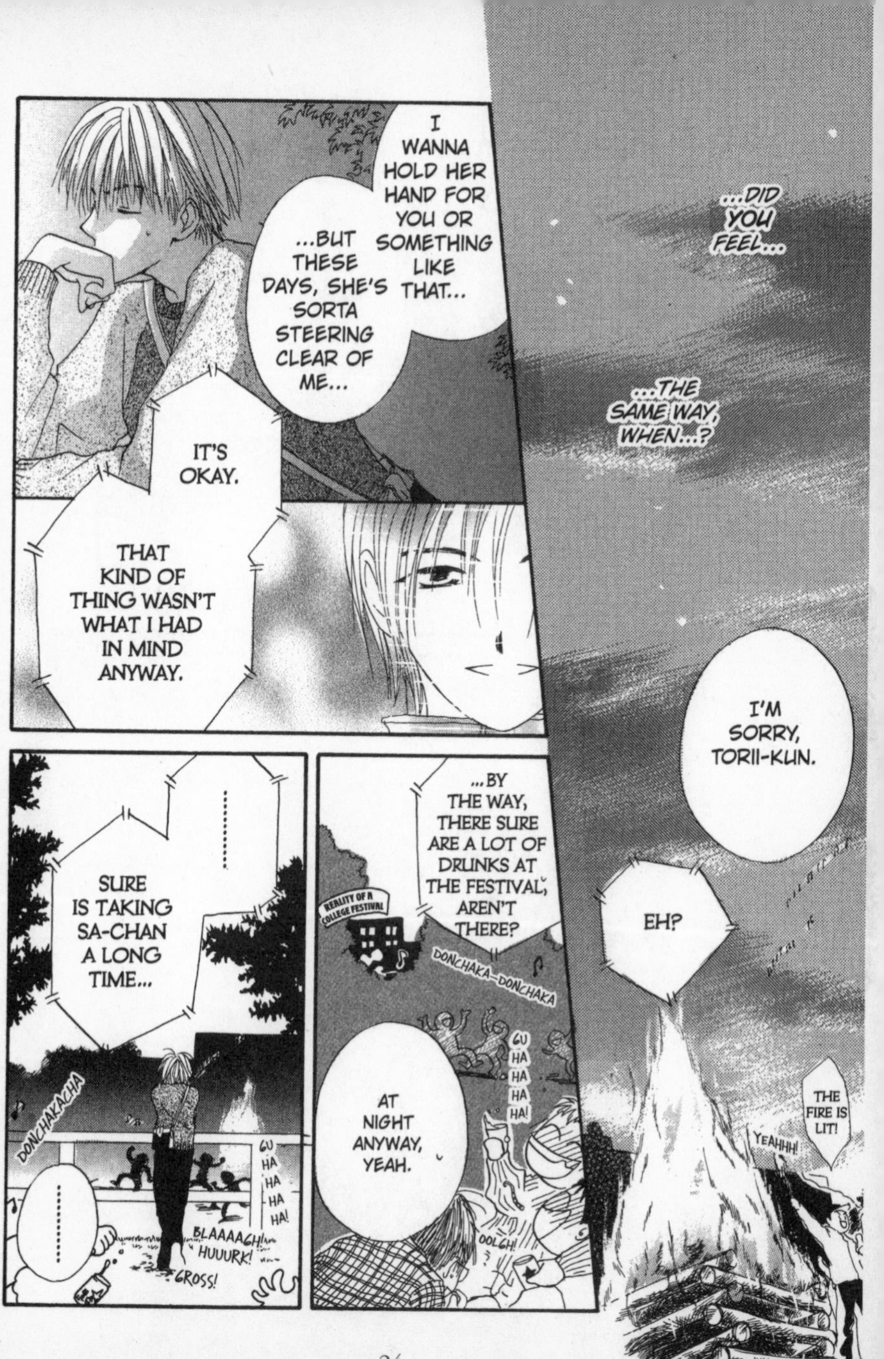
...DID YOU FEEL...
...THE SAME WAY, WHEN...?
I'M SORRY, TORII-KUN.
EH?
THE FIRE IS LIT!
YEAHHH!
I WANNA HOLD HER HAND FOR YOU OR SOMETHING LIKE THAT...
...BUT THESE DAYS, SHE'S SORTA STEERING CLEAR OF ME...
IT'S OKAY.
THAT KIND OF THING WASN'T WHAT I HAD IN MIND ANYWAY.
...BY THE WAY, THERE SURE ARE A LOT OF DRUNKS AT THE FESTIVAL, AREN'T THERE?
REALITY OF A COLLEGE FESTIVAL
DONCHAKA-DONCHAKA
GU HA HA HA HA!
AT NIGHT ANYWAY, YEAH.
OOLGH!
......
SURE IS TAKING SA-CHAN A LONG TIME...
DONCHAKACHA
GU HA HA HA HA!
BLAAAAGH!
HUUURK!
GROSS!
......

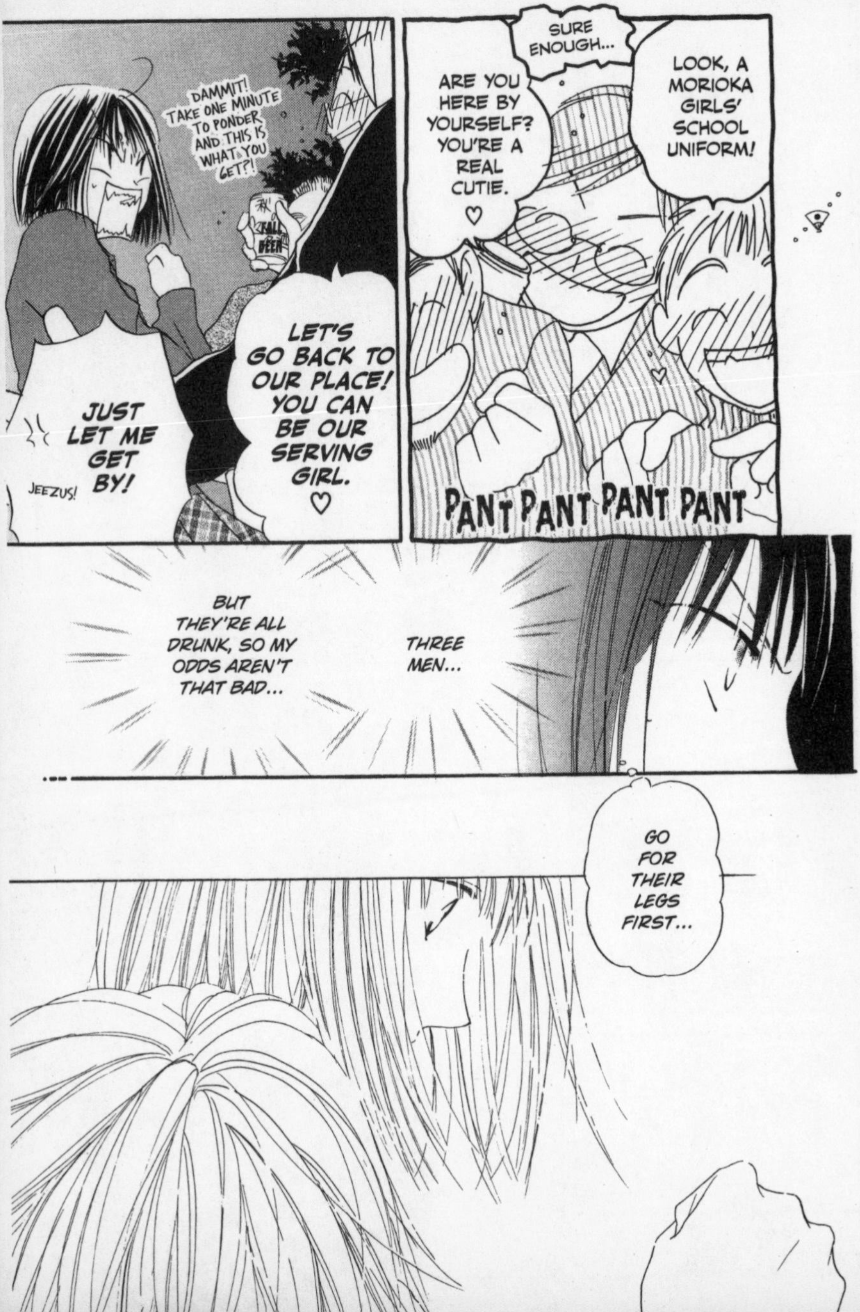
LOOK, A MORIOKA GIRLS' SCHOOL UNIFORM!
SURE ENOUGH...
ARE YOU HERE BY YOURSELF? YOU'RE A REAL CUTIE. ♡
PANT PANT PANT PANT
DAMMIT! TAKE ONE MINUTE TO PONDER AND THIS IS WHAT YOU GET?!
LET'S GO BACK TO OUR PLACE! YOU CAN BE OUR SERVING GIRL. ♡
JUST LET ME GET BY!
JEEZUS!
THREE MEN...
BUT THEY'RE ALL DRUNK, SO MY ODDS AREN'T THAT BAD...
GO FOR THEIR LEGS FIRST...

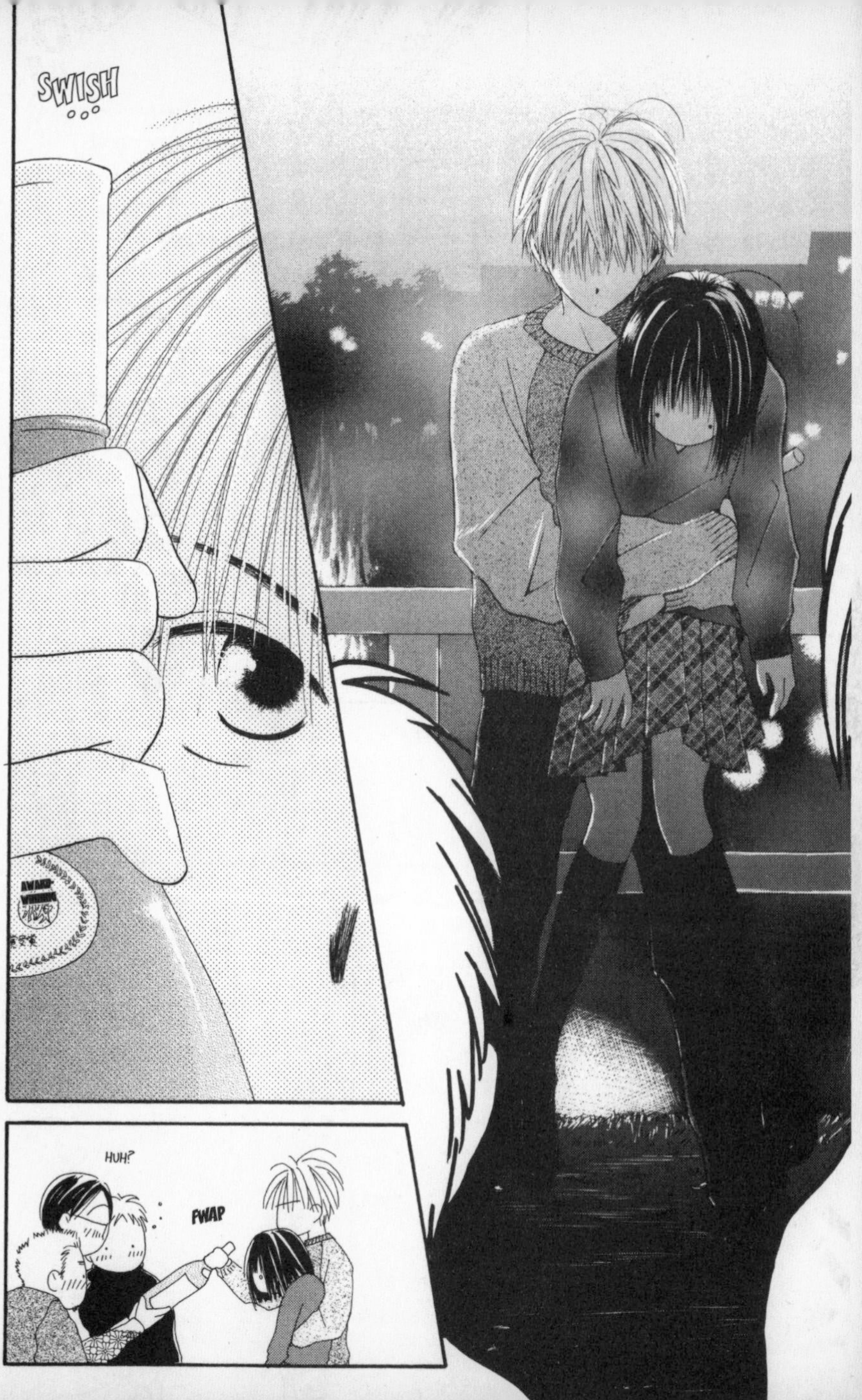
SWISH
AWARD-WINNING
HUH?
FWAP

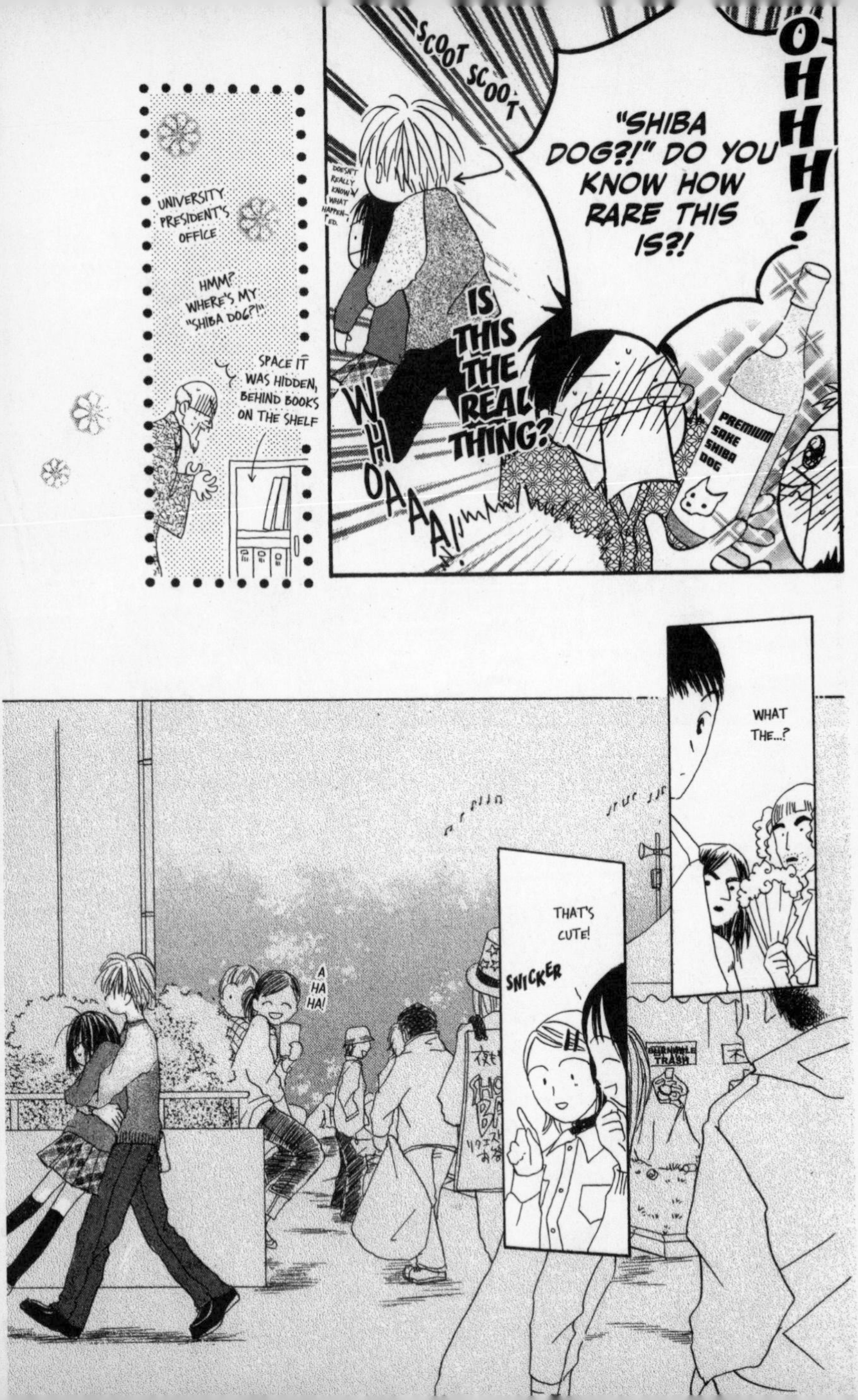
SCOOT SCOOT
OHHHH!
"SHIBA DOG?!" DO YOU KNOW HOW RARE THIS IS?!
IS THIS THE REAL THING?
WHOAAAA!
DOESN'T REALLY KNOW WHAT HAPPENED.
PREMIUM SAKE SHIBA DOG
UNIVERSITY PRESIDENT'S OFFICE
HMM? WHERE'S MY "SHIBA DOG?!"
SPACE IT WAS HIDDEN, BEHIND BOOKS ON THE SHELF
WHAT THE...?
THAT'S CUTE!
SNICKER
A HA HA!
BURNABLE TRASH

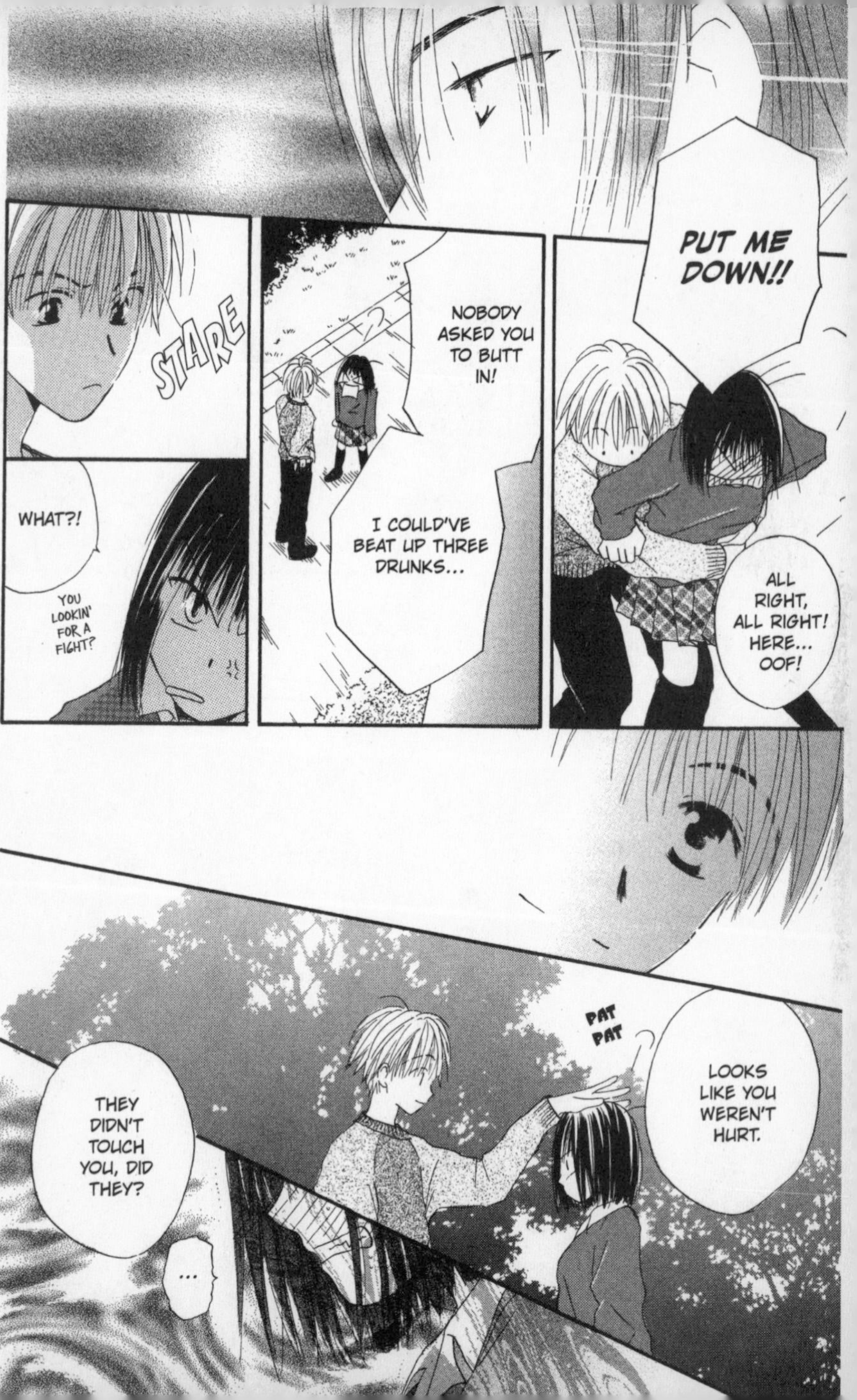
PUT ME DOWN!!
ALL RIGHT, ALL RIGHT! HERE... OOF!
NOBODY ASKED YOU TO BUTT IN!
I COULD'VE BEAT UP THREE DRUNKS...
STARE
WHAT?!
YOU LOOKIN' FOR A FIGHT?
PAT PAT
LOOKS LIKE YOU WEREN'T HURT.
THEY DIDN'T TOUCH YOU, DID THEY?
...

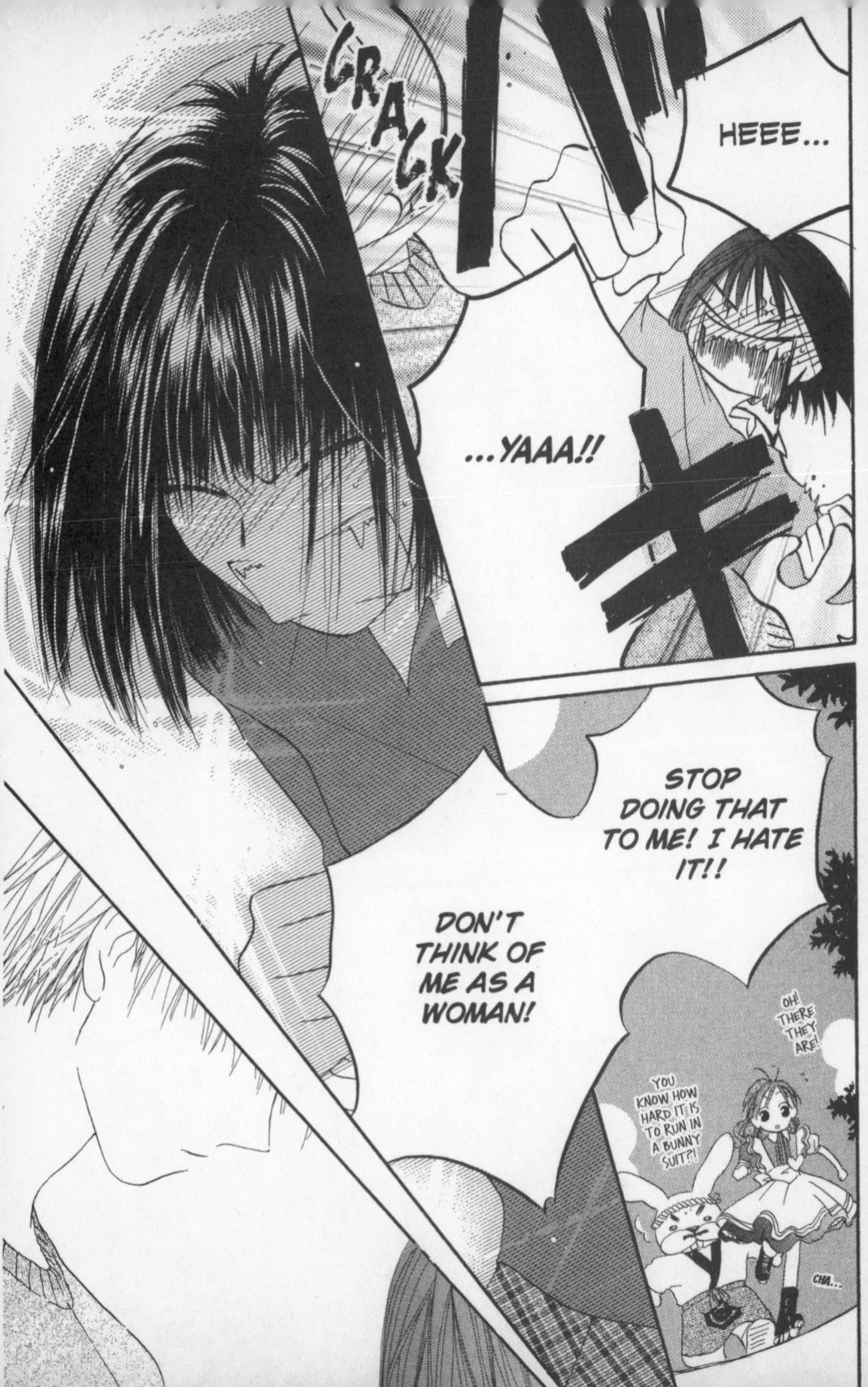
HEEE...
CRACK
...YAAA!!
STOP DOING THAT TO ME! I HATE IT!!
DON'T THINK OF ME AS A WOMAN!
OH! THERE THEY ARE!
YOU KNOW HOW HARD IT IS TO RUN IN A BUNNY SUIT?!
CHA...

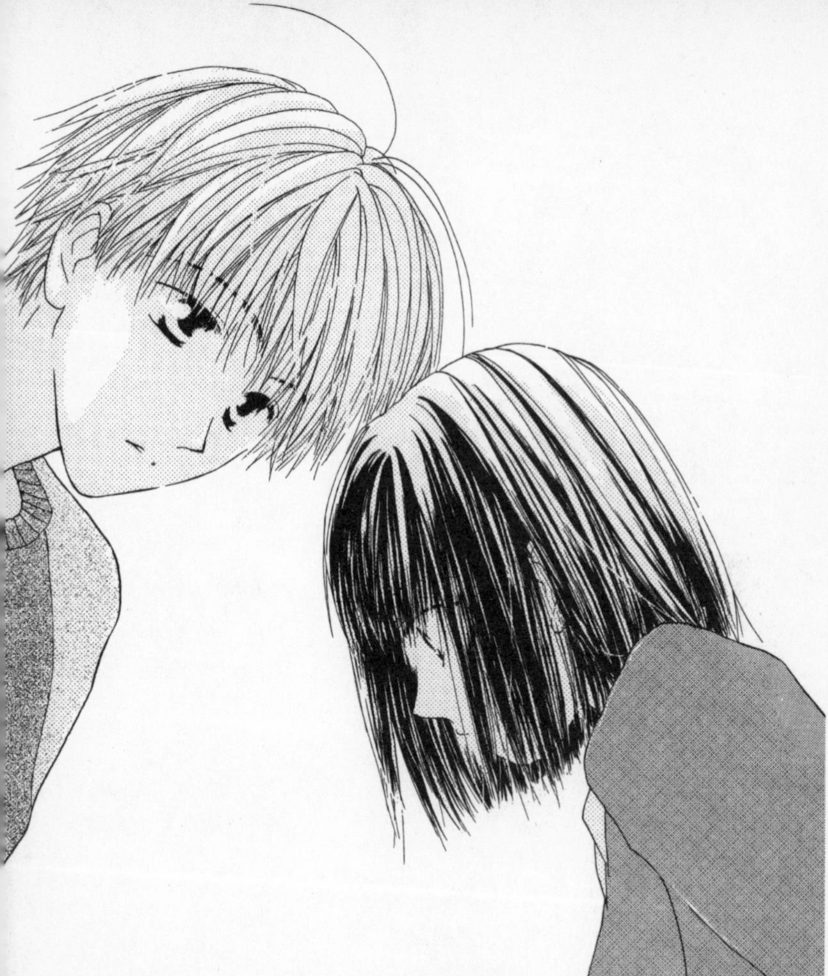
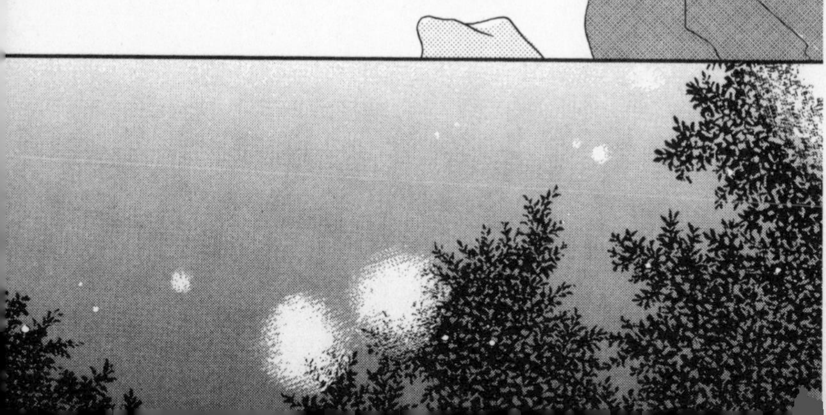

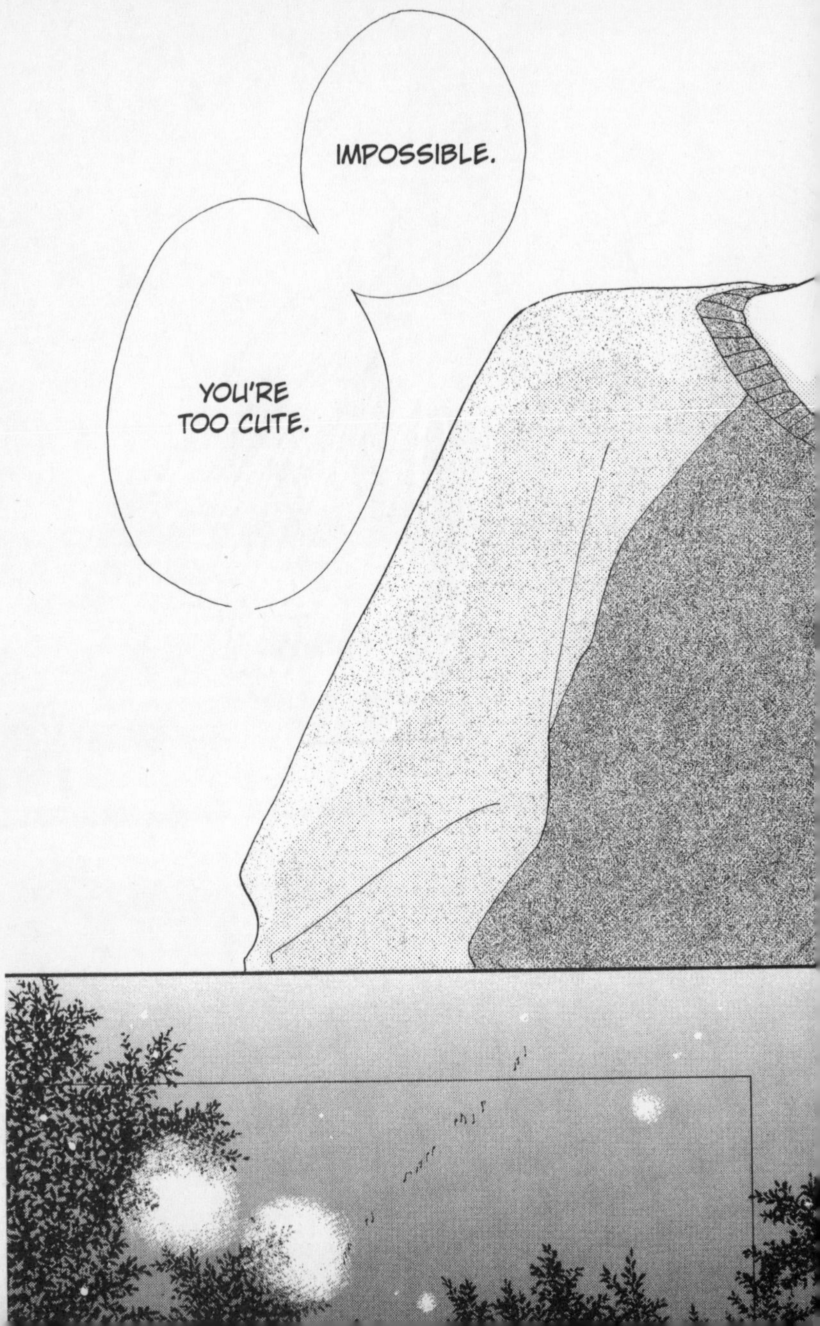
IMPOSSIBLE.
YOU'RE TOO CUTE.

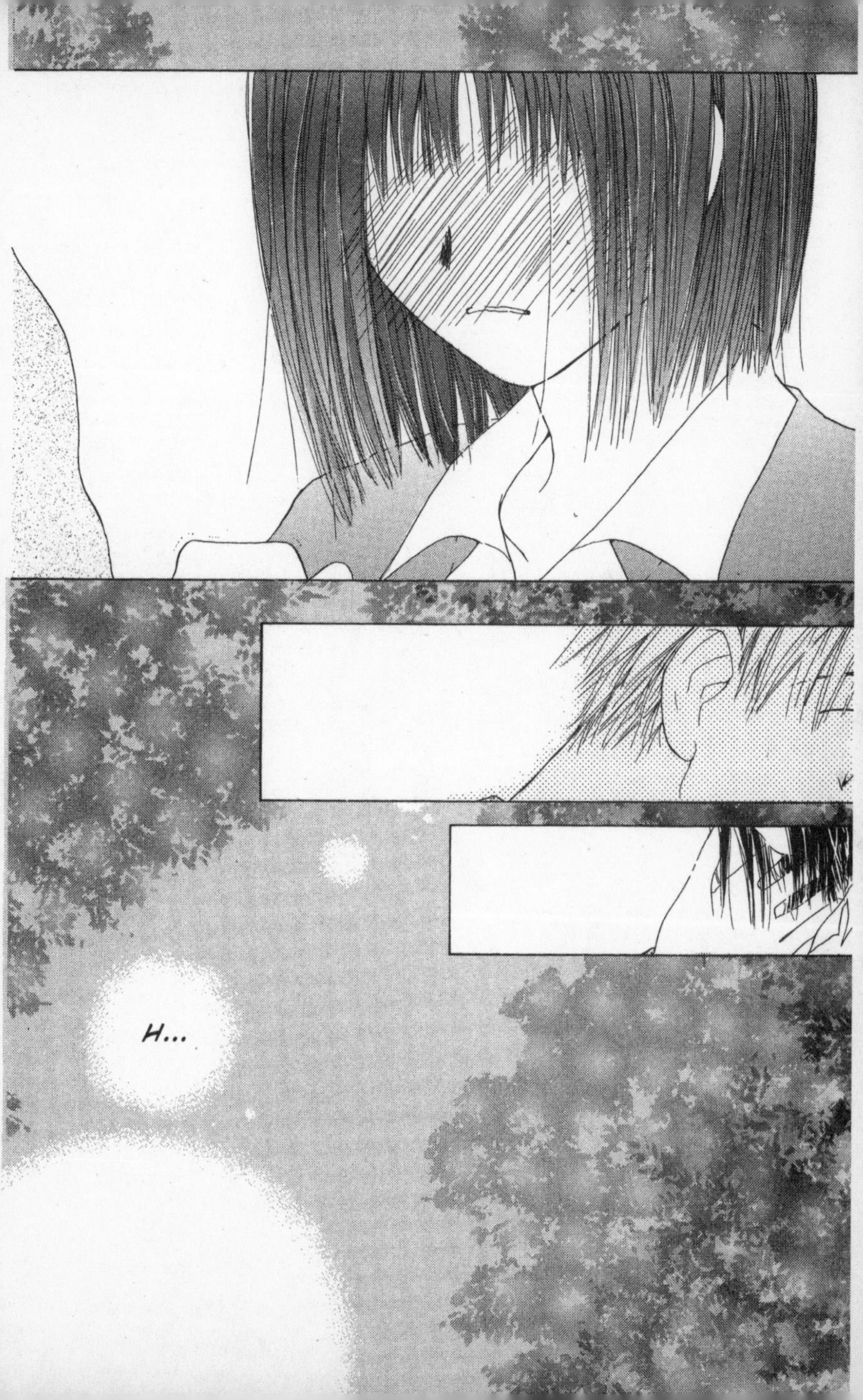
H...

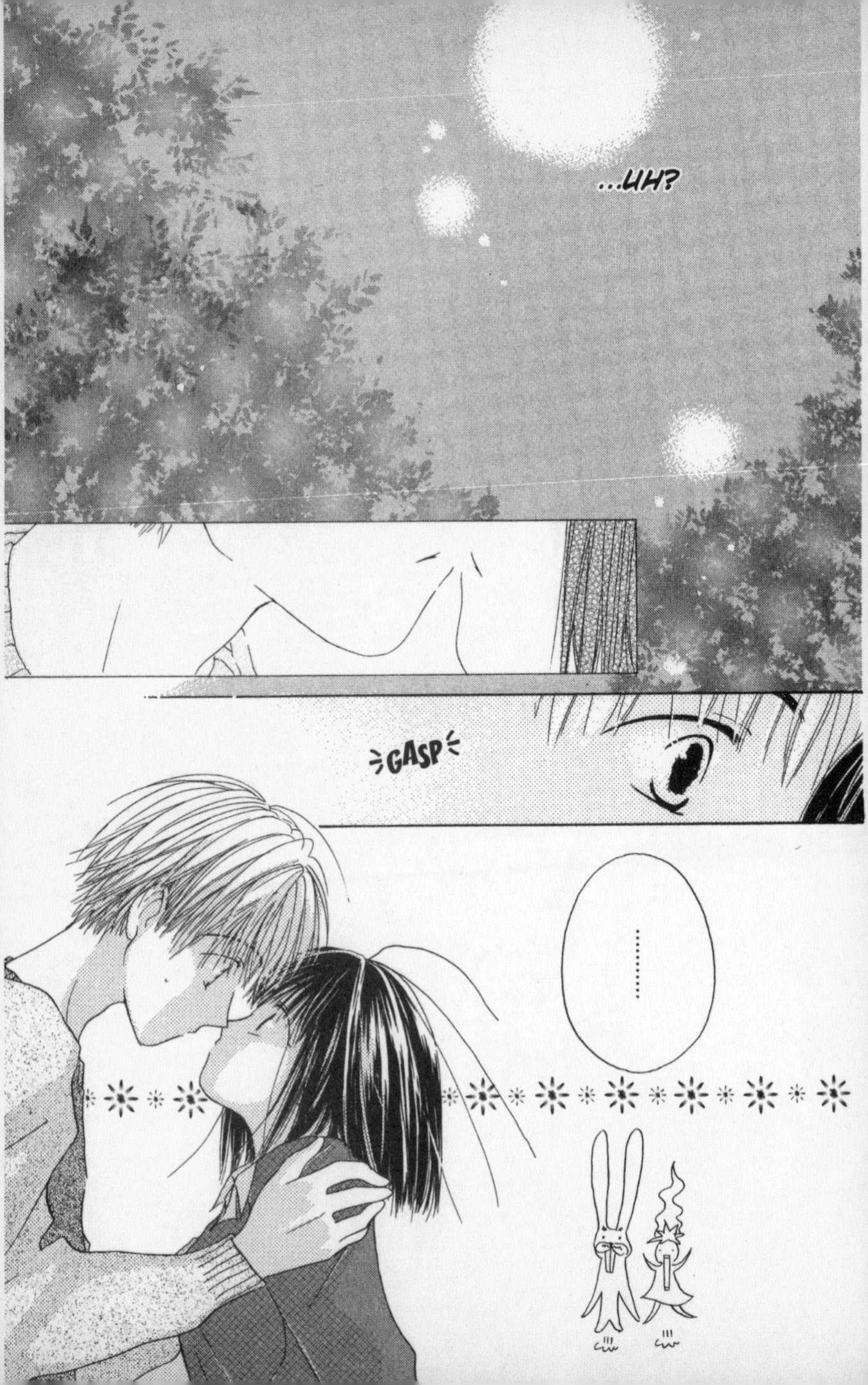
...UH?
GASP
......

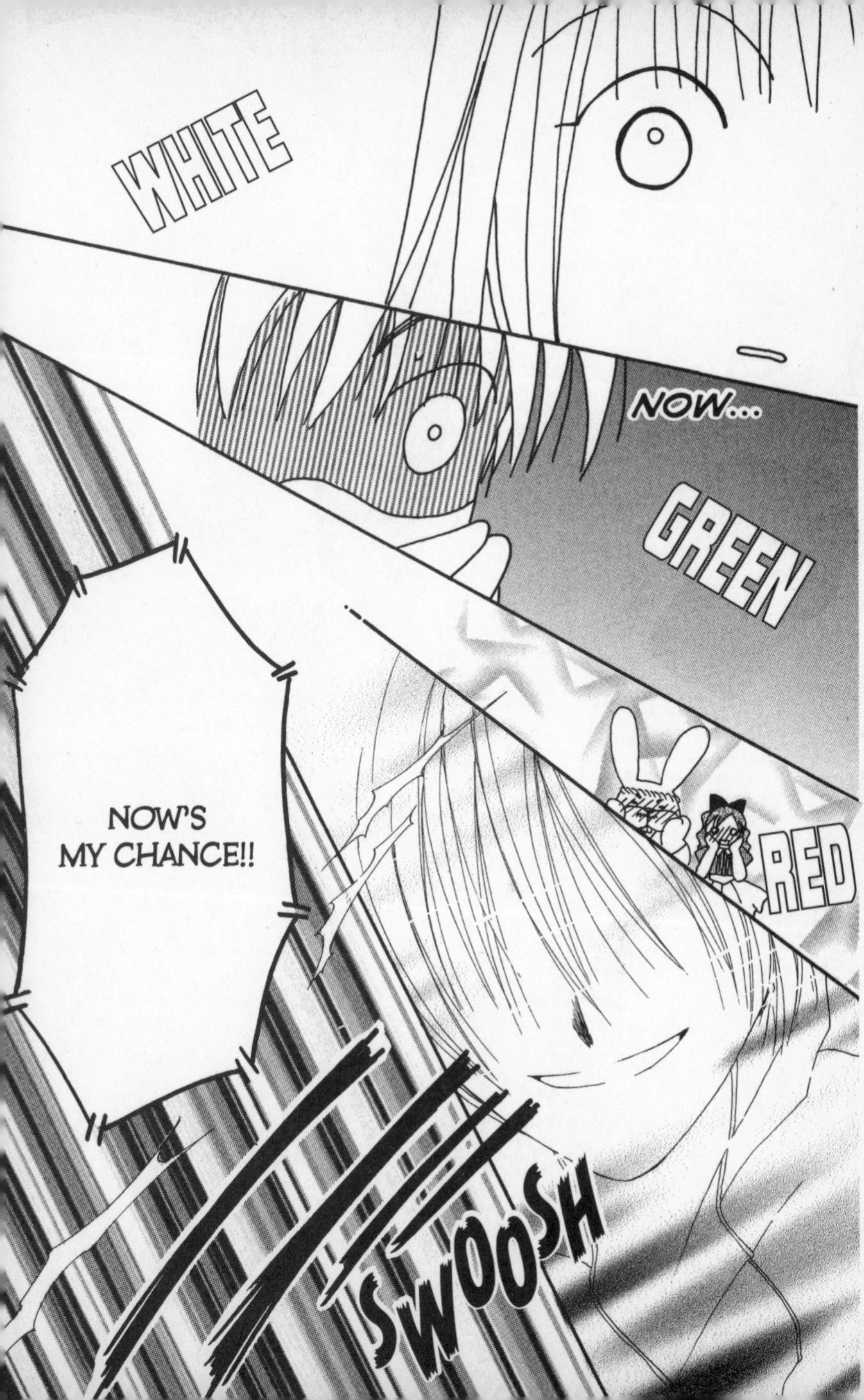
WHITE
NOW...
GREEN
RED
NOW'S MY CHANCE!!
SWOOSH

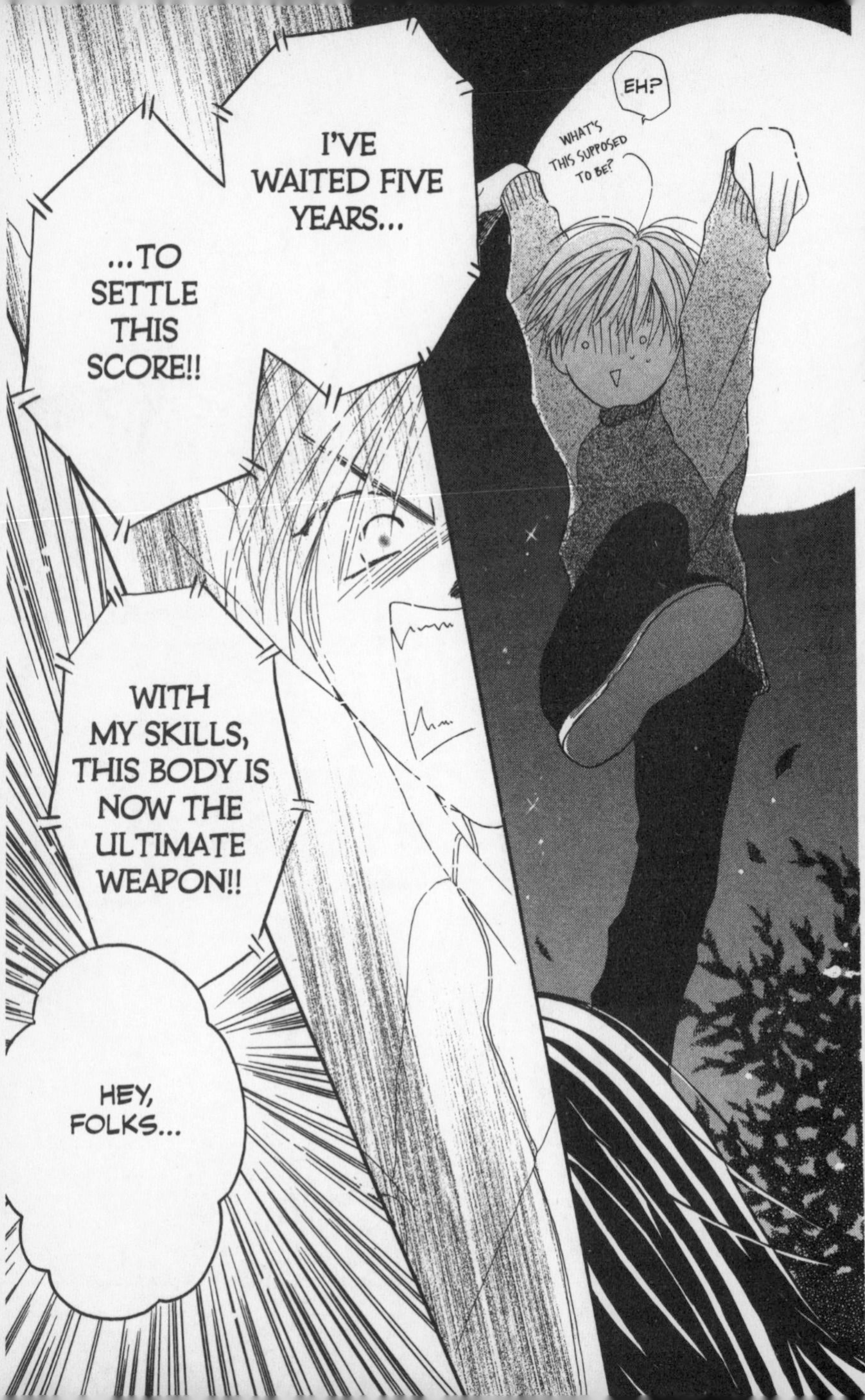
EH?
WHAT'S THIS SUPPOSED TO BE?
I'VE WAITED FIVE YEARS...
...TO SETTLE THIS SCORE!!
WITH MY SKILLS, THIS BODY IS NOW THE ULTIMATE WEAPON!!
HEY, FOLKS...

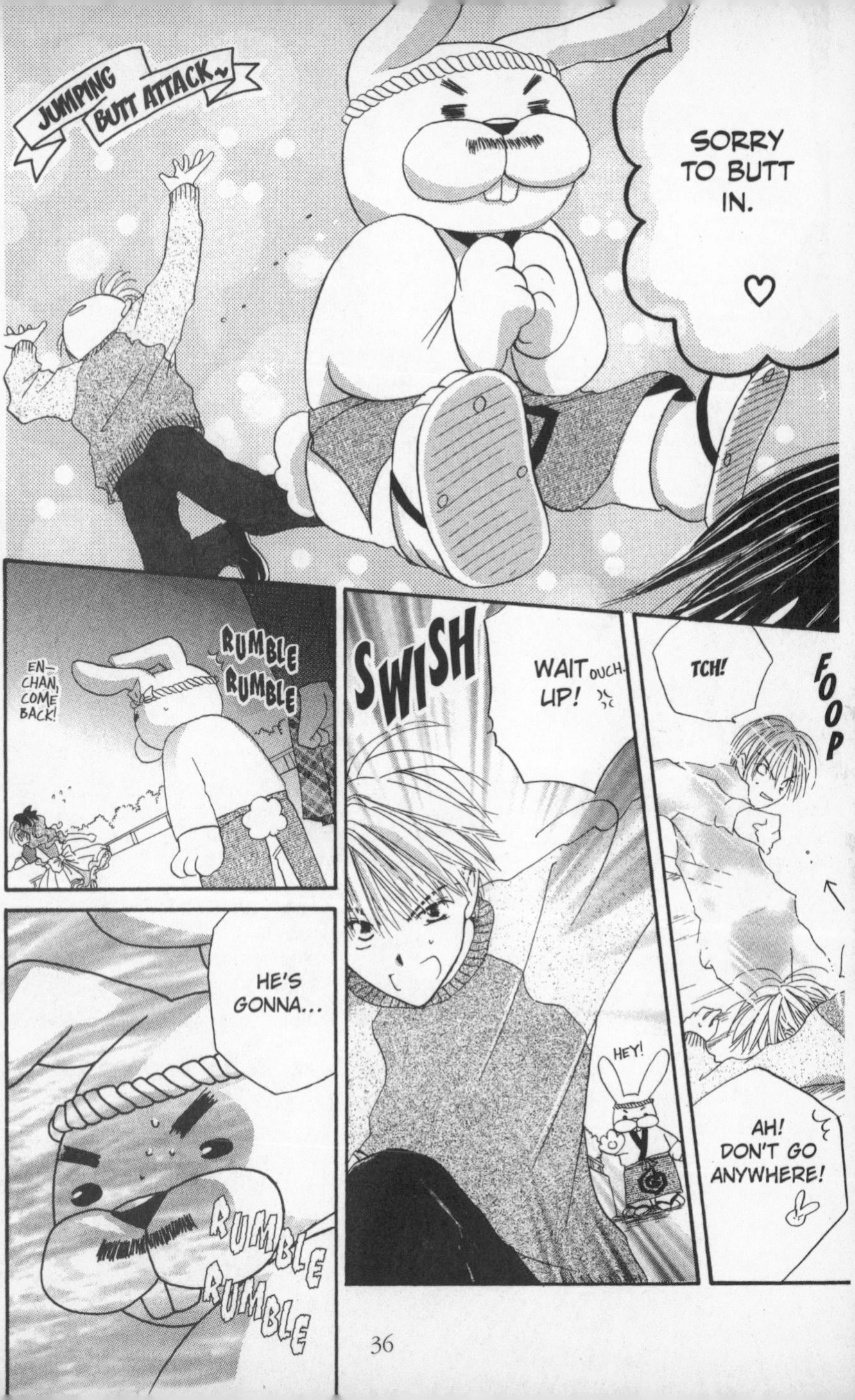
SORRY TO BUTT IN. ♡
JUMPING BUTT ATTACK~
TCH!
FOOP
AH! DON'T GO ANYWHERE!
SWISH
WAIT UP!
OUCH
HEY!
RUMBLE RUMBLE
EN-CHAN, COME BACK!
HE'S GONNA...
RUMBLE RUMBLE

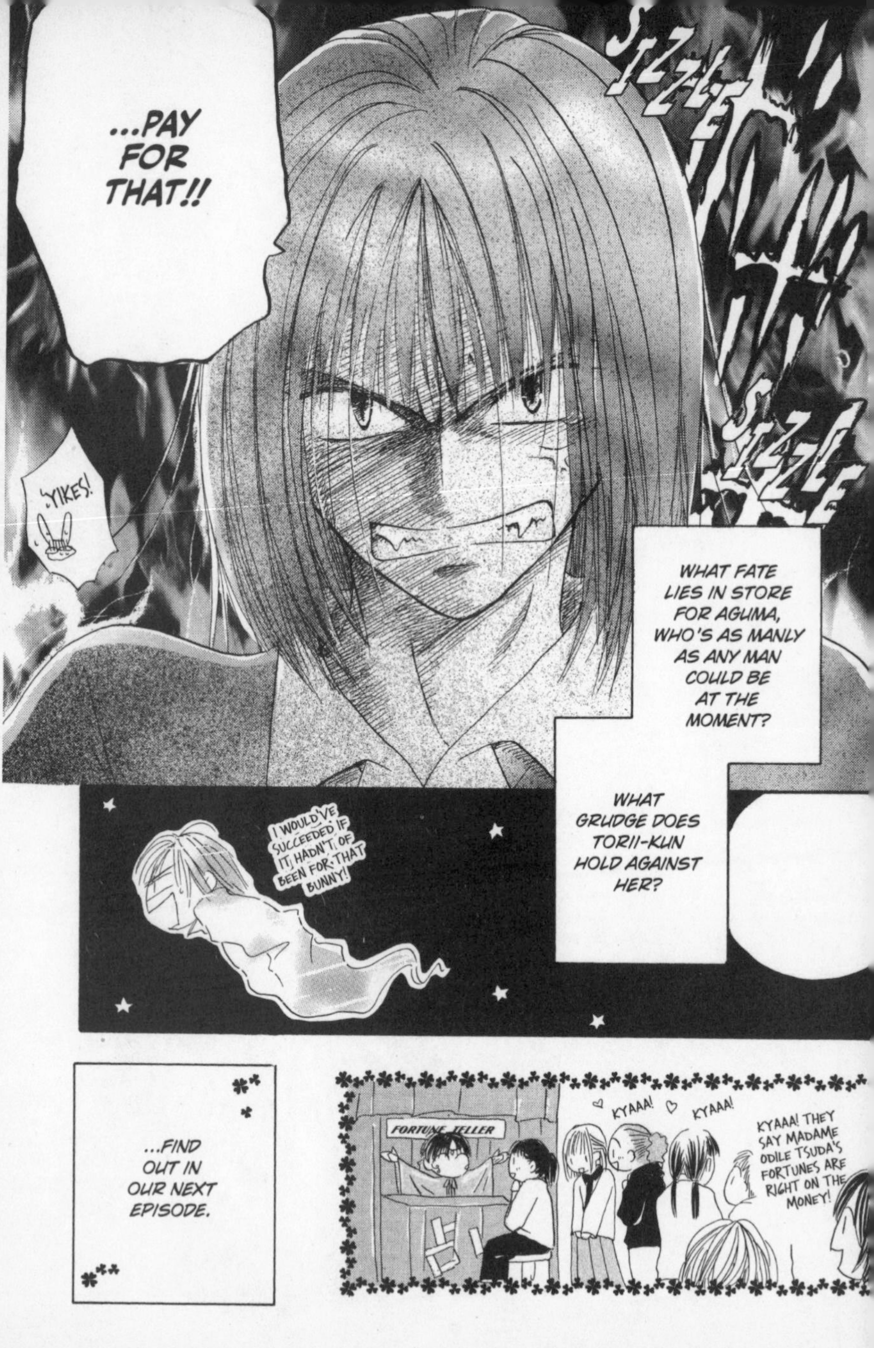

SIZZLE
SIZZLE
...PAY FOR THAT!!
YIKES!
WHAT FATE LIES IN STORE FOR AGUMA, WHO'S AS MANLY AS ANY MAN COULD BE AT THE MOMENT?
WHAT GRUDGE DOES TORII-KUN HOLD AGAINST HER?
I WOULD'VE SUCCEEDED IF IT HADN'T OF BEEN FOR THAT BUNNY!
KYAAA! THEY SAY MADAME ODILE TSUDA'S FORTUNES ARE RIGHT ON THE MONEY!
KYAAA!
KYAAA!
FORTUNE TELLER
...FIND OUT IN OUR NEXT EPISODE.

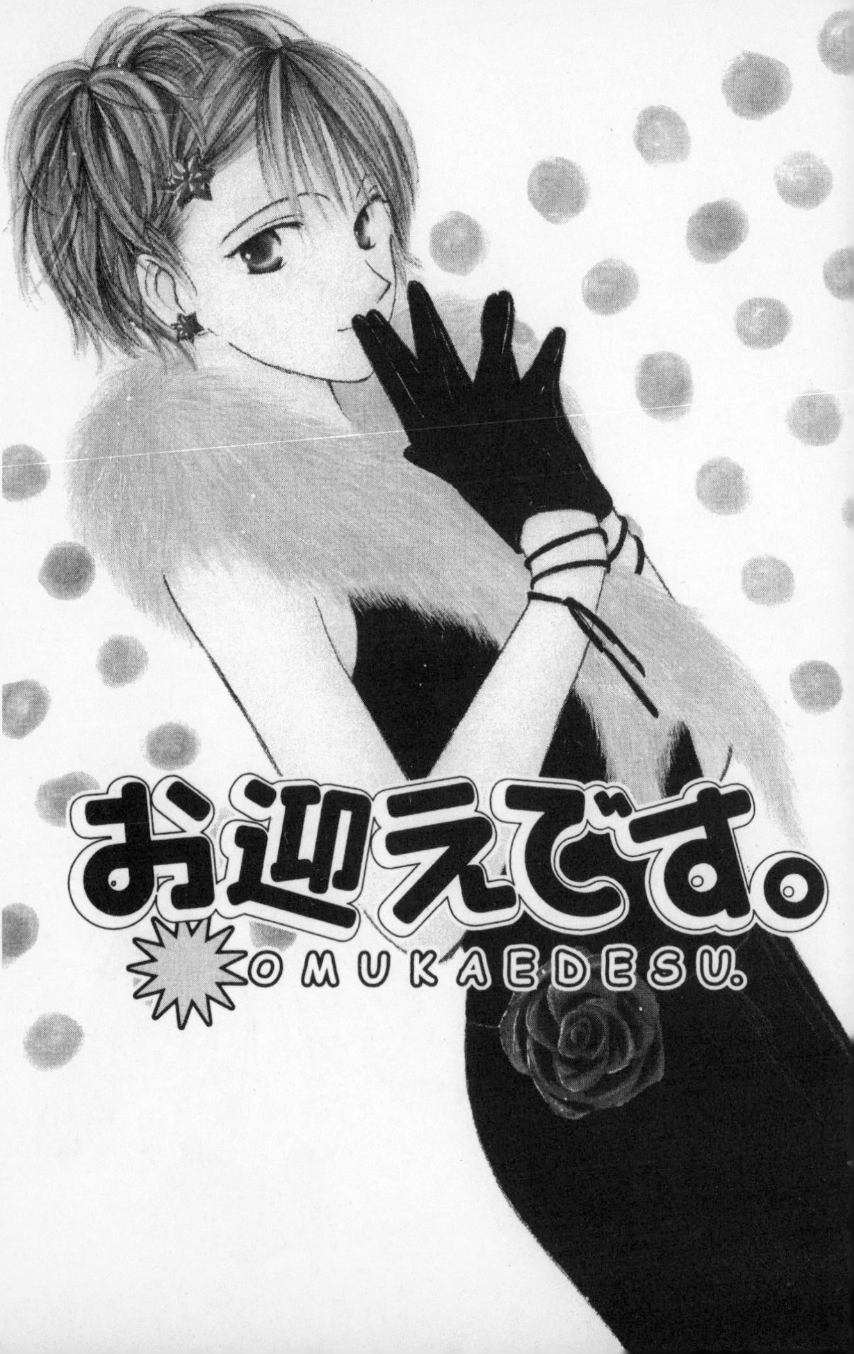
お迎えです。
OMUKAEDESU.

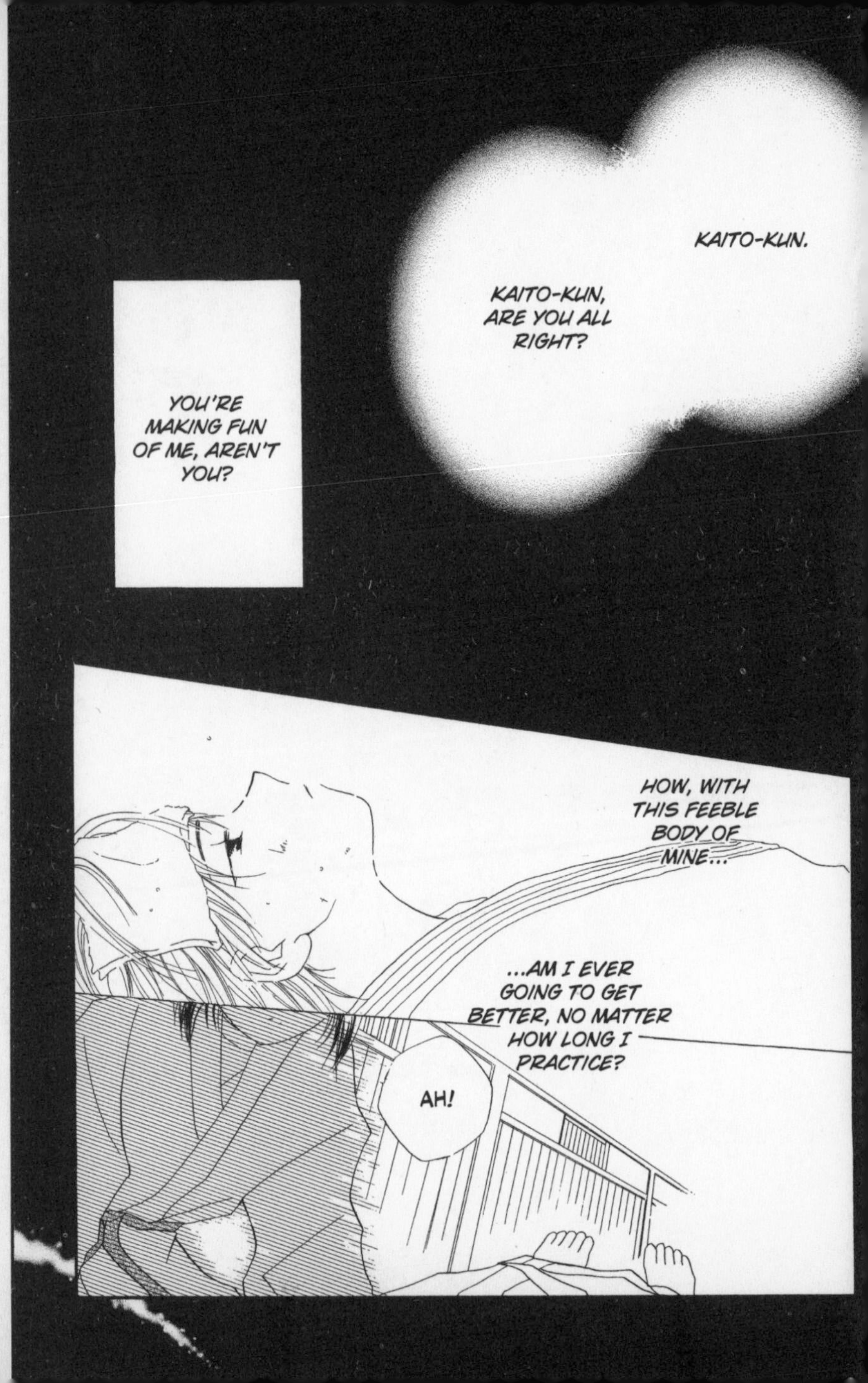
KAITO-KUN.
KAITO-KUN, ARE YOU ALL RIGHT?
YOU'RE MAKING FUN OF ME, AREN'T YOU?
HOW, WITH THIS FEEBLE BODY OF MINE...
...AM I EVER GOING TO GET BETTER, NO MATTER HOW LONG I PRACTICE?
AH!

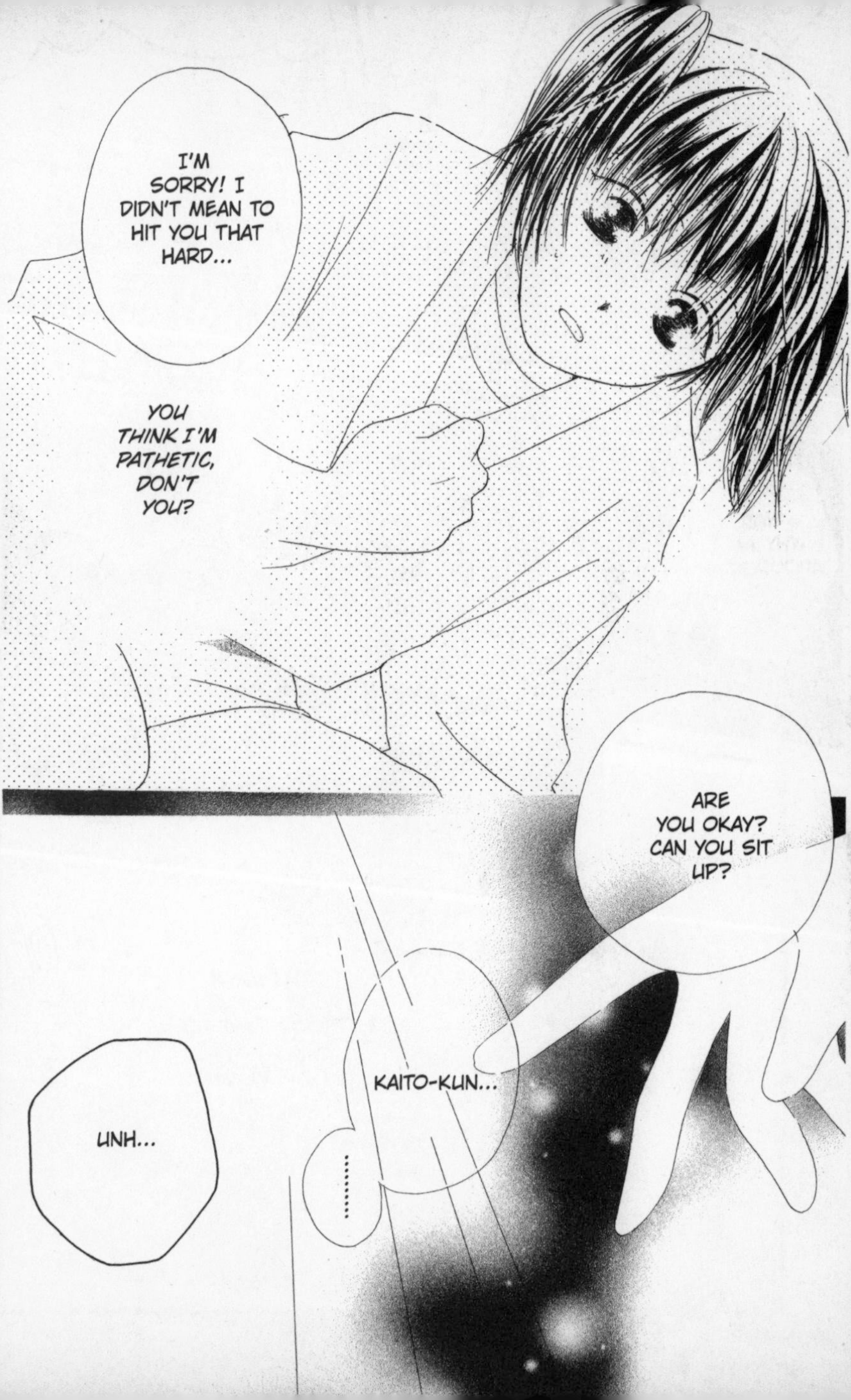
I'M SORRY! I DIDN'T MEAN TO HIT YOU THAT HARD...
YOU THINK I'M PATHETIC, DON'T YOU?
ARE YOU OKAY? CAN YOU SIT UP?
KAITO-KUN...
......
UNH...

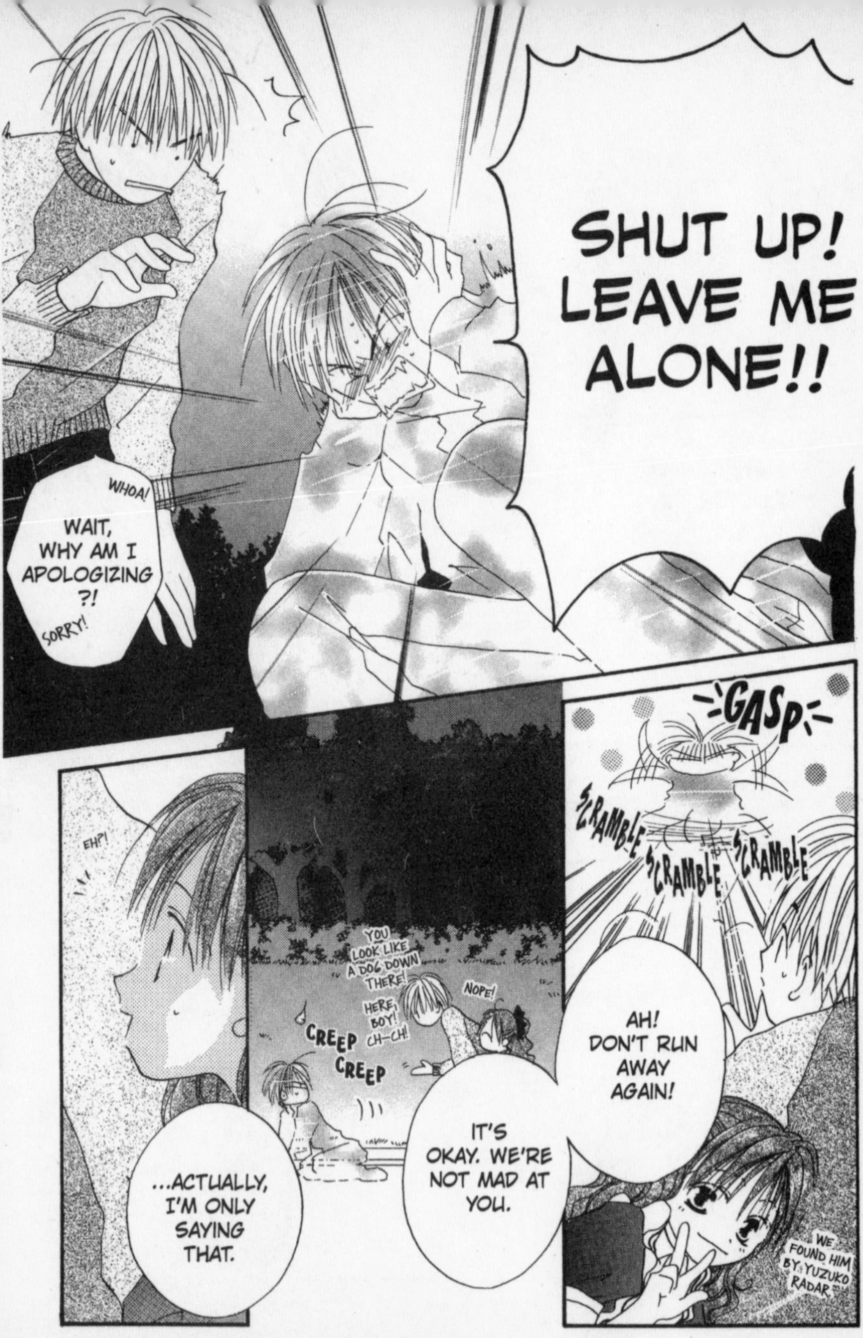
SHUT UP! LEAVE ME ALONE!!
WHOA!
WAIT, WHY AM I APOLOGIZING?!
SORRY!
GASP
SCRAMBLE SCRAMBLE SCRAMBLE
AH! DON'T RUN AWAY AGAIN!
WE FOUND HIM BY YUZUKO RADAR.
NOPE!
YOU LOOK LIKE A DOG DOWN THERE!
HERE, BOY! CH-CH!
CREEP CREEP
IT'S OKAY. WE'RE NOT MAD AT YOU.
EH?!
...ACTUALLY, I'M ONLY SAYING THAT.

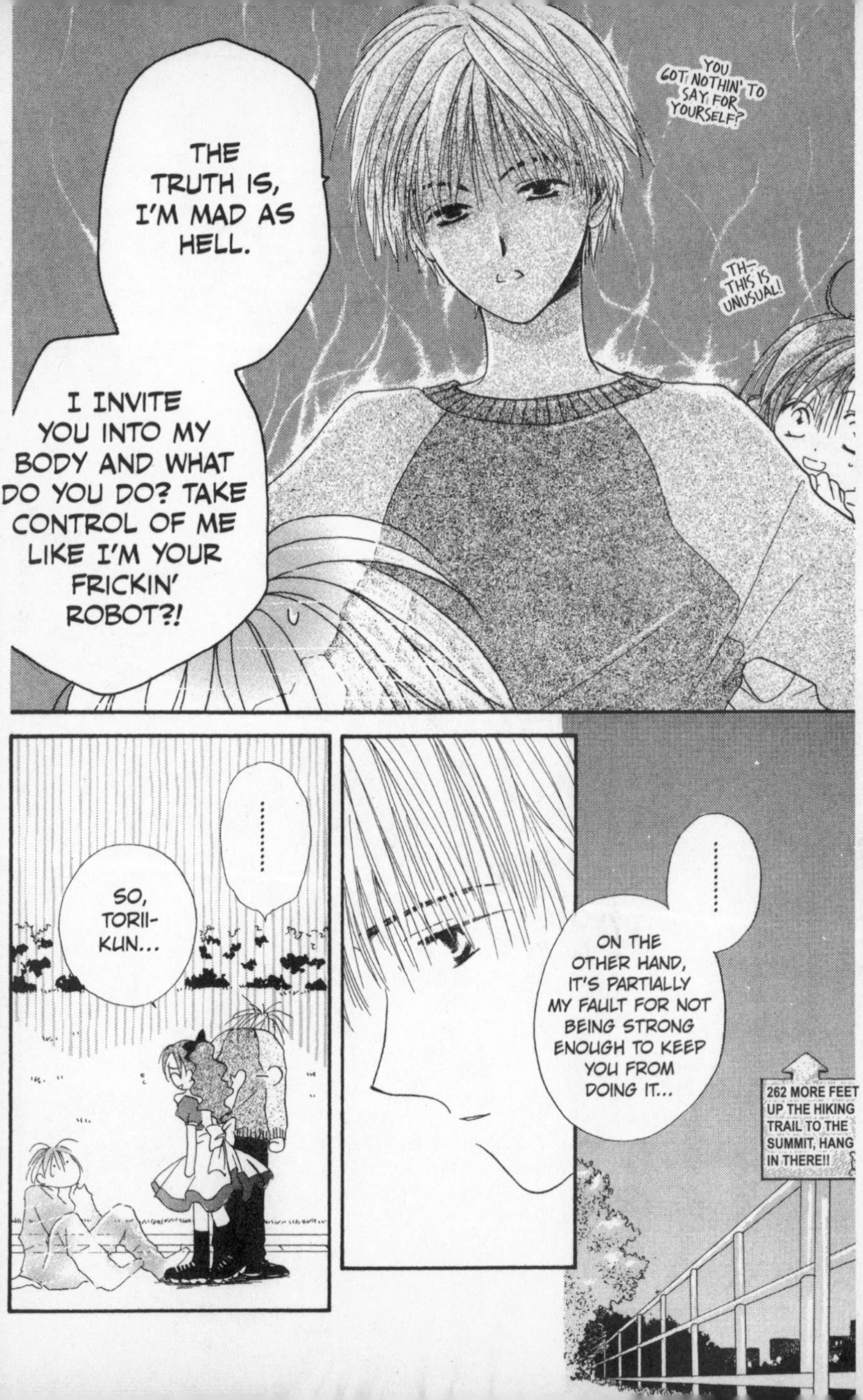
YOU GOT NOTHIN' TO SAY FOR YOURSELF?
TH- THIS IS UNUSUAL!
THE TRUTH IS, I'M MAD AS HELL.
I INVITE YOU INTO MY BODY AND WHAT DO YOU DO? TAKE CONTROL OF ME LIKE I'M YOUR FRICKIN' ROBOT?!
262 MORE FEET UP THE HIKING TRAIL TO THE SUMMIT, HANG IN THERE!!
......
ON THE OTHER HAND, IT'S PARTIALLY MY FAULT FOR NOT BEING STRONG ENOUGH TO KEEP YOU FROM DOING IT...
......
SO, TORII-KUN...

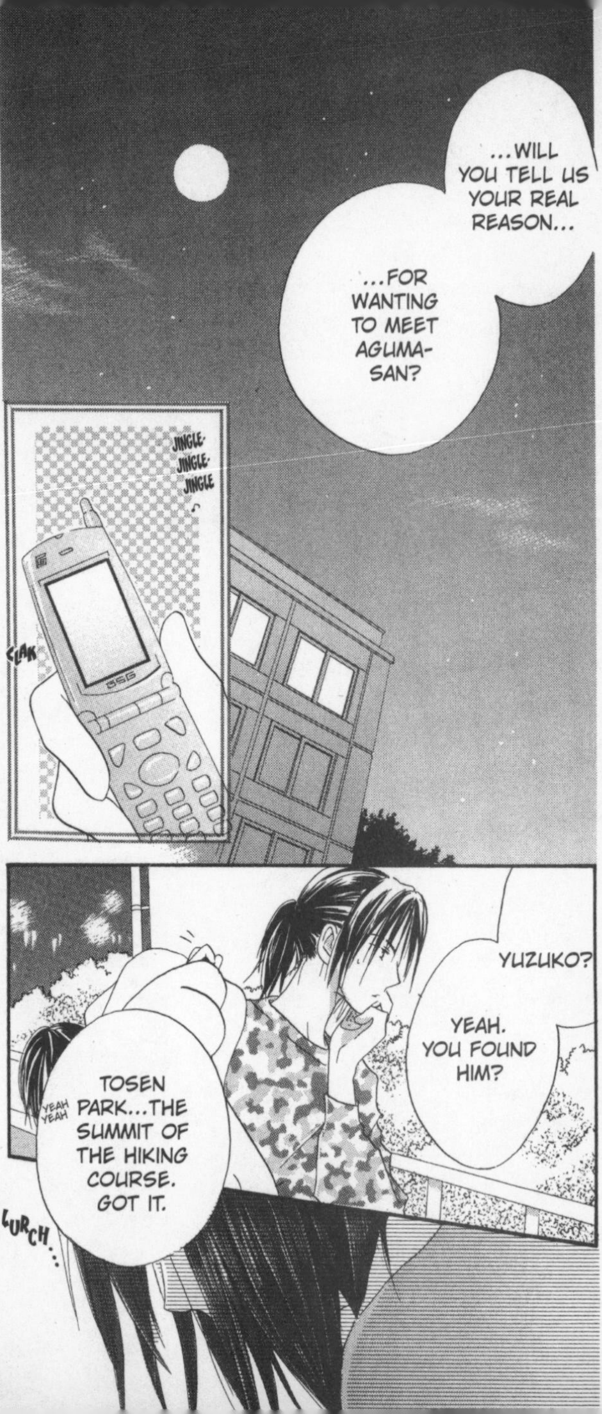
...WILL YOU TELL US YOUR REAL REASON...
...FOR WANTING TO MEET AGUMA-SAN?
JINGLE JINGLE JINGLE
CLAK
YUZUKO?
YEAH. YOU FOUND HIM?
TOSEN PARK...THE SUMMIT OF THE HIKING COURSE. GOT IT.
YEAH YEAH
LURCH...

KISS.

WHOOO, THAT WAS A HOT KISS THEY HAD, WASN'T IT? I GOT A LOT OF LETTERS FROM READERS ASKING, "WHO WAS IT, EN-CHAN OR KAITO-KUN?!"

MMM, SORRY! ACTUALLY, I'M NOT EVEN SURE MYSELF!

MAYBE IT WAS A COMBINATION OF BOTH OF THEM, WITH BOTH OF THEIR FEELINGS IN SYNCHRONICITY. WHEN I WRITE THE SCRIPT, I NEVER USE AN OUTLINE, BUT JUST PLAY IT BY EAR, SO THE CHARACTERS OFTEN SURPRISE ME.

BY THE WAY, THERE'S AN ORIGIN TO KAITO TORII-KUN'S NAME. WHEN I WENT TO A SIGNING IN HIROSHIMA, I STAYED AT AN INN IN MIYAJIMA, SO TO COMMEMORATE THAT TRIP AND MIYAJIMA'S FAMOUS TORII (GATEWAY AT THE ENTRANCE TO A SHINTO SHRINE), I USED IT HERE.

THANK YOU TO EVERYONE WHO CAME TO THE SIGNING!!

I WAS VERY UNCOOL IN THE MIDDLE OF THE SIGNING, WHEN I HAD TO RUN TO THE TOILET.

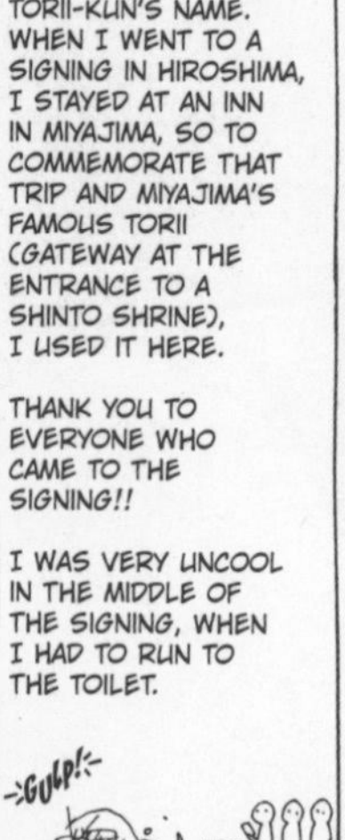
GULP!

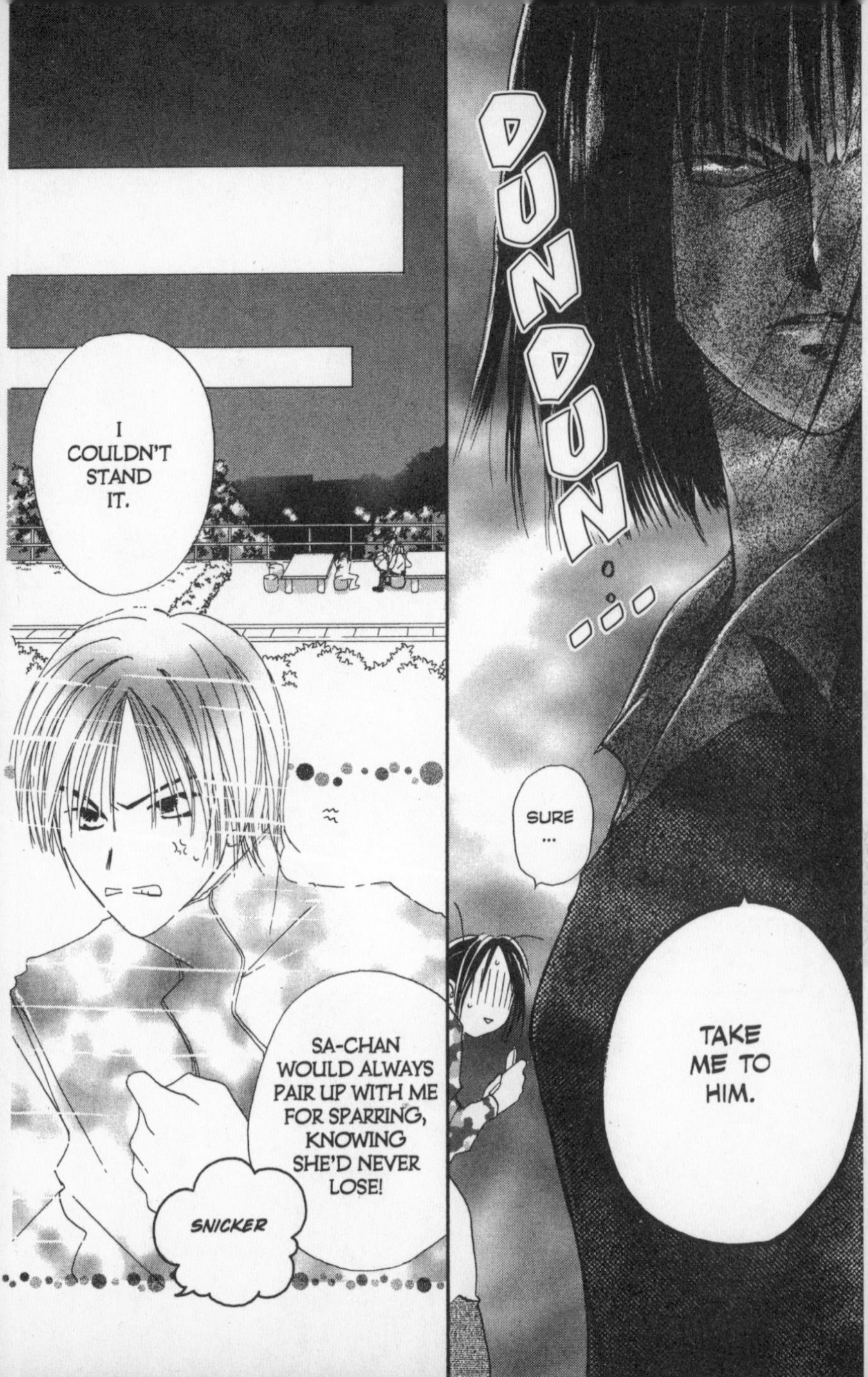
DUN DUN...
TAKE ME TO HIM.
SURE...
I COULDN'T STAND IT.
SA-CHAN WOULD ALWAYS PAIR UP WITH ME FOR SPARRING, KNOWING SHE'D NEVER LOSE!
SNICKER

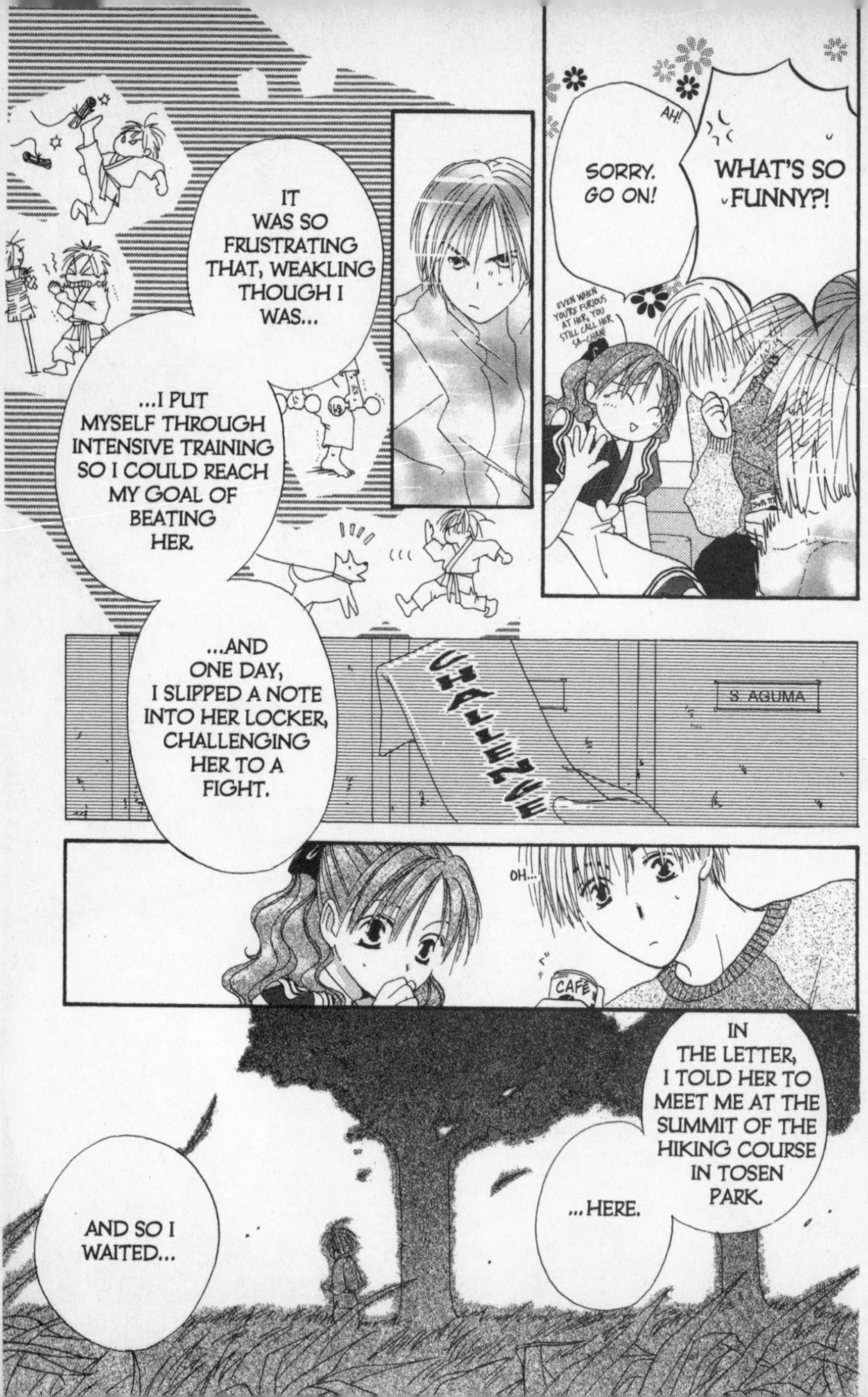
WHAT'S SO FUNNY?!
AH!
SORRY. GO ON!
EVEN WHEN YOU'RE FURIOUS AT HER, YOU STILL CALL HER SA-CHAN
IT WAS SO FRUSTRATING THAT, WEAKLING THOUGH I WAS...
...I PUT MYSELF THROUGH INTENSIVE TRAINING SO I COULD REACH MY GOAL OF BEATING HER.
S. AGUMA
CHALLENGE
...AND ONE DAY, I SLIPPED A NOTE INTO HER LOCKER, CHALLENGING HER TO A FIGHT.
OH...
CAFE
IN THE LETTER, I TOLD HER TO MEET ME AT THE SUMMIT OF THE HIKING COURSE IN TOSEN PARK.
...HERE.
AND SO I WAITED...

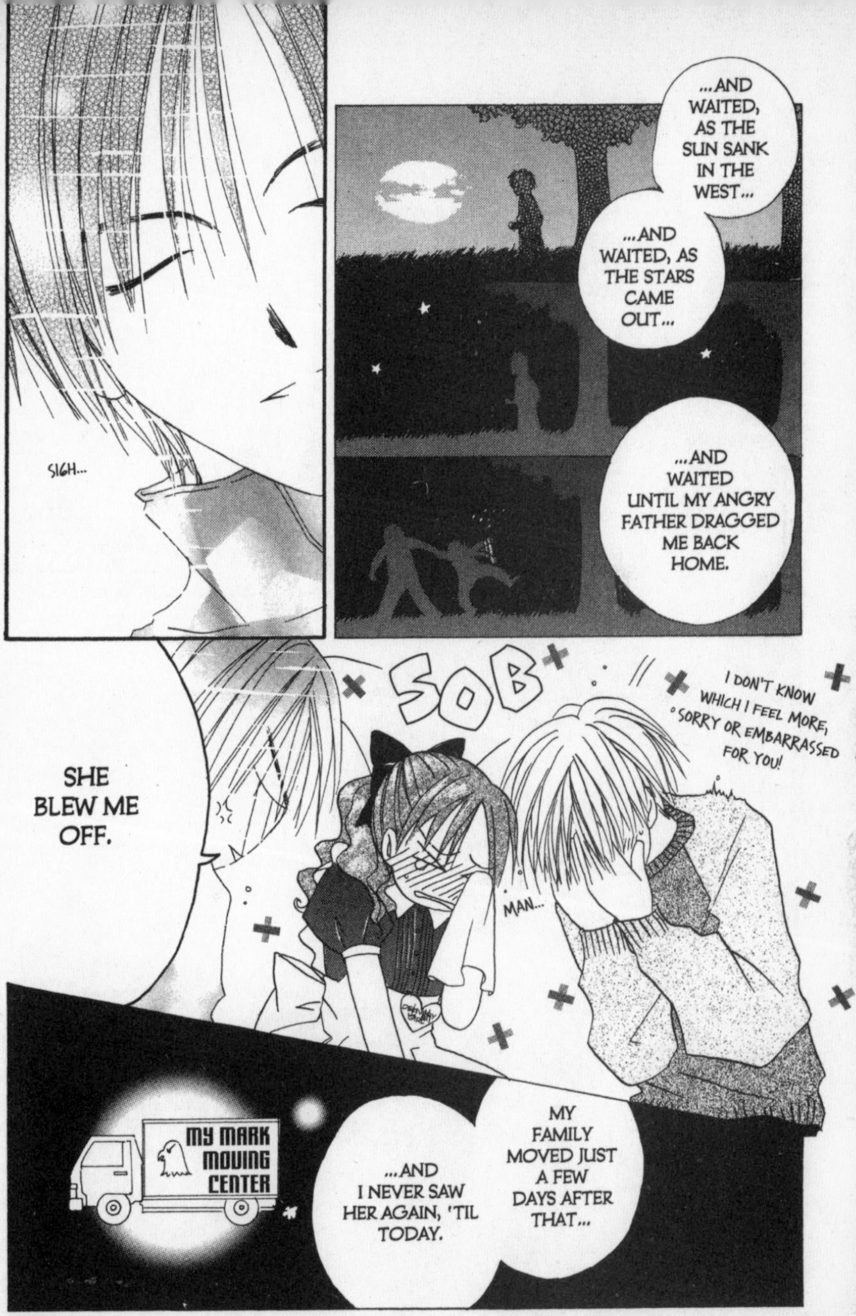
...AND WAITED, AS THE SUN SANK IN THE WEST...
...AND WAITED, AS THE STARS CAME OUT...
...AND WAITED UNTIL MY ANGRY FATHER DRAGGED ME BACK HOME.
SIGH...
I DON'T KNOW WHICH I FEEL MORE, SORRY OR EMBARRASSED FOR YOU!
SOB
SHE BLEW ME OFF.
MAN...
MY FAMILY MOVED JUST A FEW DAYS AFTER THAT...
...AND I NEVER SAW HER AGAIN, 'TIL TODAY.
MY MARK MOVING CENTER

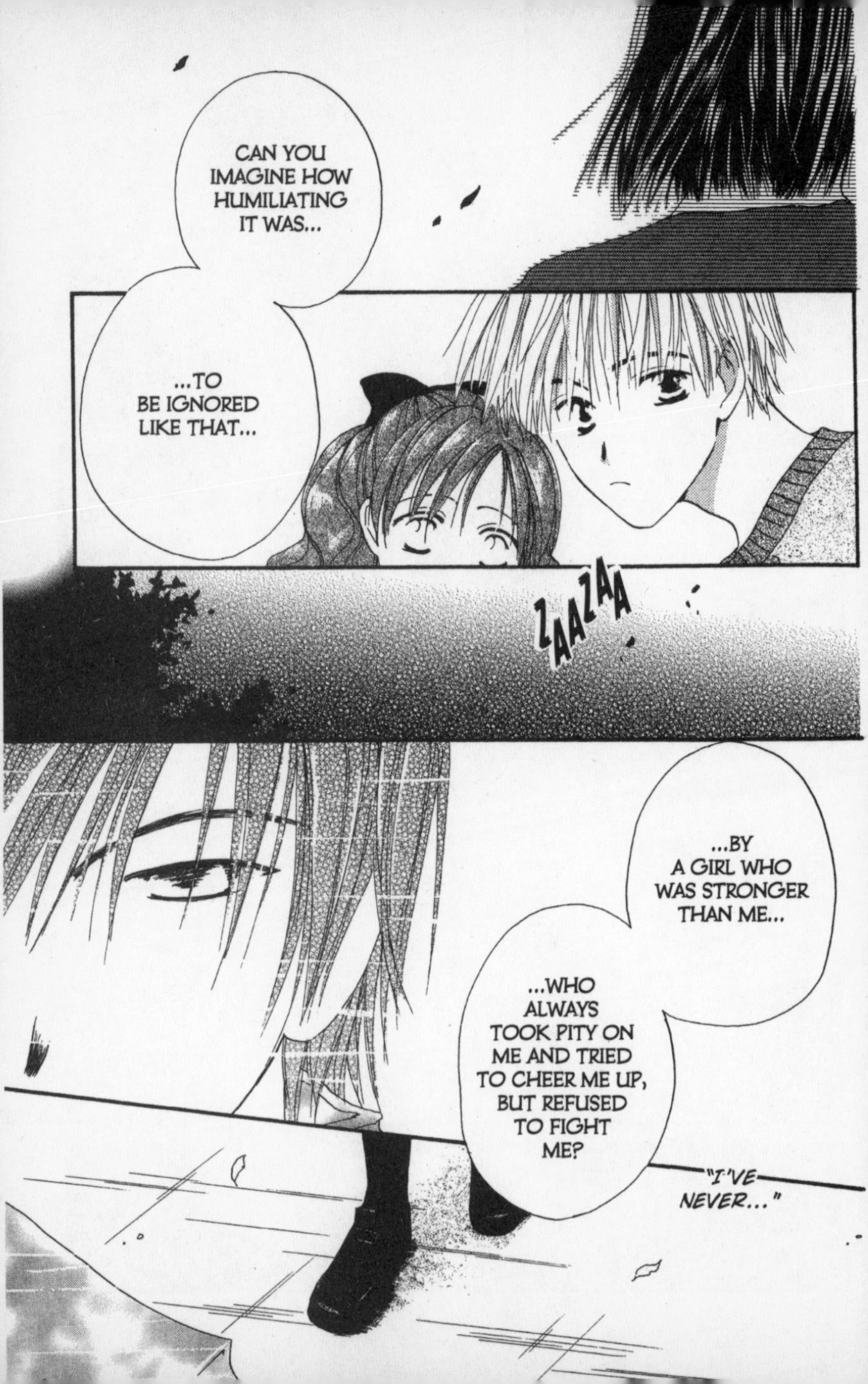

CAN YOU IMAGINE HOW HUMILIATING IT WAS...
...TO BE IGNORED LIKE THAT...
ZAAZAA
...BY A GIRL WHO WAS STRONGER THAN ME...
...WHO ALWAYS TOOK PITY ON ME AND TRIED TO CHEER ME UP, BUT REFUSED TO FIGHT ME?
"I'VE NEVER..."

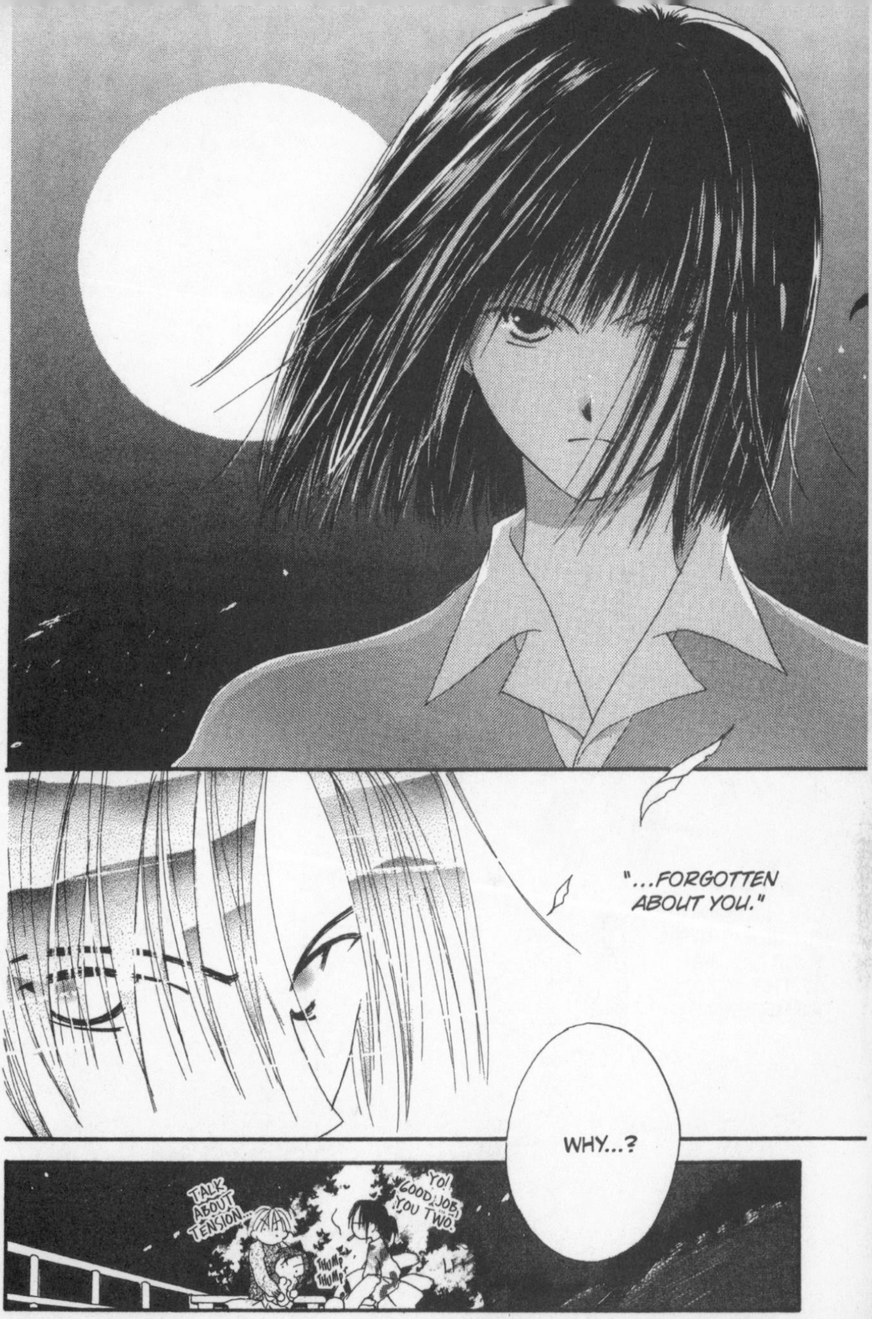
"...FORGOTTEN ABOUT YOU."
WHY...?
YO! GOOD JOB, YOU TWO.
THUMP THUMP
TALK ABOUT TENSION...

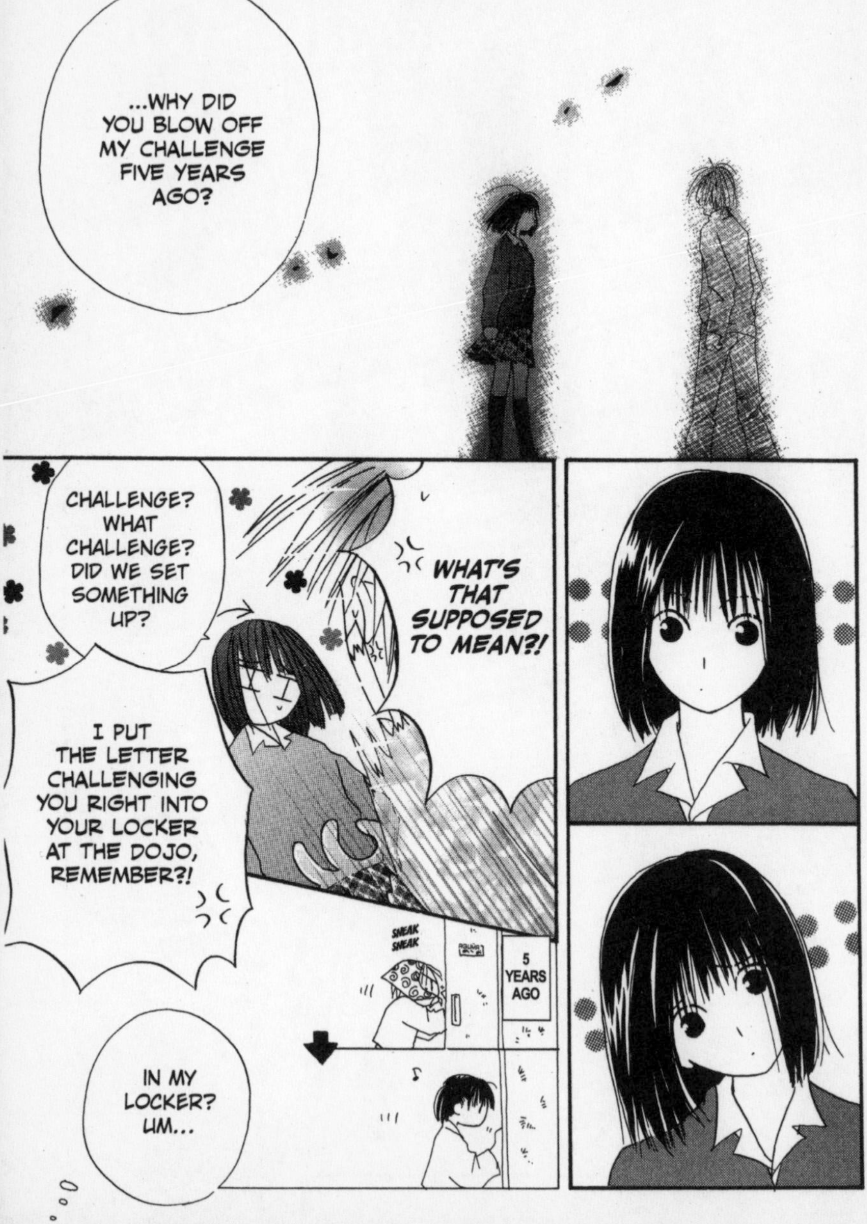
...WHY DID YOU BLOW OFF MY CHALLENGE FIVE YEARS AGO?
CHALLENGE? WHAT CHALLENGE? DID WE SET SOMETHING UP?
WHAT'S THAT SUPPOSED TO MEAN?!
I PUT THE LETTER CHALLENGING YOU RIGHT INTO YOUR LOCKER AT THE DOJO, REMEMBER?!
5 YEARS AGO
SNEAK SNEAK
IN MY LOCKER? UM...

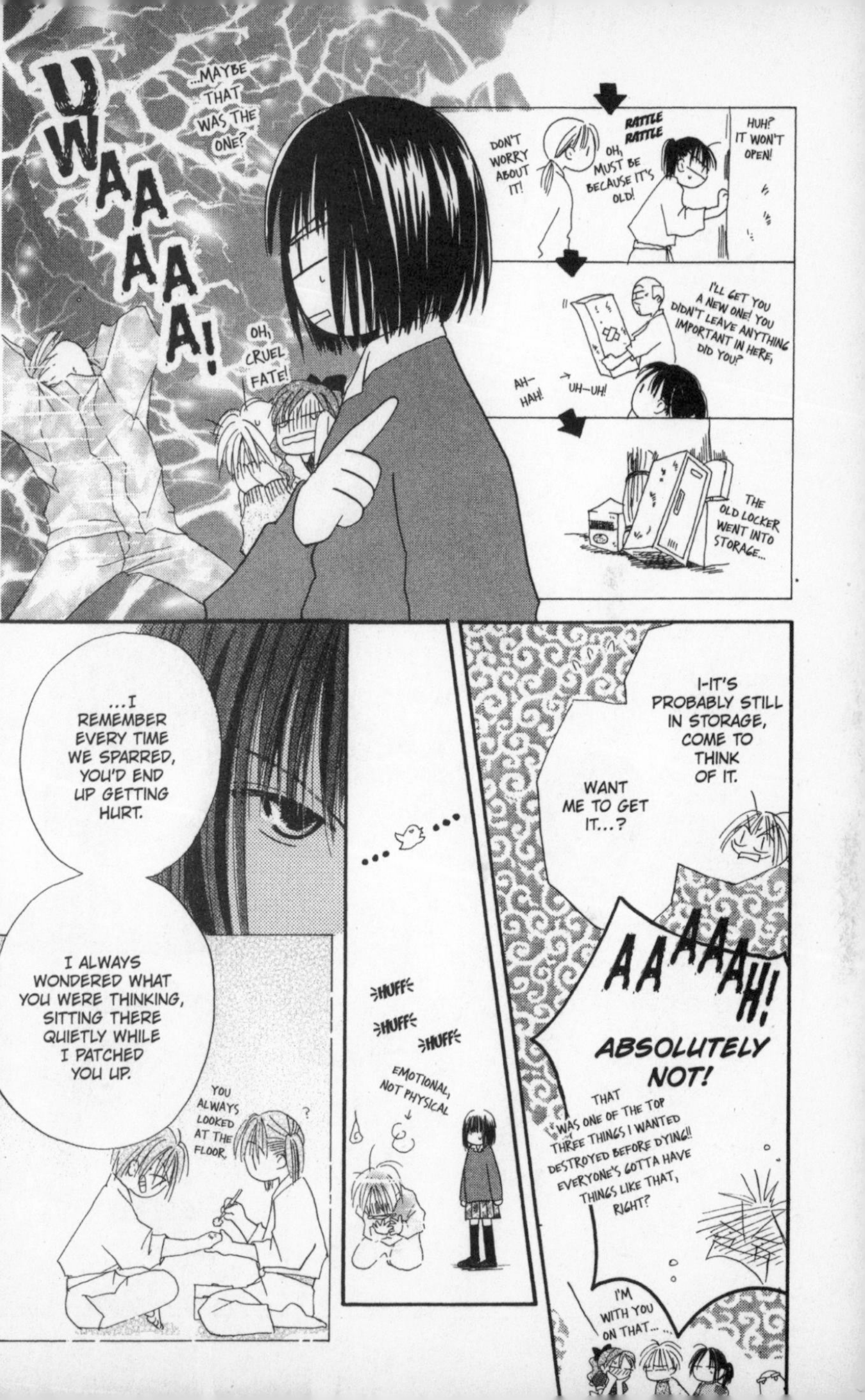
HUH? IT WON'T OPEN!
RATTLE RATTLE
OH, MUST BE BECAUSE IT'S OLD!
DON'T WORRY ABOUT IT!
I'LL GET YOU A NEW ONE! YOU DIDN'T LEAVE ANYTHING IMPORTANT IN HERE, DID YOU?
AH-HAH! → UH-UH!
THE OLD LOCKER WENT INTO STORAGE...
...MAYBE THAT WAS THE ONE?
UWAAAAA!
OH, CRUEL FATE!
I-IT'S PROBABLY STILL IN STORAGE, COME TO THINK OF IT.
WANT ME TO GET IT...?
AAAAAH!
ABSOLUTELY NOT!
THAT WAS ONE OF THE TOP THREE THINGS I WANTED DESTROYED BEFORE DYING!! EVERYONE'S GOTTA HAVE THINGS LIKE THAT, RIGHT?
I'M WITH YOU ON THAT...
... ...
HUFF
HUFF
HUFF
EMOTIONAL, NOT PHYSICAL
...I REMEMBER EVERY TIME WE SPARRED, YOU'D END UP GETTING HURT.
I ALWAYS WONDERED WHAT YOU WERE THINKING, SITTING THERE QUIETLY WHILE I PATCHED YOU UP.
YOU ALWAYS LOOKED AT THE FLOOR.

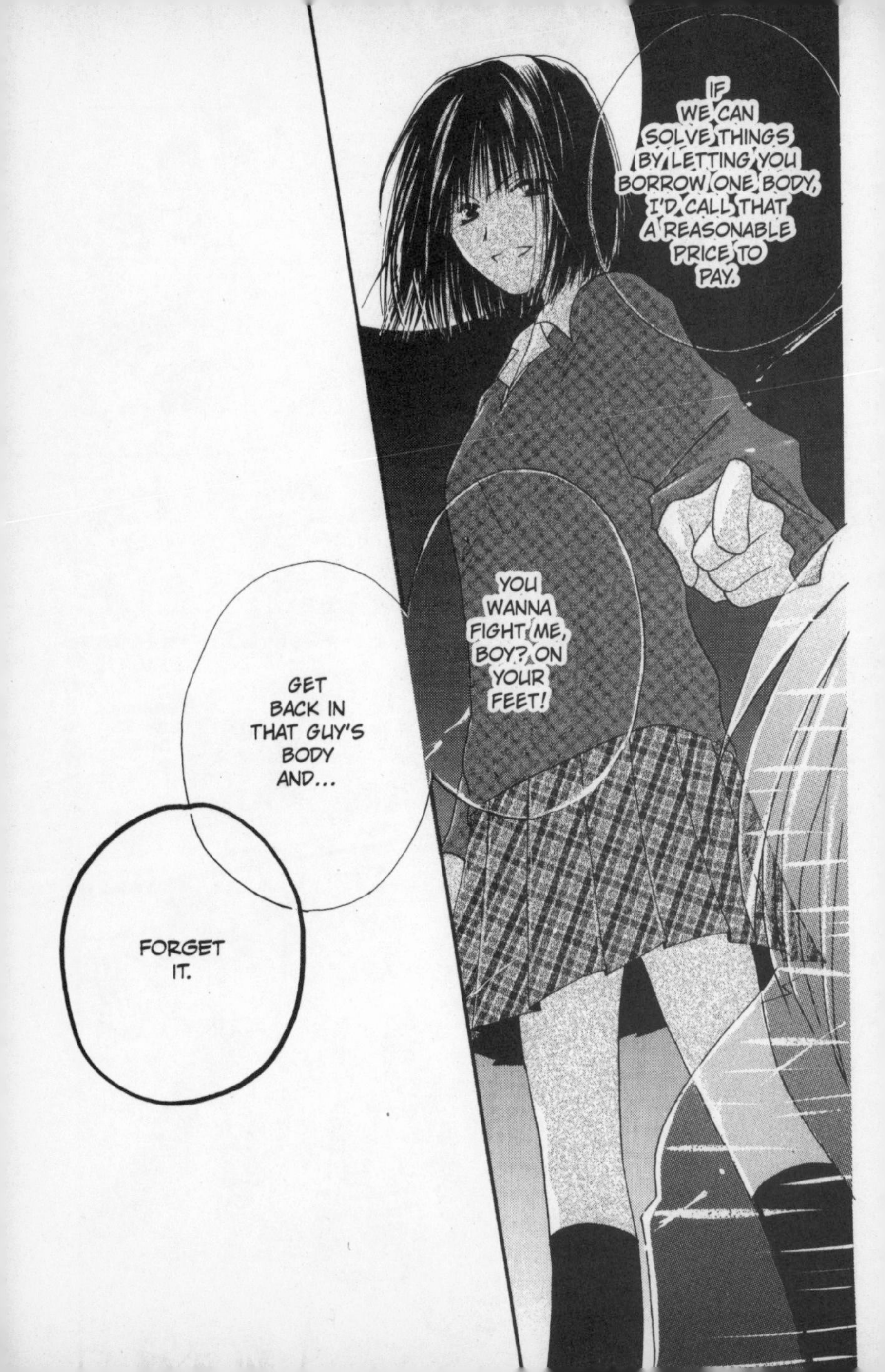
IF WE CAN SOLVE THINGS BY LETTING YOU BORROW ONE BODY, I'D CALL THAT A REASONABLE PRICE TO PAY.
YOU WANNA FIGHT ME, BOY? ON YOUR FEET!
GET BACK IN THAT GUY'S BODY AND...
FORGET IT.

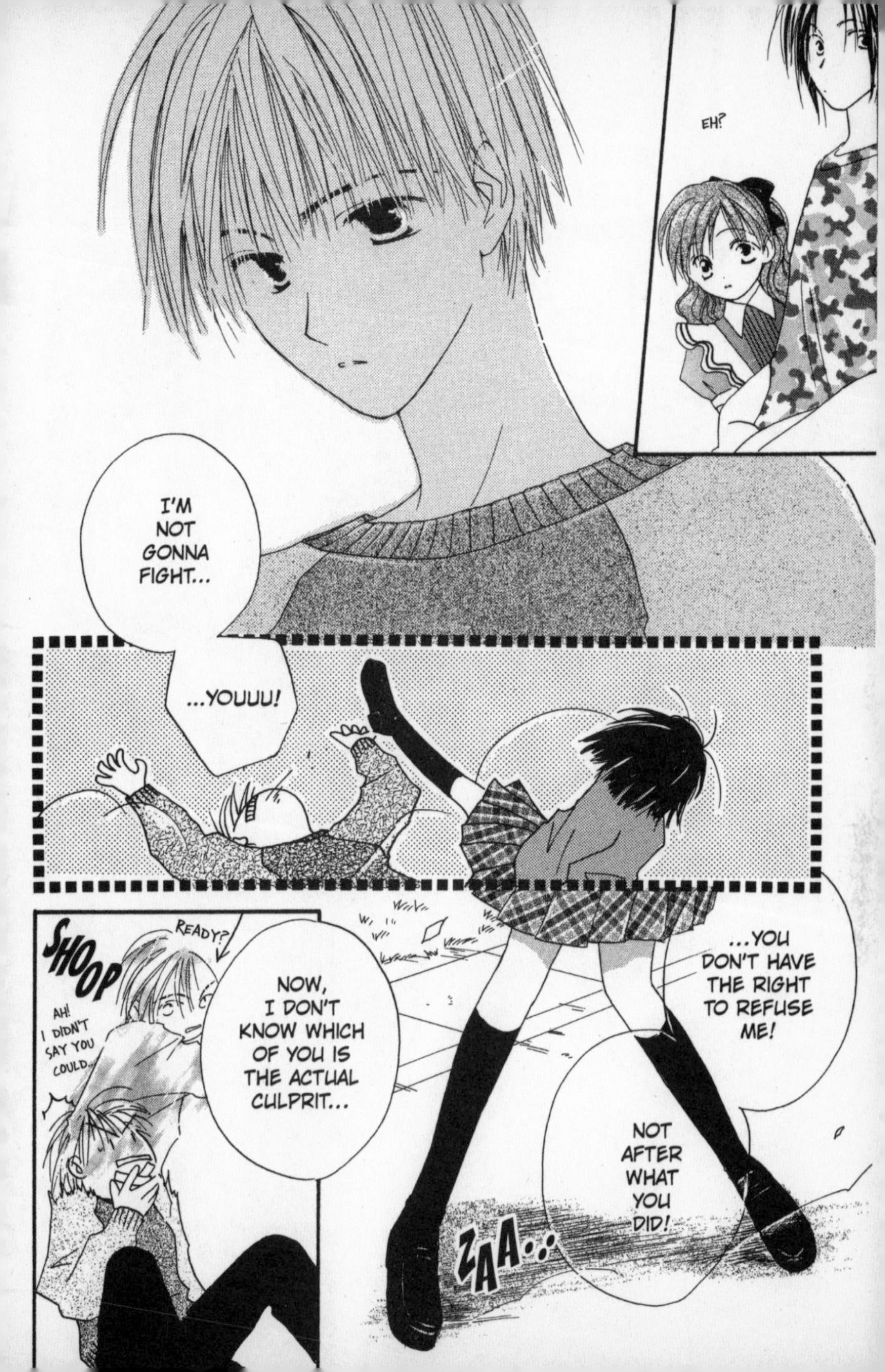
EH?
I'M NOT GONNA FIGHT...
...YOUUU!
...YOU DON'T HAVE THE RIGHT TO REFUSE ME!
NOT AFTER WHAT YOU DID!
ZAA..
NOW, I DON'T KNOW WHICH OF YOU IS THE ACTUAL CULPRIT...
READY?
SHOOP
AH! I DIDN'T SAY YOU COULD...

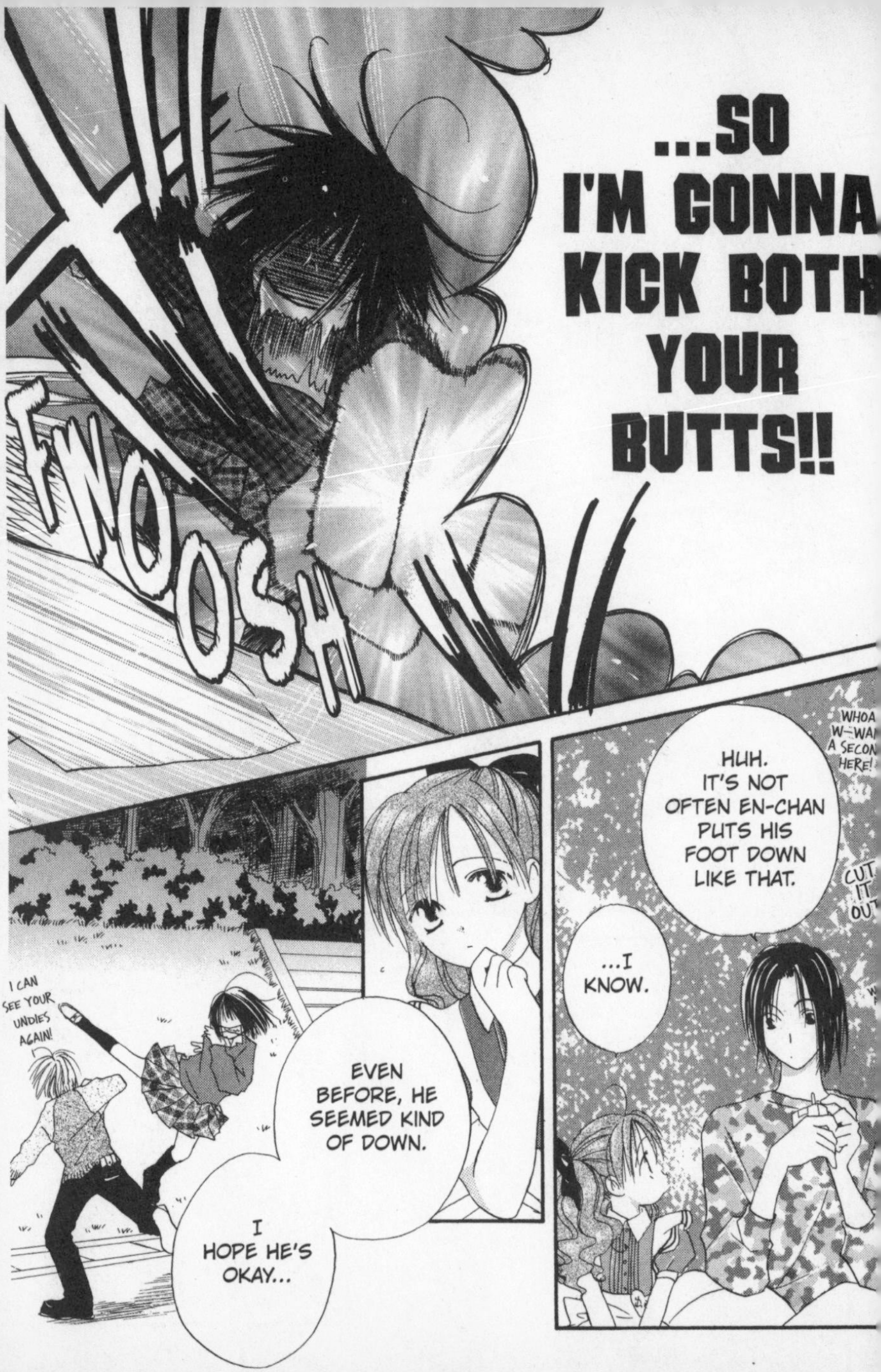
...SO I'M GONNA KICK BOTH YOUR BUTTS!!
FWOOSH
HUH. IT'S NOT OFTEN EN-CHAN PUTS HIS FOOT DOWN LIKE THAT.
...I KNOW.
EVEN BEFORE, HE SEEMED KIND OF DOWN.
I HOPE HE'S OKAY...
I CAN SEE YOUR UNDIES AGAIN!

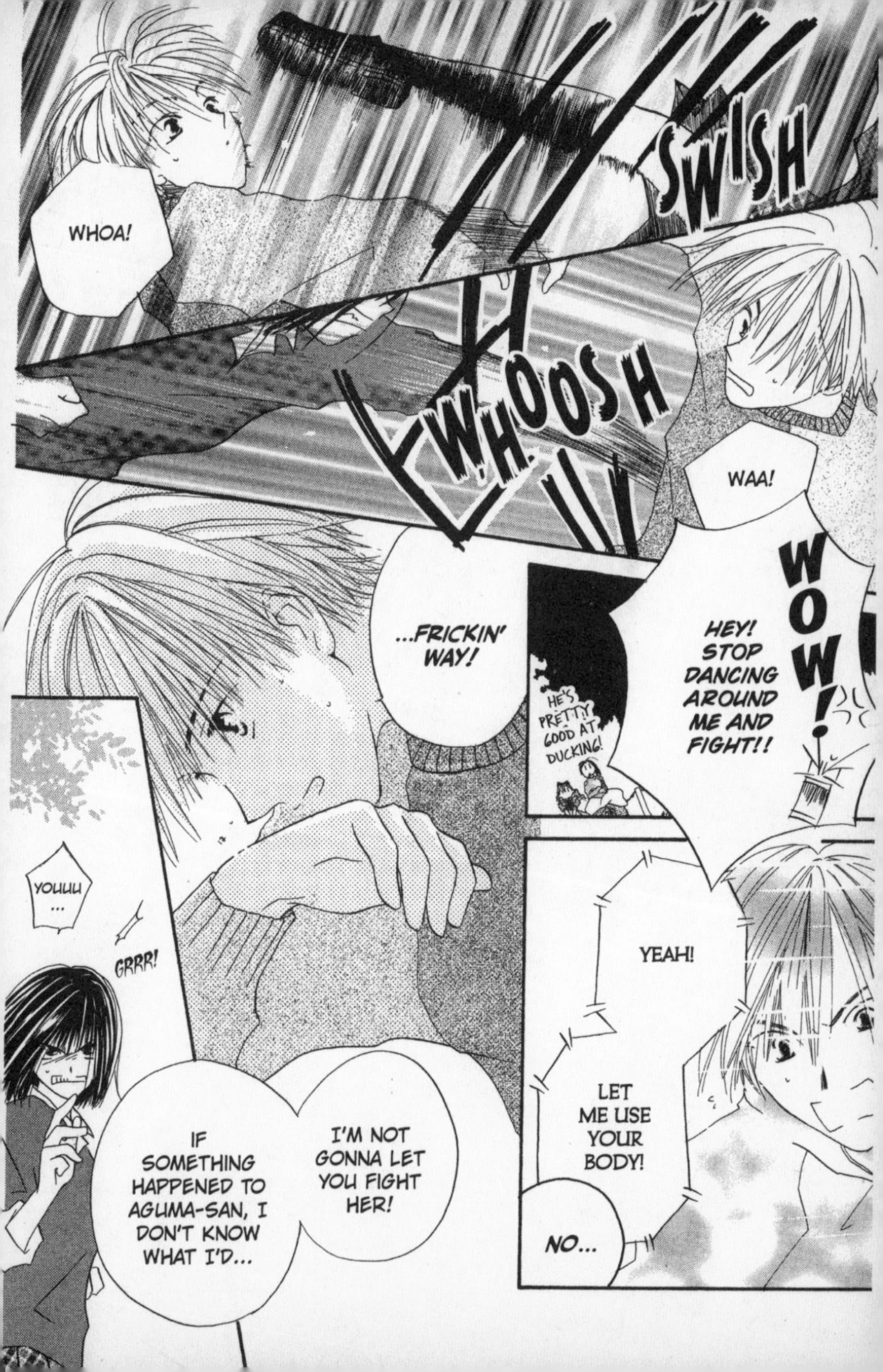
SWISH
WHOA!
WHOOSH
WAA!
WOW!
HEY! STOP DANCING AROUND ME AND FIGHT!!
HE'S PRETTY GOOD AT DUCKING!
...FRICKIN' WAY!
YEAH!
LET ME USE YOUR BODY!
NO...
YOUUU ...
GRRR!
I'M NOT GONNA LET YOU FIGHT HER!
IF SOMETHING HAPPENED TO AGUMA-SAN, I DON'T KNOW WHAT I'D...

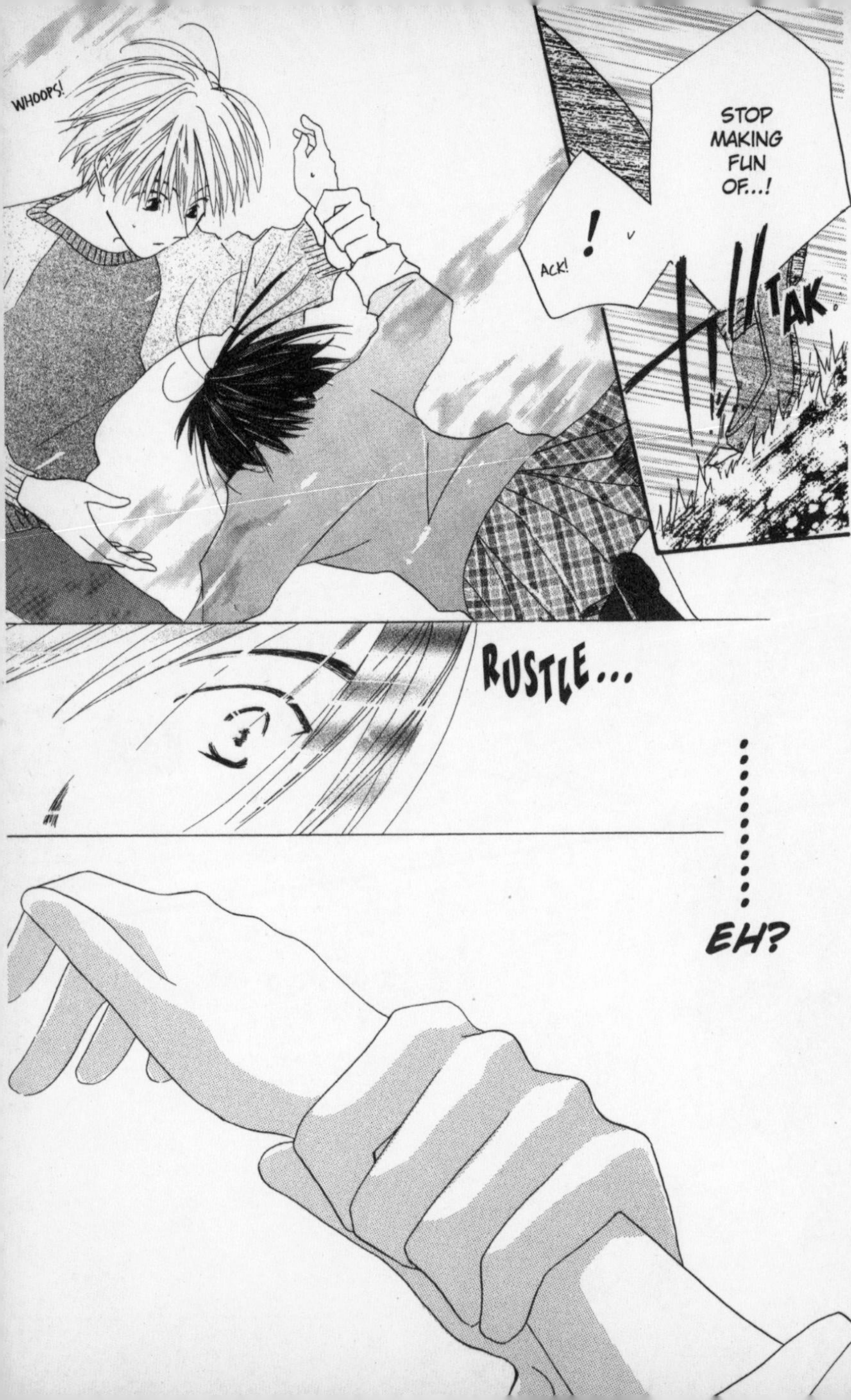
STOP MAKING FUN OF...!
TAK.
!
ACK!
WHOOPS!
RUSTLE...
....
EH?

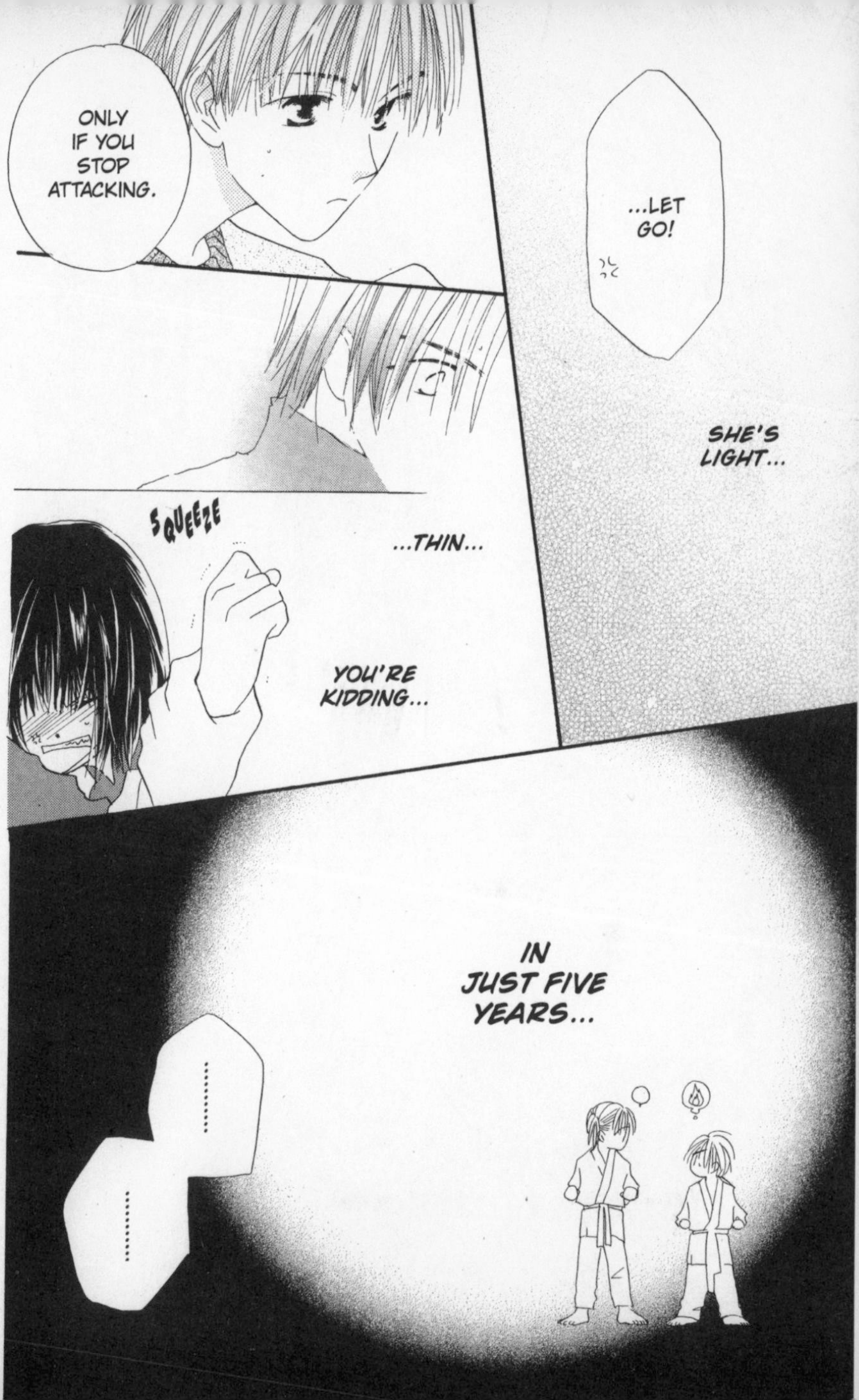
...LET GO!
SHE'S LIGHT...
ONLY IF YOU STOP ATTACKING.
SQUEEZE
...THIN...
YOU'RE KIDDING...
IN JUST FIVE YEARS...
......
......

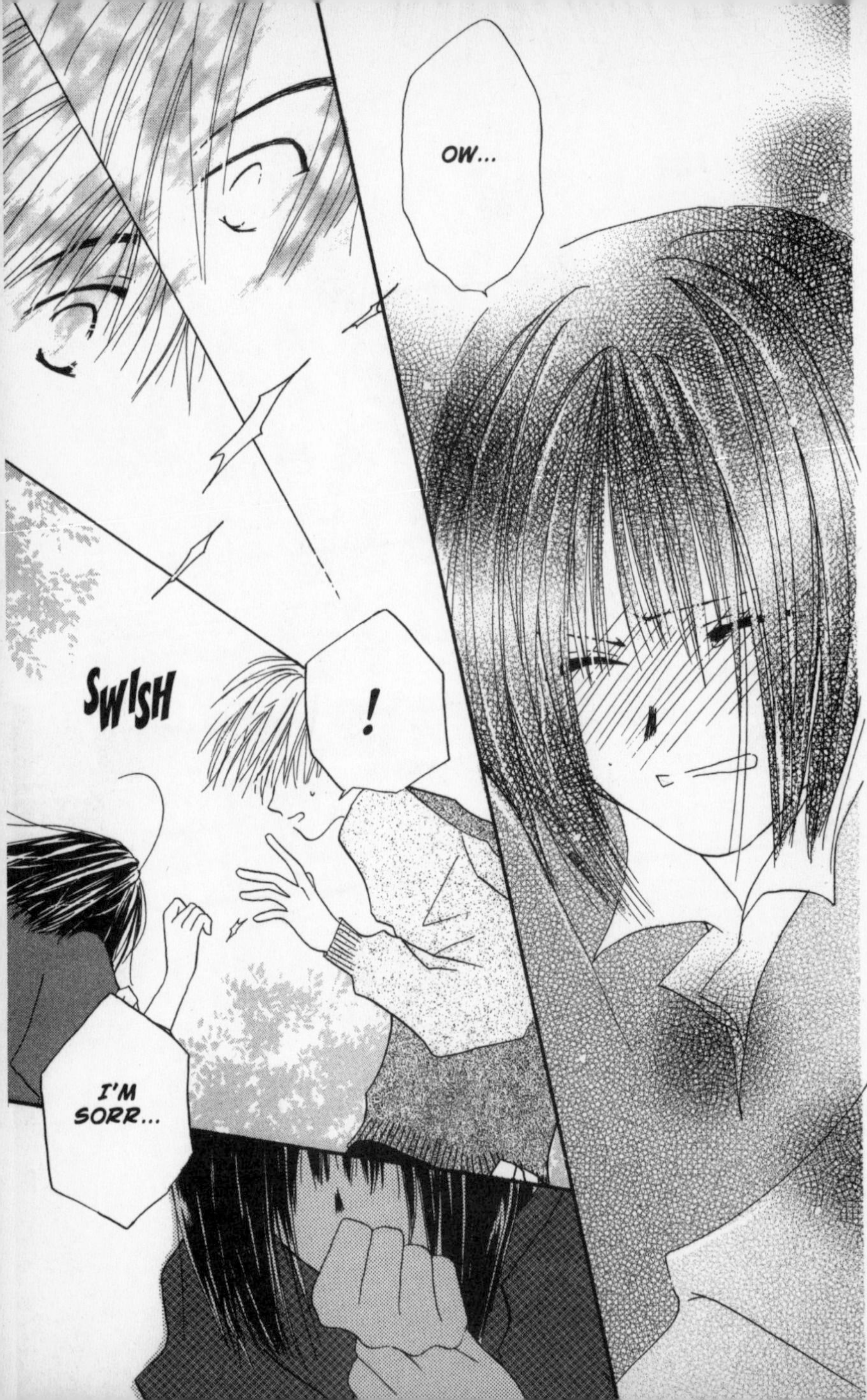
OW...
!
SWISH
I'M SORR...

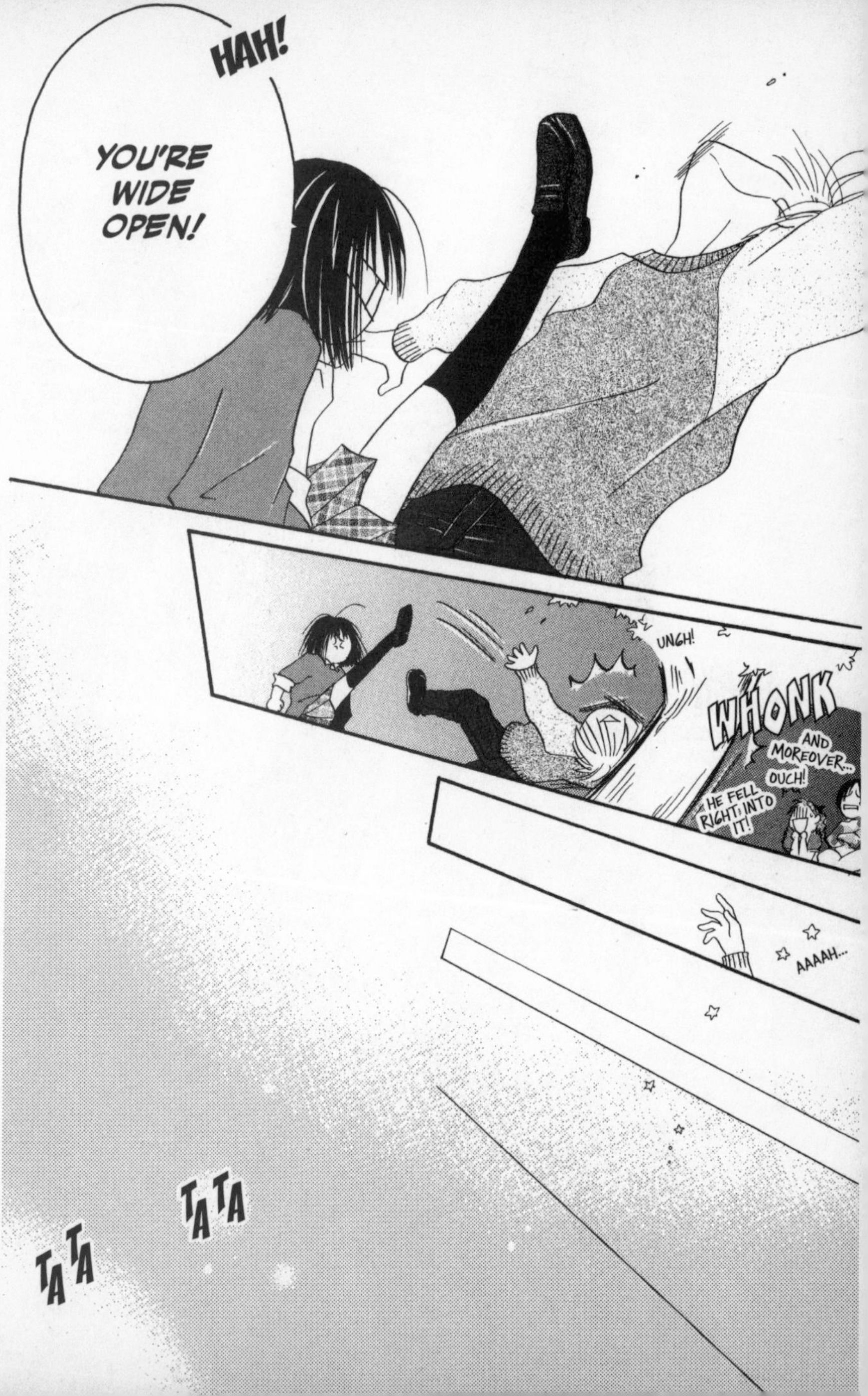
HAH!
YOU'RE WIDE OPEN!
UNGH!
WHONK
AND MOREOVER...
OUCH!
HE FELL RIGHT INTO IT!
AAAAH...
TA TA
TA TA

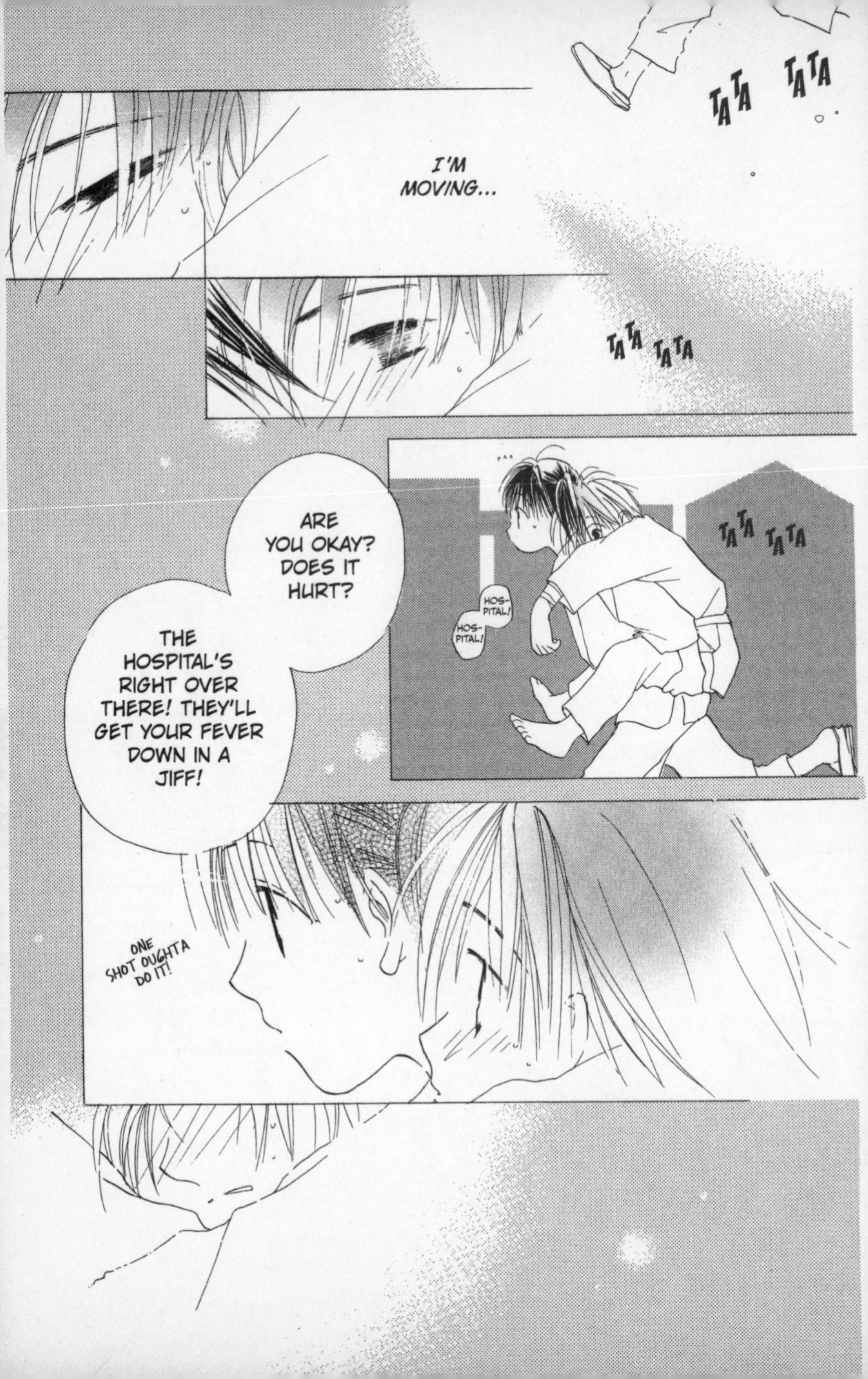
TATA TATA
I'M MOVING...
TATA TATA
TATA TATA
HOS-PITAL!
HOS-PITAL!
ARE YOU OKAY? DOES IT HURT?
THE HOSPITAL'S RIGHT OVER THERE! THEY'LL GET YOUR FEVER DOWN IN A JIFF!
ONE SHOT OUGHTA DO IT!

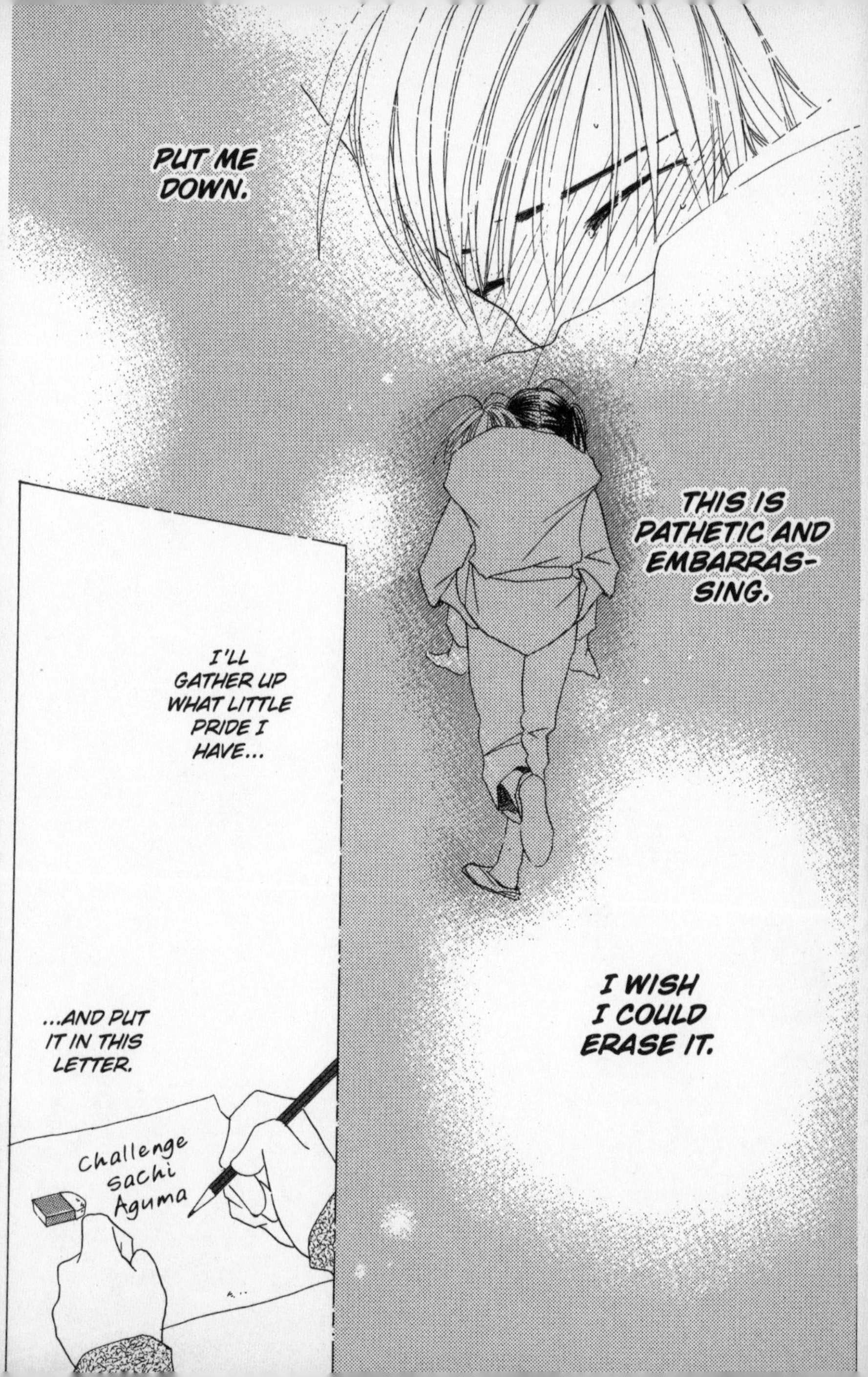
PUT ME DOWN.
THIS IS PATHETIC AND EMBARRAS-SING.
I WISH I COULD ERASE IT.
I'LL GATHER UP WHAT LITTLE PRIDE I HAVE...
...AND PUT IT IN THIS LETTER.
Challenge Sachi Aguma

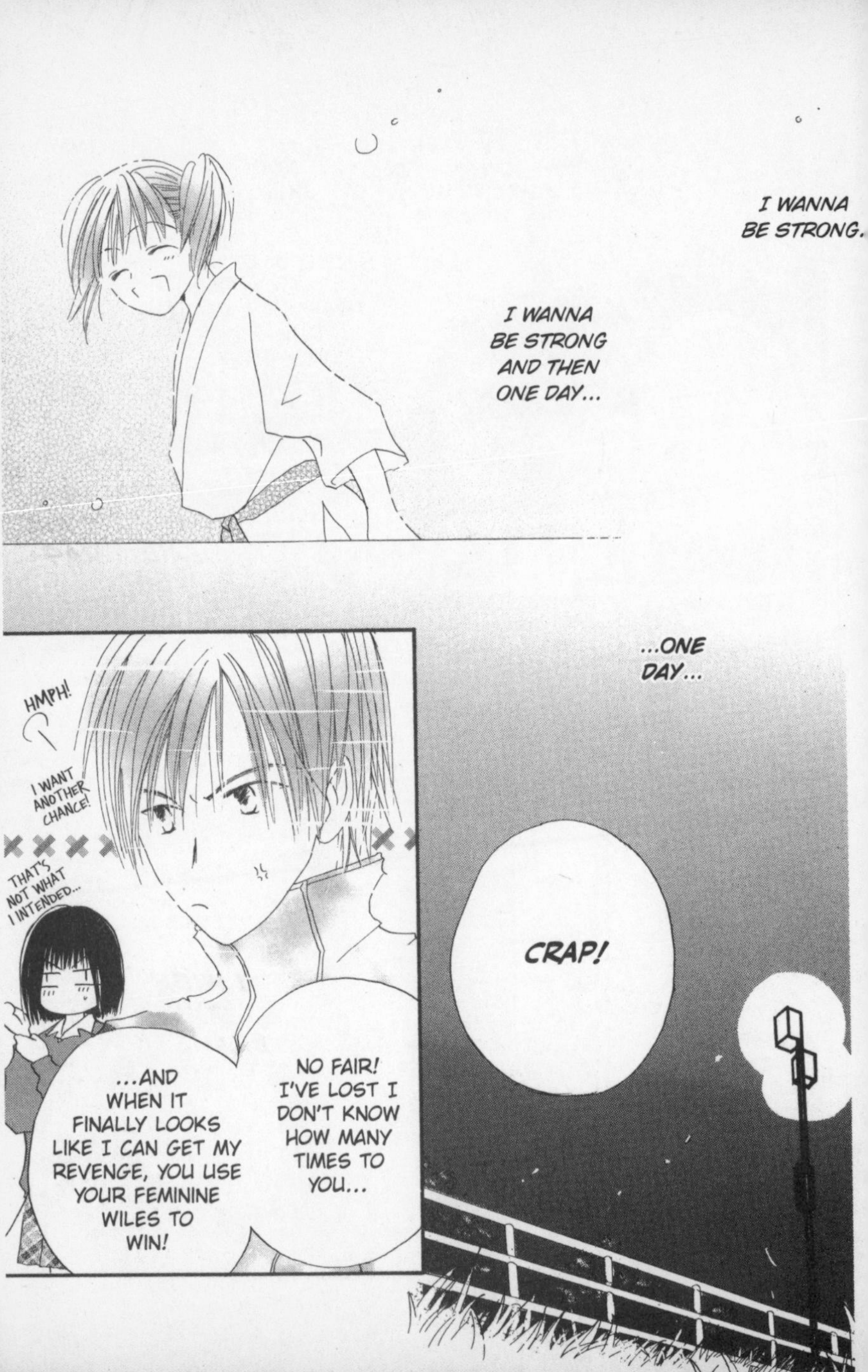
I WANNA BE STRONG.
I WANNA BE STRONG AND THEN ONE DAY...
...ONE DAY...
CRAP!
NO FAIR! I'VE LOST I DON'T KNOW HOW MANY TIMES TO YOU...
...AND WHEN IT FINALLY LOOKS LIKE I CAN GET MY REVENGE, YOU USE YOUR FEMININE WILES TO WIN!
HMPH!
I WANT ANOTHER CHANCE!
THAT'S NOT WHAT I INTENDED...

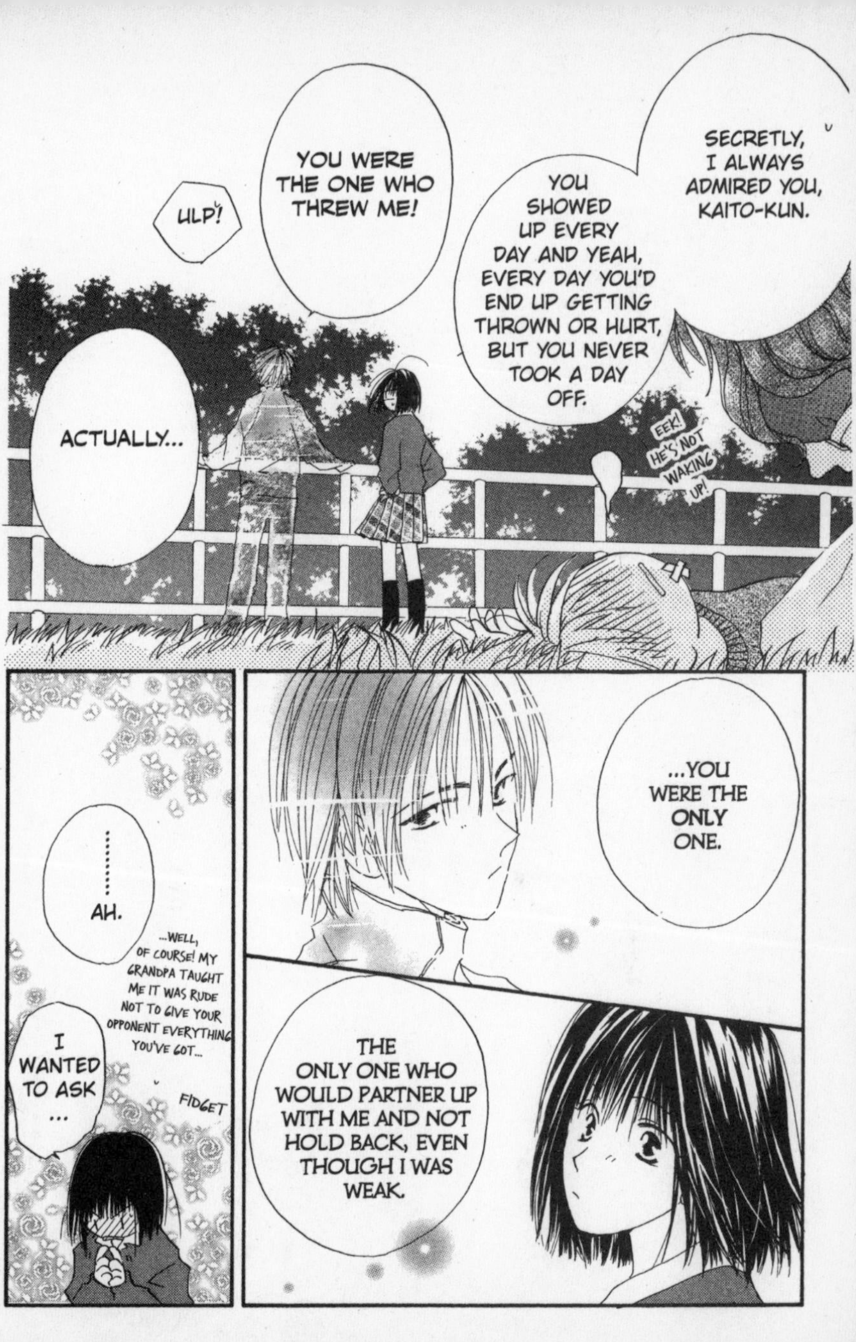
SECRETLY, I ALWAYS ADMIRED YOU, KAITO-KUN.
YOU SHOWED UP EVERY DAY AND YEAH, EVERY DAY YOU'D END UP GETTING THROWN OR HURT, BUT YOU NEVER TOOK A DAY OFF.
YOU WERE THE ONE WHO THREW ME!
ULP!
EEK! HE'S NOT WAKING UP!
ACTUALLY...
...YOU WERE THE ONLY ONE.
THE ONLY ONE WHO WOULD PARTNER UP WITH ME AND NOT HOLD BACK, EVEN THOUGH I WAS WEAK.
......AH.
...WELL, OF COURSE! MY GRANDPA TAUGHT ME IT WAS RUDE NOT TO GIVE YOUR OPPONENT EVERYTHING YOU'VE GOT...
I WANTED TO ASK ...
FIDGET

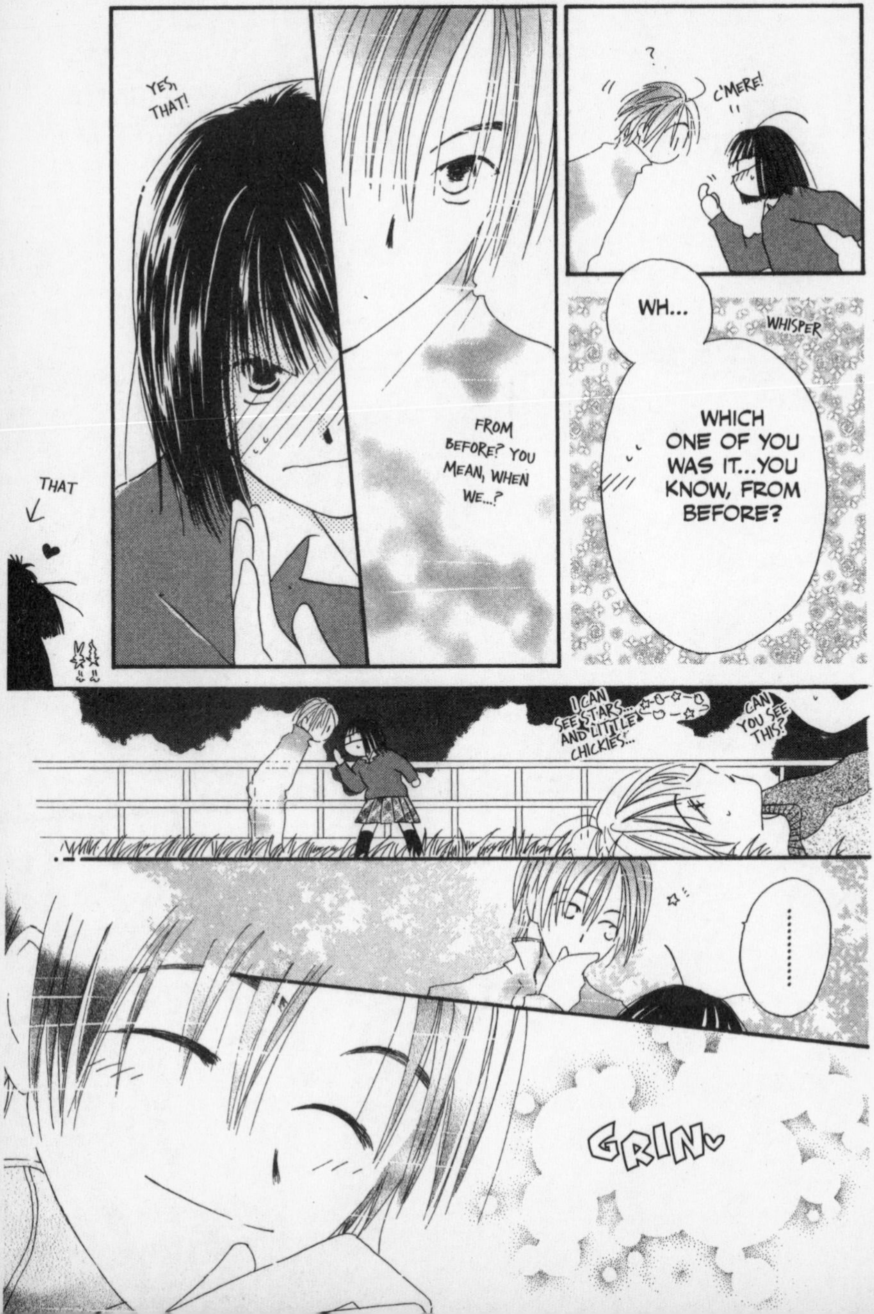
?
C'MERE!
WH...
WHISPER
WHICH ONE OF YOU WAS IT...YOU KNOW, FROM BEFORE?
FROM BEFORE? YOU MEAN, WHEN WE...?
YES, THAT!
THAT
CAN YOU SEE THIS?
I CAN SEE STARS... AND LITTLE CHICKIES...
....
GRIN

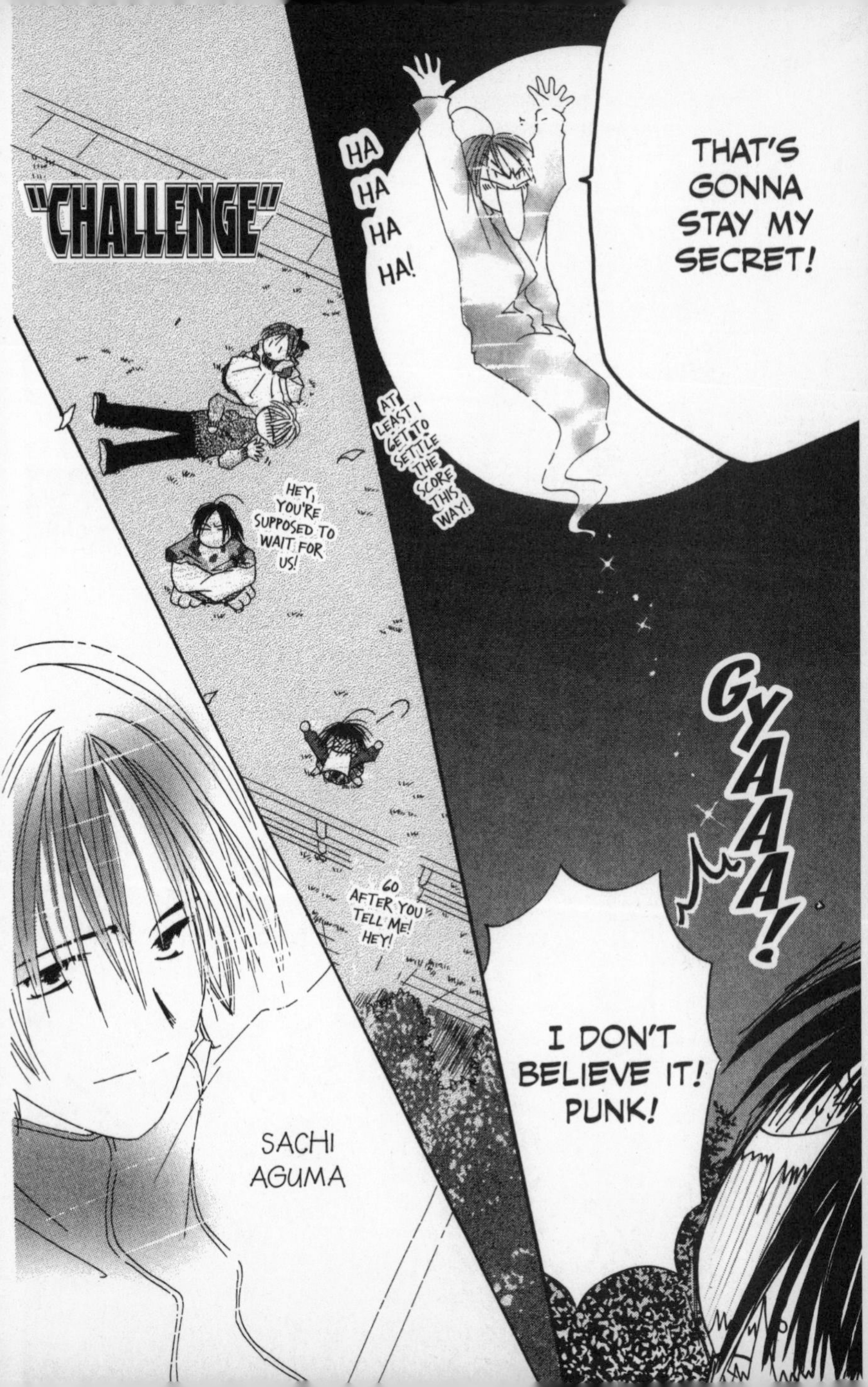
THAT'S GONNA STAY MY SECRET!
HA HA HA HA!
AT LEAST I GET TO SETTLE THE SCORE THIS WAY!
GYAAAA!
I DON'T BELIEVE IT! PUNK!
"CHALLENGE"
HEY, YOU'RE SUPPOSED TO WAIT FOR US!
GO AFTER YOU TELL ME! HEY!
SACHI AGUMA

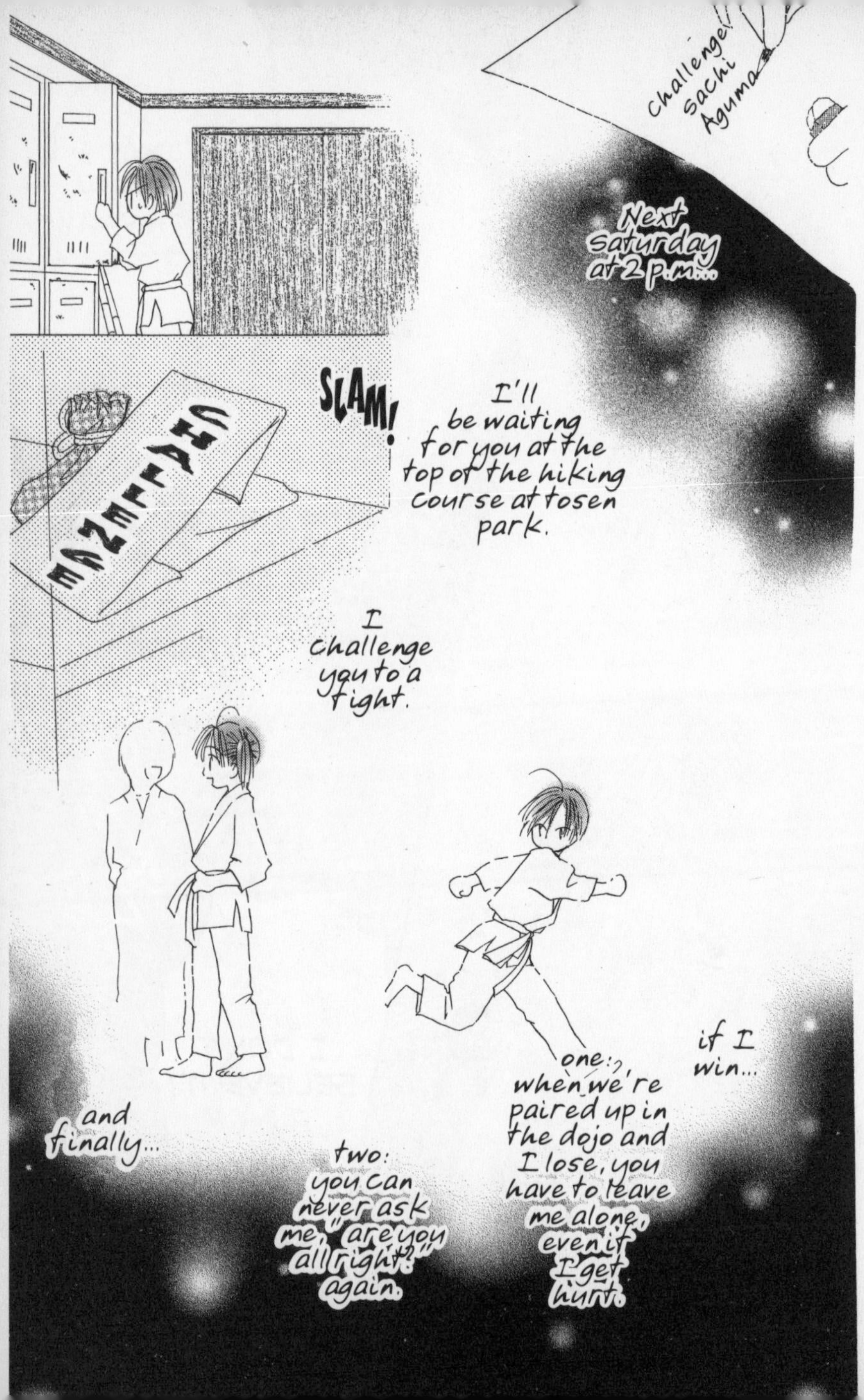
Challenge! Sachi Aguma
Next saturday at 2 p.m...
I'll be waiting for you at the top of the hiking course at tosen park.
SLAM!
CHALLENGE
I challenge you to a fight.
if I win...
one: when we're paired up in the dojo and I lose, you have to leave me alone, even if I get hurt.
two: you can never ask me, "are you all right?" again.
and finally...

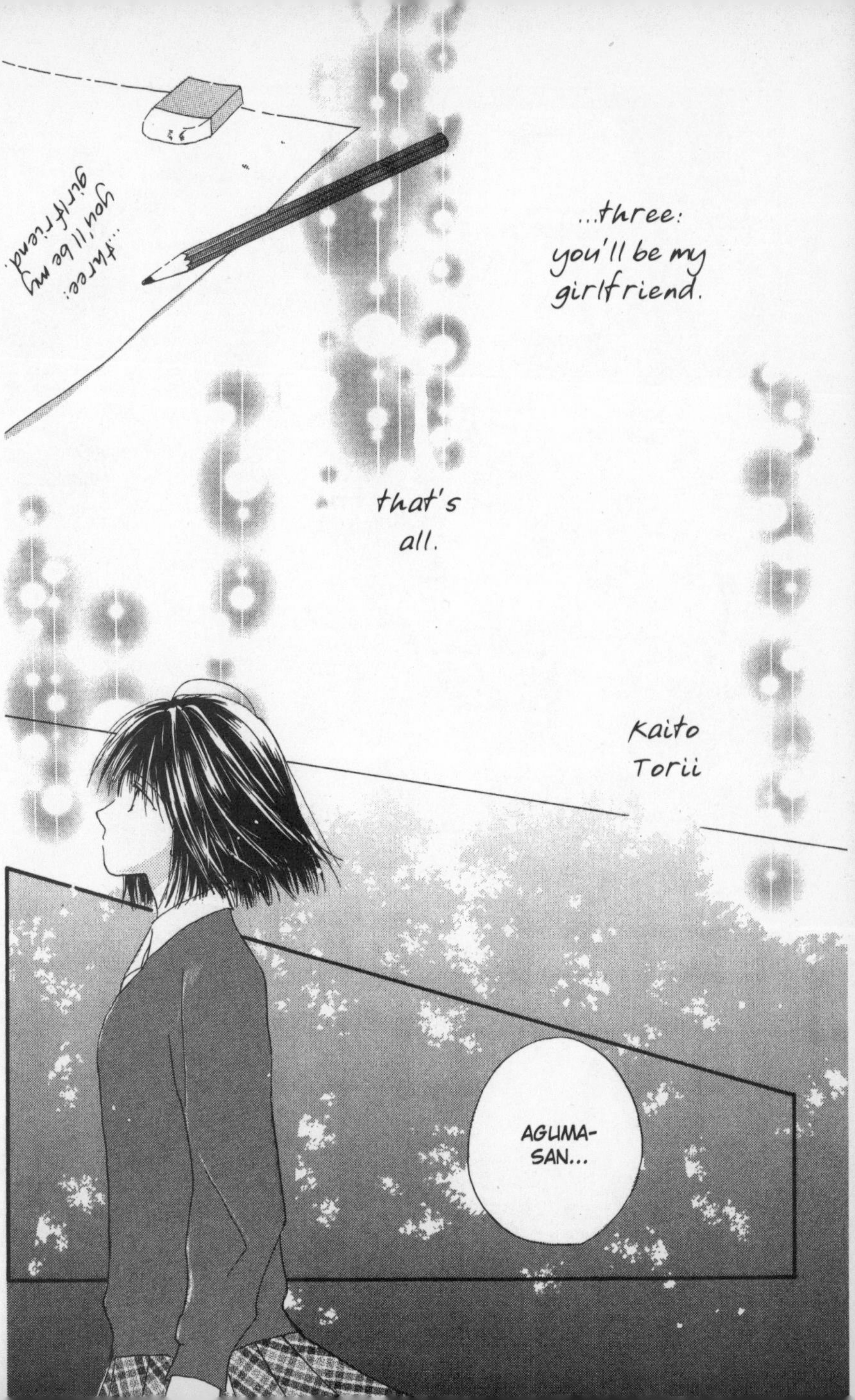
...three: you'll be my girlfriend.
...three: you'll be my girlfriend.
that's all.
Kaito Torii
AGUMA-SAN...

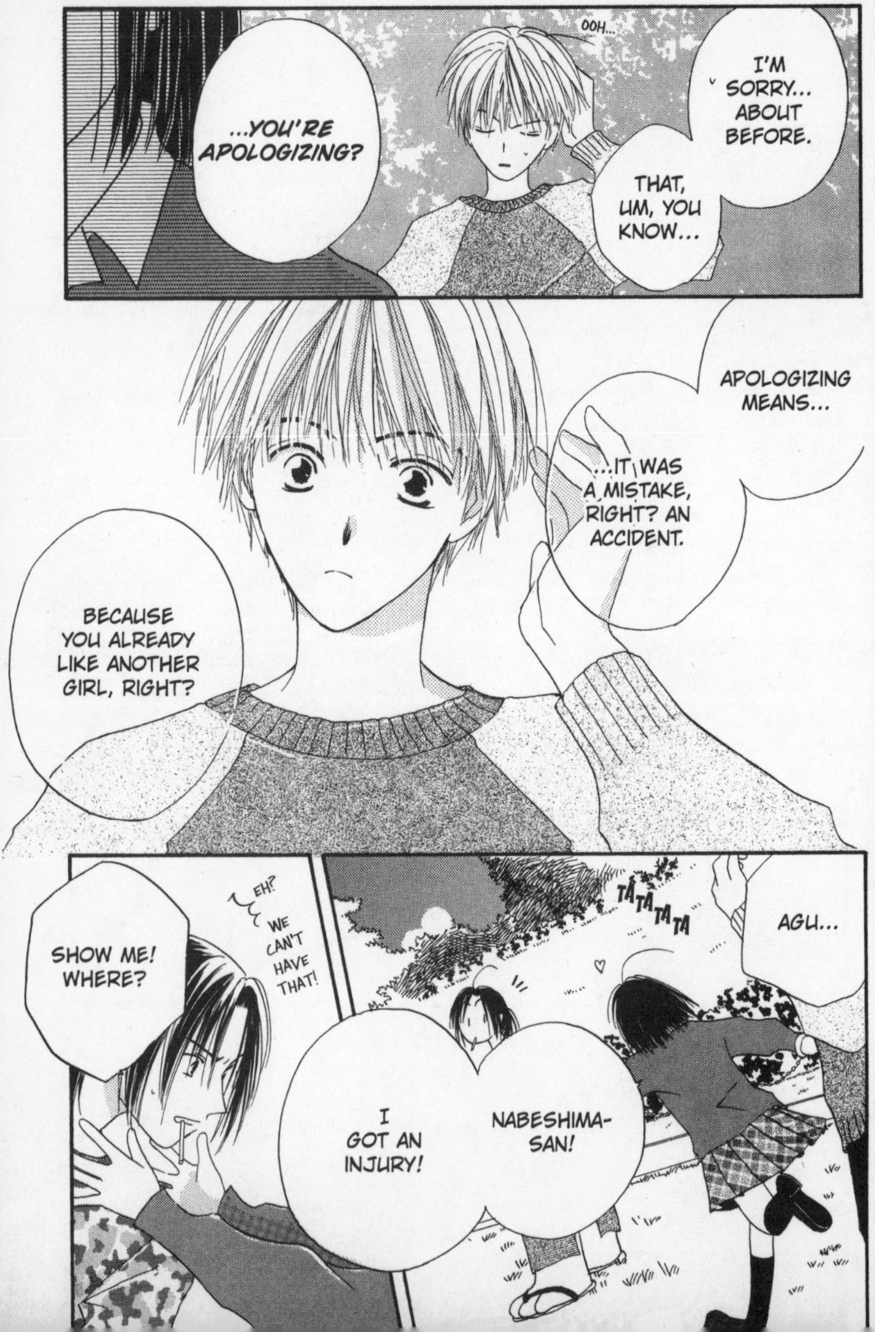
I'M SORRY... ABOUT BEFORE.
THAT, UM, YOU KNOW...
OOH...
...YOU'RE APOLOGIZING?
APOLOGIZING MEANS...
...IT WAS A MISTAKE, RIGHT? AN ACCIDENT.
BECAUSE YOU ALREADY LIKE ANOTHER GIRL, RIGHT?
AGU...
TATATATA
NABESHIMA-SAN!
I GOT AN INJURY!
EH?
WE CAN'T HAVE THAT!
SHOW ME! WHERE?

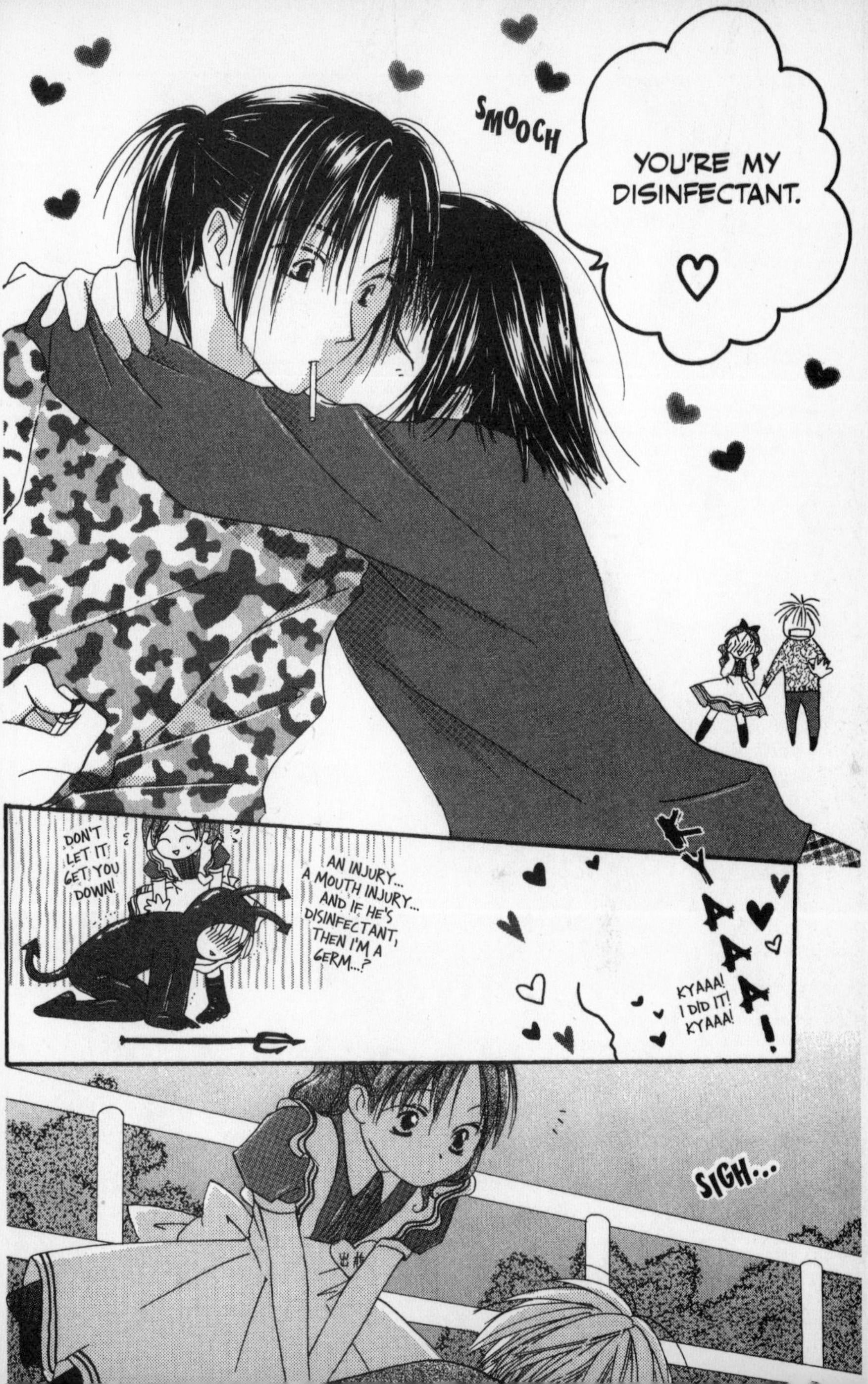
SMOOCH
YOU'RE MY DISINFECTANT. ♡
KYAAA!
KYAAA! I DID IT! KYAAA!
AN INJURY... A MOUTH INJURY... AND IF HE'S DISINFECTANT, THEN I'M A GERM...?
DON'T LET IT GET YOU DOWN!
SIGH...

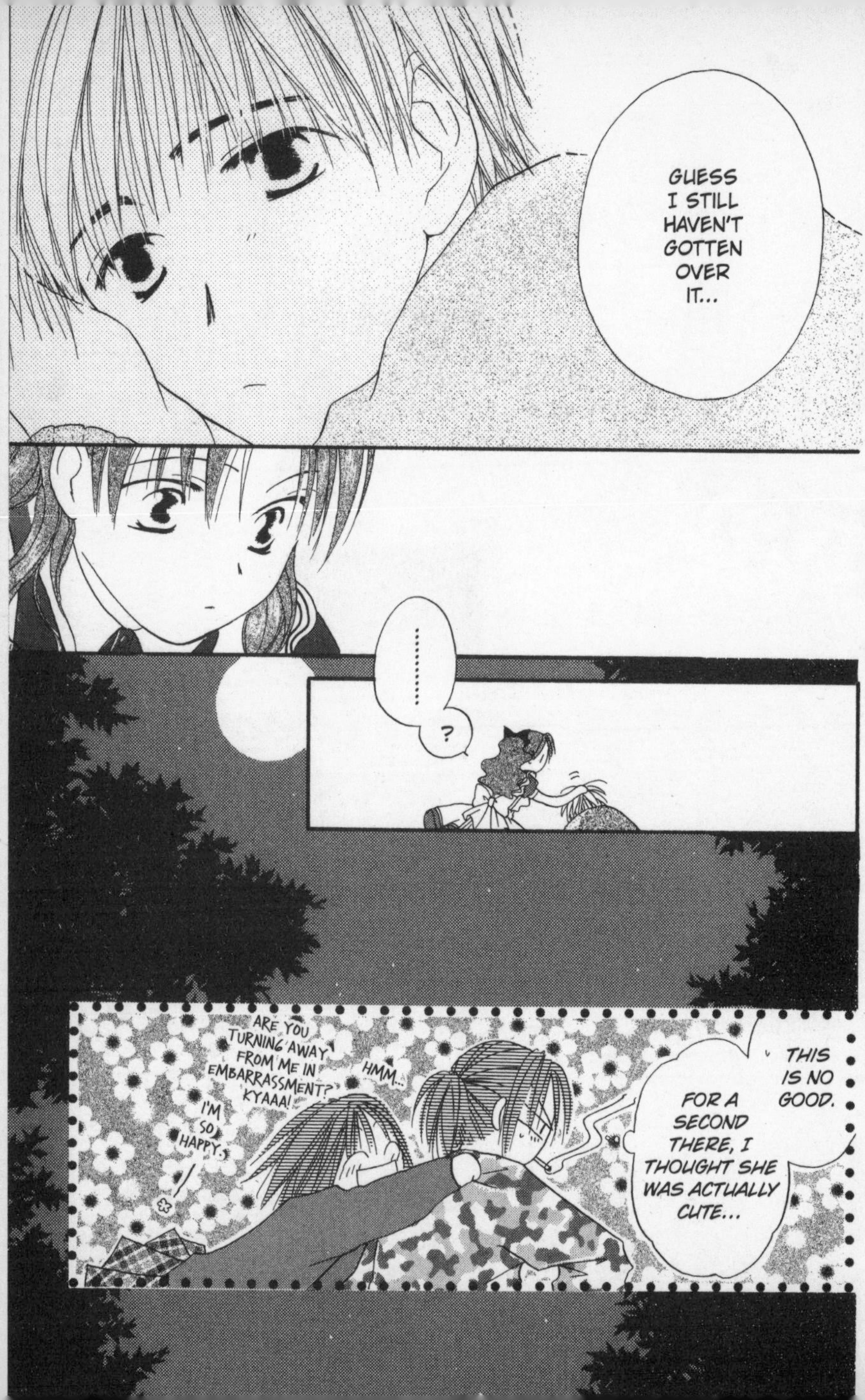
GUESS I STILL HAVEN'T GOTTEN OVER IT...
......
?
THIS IS NO GOOD.
FOR A SECOND THERE, I THOUGHT SHE WAS ACTUALLY CUTE...
HMM...
ARE YOU TURNING AWAY FROM ME IN EMBARRASSMENT? KYAAA!
I'M SO HAPPY.

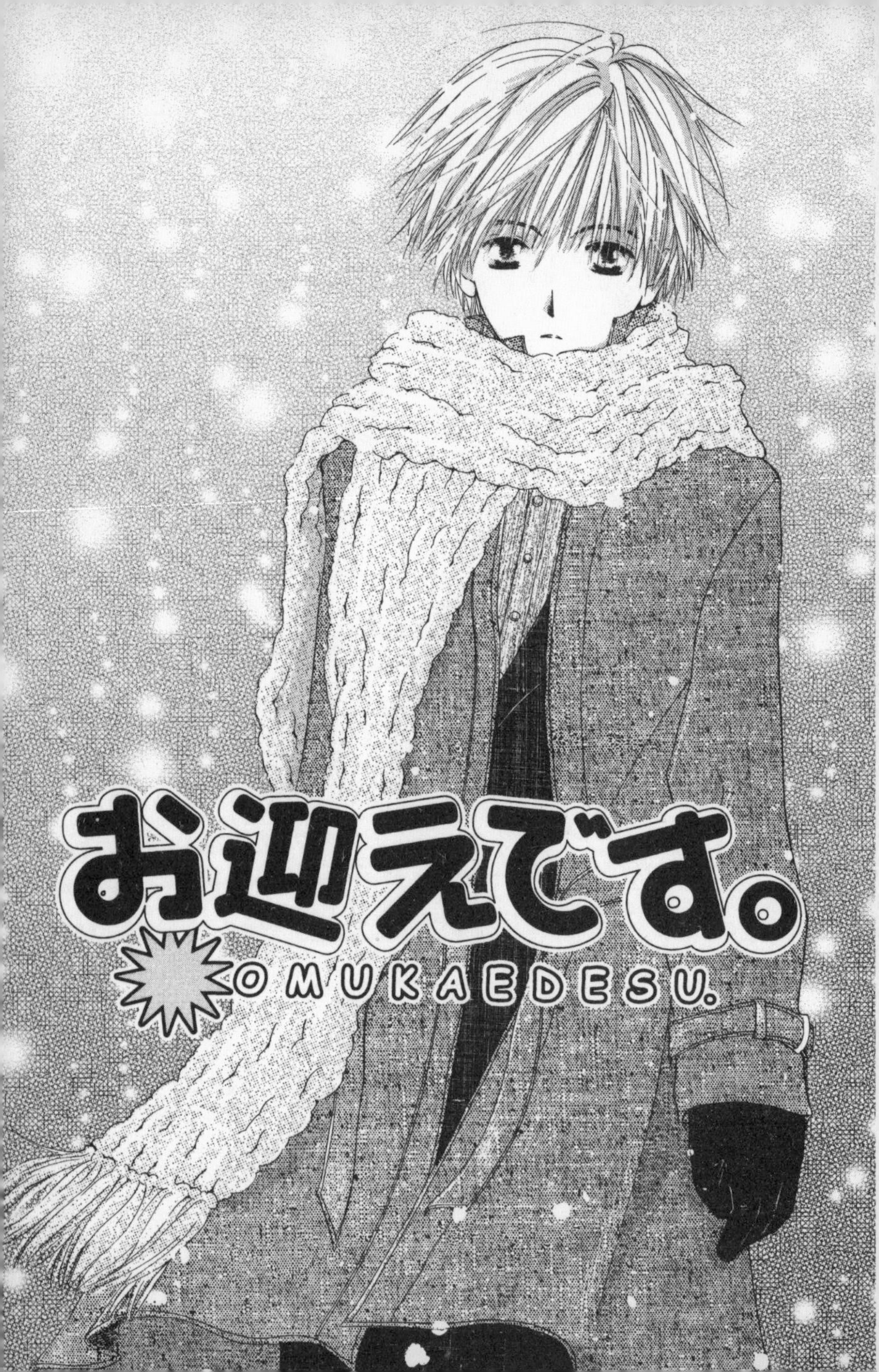
お迎えです。
OMUKAEDESU.

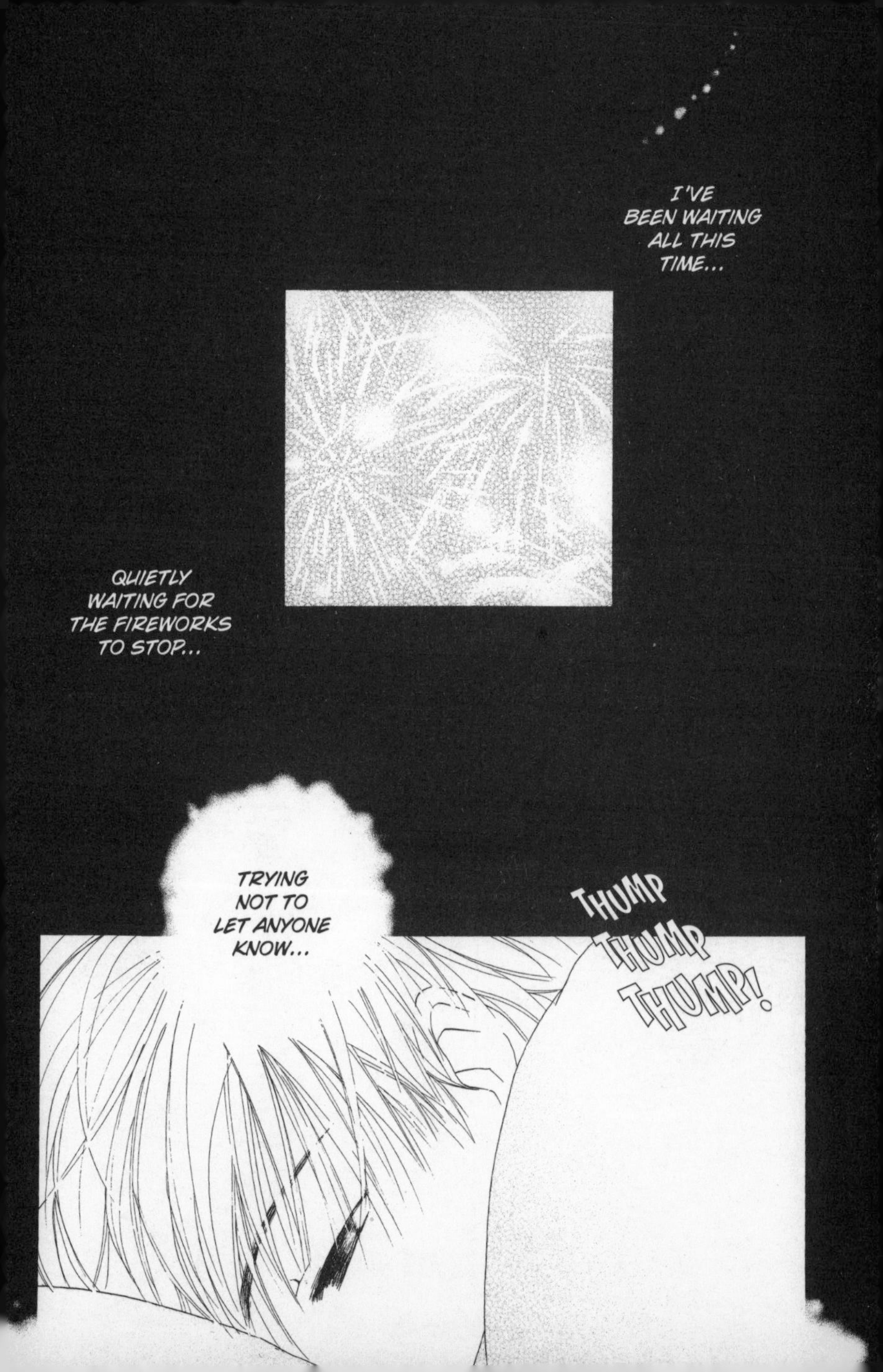
I'VE BEEN WAITING ALL THIS TIME...
QUIETLY WAITING FOR THE FIREWORKS TO STOP...
THUMP THUMP THUMP!
TRYING NOT TO LET ANYONE KNOW...

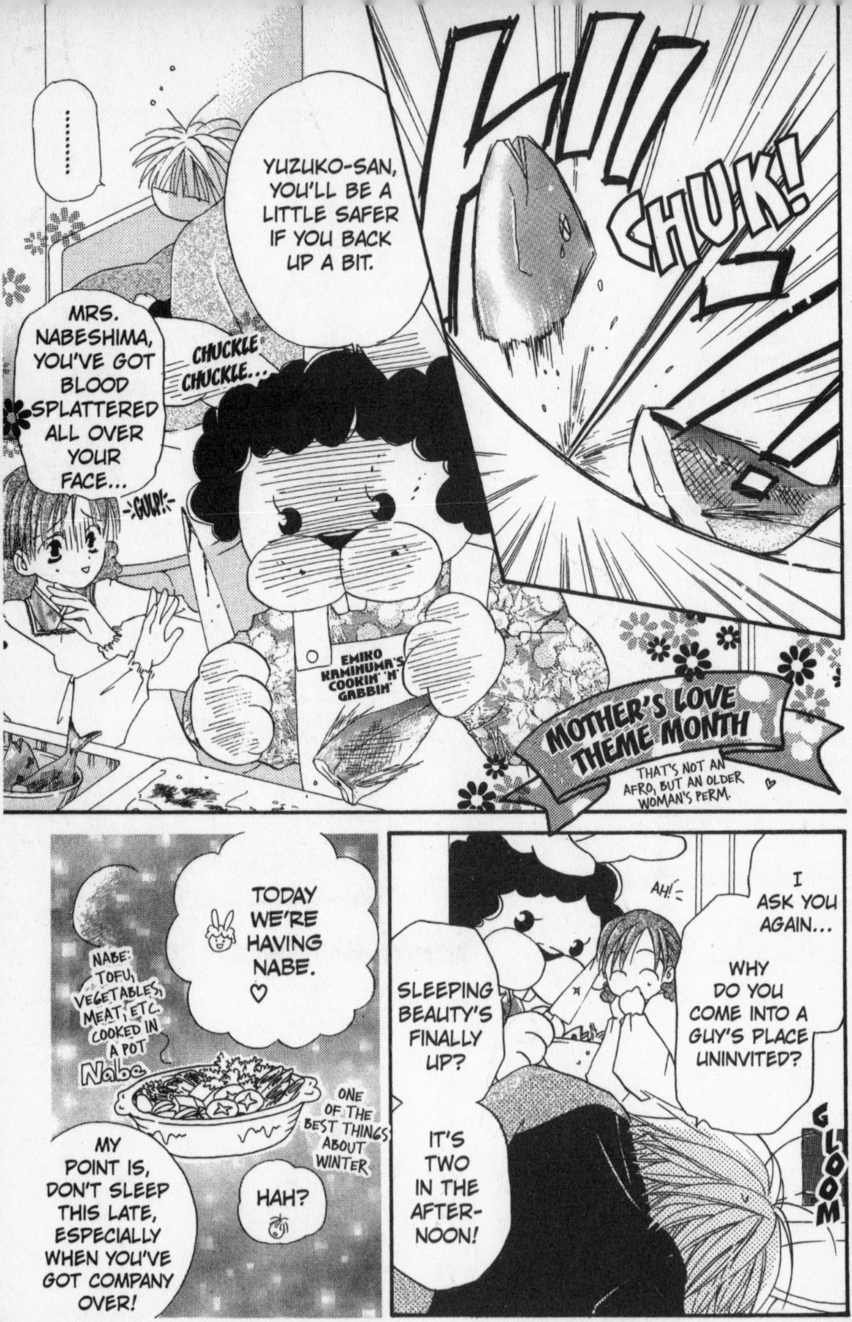
CHUK!
YUZUKO-SAN, YOU'LL BE A LITTLE SAFER IF YOU BACK UP A BIT.
......
CHUCKLE CHUCKLE...
MRS. NABESHIMA, YOU'VE GOT BLOOD SPLATTERED ALL OVER YOUR FACE...
GULP!
EMIKO KAMINUMA'S COOKIN' 'N' GABBIN'
MOTHER'S LOVE THEME MONTH
THAT'S NOT AN AFRO, BUT AN OLDER WOMAN'S PERM.
I ASK YOU AGAIN...
WHY DO YOU COME INTO A GUY'S PLACE UNINVITED?
AH!
GLOOM
SLEEPING BEAUTY'S FINALLY UP?
IT'S TWO IN THE AFTERNOON!
TODAY WE'RE HAVING NABE.
NABE: TOFU, VEGETABLES, MEAT, ETC. COOKED IN A POT
Nabe
ONE OF THE BEST THINGS ABOUT WINTER
HAH?
MY POINT IS, DON'T SLEEP THIS LATE, ESPECIALLY WHEN YOU'VE GOT COMPANY OVER!

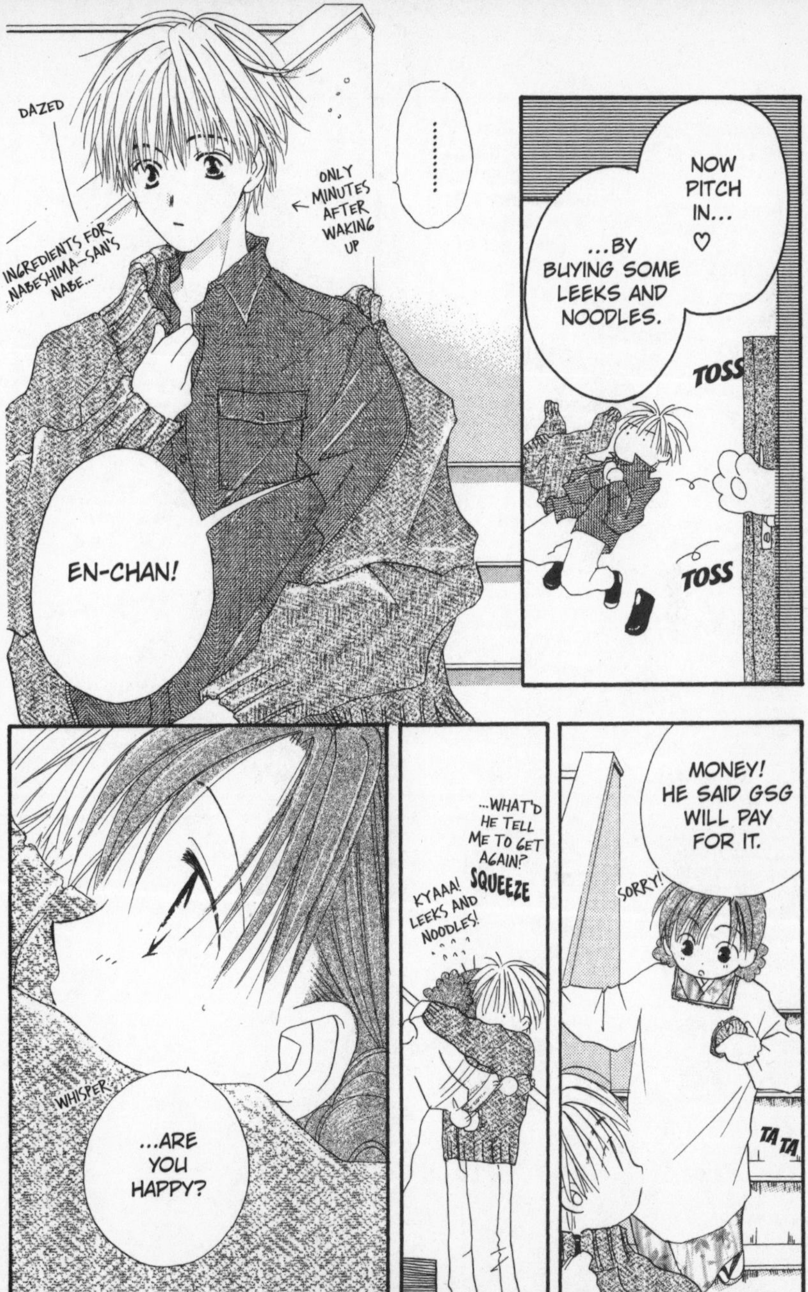
NOW PITCH IN... ♡
...BY BUYING SOME LEEKS AND NOODLES.
TOSS
TOSS
......
ONLY MINUTES AFTER WAKING UP
DAZED
INGREDIENTS FOR NABESHIMA-SAN'S NABE...
EN-CHAN!
MONEY! HE SAID GSG WILL PAY FOR IT.
SORRY!
TA TA
...WHAT'D HE TELL ME TO GET AGAIN?
SQUEEZE
KYAAA! LEEKS AND NOODLES!
WHISPER
...ARE YOU HAPPY?

LOOKING BACK A LITTLE BIT.

I THOUGHT I'D TAKE A LOOK AT VOLUME ONE.

AAAAH! AAAAH!

...PHEW, THAT ART IS BAD. WHICH IMPLIES THAT I'VE GOTTEN AT LEAST A LITTLE BETTER...I HOPE.

EVEN NOW, MY ART ISN'T CONSISTENT, SO IF IT'S HARD ON THE EYES TO LOOK AT SOMETIMES, I APOLOGIZE.

STILL, IF I THINK, "MY ART IS GREAT! PERFECT!" THEN I'LL REALLY FEEL LIKE I'VE REACHED THE END OF THE SERIES, SO THAT'S THE ATTITUDE I'LL ADOPT FROM HERE ON, ALL THE WHILE SQUINTING SUSPICIOUSLY AT MYSELF. OF COURSE I'M ONLY FOOLING MYSELF! EVEN I'M NOT FOOLED BY THAT!

IN THIS VOLUME, ALL OF THE CHARACTERS HAVE WELL-DEFINED FEATURES FOR SOME REASON...

AND EN-CHAN'S EYES ARE HUGE...

DON'T TELL ANYONE.

EVEN SO, COMPARING THE ART HERE TO THAT OF VOLUME 1, YOU CAN SEE HOW EN-CHAN'S CHANGED. IN THE VERY FIRST EPISODE, WHEN HE WAS STILL A HIGH SCHOOL STUDENT, HE SEEMS MUCH OLDER THAN HE DOES HERE...

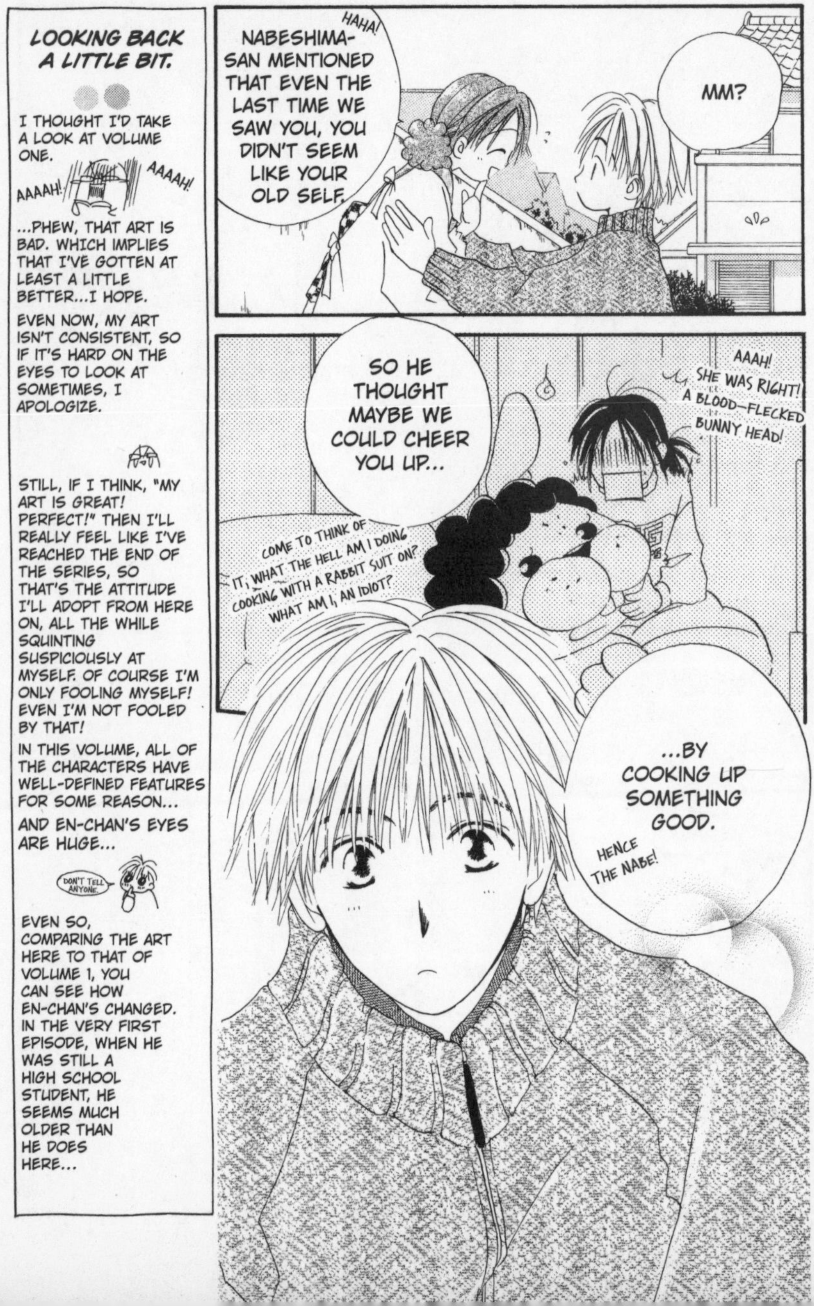
MM?
HAHA!
NABESHIMA-SAN MENTIONED THAT EVEN THE LAST TIME WE SAW YOU, YOU DIDN'T SEEM LIKE YOUR OLD SELF.
AAAH! SHE WAS RIGHT! A BLOOD-FLECKED BUNNY HEAD!
SO HE THOUGHT MAYBE WE COULD CHEER YOU UP...
COME TO THINK OF IT, WHAT THE HELL AM I DOING COOKING WITH A RABBIT SUIT ON? WHAT AM I, AN IDIOT?
...BY COOKING UP SOMETHING GOOD.
HENCE THE NABE!

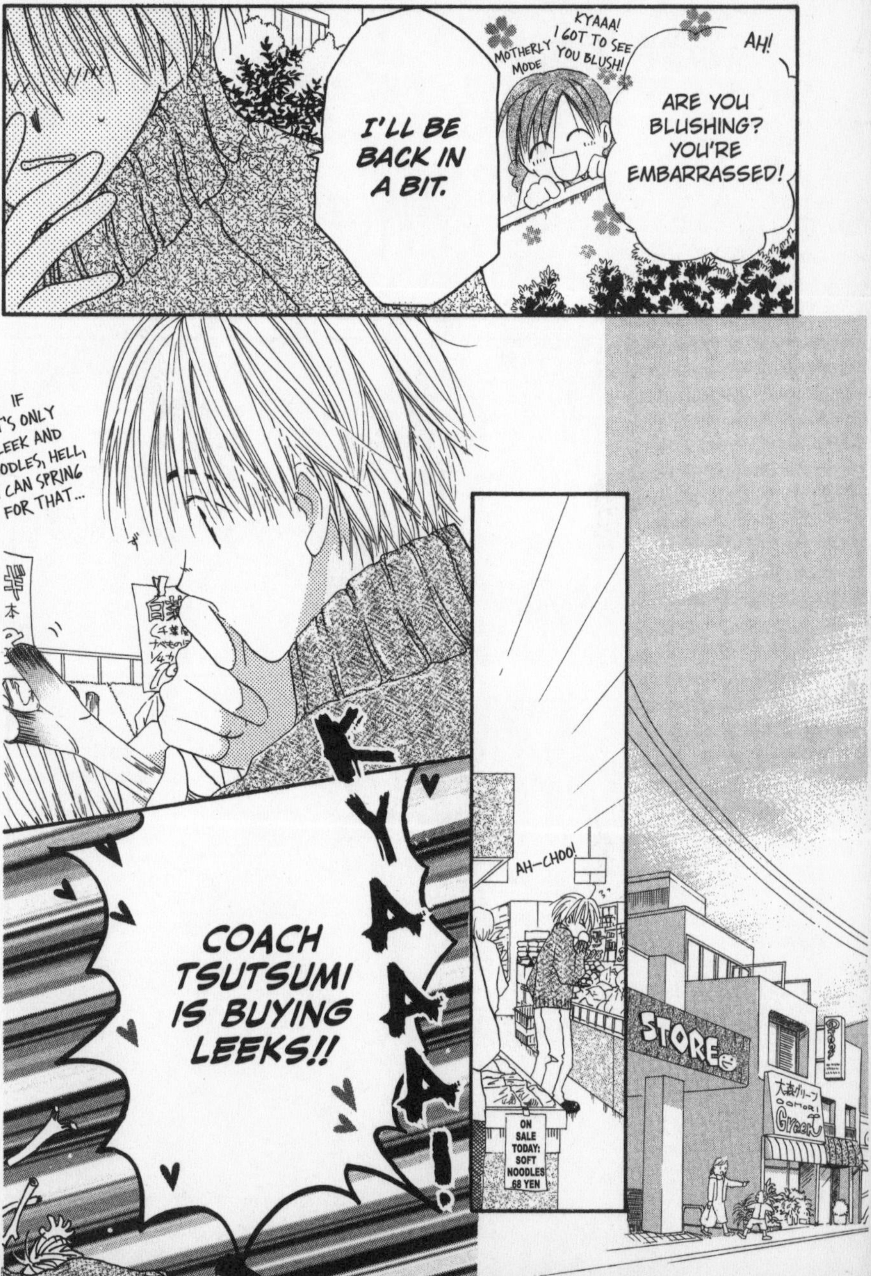
AH!
ARE YOU BLUSHING? YOU'RE EMBARRASSED!
KYAAA! I GOT TO SEE YOU BLUSH!
MOTHERLY MODE
I'LL BE BACK IN A BIT.
STORE
大森グリーン OOMORI Green
AH-CHOO!
ON SALE TODAY: SOFT NOODLES 68 YEN
IF IT'S ONLY LEEK AND NOODLES, HELL, I CAN SPRING FOR THAT...
KYAAAA!
COACH TSUTSUMI IS BUYING LEEKS!!

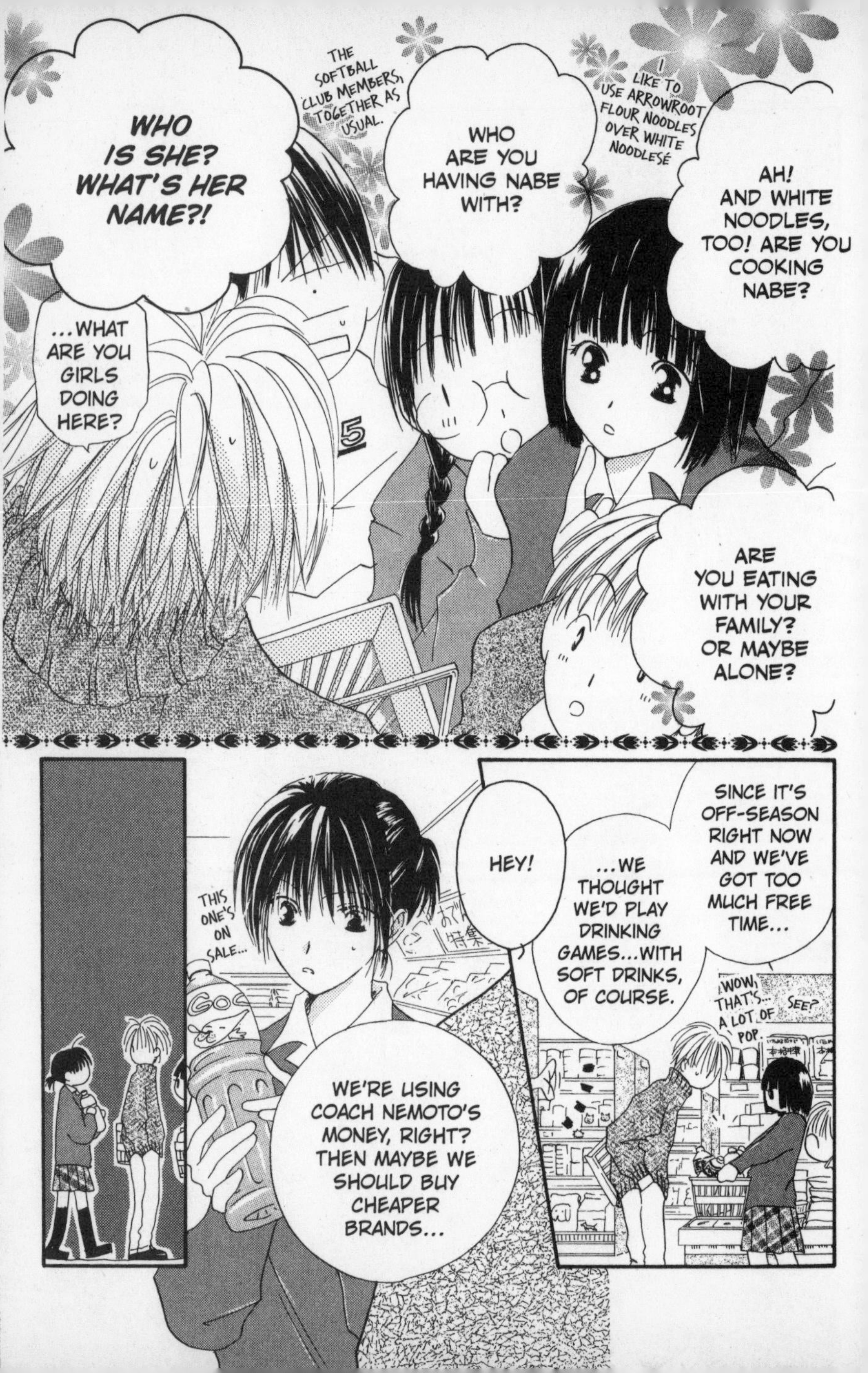
AH! AND WHITE NOODLES, TOO! ARE YOU COOKING NABE?
I LIKE TO USE ARROWROOT FLOUR NOODLES OVER WHITE NOODLES
WHO ARE YOU HAVING NABE WITH?
THE SOFTBALL CLUB MEMBERS, TOGETHER AS USUAL.
WHO IS SHE? WHAT'S HER NAME?!
...WHAT ARE YOU GIRLS DOING HERE?
ARE YOU EATING WITH YOUR FAMILY? OR MAYBE ALONE?
SINCE IT'S OFF-SEASON RIGHT NOW AND WE'VE GOT TOO MUCH FREE TIME...
...WE THOUGHT WE'D PLAY DRINKING GAMES...WITH SOFT DRINKS, OF COURSE.
HEY!
SEE?
WOW, THAT'S... A LOT OF POP.
THIS ONE'S ON SALE...
WE'RE USING COACH NEMOTO'S MONEY, RIGHT? THEN MAYBE WE SHOULD BUY CHEAPER BRANDS...

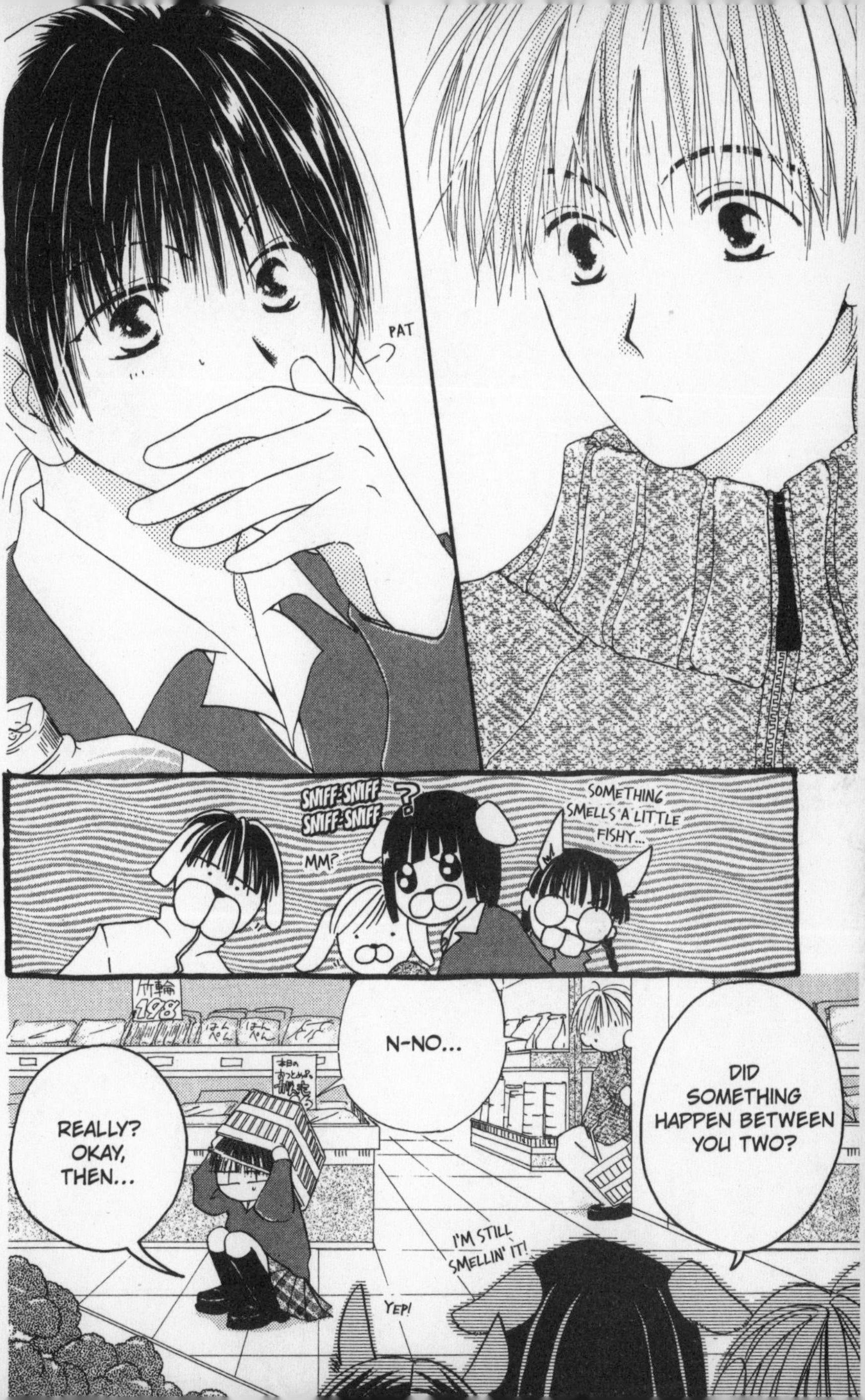
PAT
...
SOMETHING SMELLS A LITTLE FISHY...
SNIFF-SNIFF SNIFF-SNIFF
MM?
198
DID SOMETHING HAPPEN BETWEEN YOU TWO?
N-NO...
REALLY? OKAY, THEN...
I'M STILL SMELLIN' IT!
YEP!

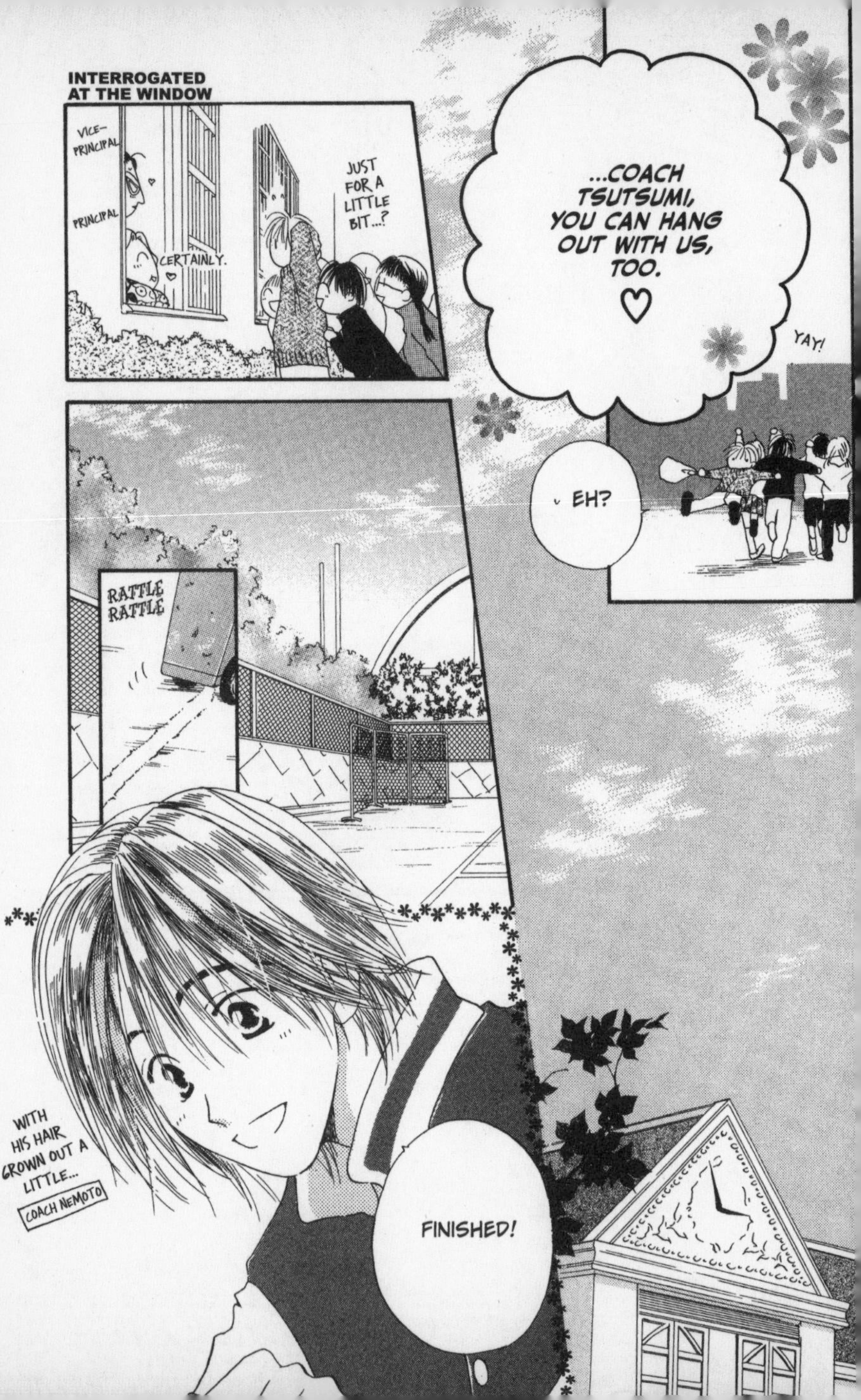
...COACH TSUTSUMI, YOU CAN HANG OUT WITH US, TOO. ♡
YAY!
EH?
INTERROGATED AT THE WINDOW
VICE-PRINCIPAL
PRINCIPAL
JUST FOR A LITTLE BIT...?
CERTAINLY.
RATTLE RATTLE
FINISHED!
WITH HIS HAIR GROWN OUT A LITTLE...
COACH NEMOTO

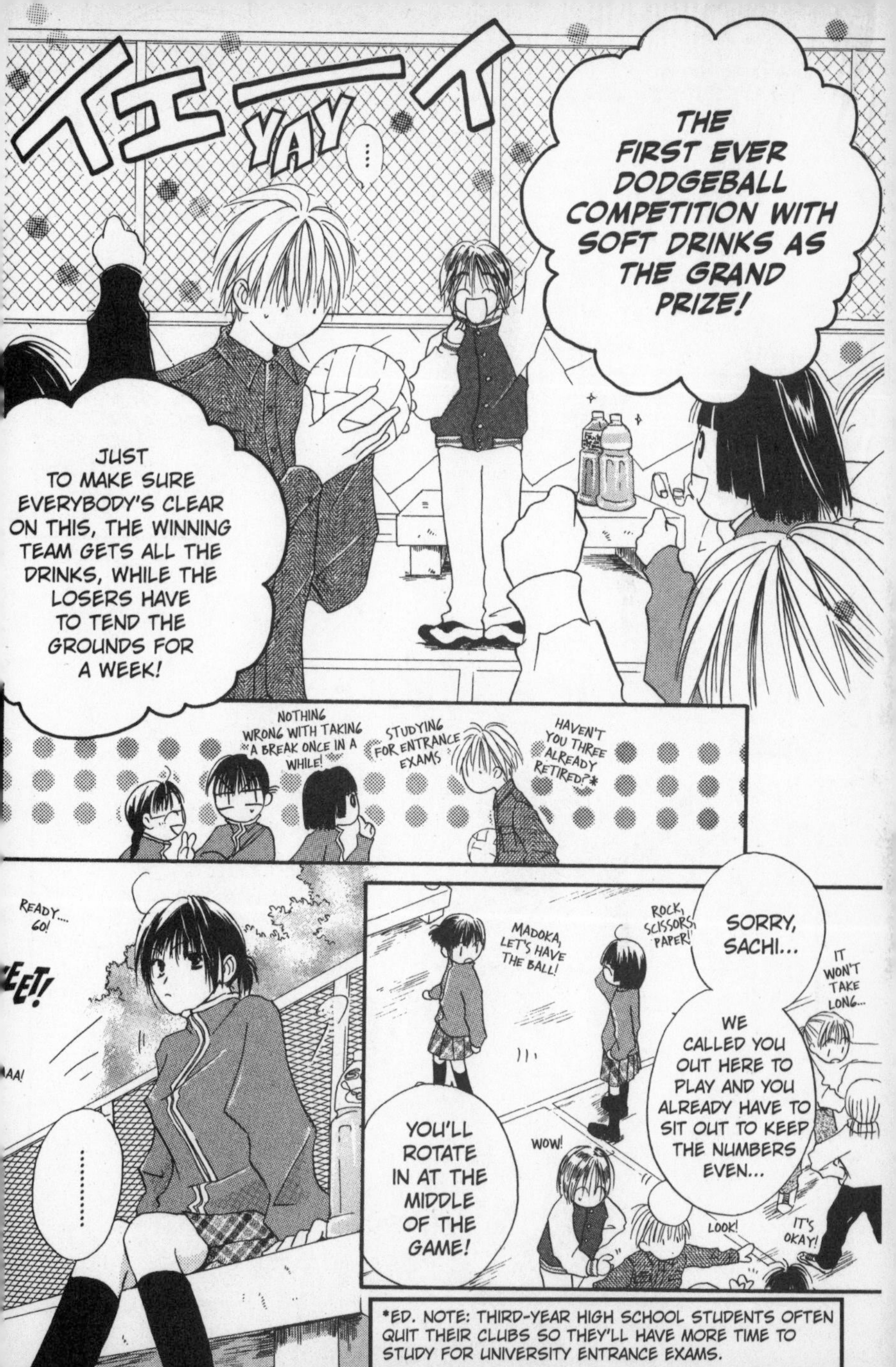
イエーイ
YAY
...
THE FIRST EVER DODGEBALL COMPETITION WITH SOFT DRINKS AS THE GRAND PRIZE!
JUST TO MAKE SURE EVERYBODY'S CLEAR ON THIS, THE WINNING TEAM GETS ALL THE DRINKS, WHILE THE LOSERS HAVE TO TEND THE GROUNDS FOR A WEEK!
HAVEN'T YOU THREE ALREADY RETIRED?*
STUDYING FOR ENTRANCE EXAMS
NOTHING WRONG WITH TAKING A BREAK ONCE IN A WHILE!
SORRY, SACHI...
WE CALLED YOU OUT HERE TO PLAY AND YOU ALREADY HAVE TO SIT OUT TO KEEP THE NUMBERS EVEN...
IT WON'T TAKE LONG...
ROCK, SCISSORS, PAPER!
MADOKA, LET'S HAVE THE BALL!
YOU'LL ROTATE IN AT THE MIDDLE OF THE GAME!
WOW!
LOOK!
IT'S OKAY!
READY... GO!
....

*ED. NOTE: THIRD-YEAR HIGH SCHOOL STUDENTS OFTEN QUIT THEIR CLUBS SO THEY'LL HAVE MORE TIME TO STUDY FOR UNIVERSITY ENTRANCE EXAMS.

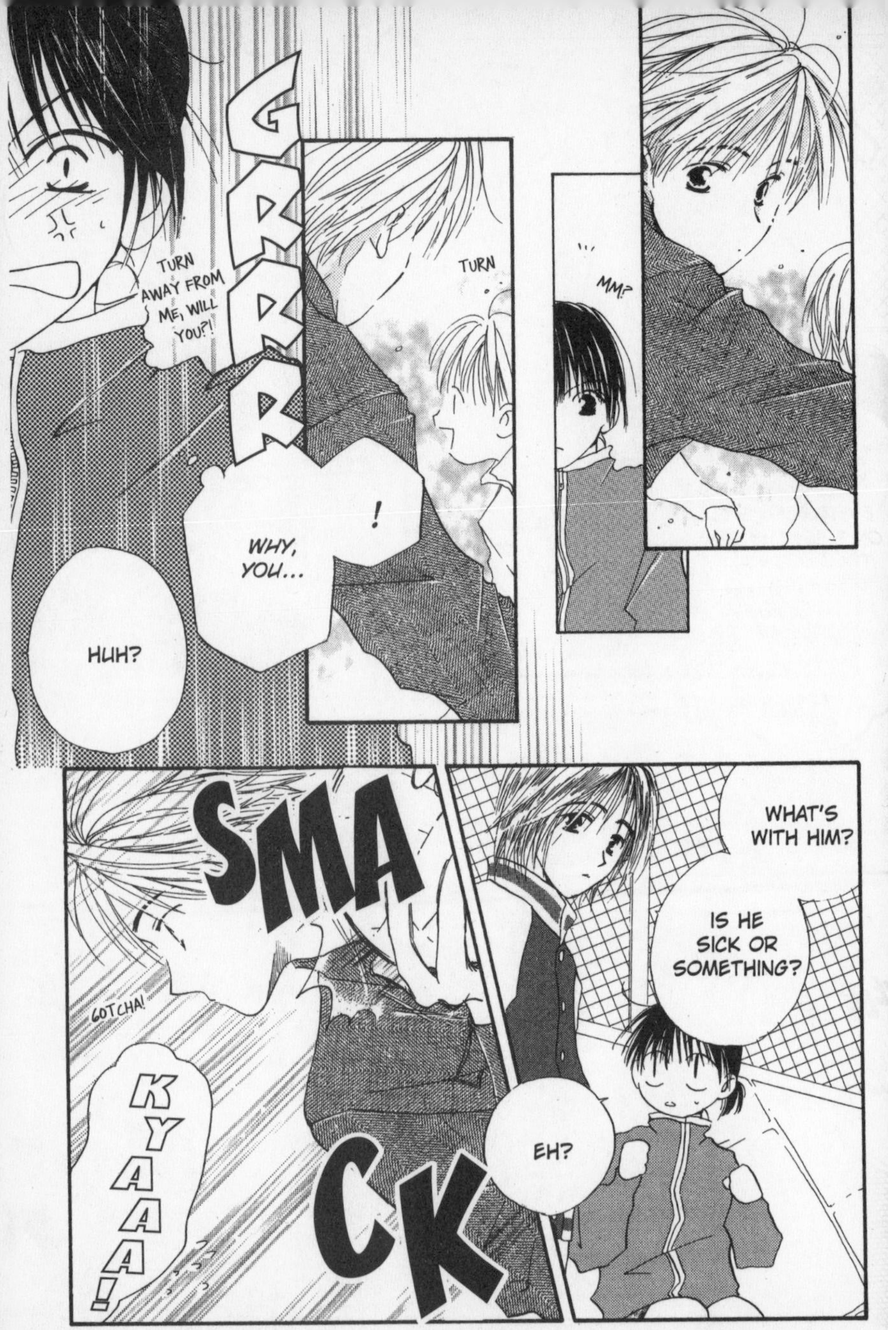
MM?
TURN
!
WHY, YOU...
GRRR
TURN AWAY FROM ME, WILL YOU?!
HUH?
WHAT'S WITH HIM?
IS HE SICK OR SOMETHING?
EH?
SMACK
GOTCHA!
KYAAAA!

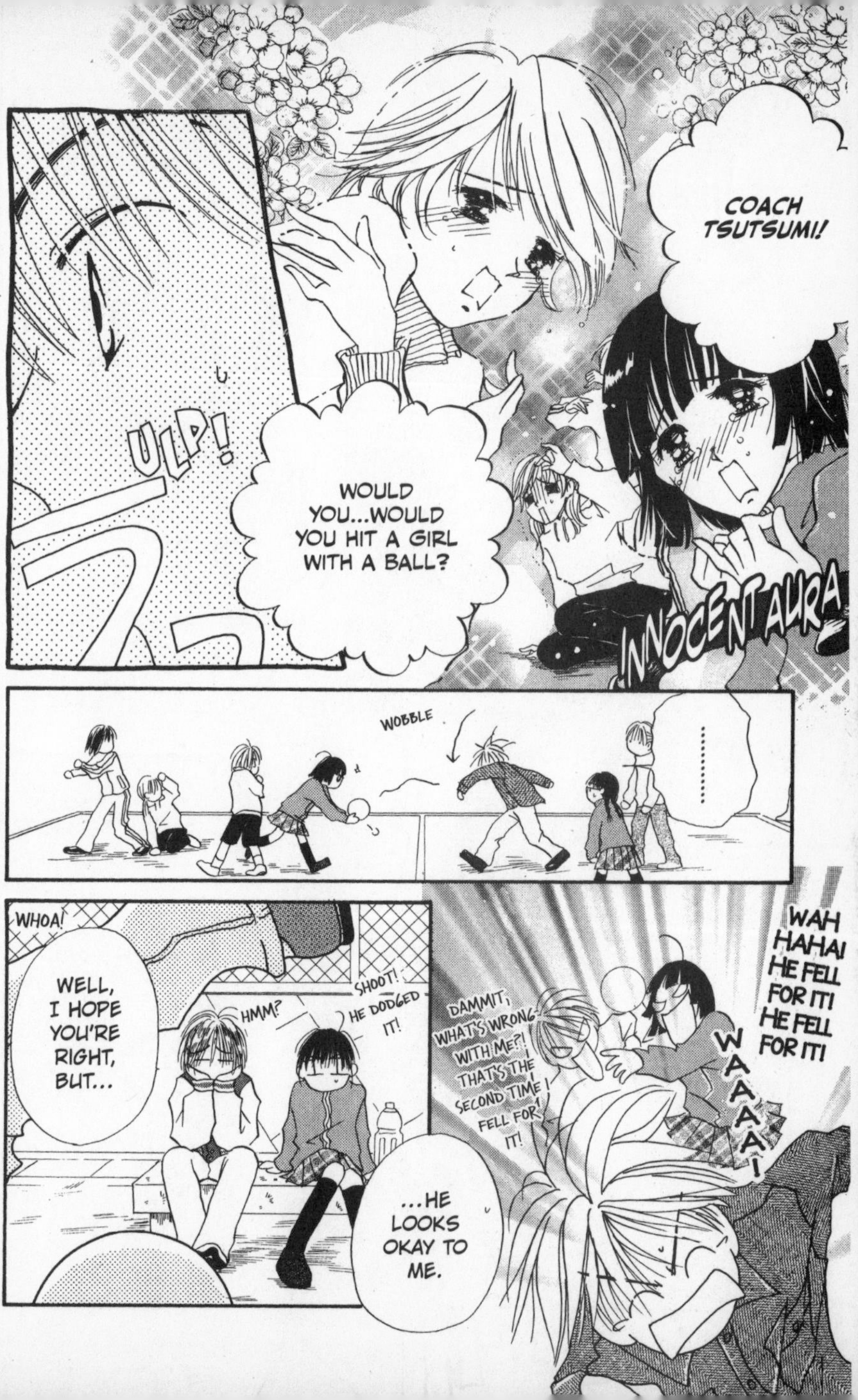
COACH TSUTSUMI!
WOULD YOU...WOULD YOU HIT A GIRL WITH A BALL?
INNOCENT AURA
ULP!
......
WOBBLE
WAH HAHA! HE FELL FOR IT! HE FELL FOR IT!
WAAAA!
DAMMIT, WHAT'S WRONG WITH ME?! THAT'S THE SECOND TIME I FELL FOR IT!
WHOA!
SHOOT! HE DODGED IT!
HMM?
WELL, I HOPE YOU'RE RIGHT, BUT...
...HE LOOKS OKAY TO ME.

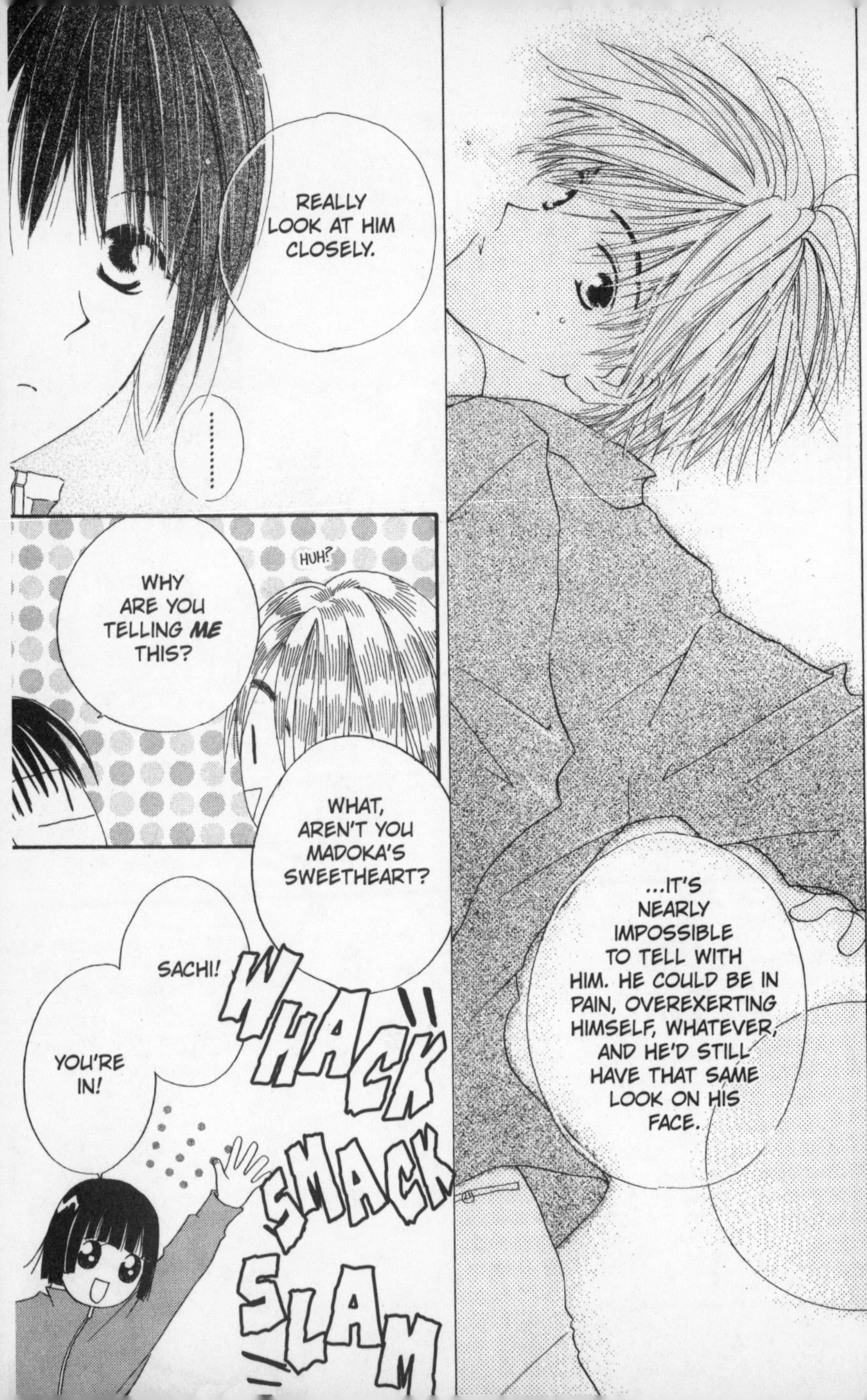
...IT'S NEARLY IMPOSSIBLE TO TELL WITH HIM. HE COULD BE IN PAIN, OVEREXERTING HIMSELF, WHATEVER, AND HE'D STILL HAVE THAT SAME LOOK ON HIS FACE.
REALLY LOOK AT HIM CLOSELY.
......
HUH?
WHY ARE YOU TELLING *ME* THIS?
WHAT, AREN'T YOU MADOKA'S SWEETHEART?
WHACK
SACHI!
YOU'RE IN!
SMACK
SLAM

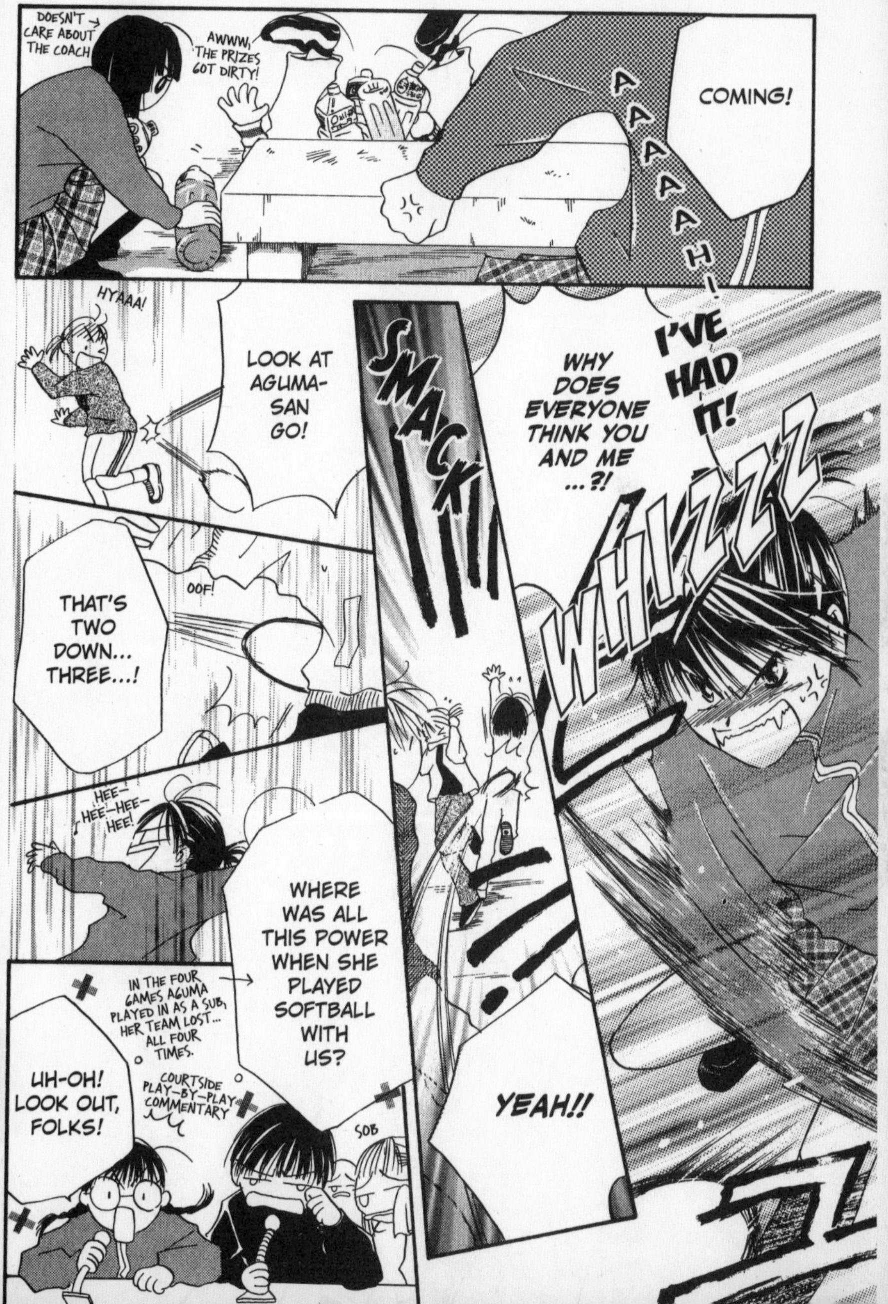
COMING!
AAAAAH!
AWWW, THE PRIZES GOT DIRTY!
DOESN'T CARE ABOUT THE COACH
I'VE HAD IT!
WHY DOES EVERYONE THINK YOU AND ME ...?!
WHIZZZ
YEAH!!
SMACK!
HYAAA!
LOOK AT AGUMA-SAN GO!
THAT'S TWO DOWN... THREE...!
OOF!
HEE-HEE-HEE-HEE!
WHERE WAS ALL THIS POWER WHEN SHE PLAYED SOFTBALL WITH US?
IN THE FOUR GAMES AGUMA PLAYED IN AS A SUB, HER TEAM LOST... ALL FOUR TIMES.
SOB
COURTSIDE PLAY-BY-PLAY COMMENTARY
UH-OH! LOOK OUT, FOLKS!

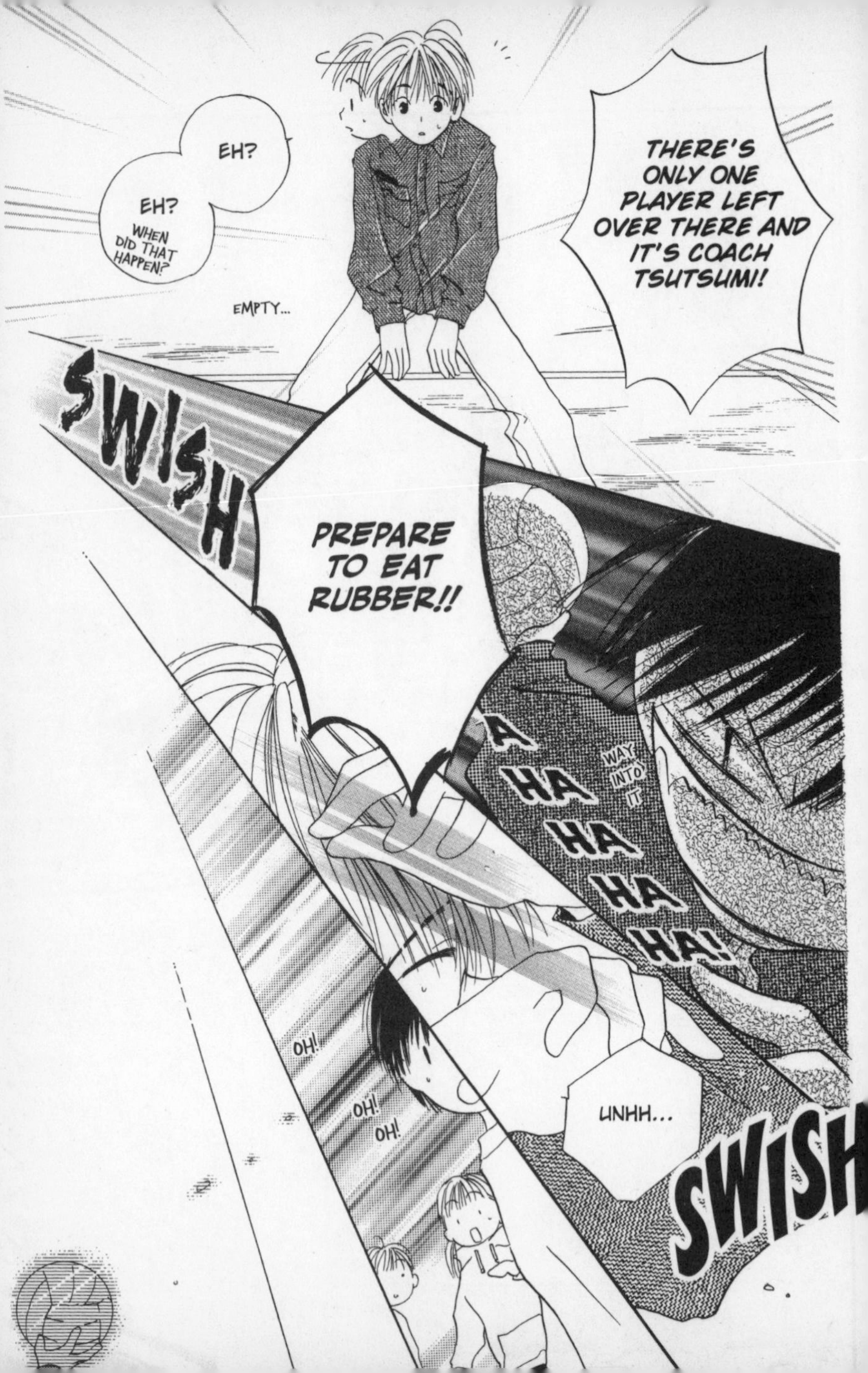
THERE'S ONLY ONE PLAYER LEFT OVER THERE AND IT'S COACH TSUTSUMI!
EH?
EH? WHEN DID THAT HAPPEN?
EMPTY...
SWISH
PREPARE TO EAT RUBBER!!
A HA HA HA HA HA!
WAY INTO IT
UNHH...
SWISH
OH!
OH!
OH!

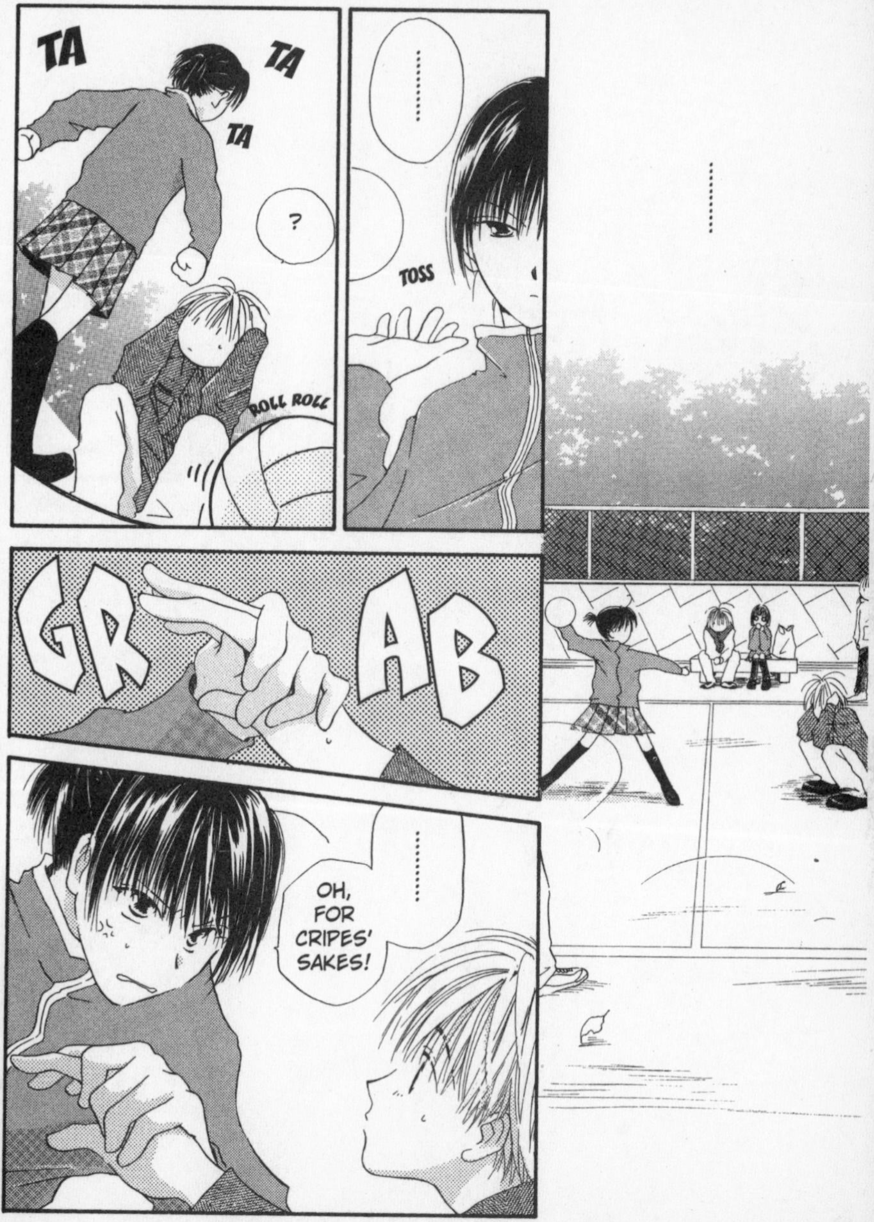
......
......
TOSS
TA
TA
TA
?
ROLL ROLL
GR AB
......
OH, FOR CRIPES' SAKES!

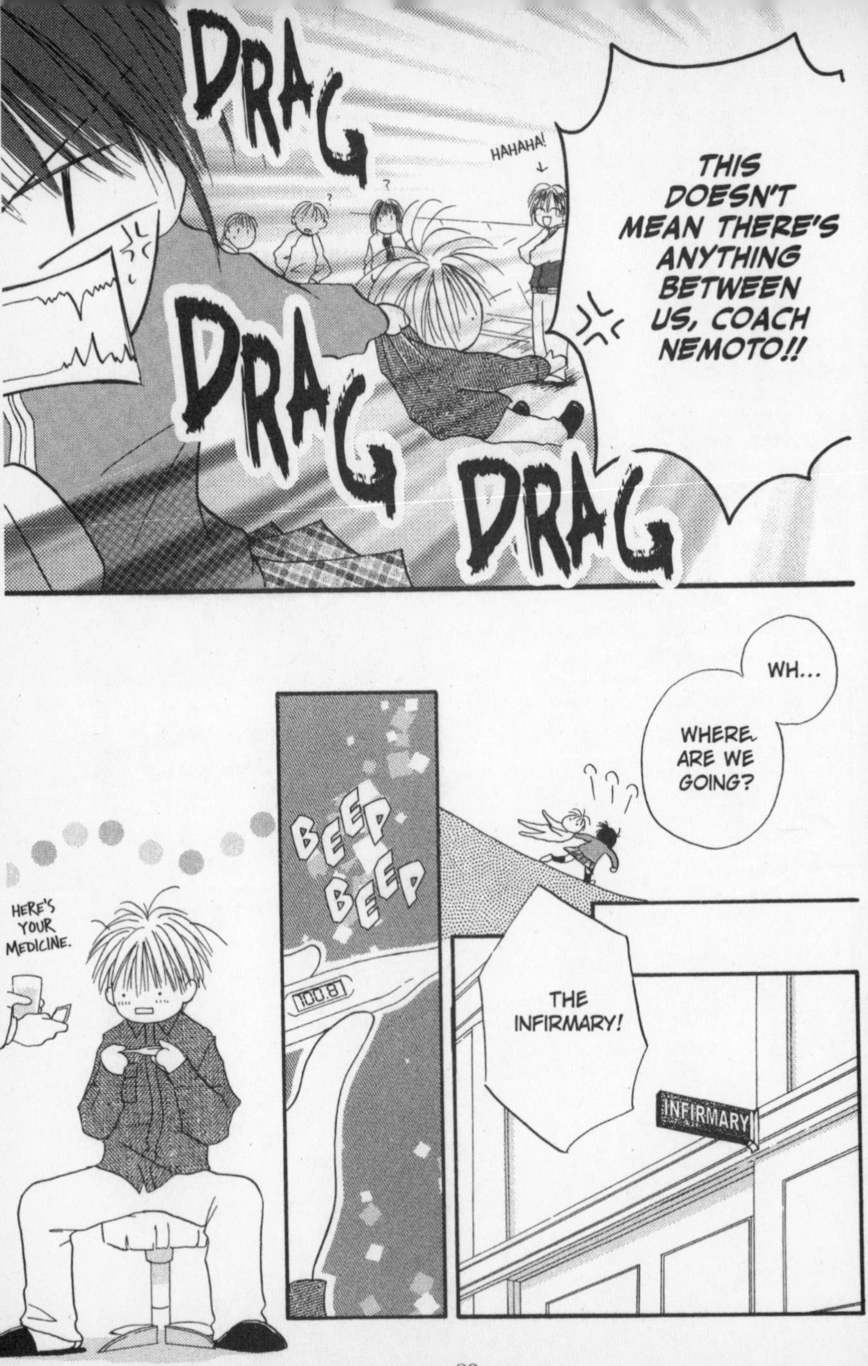
THIS DOESN'T MEAN THERE'S ANYTHING BETWEEN US, COACH NEMOTO!!
HAHAHA!
DRAG
DRAG
DRAG
WH...
WHERE ARE WE GOING?
THE INFIRMARY!
INFIRMARY
BEEP BEEP
100.8
HERE'S YOUR MEDICINE.

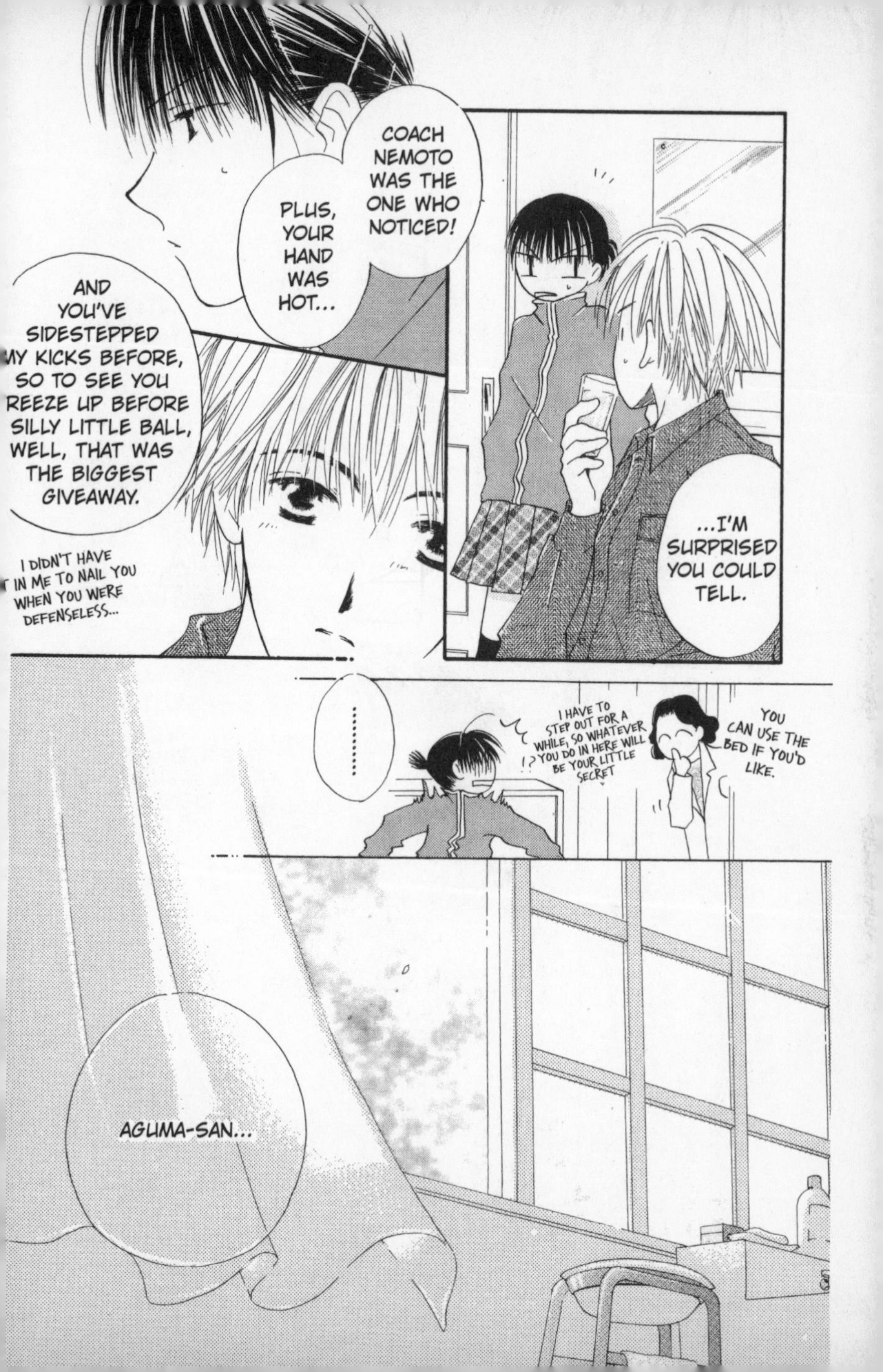
...I'M SURPRISED YOU COULD TELL.
COACH NEMOTO WAS THE ONE WHO NOTICED!
PLUS, YOUR HAND WAS HOT...
AND YOU'VE SIDESTEPPED MY KICKS BEFORE, SO TO SEE YOU REEZE UP BEFORE SILLY LITTLE BALL, WELL, THAT WAS THE BIGGEST GIVEAWAY.
I DIDN'T HAVE IN ME TO NAIL YOU WHEN YOU WERE DEFENSELESS...
YOU CAN USE THE BED IF YOU'D LIKE.
I HAVE TO STEP OUT FOR A WHILE, SO WHATEVER YOU DO IN HERE WILL BE YOUR LITTLE SECRET
!?
....
AGUMA-SAN...

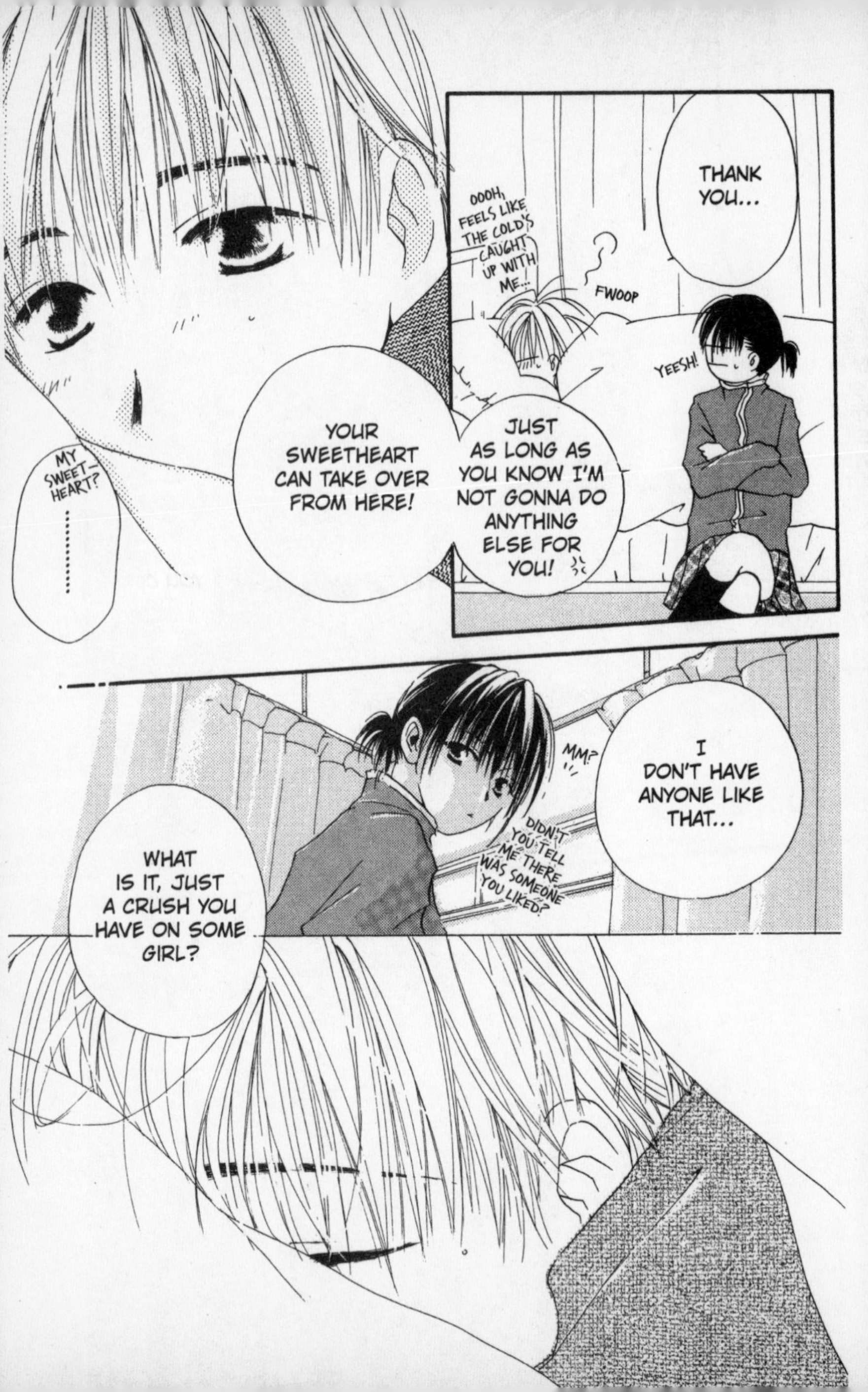
THANK YOU...
YEESH!
FWOOP
OOOH, FEELS LIKE THE COLD'S CAUGHT UP WITH ME...
JUST AS LONG AS YOU KNOW I'M NOT GONNA DO ANYTHING ELSE FOR YOU!
YOUR SWEETHEART CAN TAKE OVER FROM HERE!
MY SWEET-HEART?
......
MM?
I DON'T HAVE ANYONE LIKE THAT...
DIDN'T YOU TELL ME THERE WAS SOMEONE YOU LIKED?
WHAT IS IT, JUST A CRUSH YOU HAVE ON SOME GIRL?

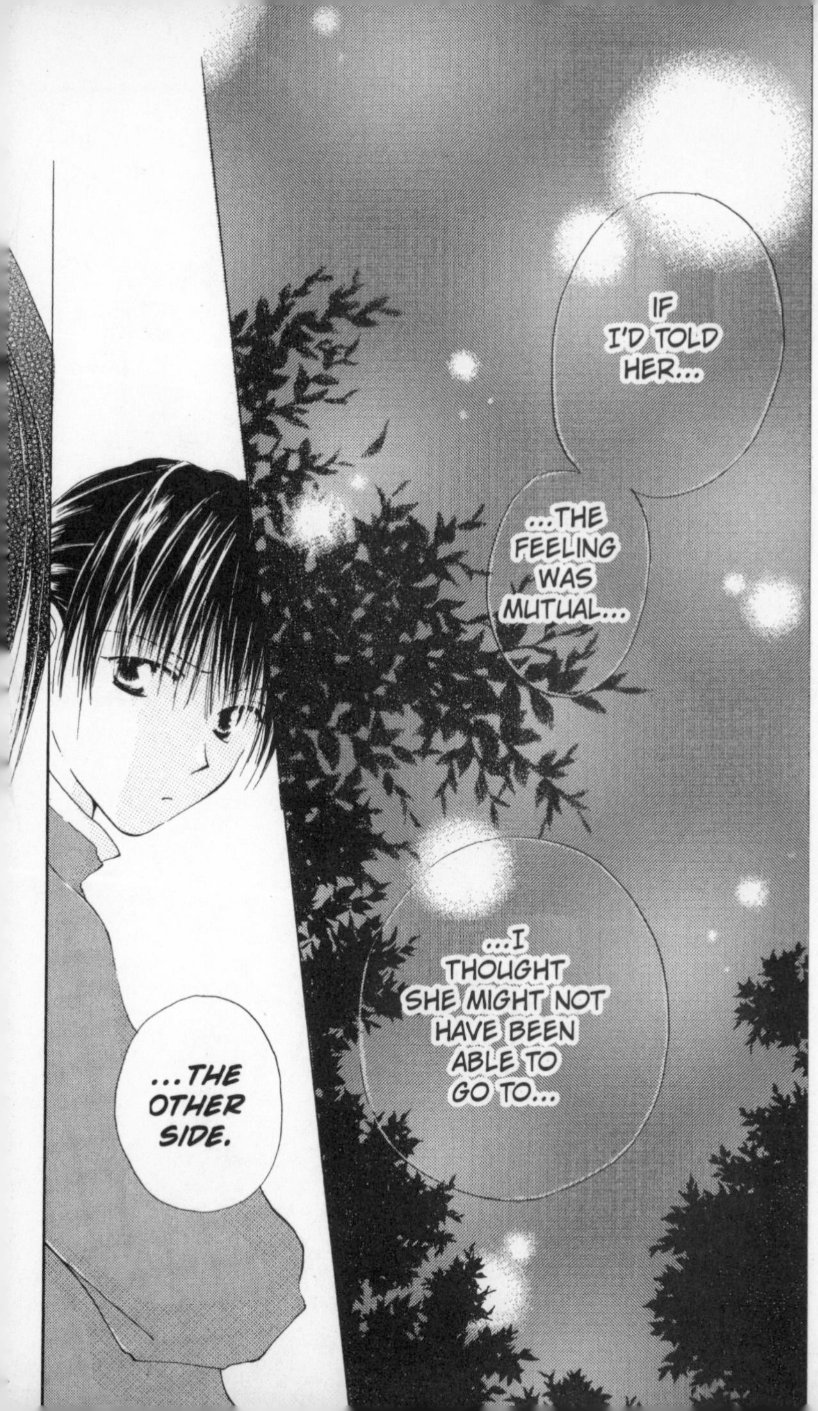
IF I'D TOLD HER...
...THE FEELING WAS MUTUAL...
...I THOUGHT SHE MIGHT NOT HAVE BEEN ABLE TO GO TO...
...THE OTHER SIDE.

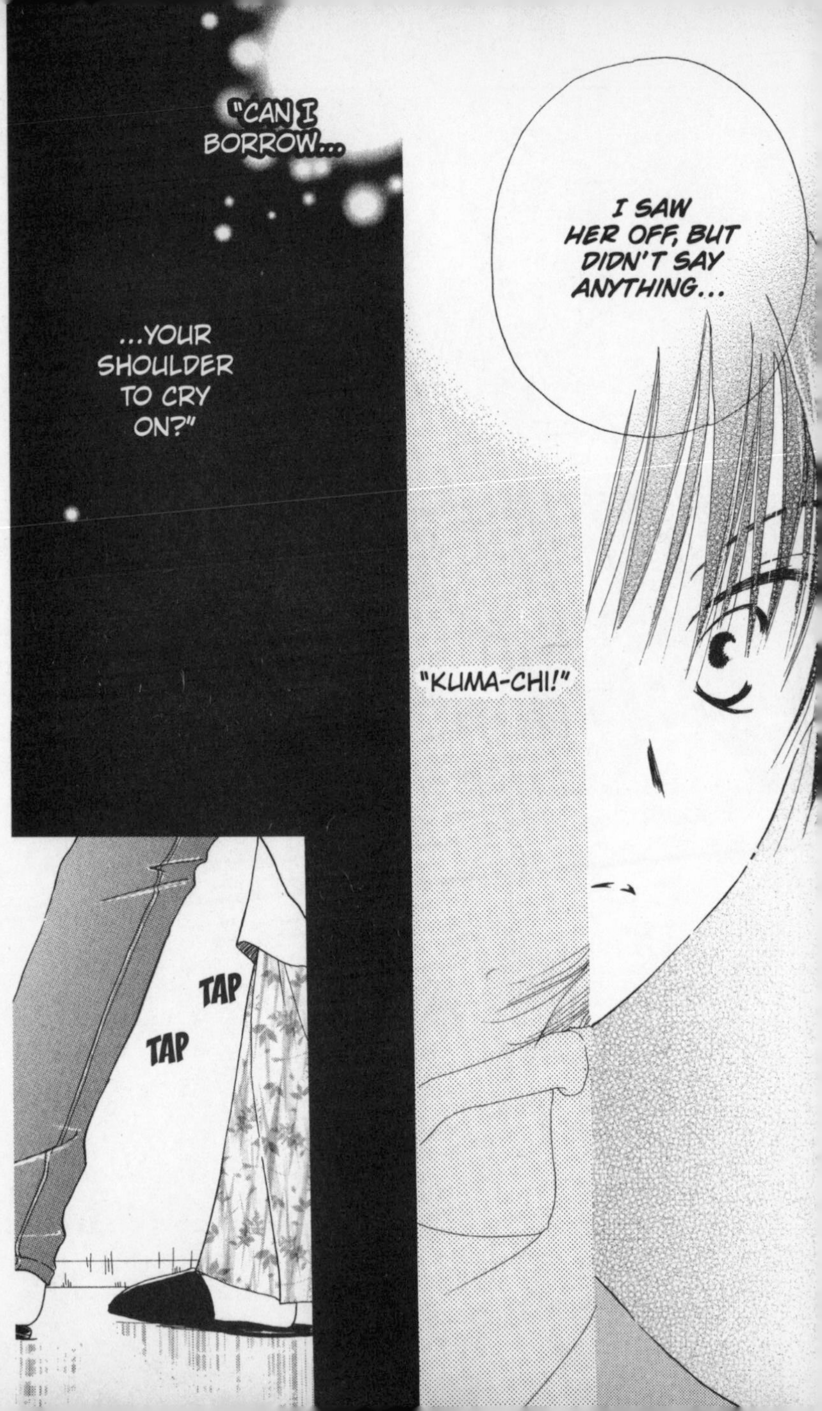
I SAW HER OFF, BUT DIDN'T SAY ANYTHING...
"KUMA-CHI!"
"CAN I BORROW...
...YOUR SHOULDER TO CRY ON?"
TAP
TAP

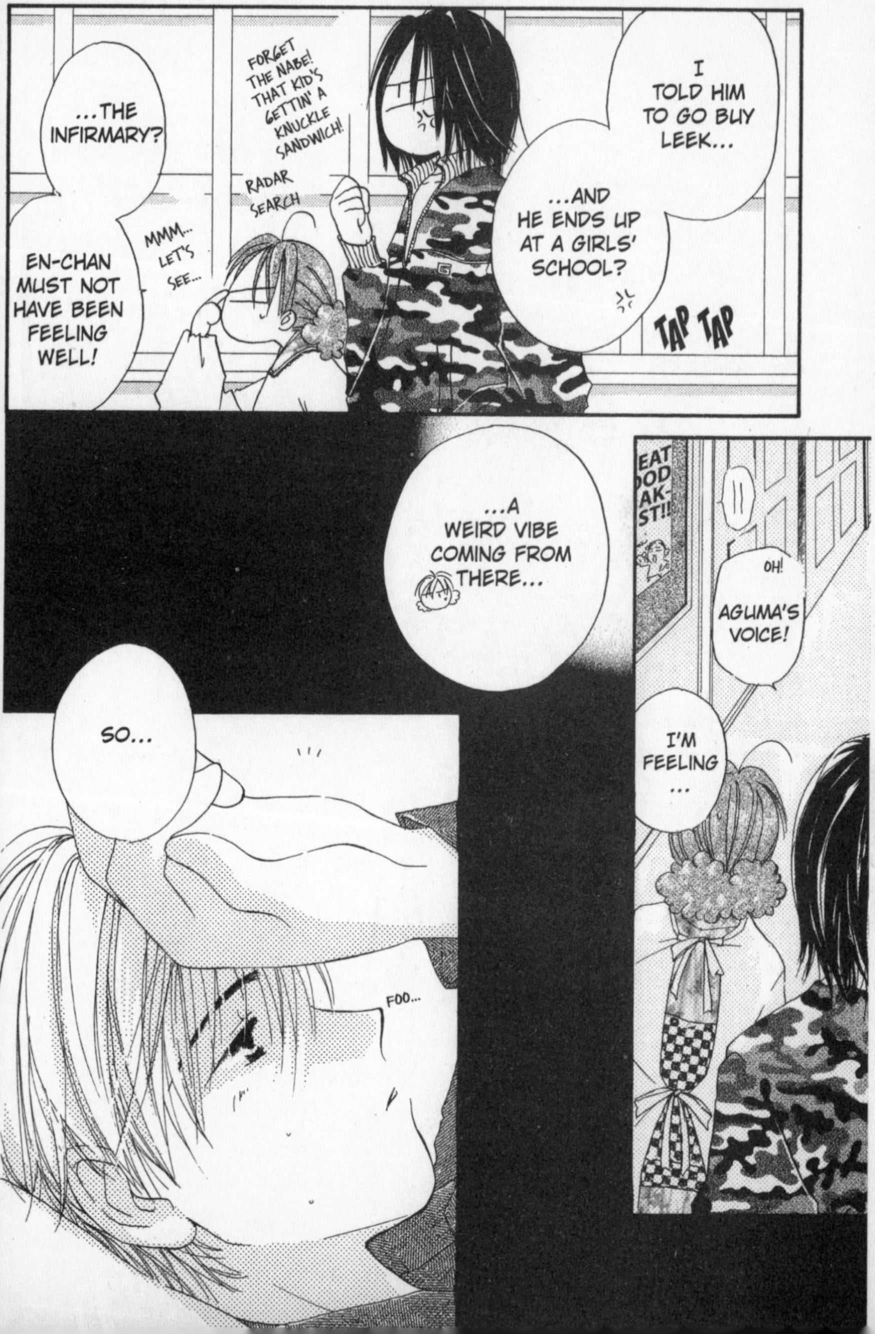
I TOLD HIM TO GO BUY LEEK...
...AND HE ENDS UP AT A GIRLS' SCHOOL?
TAP TAP
FORGET THE NABE! THAT KID'S GETTIN' A KNUCKLE SANDWICH!
RADAR SEARCH
MMM... LET'S SEE...
...THE INFIRMARY?
EN-CHAN MUST NOT HAVE BEEN FEELING WELL!
OH!
AGUMA'S VOICE!
I'M FEELING ...
...A WEIRD VIBE COMING FROM THERE...
SO...
FOO...

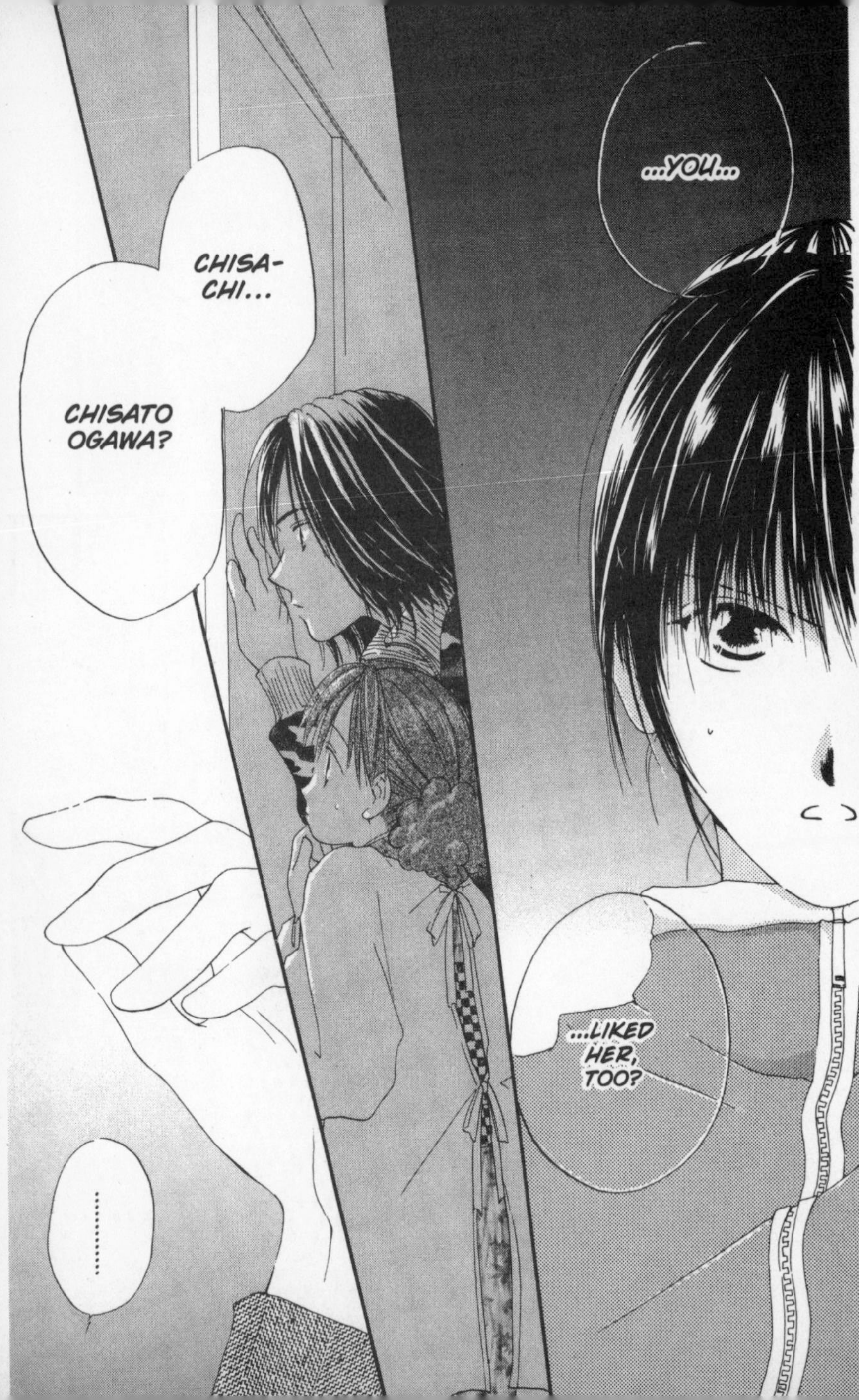
...YOU...
...LIKED HER, TOO?
CHISA-CHI...
CHISATO OGAWA?
......

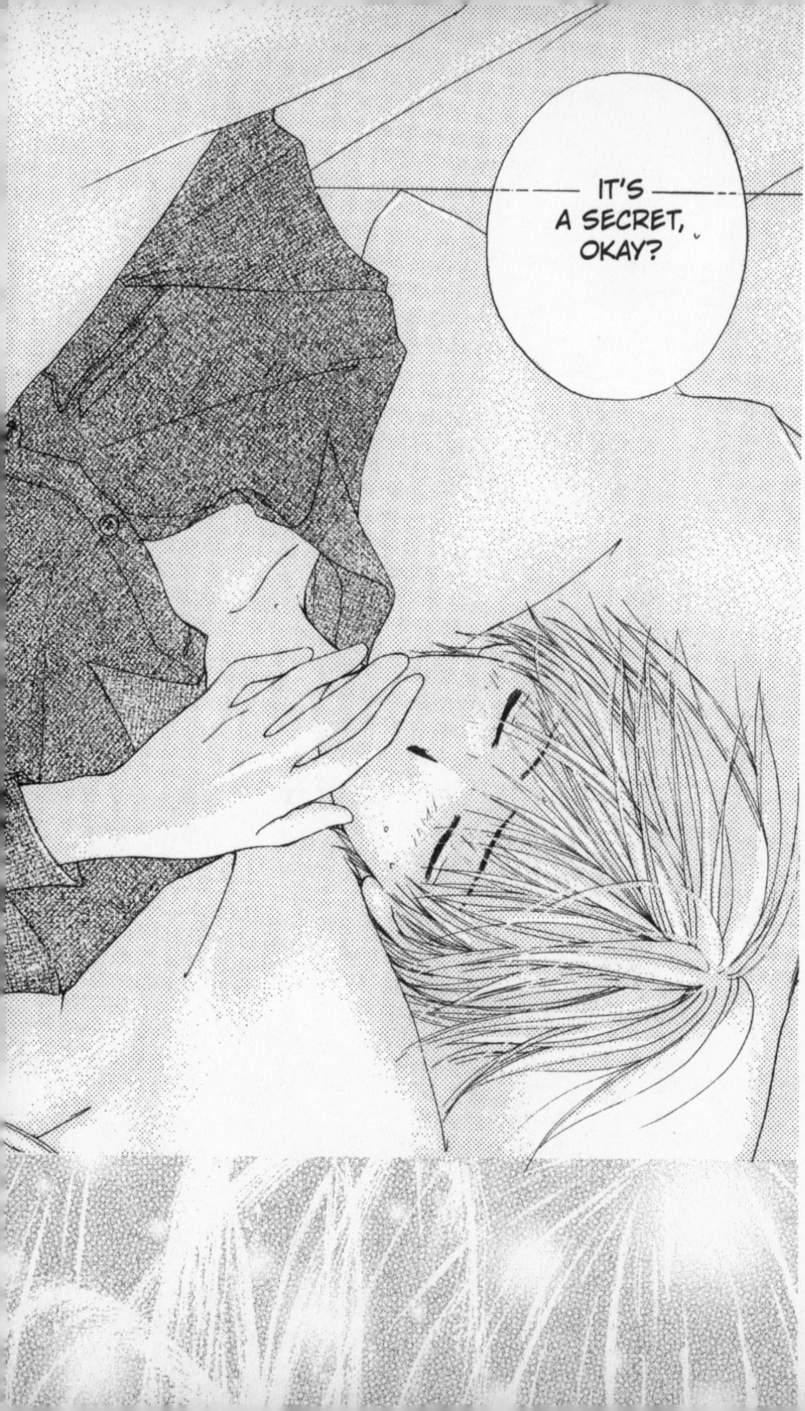
IT'S A SECRET, OKAY?

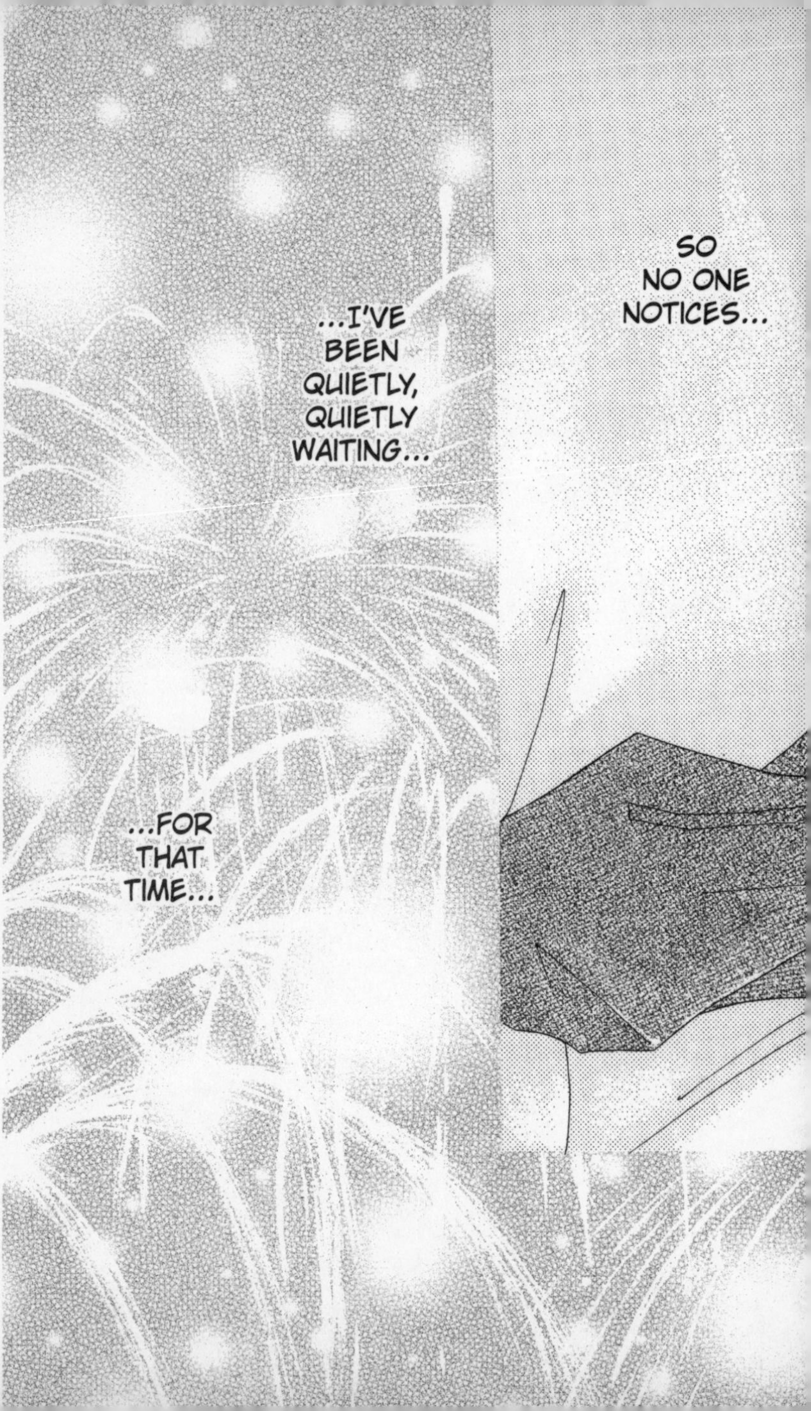
SO NO ONE NOTICES...
...I'VE BEEN QUIETLY, QUIETLY WAITING...
...FOR THAT TIME...

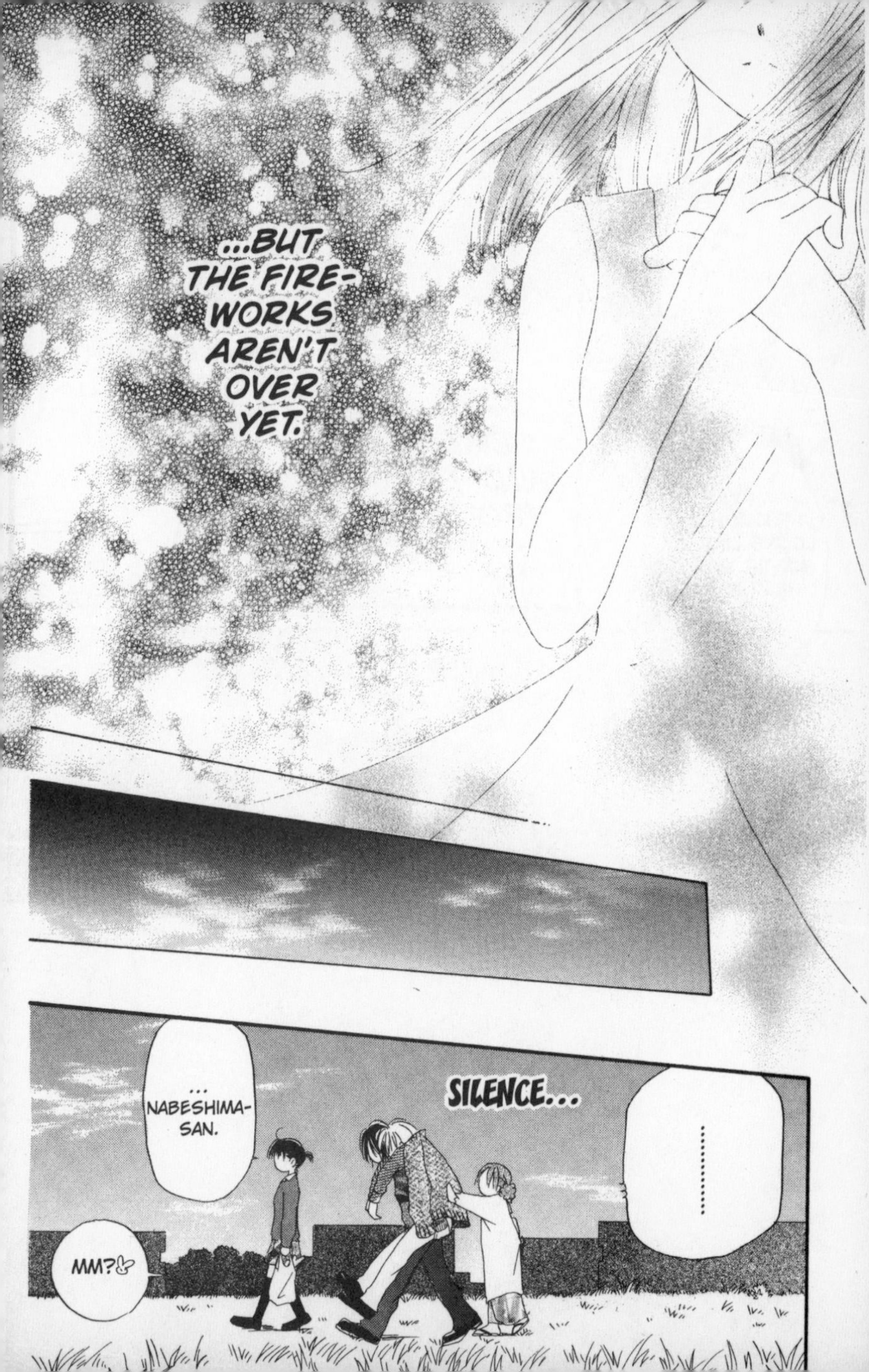
...BUT THE FIRE-WORKS AREN'T OVER YET.
....
SILENCE...
...NABESHIMA-SAN.
MM?

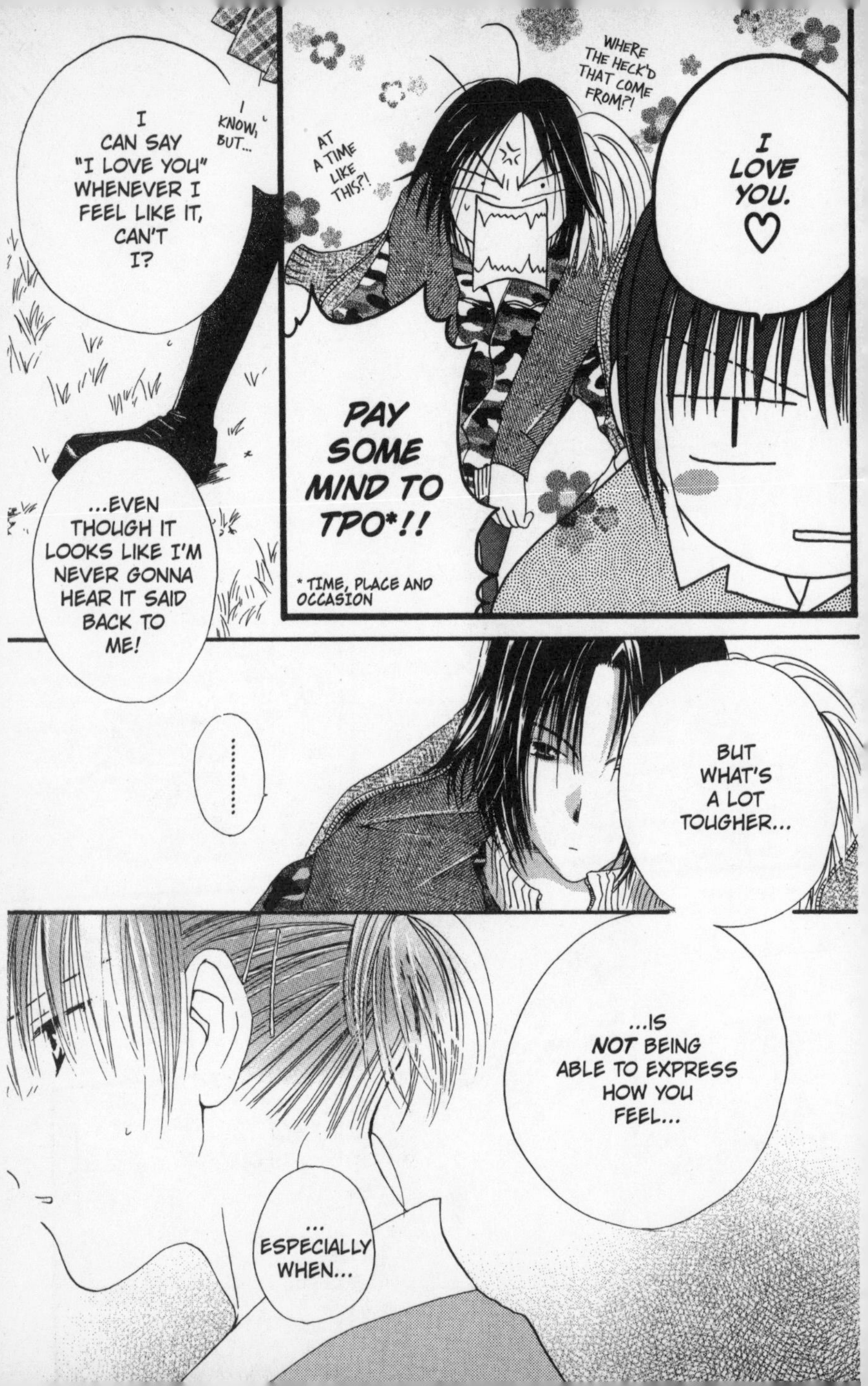
I LOVE YOU. ♡
WHERE THE HECK'D THAT COME FROM?!
AT A TIME LIKE THIS?!
PAY SOME MIND TO TPO*!!
* TIME, PLACE AND OCCASION
I KNOW, BUT...
I CAN SAY "I LOVE YOU" WHENEVER I FEEL LIKE IT, CAN'T I?
...EVEN THOUGH IT LOOKS LIKE I'M NEVER GONNA HEAR IT SAID BACK TO ME!
BUT WHAT'S A LOT TOUGHER...
....
...IS NOT BEING ABLE TO EXPRESS HOW YOU FEEL...
... ESPECIALLY WHEN...

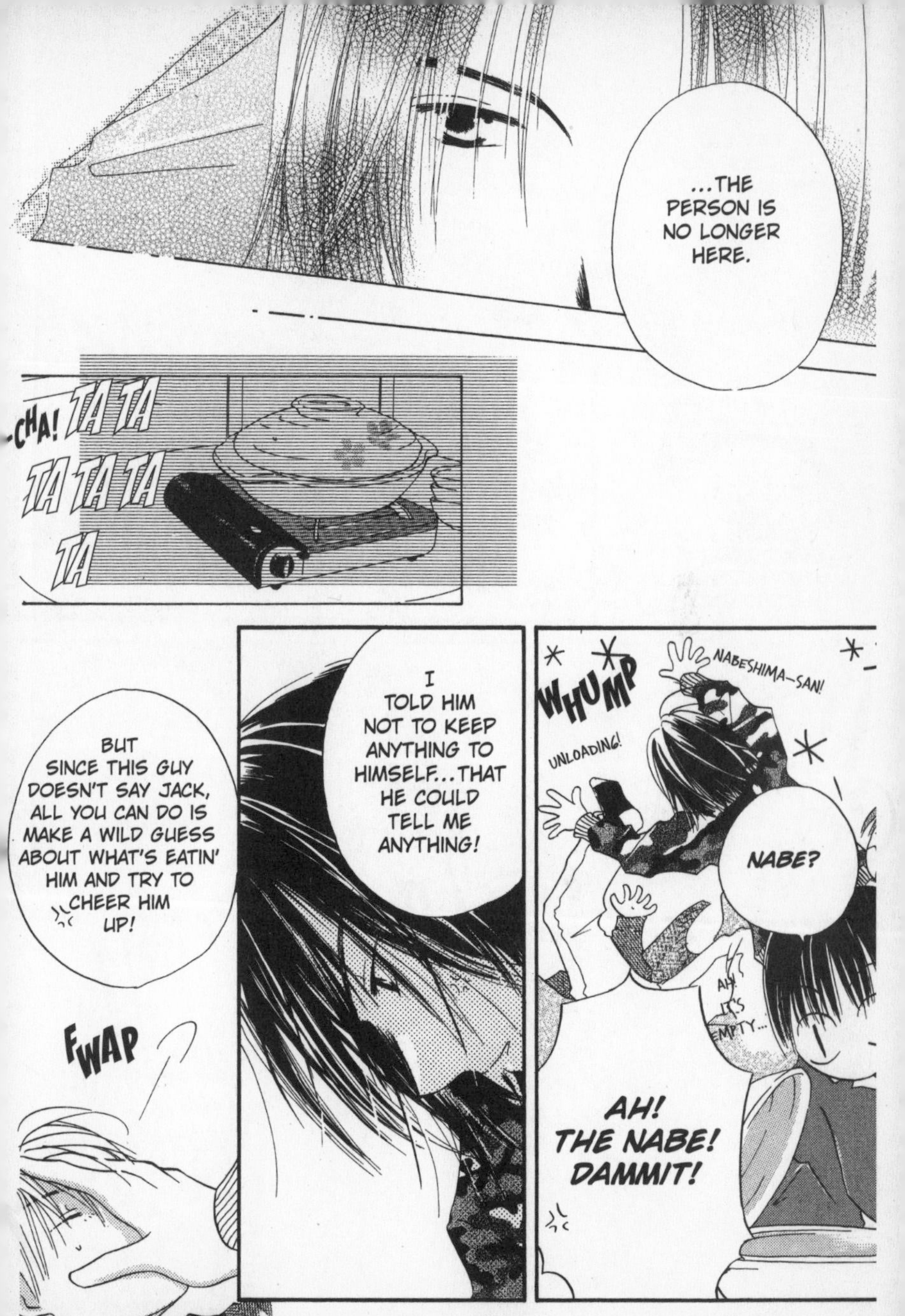
...THE PERSON IS NO LONGER HERE.
-CHA! TA TA TA TA TA TA
NABESHIMA-SAN!
WHUMP
NABE?
UNLOADING!
AH! IT'S EMPTY...
AH! THE NABE! DAMMIT!
I TOLD HIM NOT TO KEEP ANYTHING TO HIMSELF...THAT HE COULD TELL ME ANYTHING!
BUT SINCE THIS GUY DOESN'T SAY JACK, ALL YOU CAN DO IS MAKE A WILD GUESS ABOUT WHAT'S EATIN' HIM AND TRY TO CHEER HIM UP!
FWAP

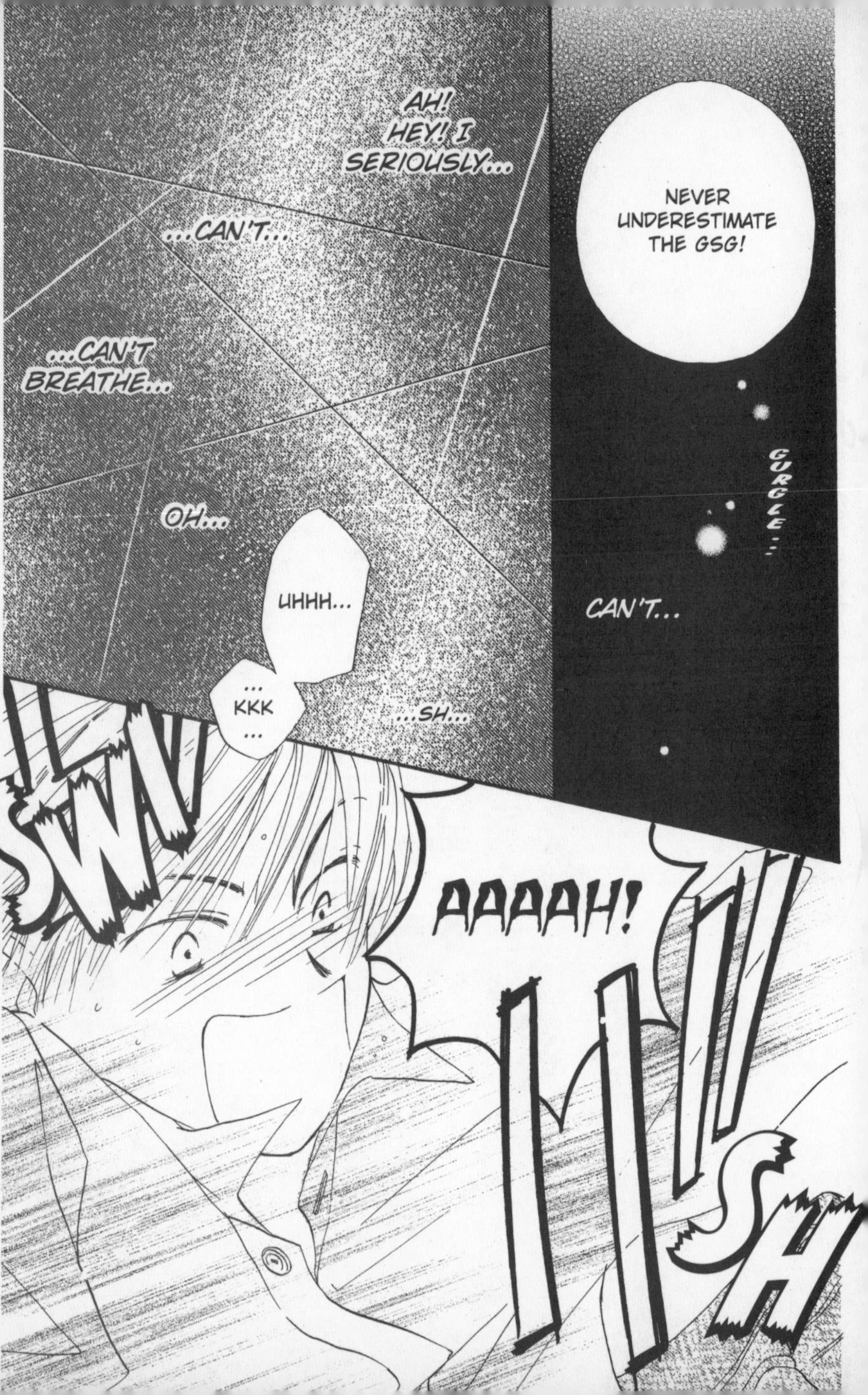
NEVER UNDERESTIMATE THE GSG!
GURGLE...
CAN'T...
AH! HEY! I SERIOUSLY...
...CAN'T...
...CAN'T BREATHE...
OH...
UHHH...
...KKK...
...SH...
AAAAH!

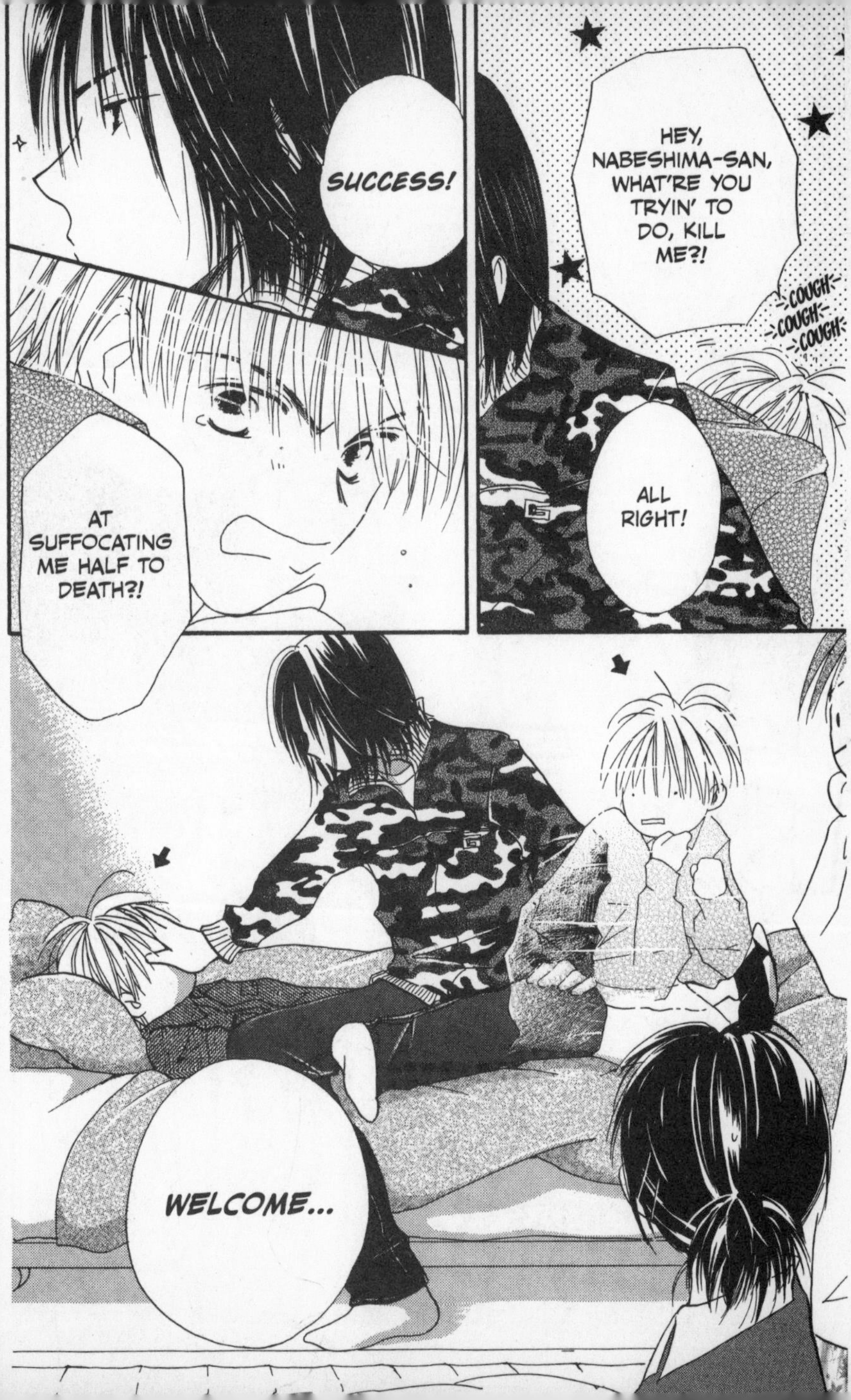
HEY, NABESHIMA-SAN, WHAT'RE YOU TRYIN' TO DO, KILL ME?!
COUGH COUGH COUGH
ALL RIGHT!
SUCCESS!
AT SUFFOCATING ME HALF TO DEATH?!
WELCOME...

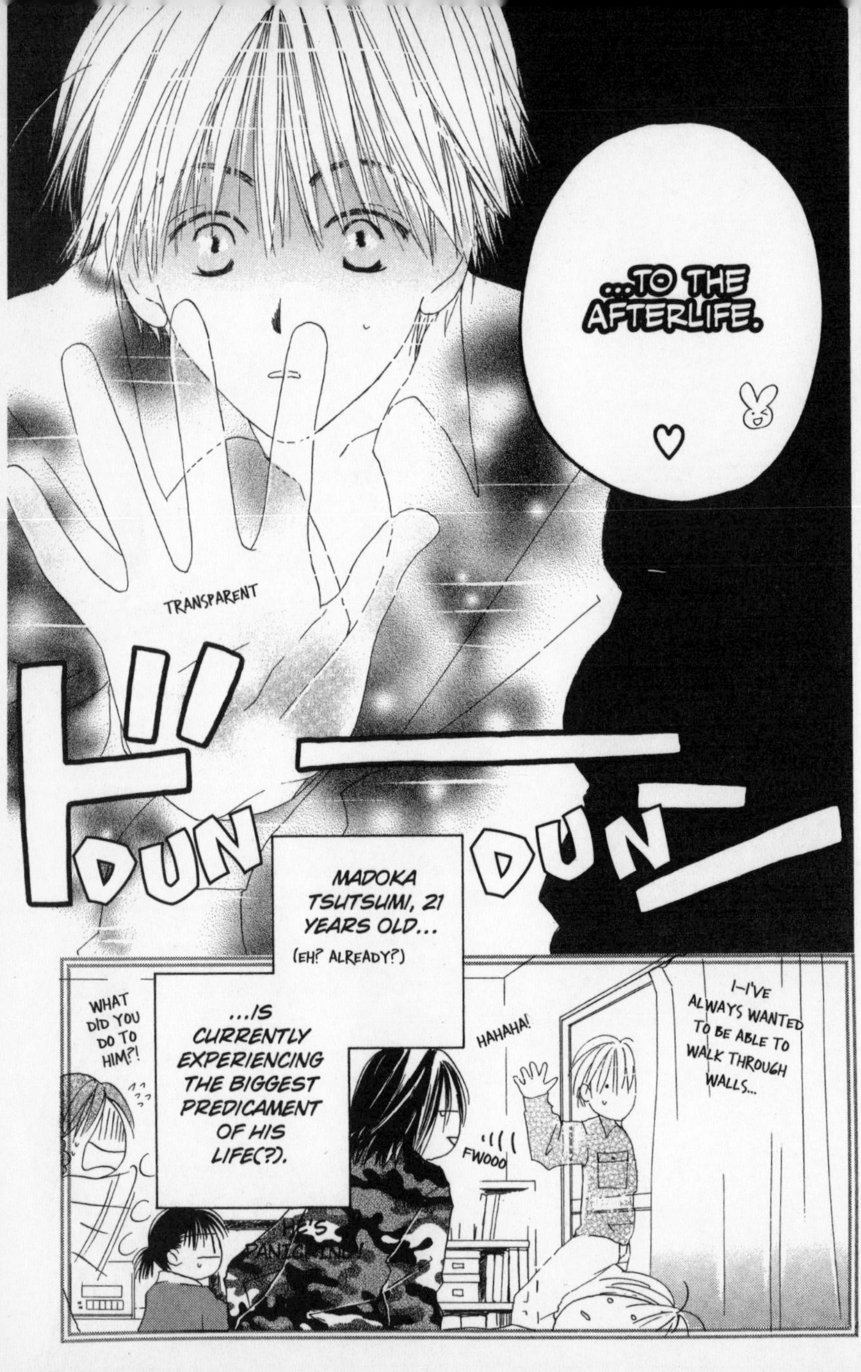
...TO THE AFTERLIFE.
TRANSPARENT
DUN
DUN
MADOKA TSUTSUMI, 21 YEARS OLD...
(EH? ALREADY?)
I-I'VE ALWAYS WANTED TO BE ABLE TO WALK THROUGH WALLS...
HAHAHA!
FWOOO
...IS CURRENTLY EXPERIENCING THE BIGGEST PREDICAMENT OF HIS LIFE(?).
WHAT DID YOU DO TO HIM?!
HE'S PANICKING!

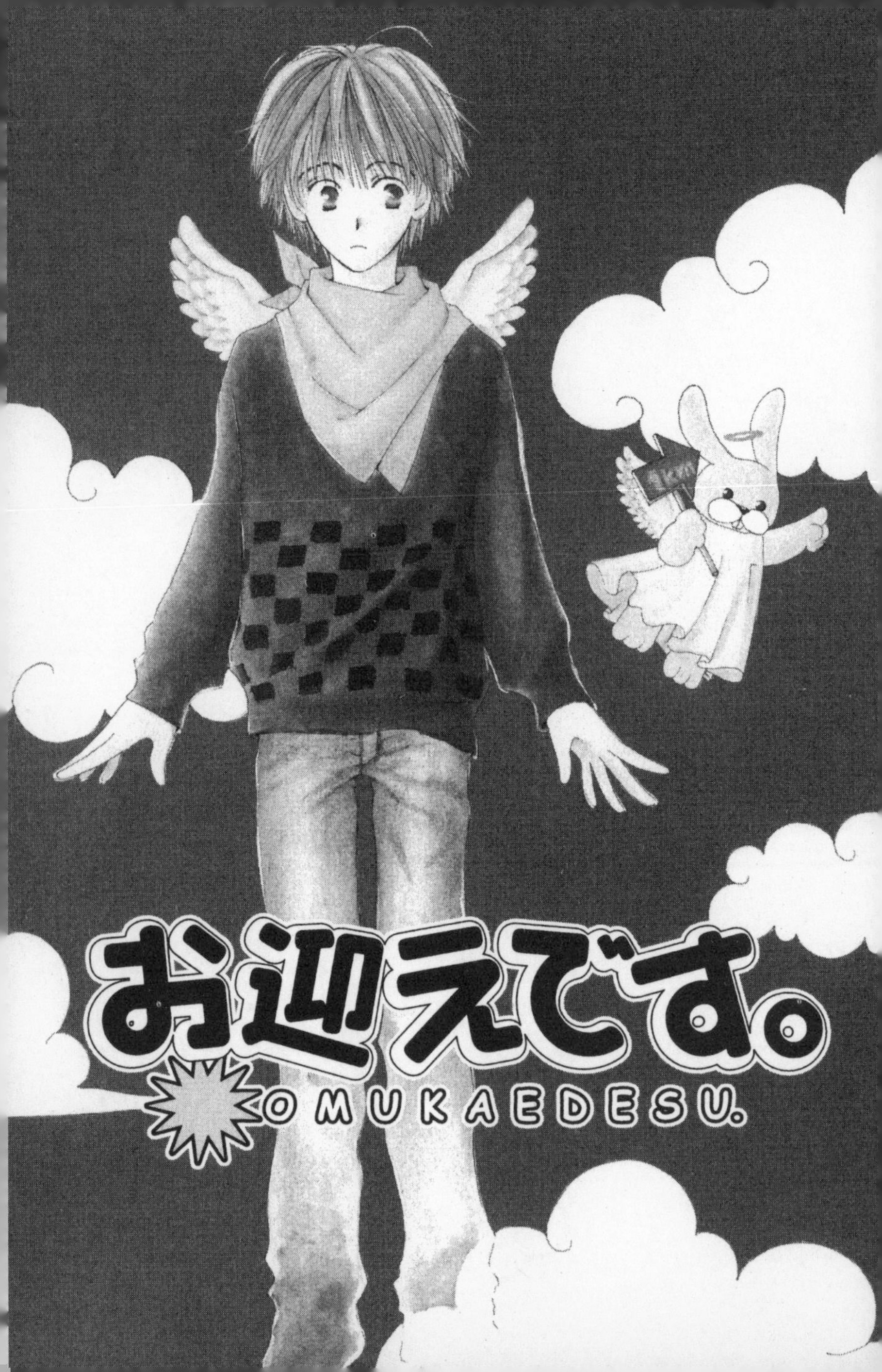
お迎えです。
OMUKAEDESU.

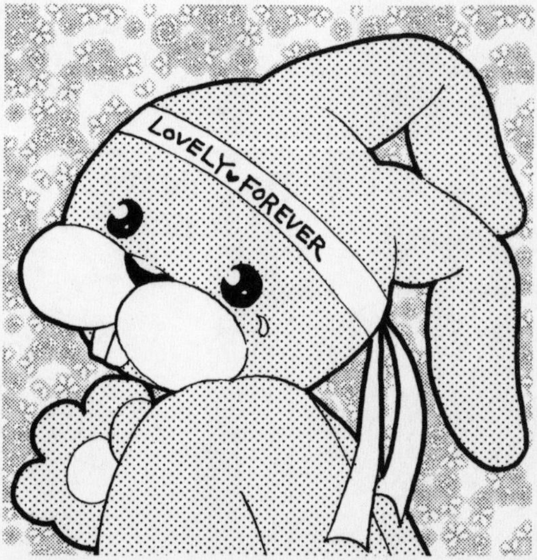
LOVELY♥FOREVER

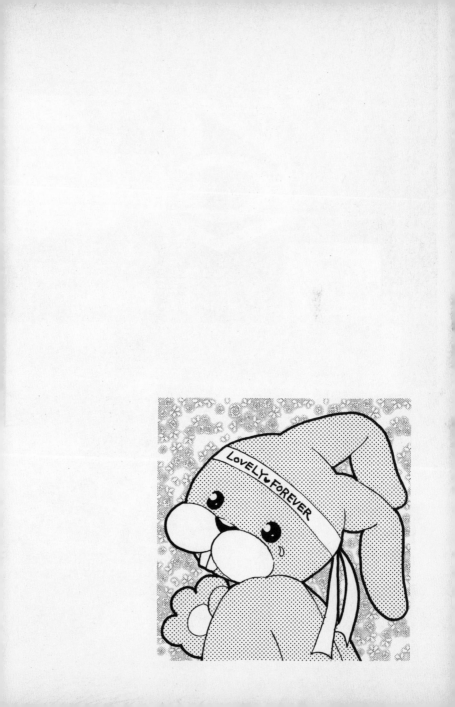

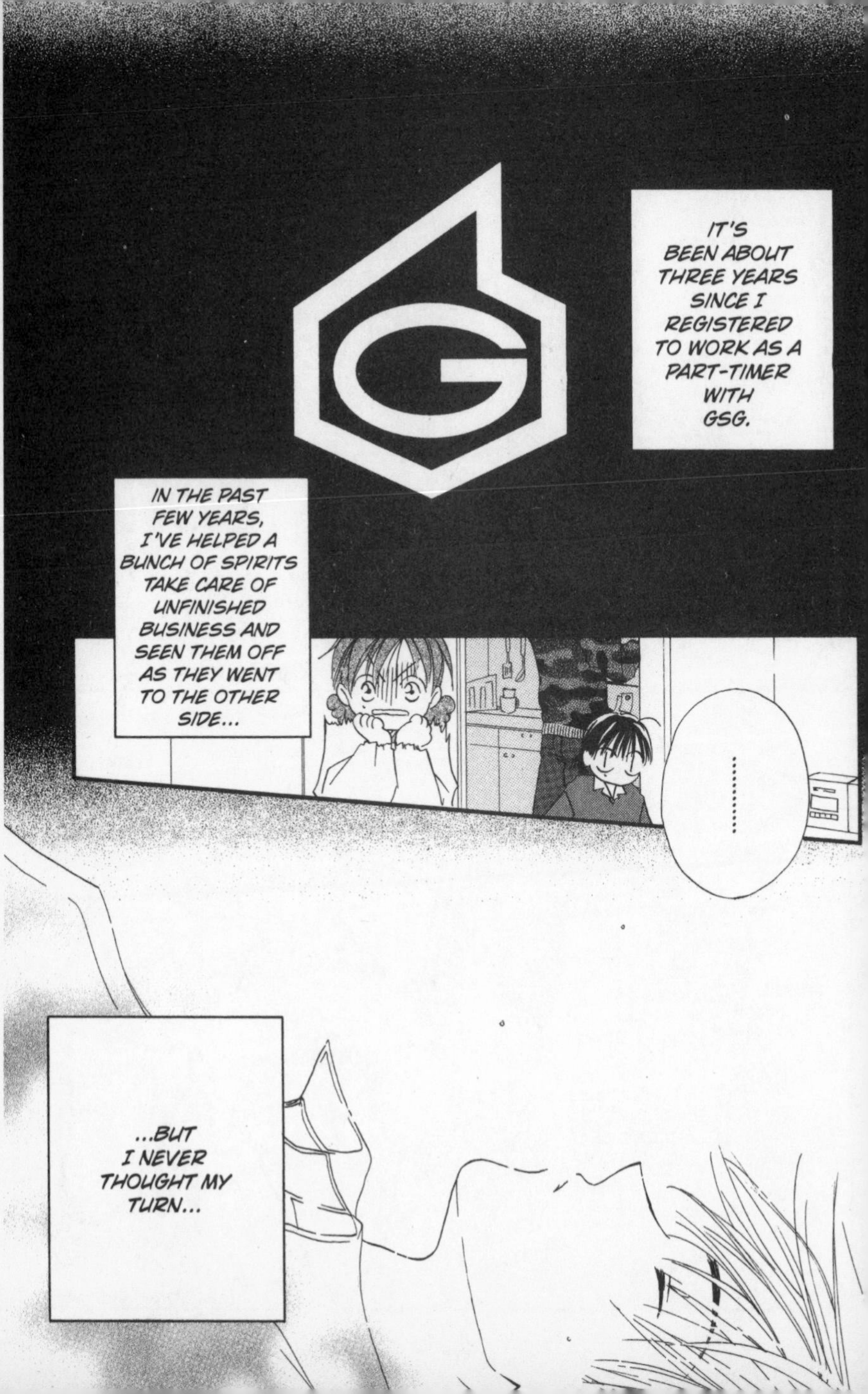
IT'S BEEN ABOUT THREE YEARS SINCE I REGISTERED TO WORK AS A PART-TIMER WITH GSG.
IN THE PAST FEW YEARS, I'VE HELPED A BUNCH OF SPIRITS TAKE CARE OF UNFINISHED BUSINESS AND SEEN THEM OFF AS THEY WENT TO THE OTHER SIDE...
......
...BUT I NEVER THOUGHT MY TURN...

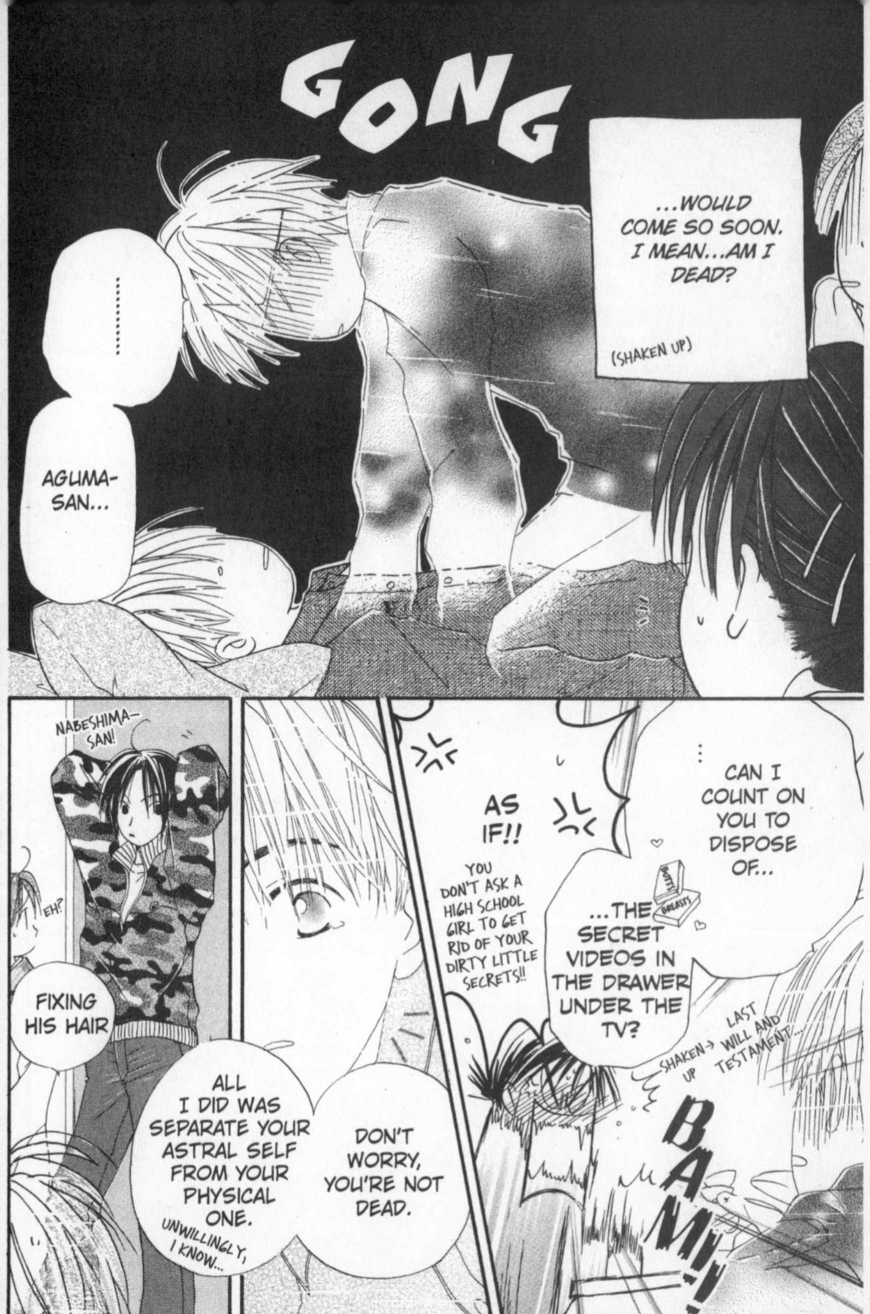
GONG
...WOULD COME SO SOON. I MEAN...AM I DEAD?
(SHAKEN UP)
......
AGUMA-SAN...
...CAN I COUNT ON YOU TO DISPOSE OF...
...THE SECRET VIDEOS IN THE DRAWER UNDER THE TV?
BUTTS
BREASTS
LAST WILL AND TESTAMENT...
SHAKEN UP
AS IF!!
YOU DON'T ASK A HIGH SCHOOL GIRL TO GET RID OF YOUR DIRTY LITTLE SECRETS!!
BAM!!
DON'T WORRY, YOU'RE NOT DEAD.
ALL I DID WAS SEPARATE YOUR ASTRAL SELF FROM YOUR PHYSICAL ONE.
UNWILLINGLY, I KNOW...
NABESHIMA-SAN!
EH?
FIXING HIS HAIR

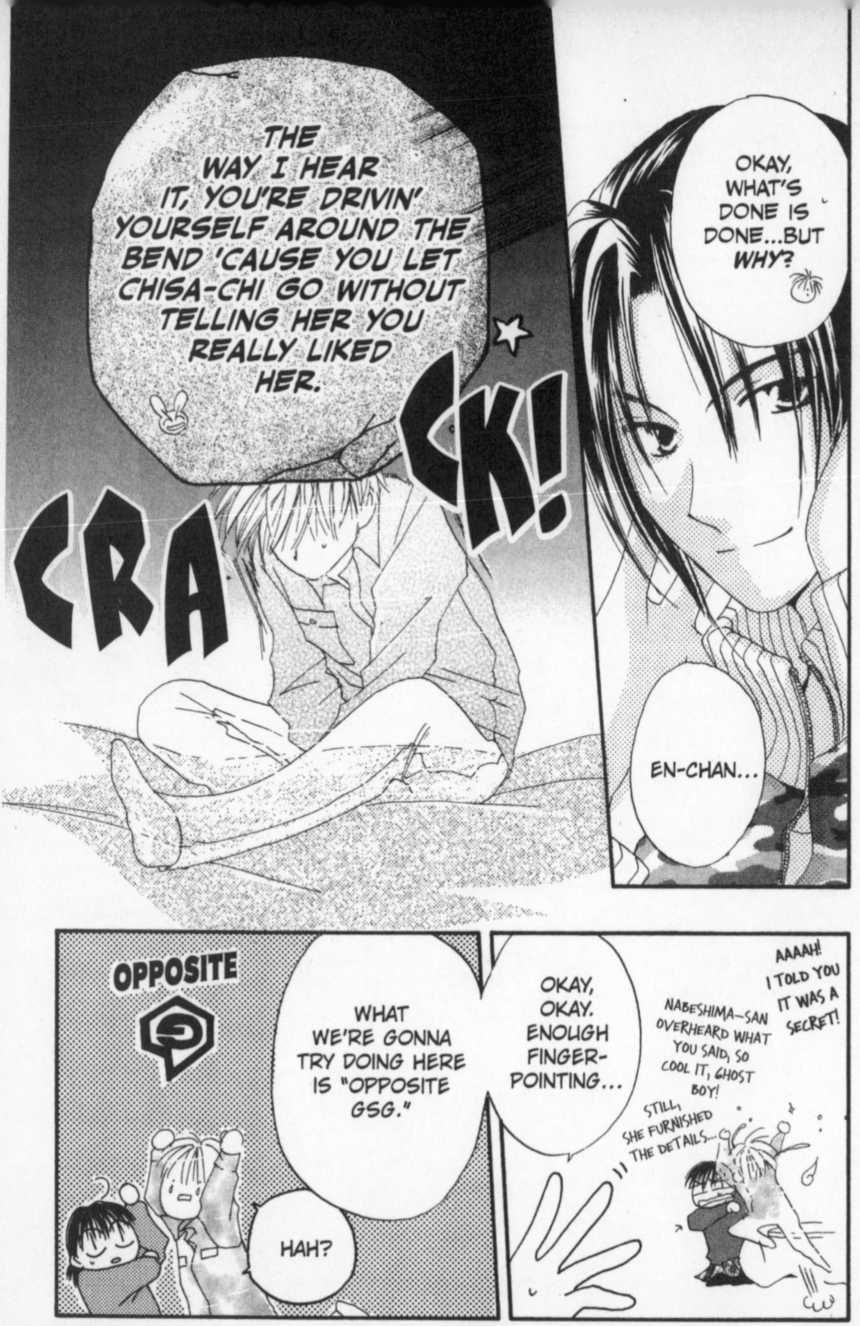
OKAY, WHAT'S DONE IS DONE...BUT WHY?
EN-CHAN...
THE WAY I HEAR IT, YOU'RE DRIVIN' YOURSELF AROUND THE BEND 'CAUSE YOU LET CHISA-CHI GO WITHOUT TELLING HER YOU REALLY LIKED HER.
CRACK!
AAAAH! I TOLD YOU IT WAS A SECRET!
OKAY, OKAY. ENOUGH FINGER-POINTING...
NABESHIMA-SAN OVERHEARD WHAT YOU SAID, SO COOL IT, GHOST BOY!
STILL, SHE FURNISHED THE DETAILS...
WHAT WE'RE GONNA TRY DOING HERE IS "OPPOSITE GSG."
OPPOSITE
HAH?

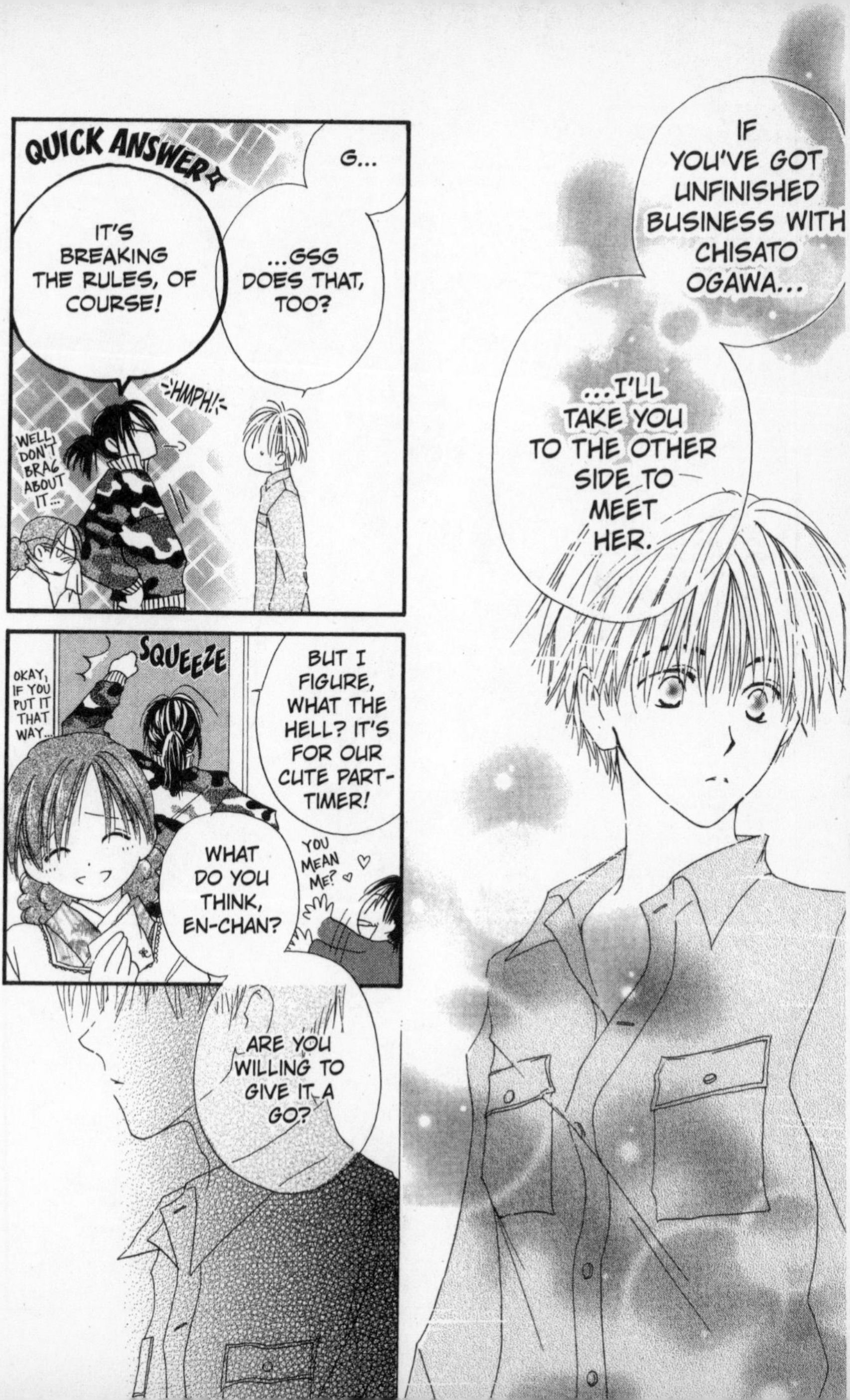
IF YOU'VE GOT UNFINISHED BUSINESS WITH CHISATO OGAWA...
...I'LL TAKE YOU TO THE OTHER SIDE TO MEET HER.
G...
...GSG DOES THAT, TOO?
QUICK ANSWER
IT'S BREAKING THE RULES, OF COURSE!
HMPH!
WELL DON'T BRAG ABOUT IT...
BUT I FIGURE, WHAT THE HELL? IT'S FOR OUR CUTE PART-TIMER!
SQUEEZE
OKAY, IF YOU PUT IT THAT WAY...
YOU MEAN ME?
WHAT DO YOU THINK, EN-CHAN?
ARE YOU WILLING TO GIVE IT A GO?

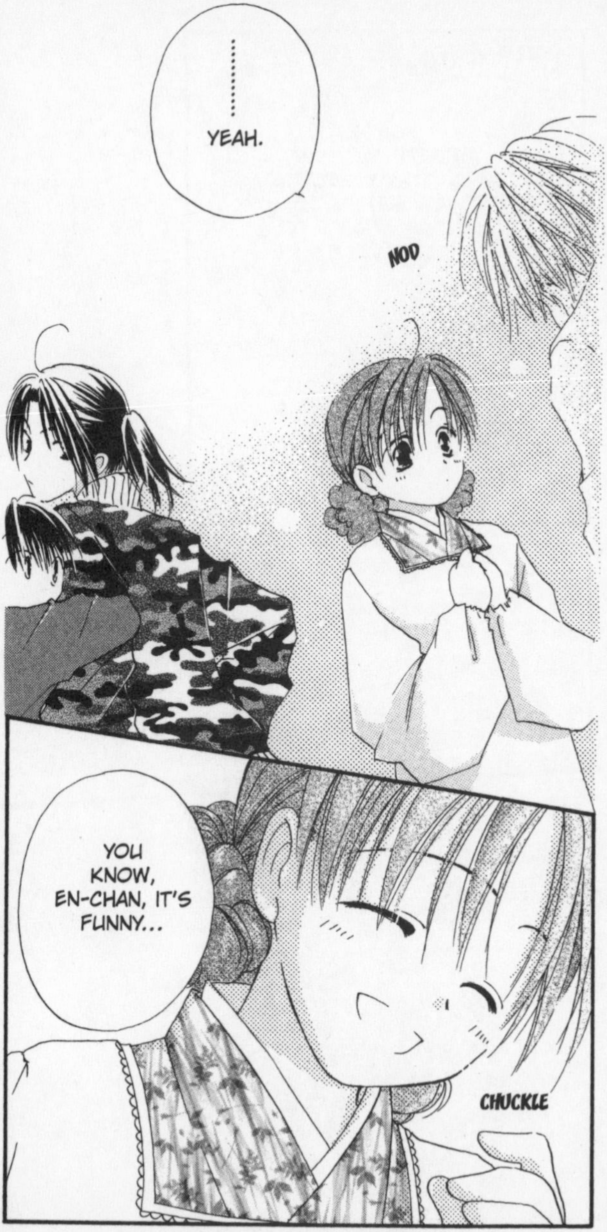
......
YEAH.
NOD
YOU KNOW, EN-CHAN, IT'S FUNNY...
CHUCKLE

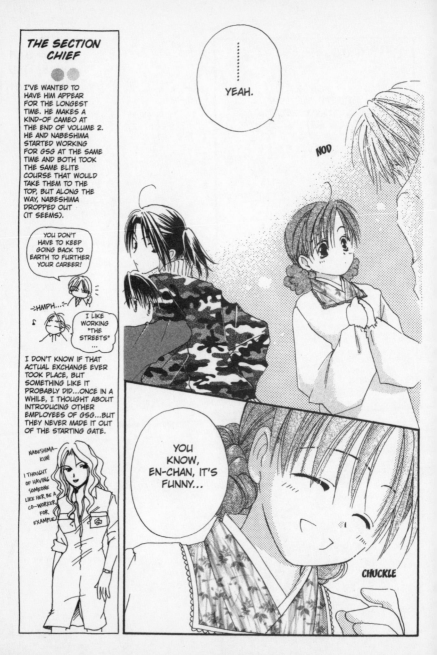

THE SECTION CHIEF

I'VE WANTED TO HAVE HIM APPEAR FOR THE LONGEST TIME. HE MAKES A KIND-OF CAMEO AT THE END OF VOLUME 2. HE AND NABESHIMA STARTED WORKING FOR GSG AT THE SAME TIME AND BOTH TOOK THE SAME ELITE COURSE THAT WOULD TAKE THEM TO THE TOP, BUT ALONG THE WAY, NABESHIMA DROPPED OUT (IT SEEMS).

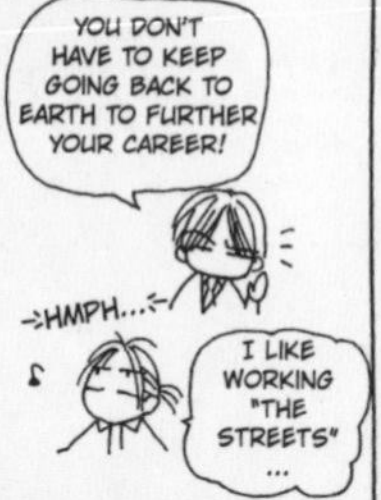
YOU DON'T HAVE TO KEEP GOING BACK TO EARTH TO FURTHER YOUR CAREER!
HMPH...
I LIKE WORKING "THE STREETS" ...

I DON'T KNOW IF THAT ACTUAL EXCHANGE EVER TOOK PLACE, BUT SOMETHING LIKE IT PROBABLY DID...ONCE IN A WHILE, I THOUGHT ABOUT INTRODUCING OTHER EMPLOYEES OF GSG...BUT THEY NEVER MADE IT OUT OF THE STARTING GATE.

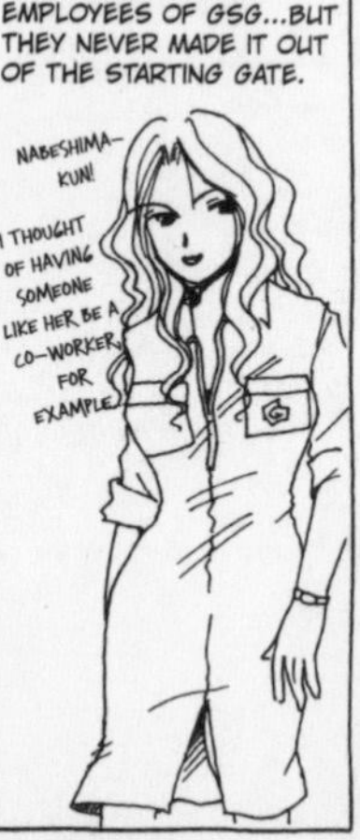
NABESHIMA-KUN!
I THOUGHT OF HAVING SOMEONE LIKE HER BE A CO-WORKER, FOR EXAMPLE.

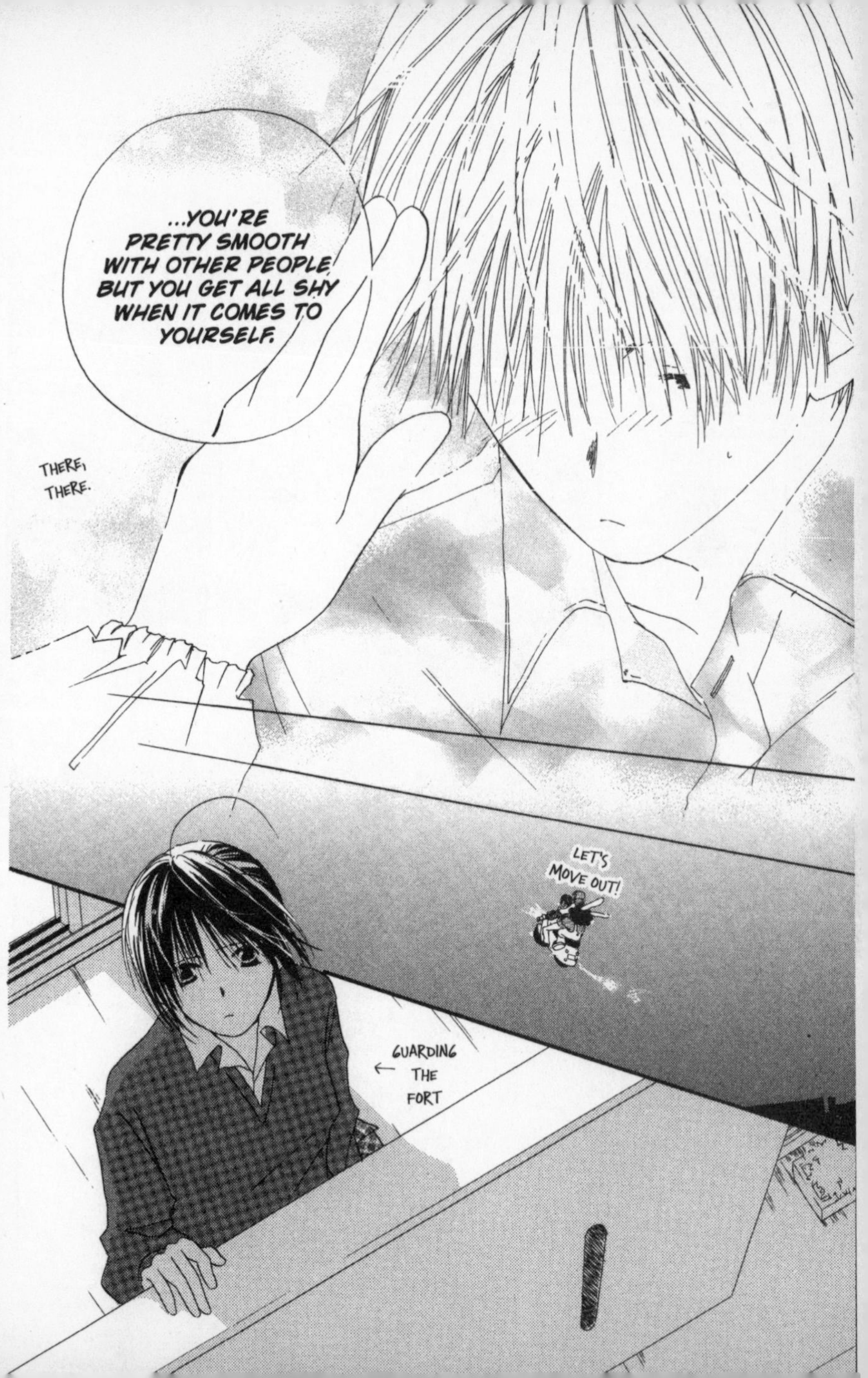

...YOU'RE PRETTY SMOOTH WITH OTHER PEOPLE, BUT YOU GET ALL SHY WHEN IT COMES TO YOURSELF.
THERE, THERE.
LET'S MOVE OUT!
← GUARDING THE FORT

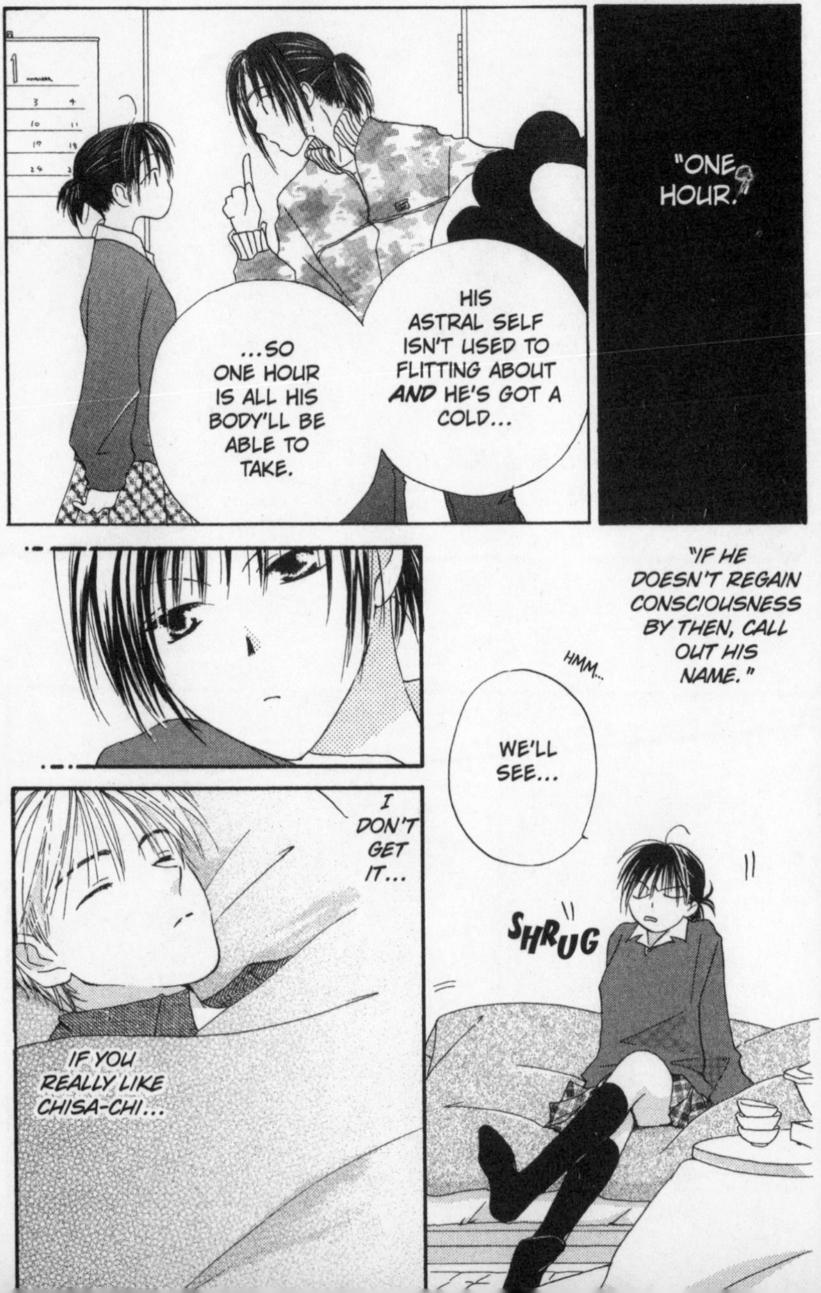
"ONE HOUR."
HIS ASTRAL SELF ISN'T USED TO FLITTING ABOUT AND HE'S GOT A COLD...
...SO ONE HOUR IS ALL HIS BODY'LL BE ABLE TO TAKE.
"IF HE DOESN'T REGAIN CONSCIOUSNESS BY THEN, CALL OUT HIS NAME."
HMM...
WE'LL SEE...
SHRUG
I DON'T GET IT...
IF YOU REALLY LIKE CHISA-CHI...

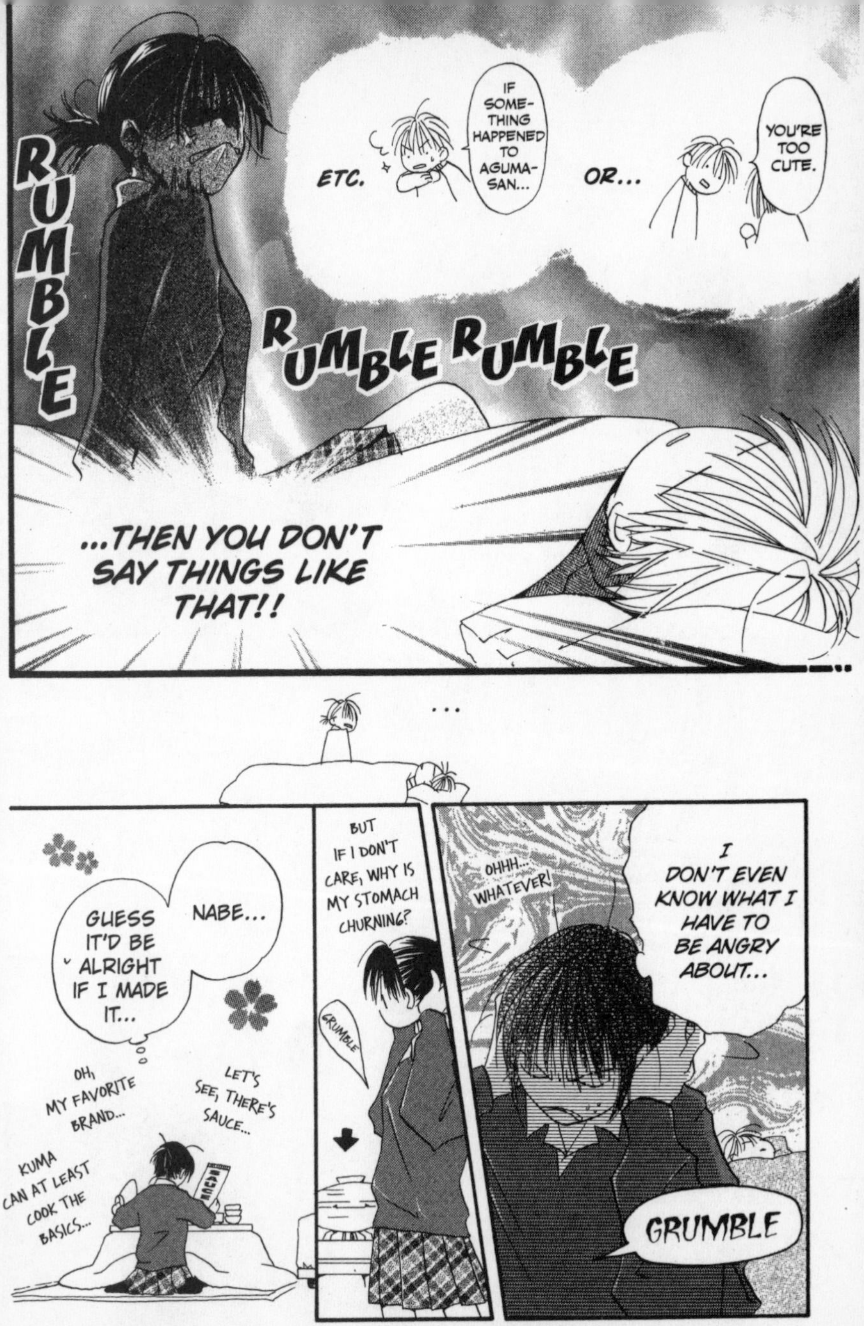
RUMBLE
YOU'RE TOO CUTE.
OR...
IF SOMETHING HAPPENED TO AGUMA-SAN...
ETC.
RUMBLE RUMBLE
...THEN YOU DON'T SAY THINGS LIKE THAT!!
...
I DON'T EVEN KNOW WHAT I HAVE TO BE ANGRY ABOUT...
OHHH... WHATEVER!
GRUMBLE
BUT IF I DON'T CARE, WHY IS MY STOMACH CHURNING?
GRUMBLE
NABE...
GUESS IT'D BE ALRIGHT IF I MADE IT...
LET'S SEE, THERE'S SAUCE...
OH, MY FAVORITE BRAND...
SAUCE
KUMA CAN AT LEAST COOK THE BASICS...

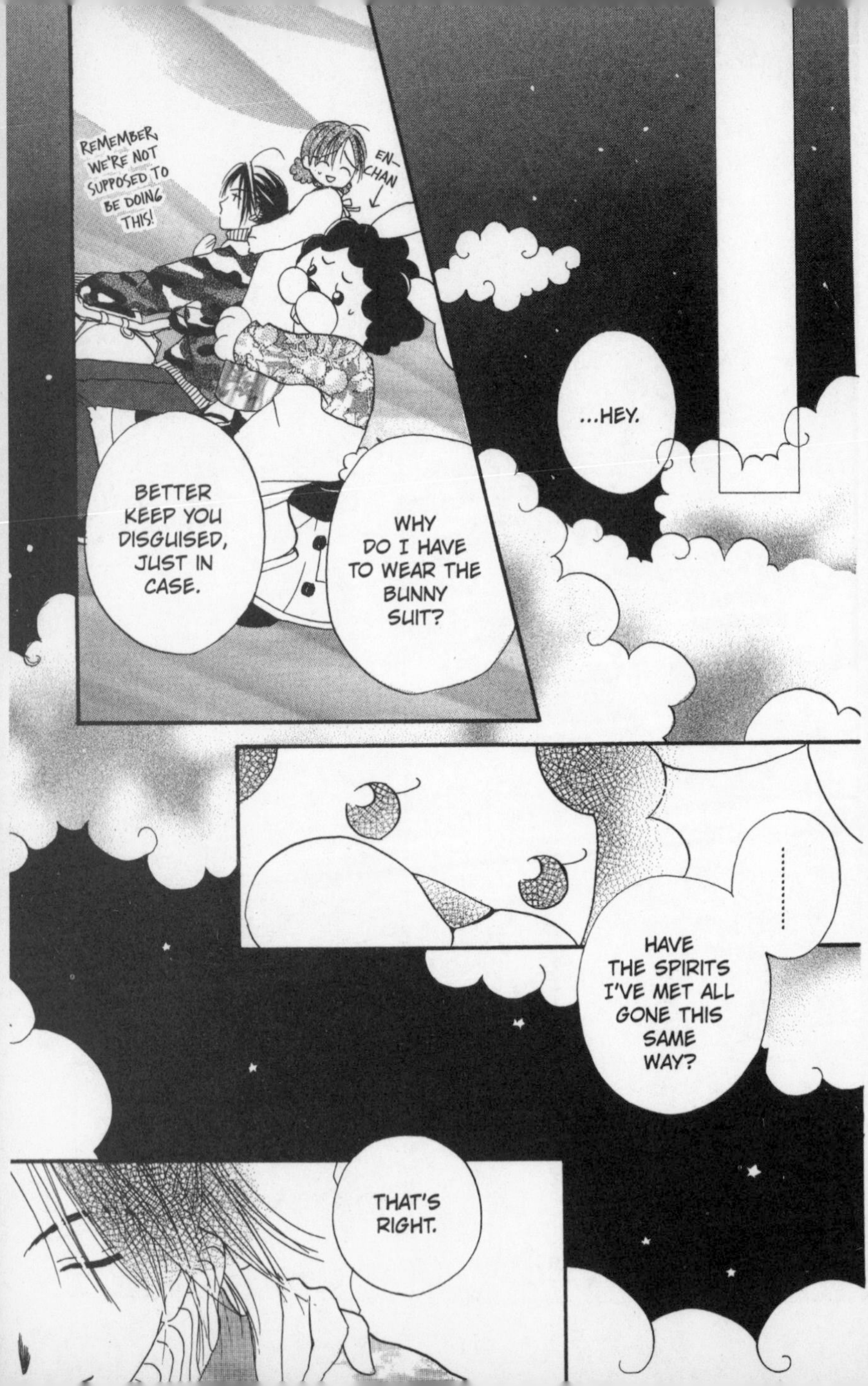
...HEY.
WHY DO I HAVE TO WEAR THE BUNNY SUIT?
BETTER KEEP YOU DISGUISED, JUST IN CASE.
REMEMBER, WE'RE NOT SUPPOSED TO BE DOING THIS!
EN-CHAN
......
HAVE THE SPIRITS I'VE MET ALL GONE THIS SAME WAY?
THAT'S RIGHT.

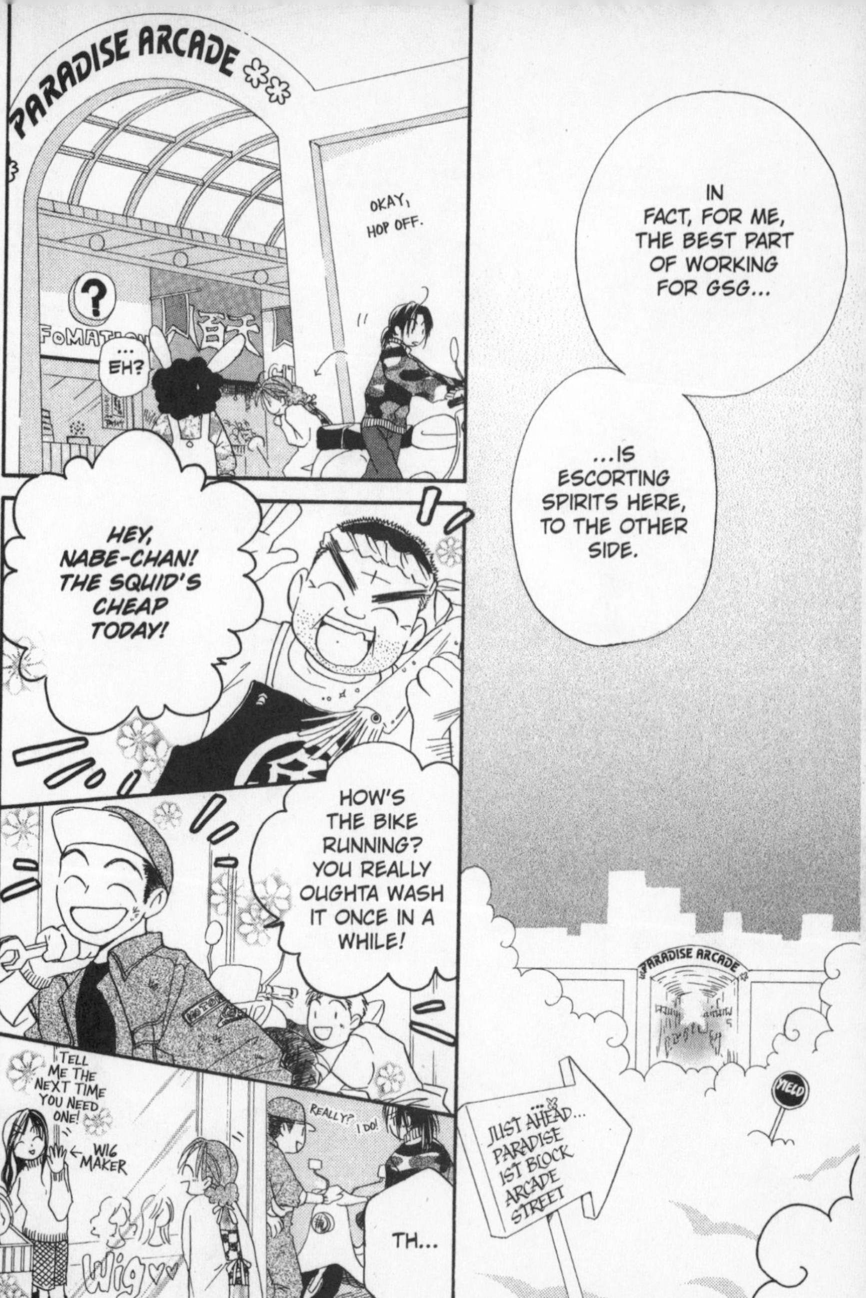
IN FACT, FOR ME, THE BEST PART OF WORKING FOR GSG...
...IS ESCORTING SPIRITS HERE, TO THE OTHER SIDE.
PARADISE ARCADE
JUST AHEAD... PARADISE 1ST BLOCK ARCADE STREET
YIELD
PARADISE ARCADE
OKAY, HOP OFF.
...EH?
HEY, NABE-CHAN! THE SQUID'S CHEAP TODAY!
HOW'S THE BIKE RUNNING? YOU REALLY OUGHTA WASH IT ONCE IN A WHILE!
TH...
REALLY? I DO!
TELL ME THE NEXT TIME YOU NEED ONE!
← WIG MAKER
Wig

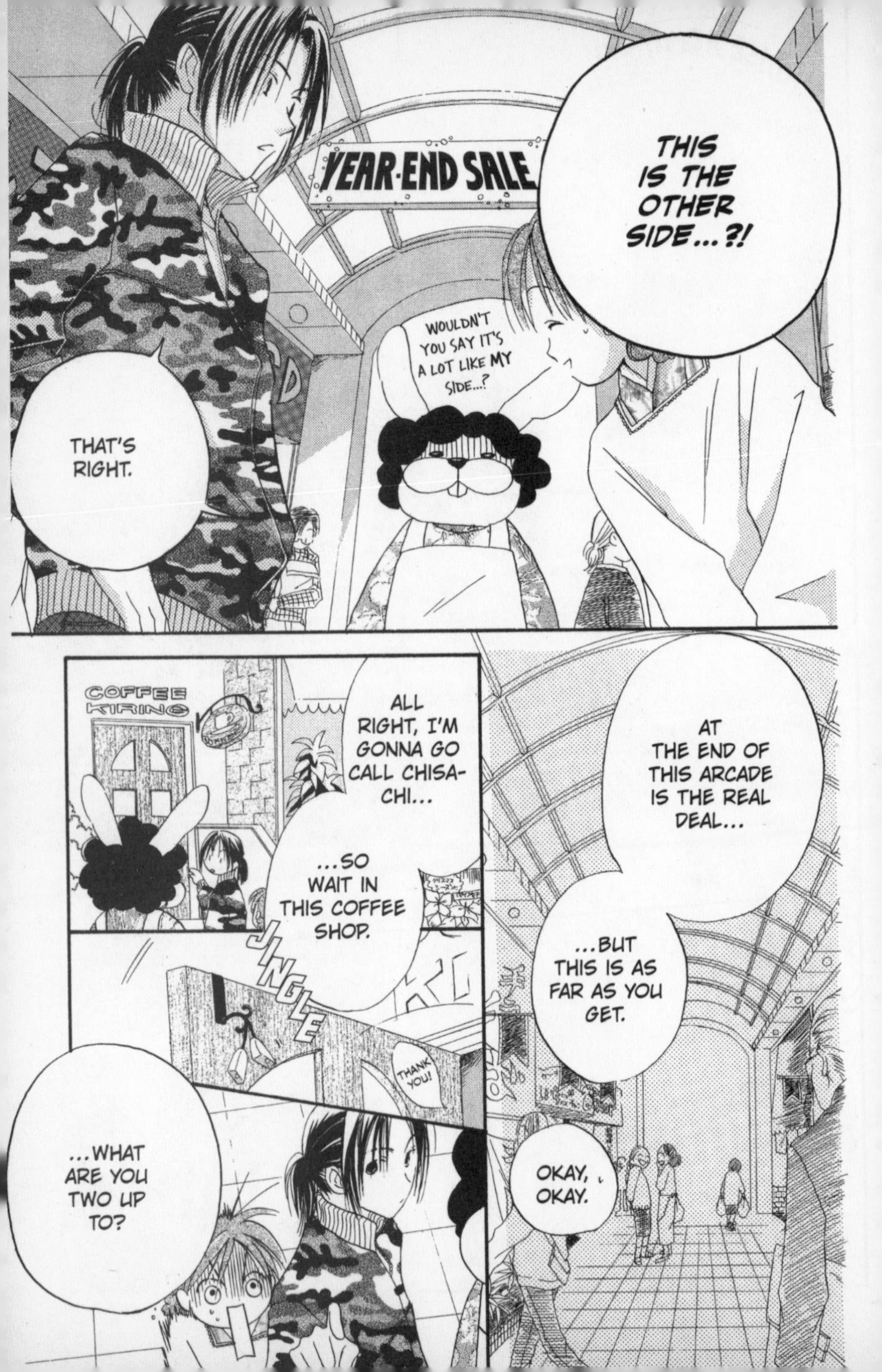
YEAR-END SALE
THIS IS THE OTHER SIDE...?!
WOULDN'T YOU SAY IT'S A LOT LIKE MY SIDE...?
THAT'S RIGHT.
AT THE END OF THIS ARCADE IS THE REAL DEAL...
...BUT THIS IS AS FAR AS YOU GET.
OKAY, OKAY.
COFFEE KIRING
ALL RIGHT, I'M GONNA GO CALL CHISA-CHI...
...SO WAIT IN THIS COFFEE SHOP.
JINGLE
THANK YOU!
...WHAT ARE YOU TWO UP TO?

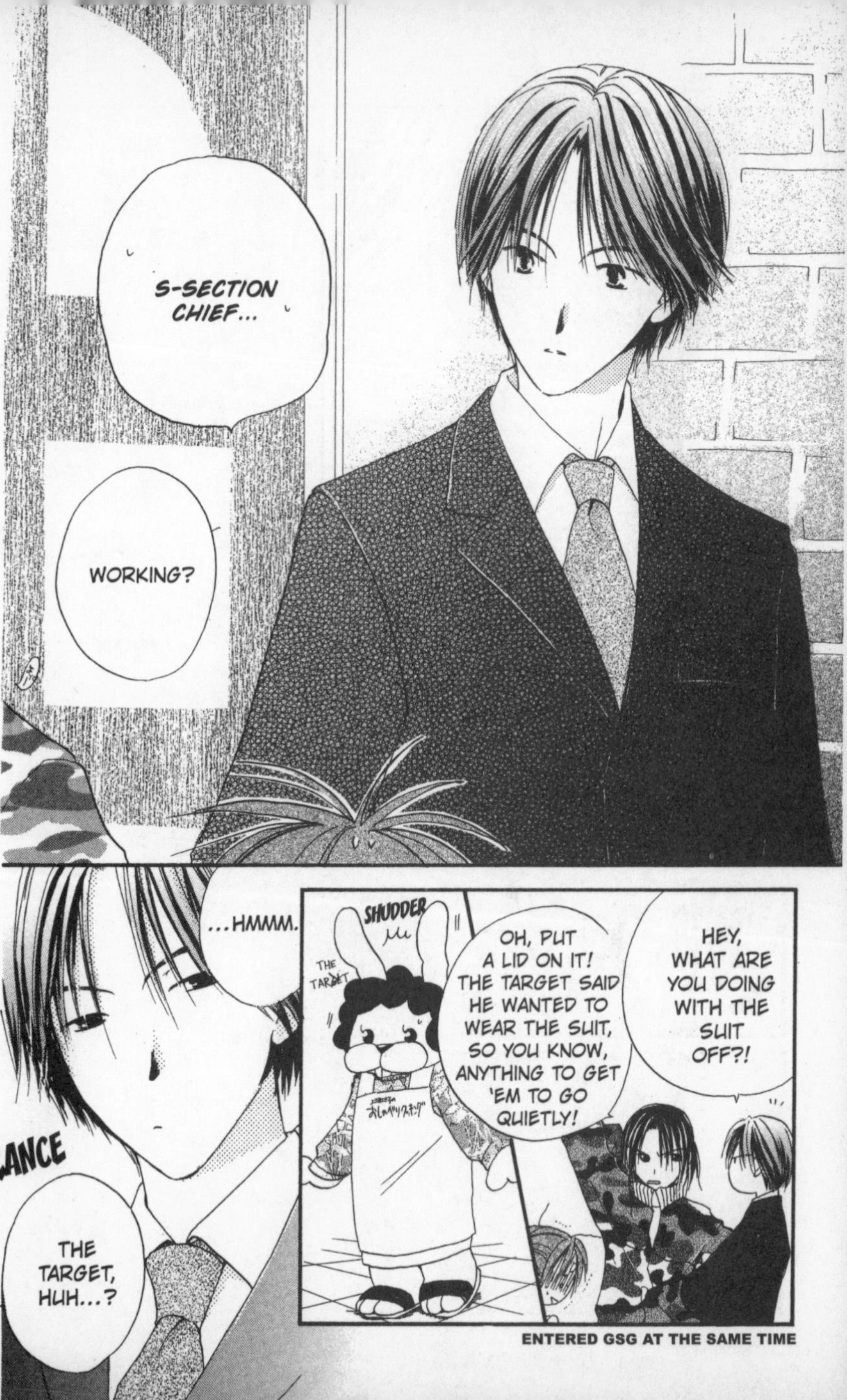
S-SECTION CHIEF...
WORKING?
HEY, WHAT ARE YOU DOING WITH THE SUIT OFF?!
OH, PUT A LID ON IT! THE TARGET SAID HE WANTED TO WEAR THE SUIT, SO YOU KNOW, ANYTHING TO GET 'EM TO GO QUIETLY!
SHUDDER
THE TARGET
ENTERED GSG AT THE SAME TIME
...HMMM.
GLANCE
THE TARGET, HUH...?

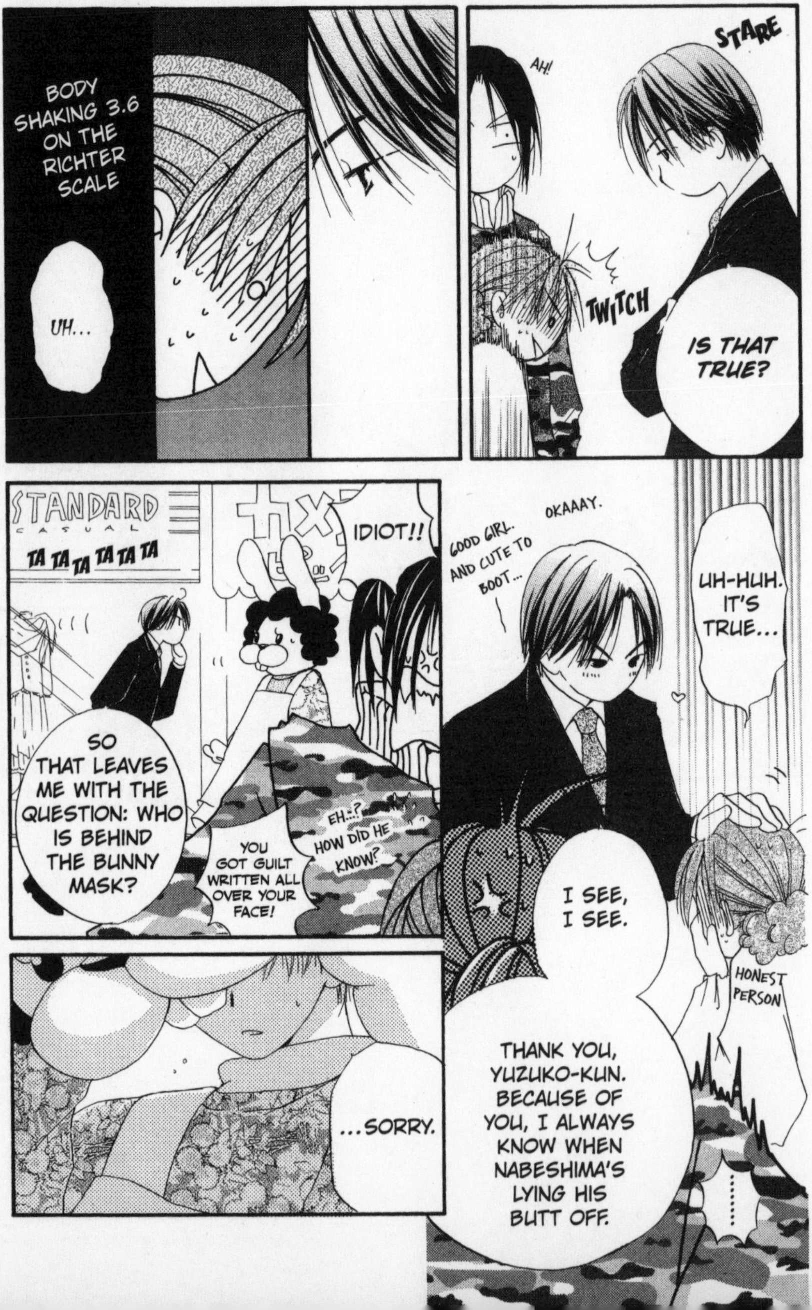
STARE
AH!
TWITCH
IS THAT TRUE?
BODY SHAKING 3.6 ON THE RICHTER SCALE
UH...
UH-HUH. IT'S TRUE...
OKAAAY.
GOOD GIRL. AND CUTE TO BOOT...
I SEE, I SEE.
HONEST PERSON
THANK YOU, YUZUKO-KUN. BECAUSE OF YOU, I ALWAYS KNOW WHEN NABESHIMA'S LYING HIS BUTT OFF.
......
STANDARD
CASUAL
TA TA TA TA TA TA
IDIOT!!
SO THAT LEAVES ME WITH THE QUESTION: WHO IS BEHIND THE BUNNY MASK?
EH...? HOW DID HE KNOW?
YOU GOT GUILT WRITTEN ALL OVER YOUR FACE!
...SORRY.

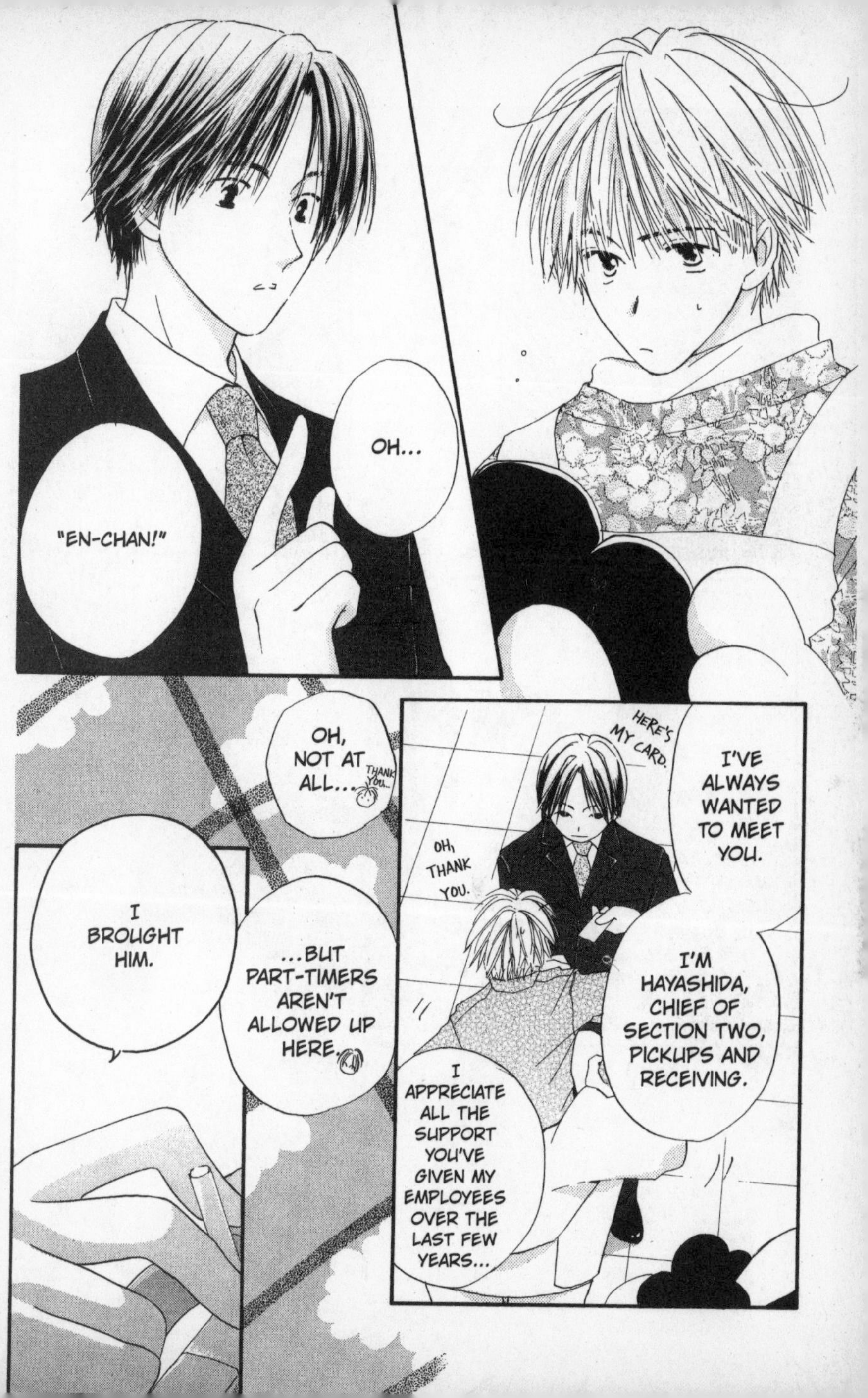
OH...
"EN-CHAN!"
I'VE ALWAYS WANTED TO MEET YOU.
HERE'S MY CARD.
I'M HAYASHIDA, CHIEF OF SECTION TWO, PICKUPS AND RECEIVING.
OH, THANK YOU.
I APPRECIATE ALL THE SUPPORT YOU'VE GIVEN MY EMPLOYEES OVER THE LAST FEW YEARS...
OH, NOT AT ALL...
THANK YOU...
...BUT PART-TIMERS AREN'T ALLOWED UP HERE.
I BROUGHT HIM.

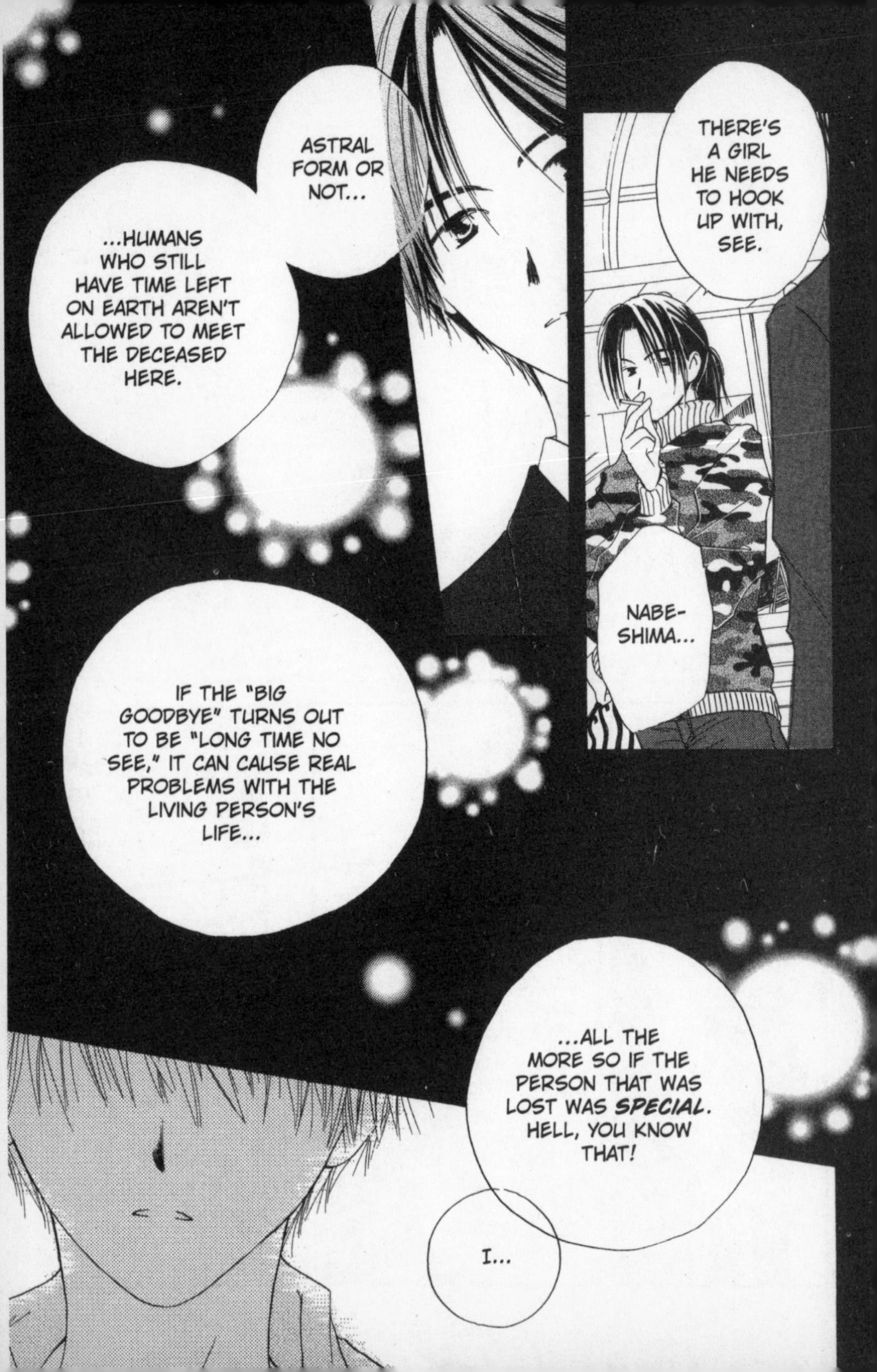
THERE'S A GIRL HE NEEDS TO HOOK UP WITH, SEE.
NABE-SHIMA...
ASTRAL FORM OR NOT...
...HUMANS WHO STILL HAVE TIME LEFT ON EARTH AREN'T ALLOWED TO MEET THE DECEASED HERE.
IF THE "BIG GOODBYE" TURNS OUT TO BE "LONG TIME NO SEE," IT CAN CAUSE REAL PROBLEMS WITH THE LIVING PERSON'S LIFE...
...ALL THE MORE SO IF THE PERSON THAT WAS LOST WAS *SPECIAL*. HELL, YOU KNOW THAT!
I...

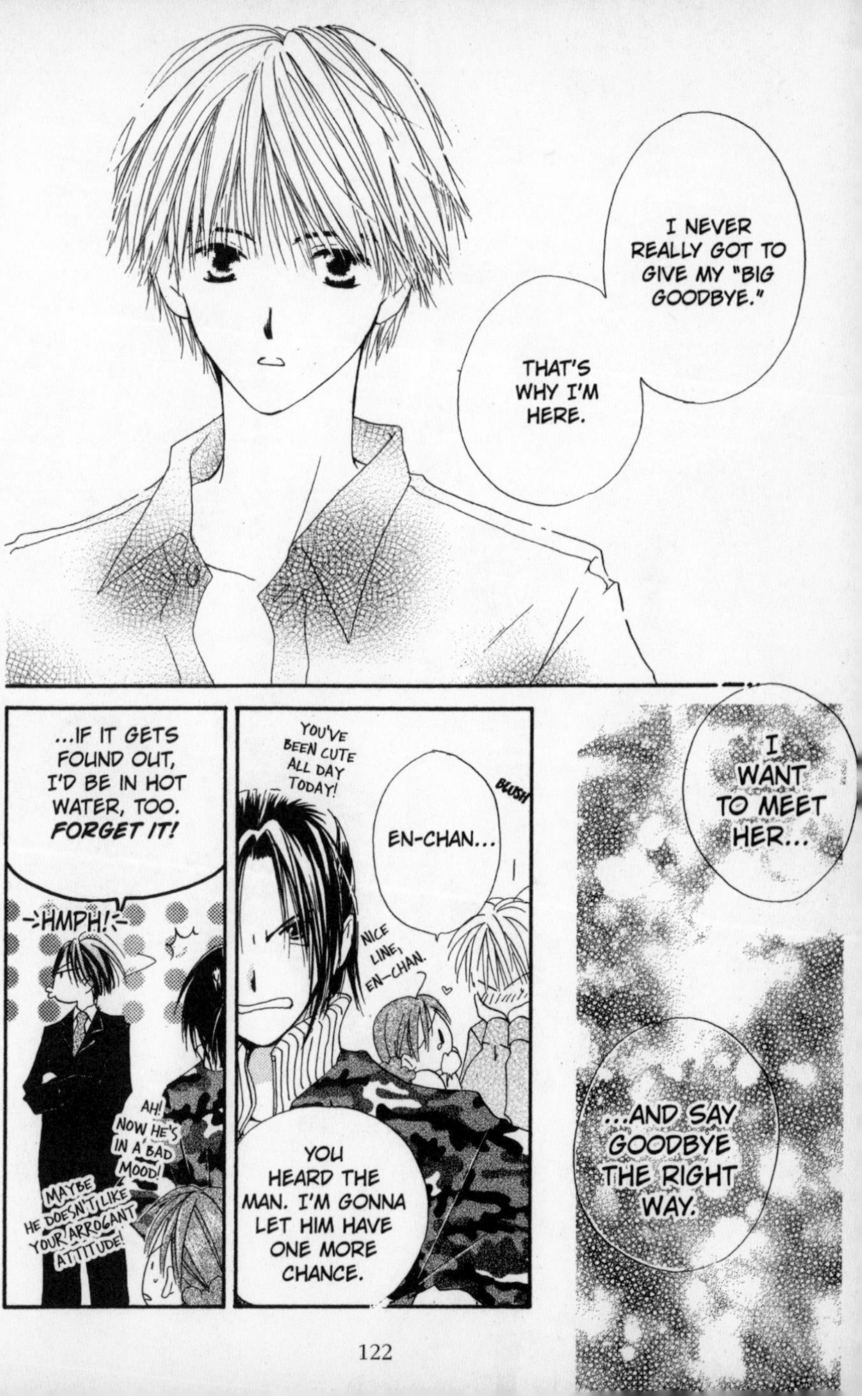
I NEVER REALLY GOT TO GIVE MY "BIG GOODBYE."
THAT'S WHY I'M HERE.
I WANT TO MEET HER...
...AND SAY GOODBYE THE RIGHT WAY.
BLUSH
EN-CHAN...
YOU'VE BEEN CUTE ALL DAY TODAY!
NICE LINE, EN-CHAN.
YOU HEARD THE MAN. I'M GONNA LET HIM HAVE ONE MORE CHANCE.
...IF IT GETS FOUND OUT, I'D BE IN HOT WATER, TOO. *FORGET IT!*
-HMPH!-
AH! NOW HE'S IN A BAD MOOD!
MAYBE HE DOESN'T LIKE YOUR ARROGANT ATTITUDE!

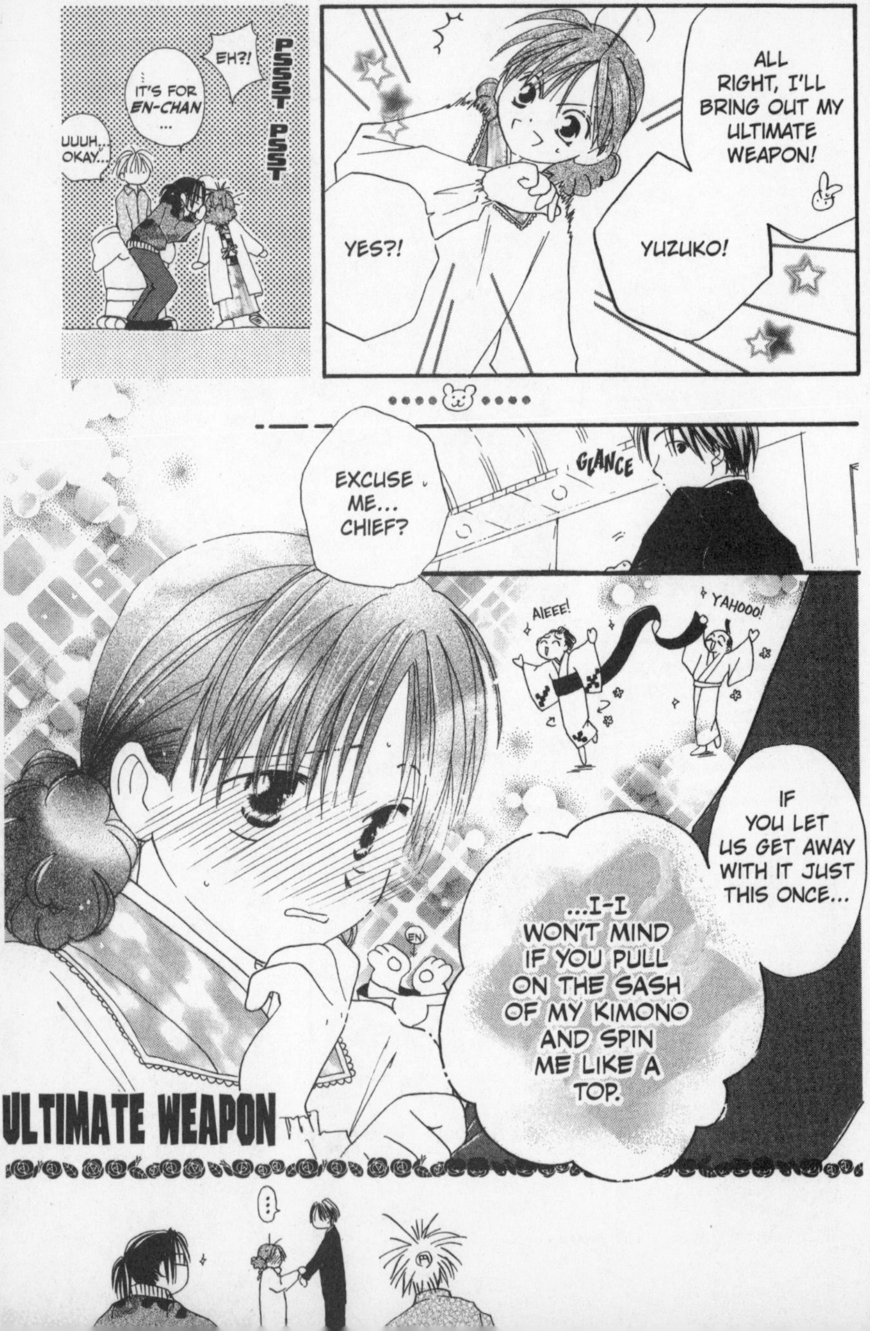
ALL RIGHT, I'LL BRING OUT MY ULTIMATE WEAPON!
YUZUKO!
YES?!
PSSST PSSST
EH?!
IT'S FOR EN-CHAN ...
UUUH, OKAY...
EXCUSE ME... CHIEF?
GLANCE
YAHOOO!
AIEEE!
IF YOU LET US GET AWAY WITH IT JUST THIS ONCE...
...I-I WON'T MIND IF YOU PULL ON THE SASH OF MY KIMONO AND SPIN ME LIKE A TOP.
EN
ULTIMATE WEAPON
...

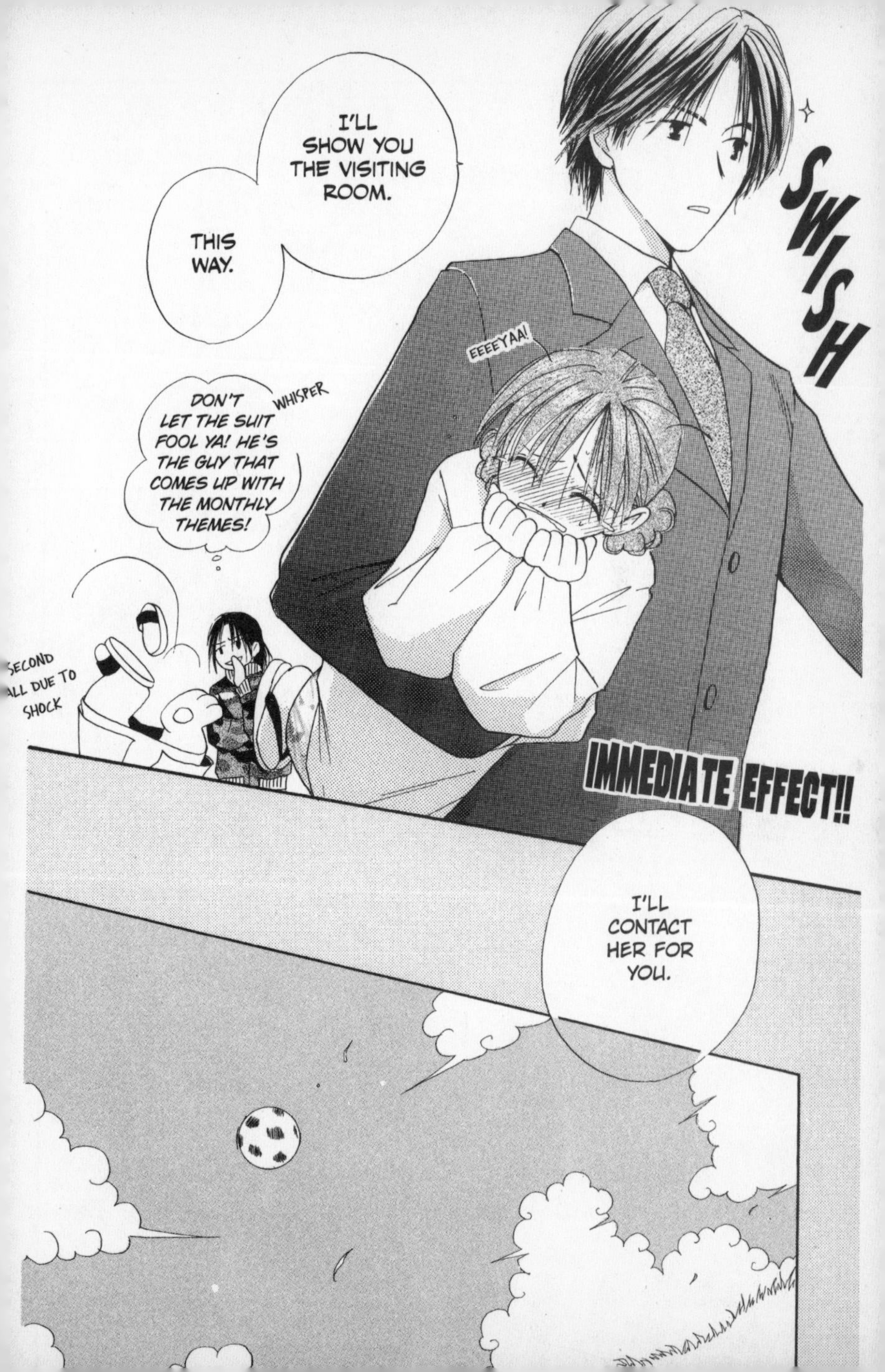
SWISH
I'LL SHOW YOU THE VISITING ROOM.
THIS WAY.
EEEEYAA!
IMMEDIATE EFFECT!!
WHISPER
DON'T LET THE SUIT FOOL YA! HE'S THE GUY THAT COMES UP WITH THE MONTHLY THEMES!
SECOND
ALL DUE TO
SHOCK
I'LL CONTACT HER FOR YOU.

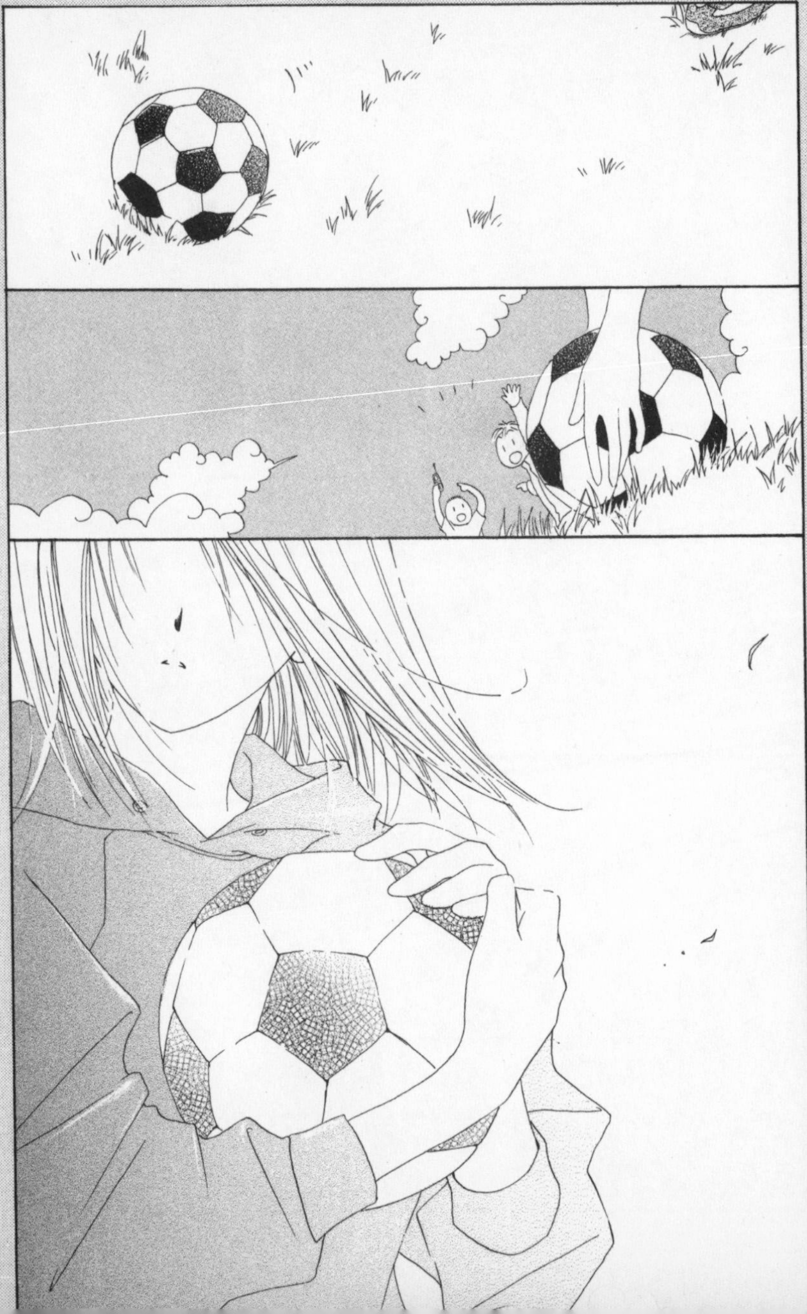

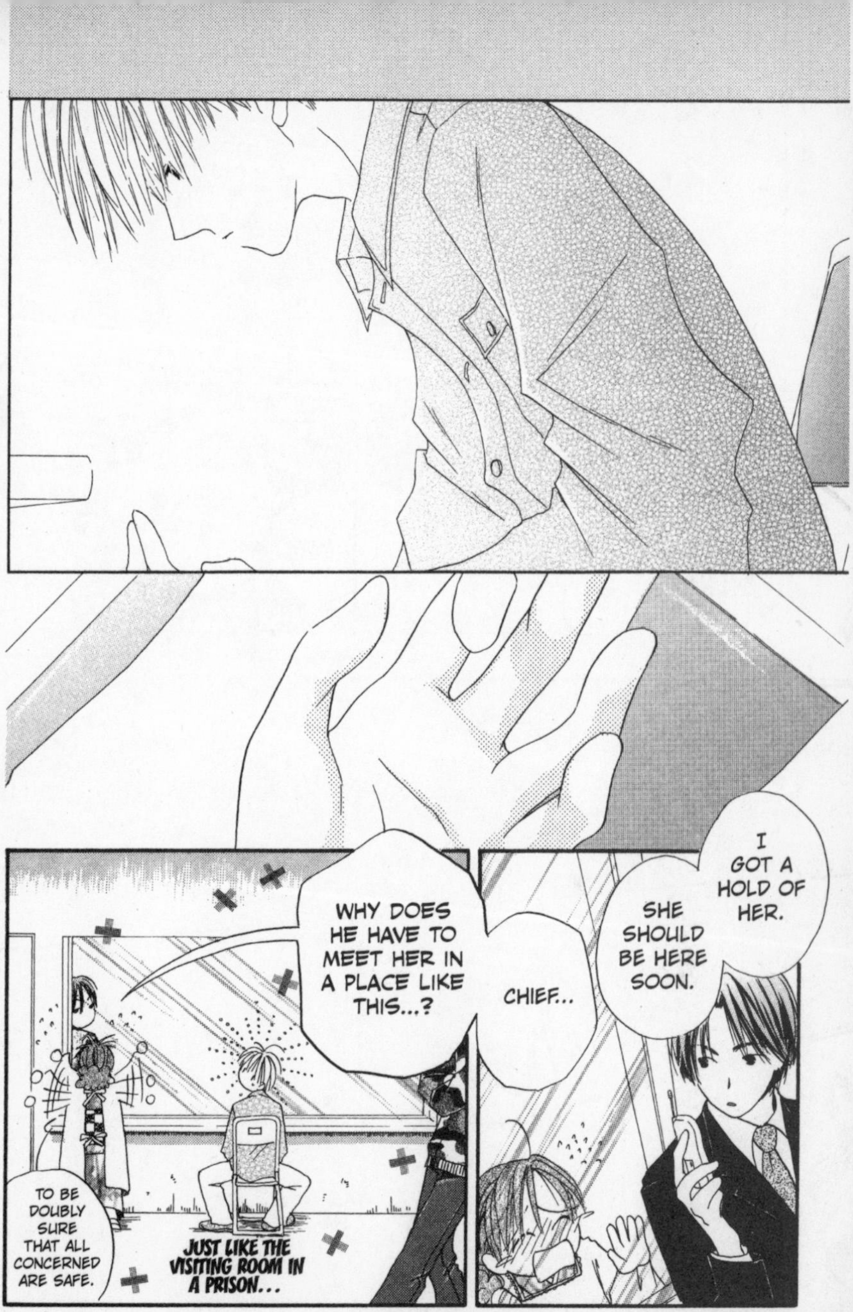
I GOT A HOLD OF HER.
SHE SHOULD BE HERE SOON.
CHIEF...
WHY DOES HE HAVE TO MEET HER IN A PLACE LIKE THIS...?
JUST LIKE THE VISITING ROOM IN A PRISON...
TO BE DOUBLY SURE THAT ALL CONCERNED ARE SAFE.

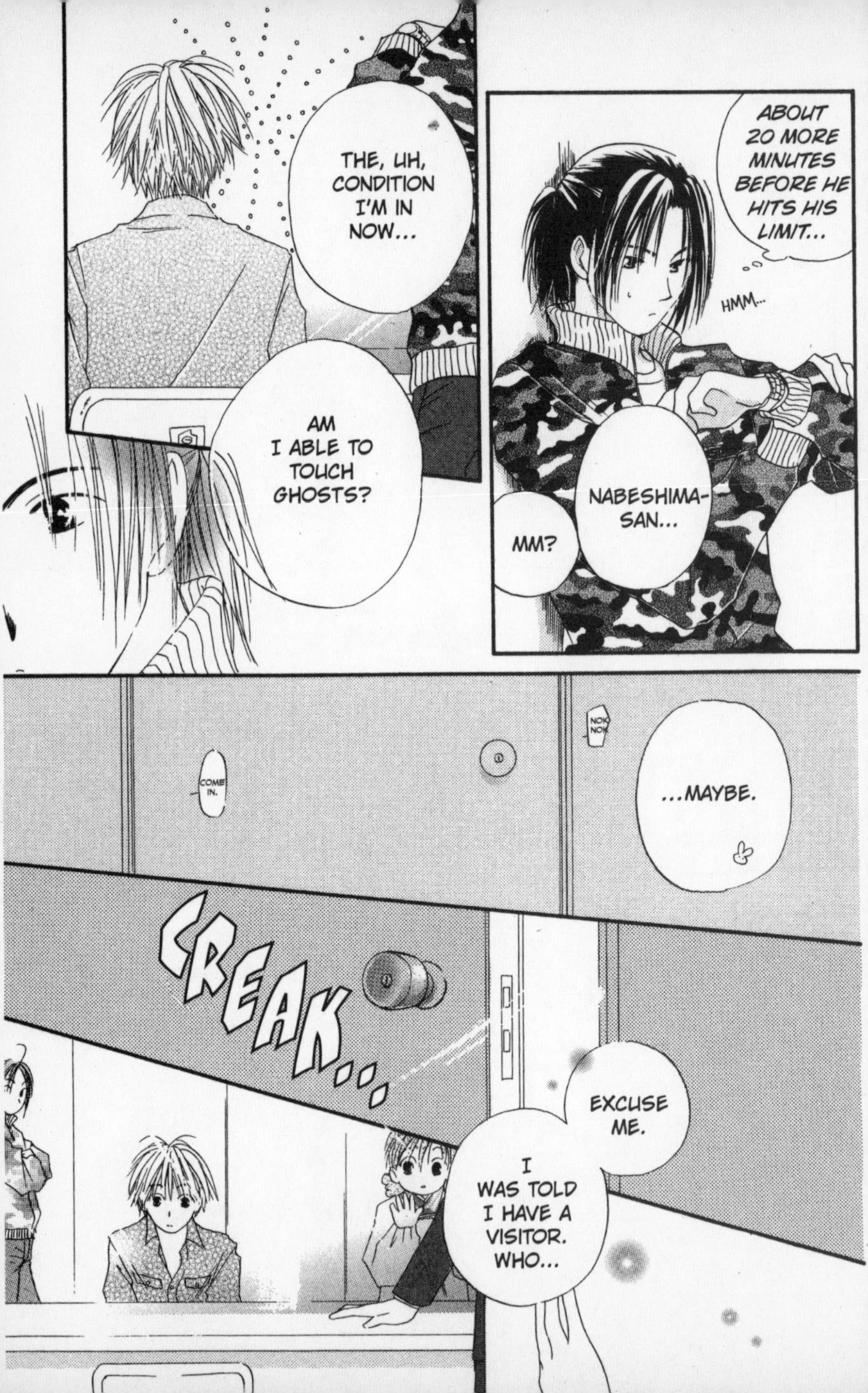
ABOUT 20 MORE MINUTES BEFORE HE HITS HIS LIMIT...
HMM...
NABESHIMA-SAN...
MM?
THE, UH, CONDITION I'M IN NOW...
AM I ABLE TO TOUCH GHOSTS?
...MAYBE.
NOK NOK
COME IN.
CREAK...
EXCUSE ME.
I WAS TOLD I HAVE A VISITOR. WHO...

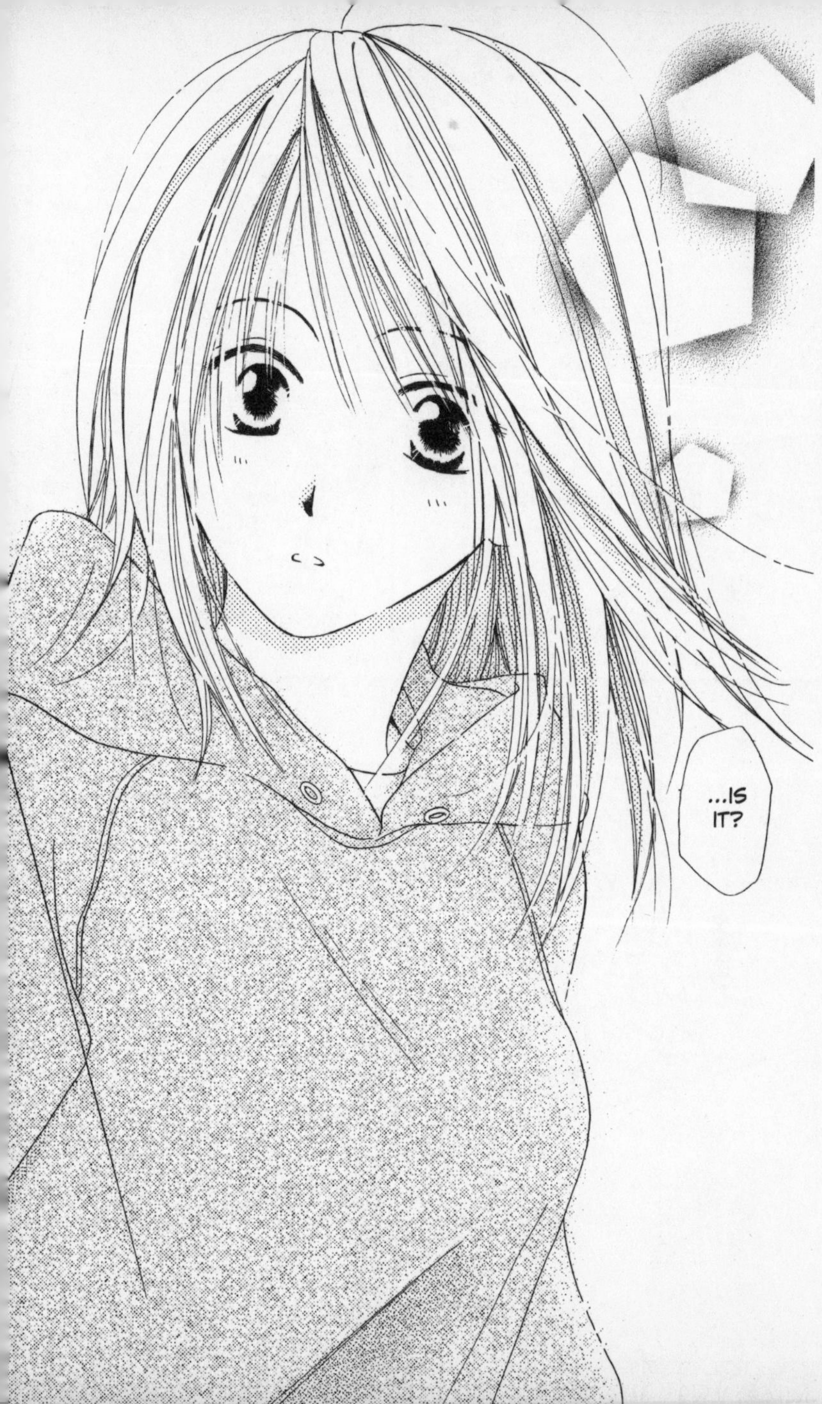
...IS IT?

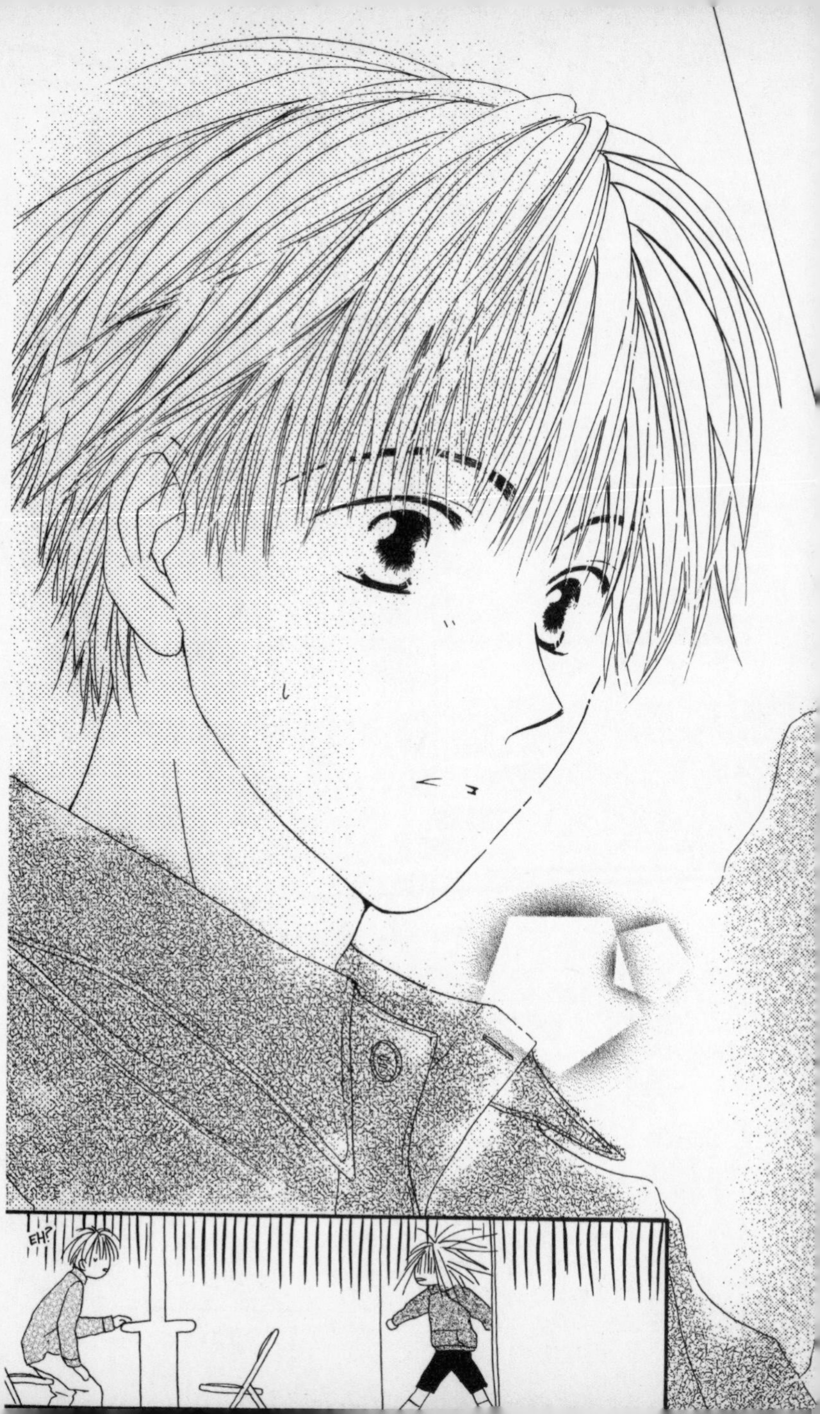
EH?

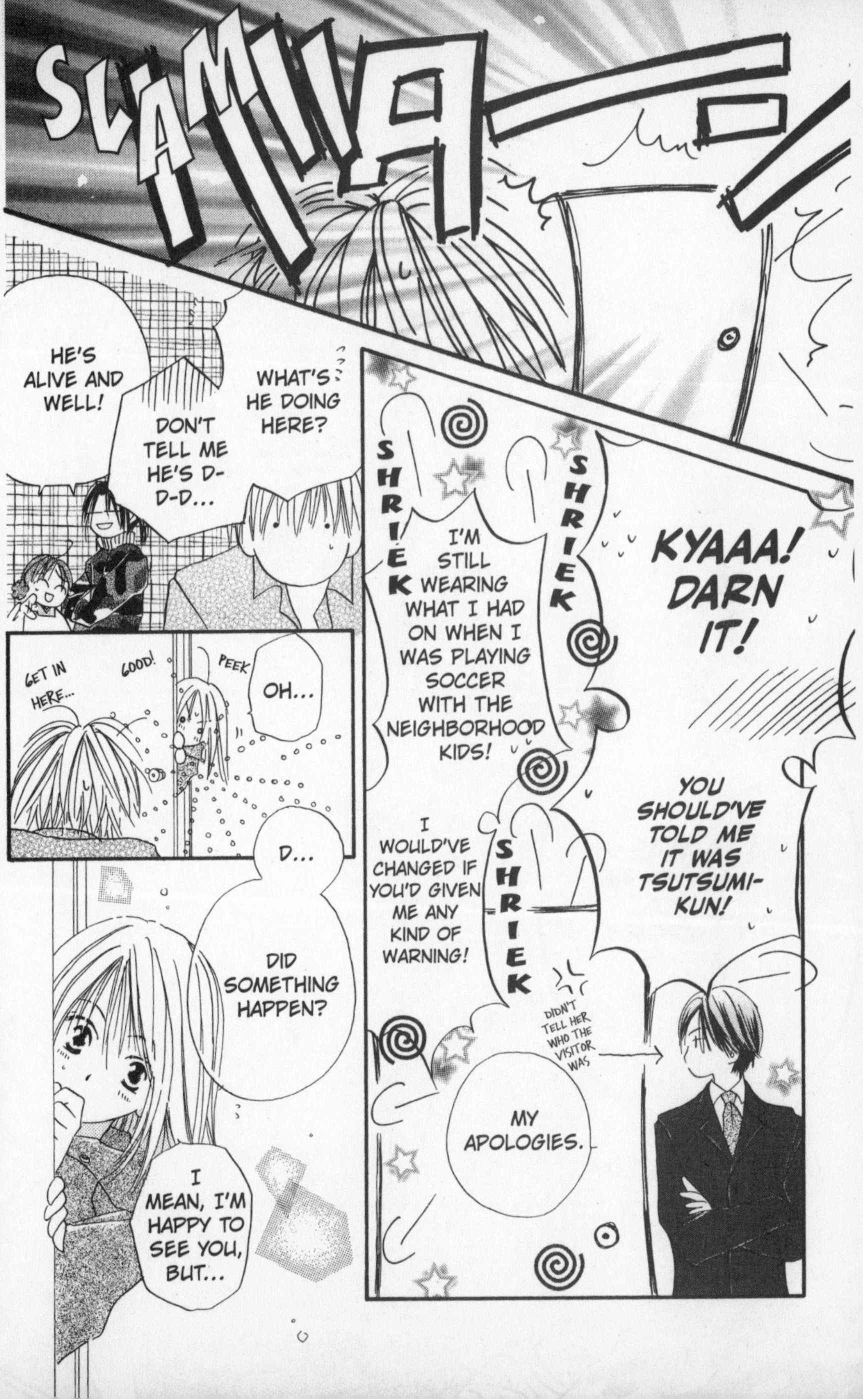
SLAM
KYAAA! DARN IT!
SHRIEK
I'M STILL WEARING WHAT I HAD ON WHEN I WAS PLAYING SOCCER WITH THE NEIGHBORHOOD KIDS!
SHRIEK
YOU SHOULD'VE TOLD ME IT WAS TSUTSUMI-KUN!
SHRIEK
I WOULD'VE CHANGED IF YOU'D GIVEN ME ANY KIND OF WARNING!
DIDN'T TELL HER WHO THE VISITOR WAS
MY APOLOGIES.
WHAT'S HE DOING HERE?
DON'T TELL ME HE'S D-D-D...
HE'S ALIVE AND WELL!
PEEK
OH...
GOOD!
GET IN HERE...
D...
DID SOMETHING HAPPEN?
I MEAN, I'M HAPPY TO SEE YOU, BUT...

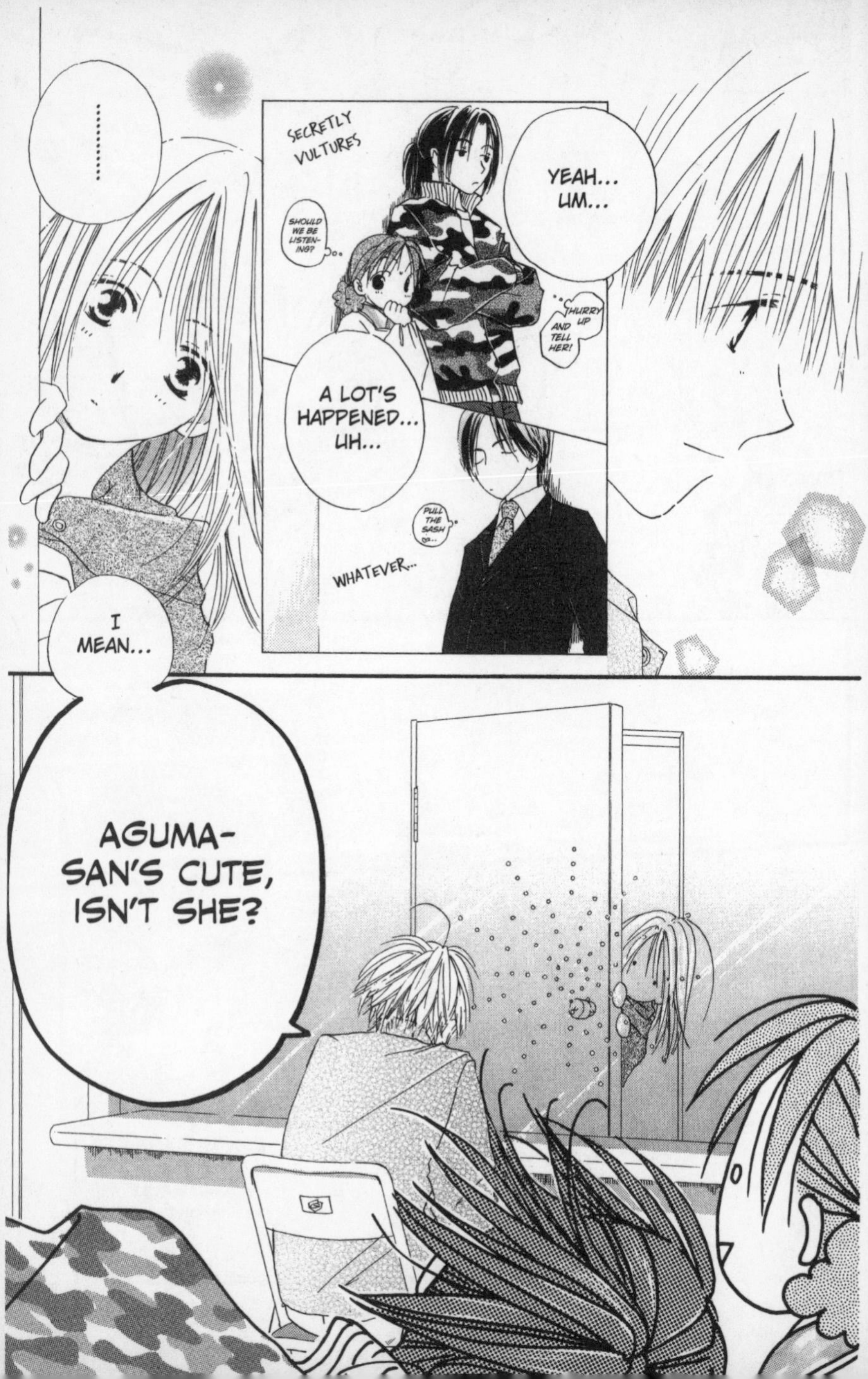
YEAH... UM...
HURRY UP AND TELL HER!
SECRETLY VULTURES
SHOULD WE BE LISTENING?
A LOT'S HAPPENED... UH...
PULL THE SASH...
WHATEVER...
......
I MEAN...
AGUMA-SAN'S CUTE, ISN'T SHE?

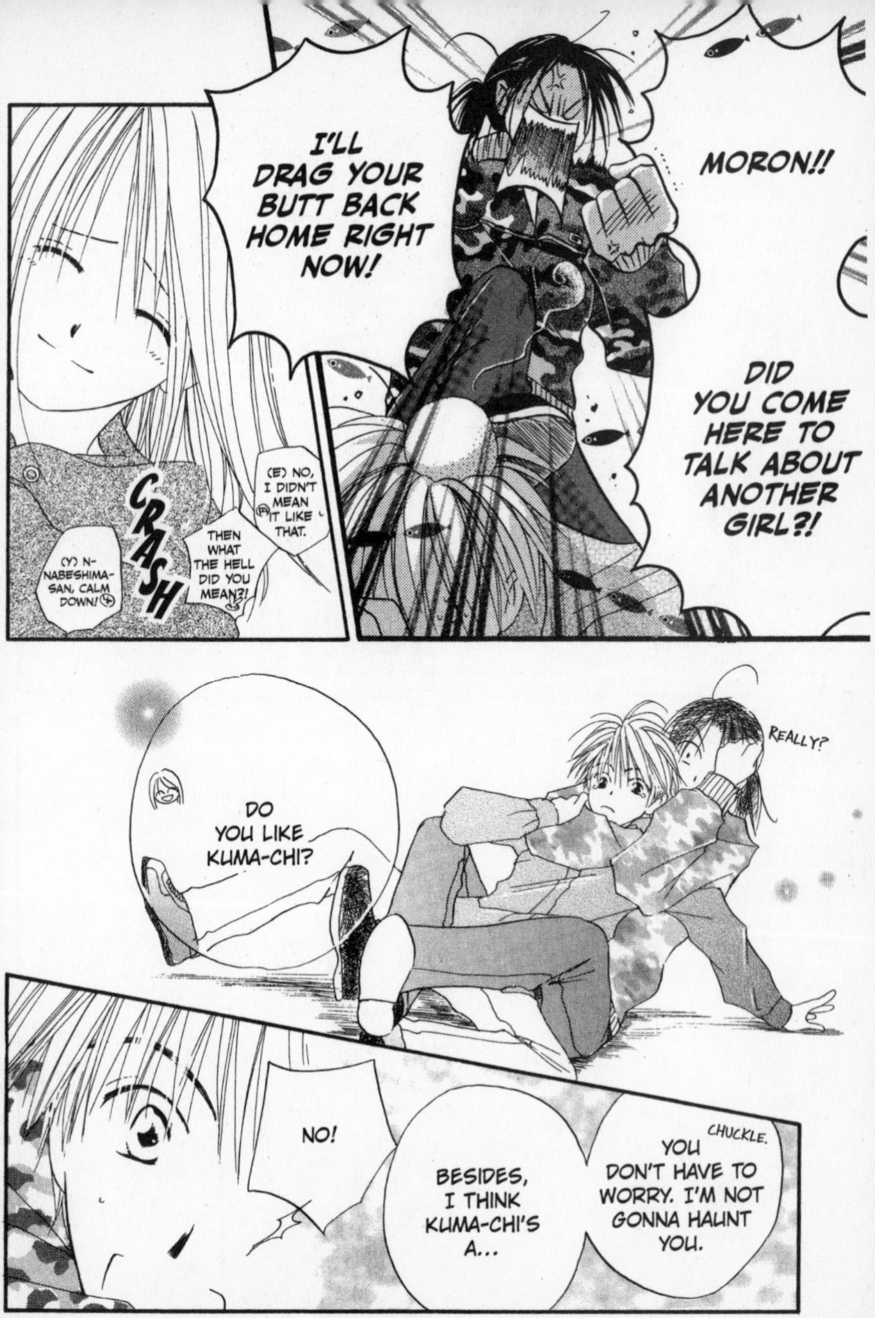
MORON!!
DID YOU COME HERE TO TALK ABOUT ANOTHER GIRL?!
I'LL DRAG YOUR BUTT BACK HOME RIGHT NOW!
(E) NO, I DIDN'T MEAN IT LIKE THAT.
THEN WHAT THE HELL DID YOU MEAN?!
CRASH
(Y) N-NABESHIMA-SAN, CALM DOWN!
REALLY?
DO YOU LIKE KUMA-CHI?
CHUCKLE.
YOU DON'T HAVE TO WORRY. I'M NOT GONNA HAUNT YOU.
BESIDES, I THINK KUMA-CHI'S A...
NO!

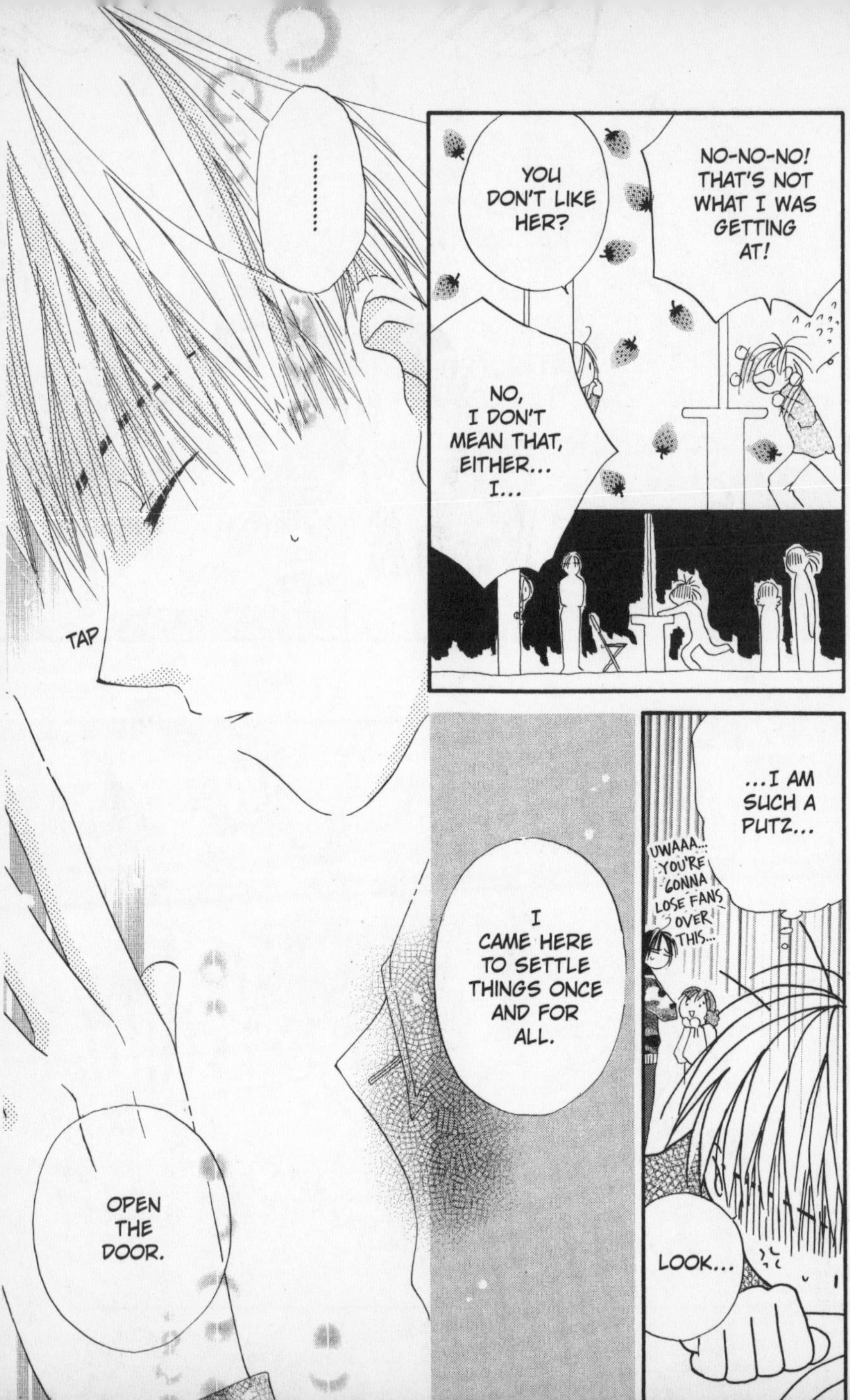
NO-NO-NO! THAT'S NOT WHAT I WAS GETTING AT!
YOU DON'T LIKE HER?
NO, I DON'T MEAN THAT, EITHER... I...
...I AM SUCH A PUTZ...
UWAAA... YOU'RE GONNA LOSE FANS OVER THIS...
LOOK...
I CAME HERE TO SETTLE THINGS ONCE AND FOR ALL.
......
TAP
OPEN THE DOOR.

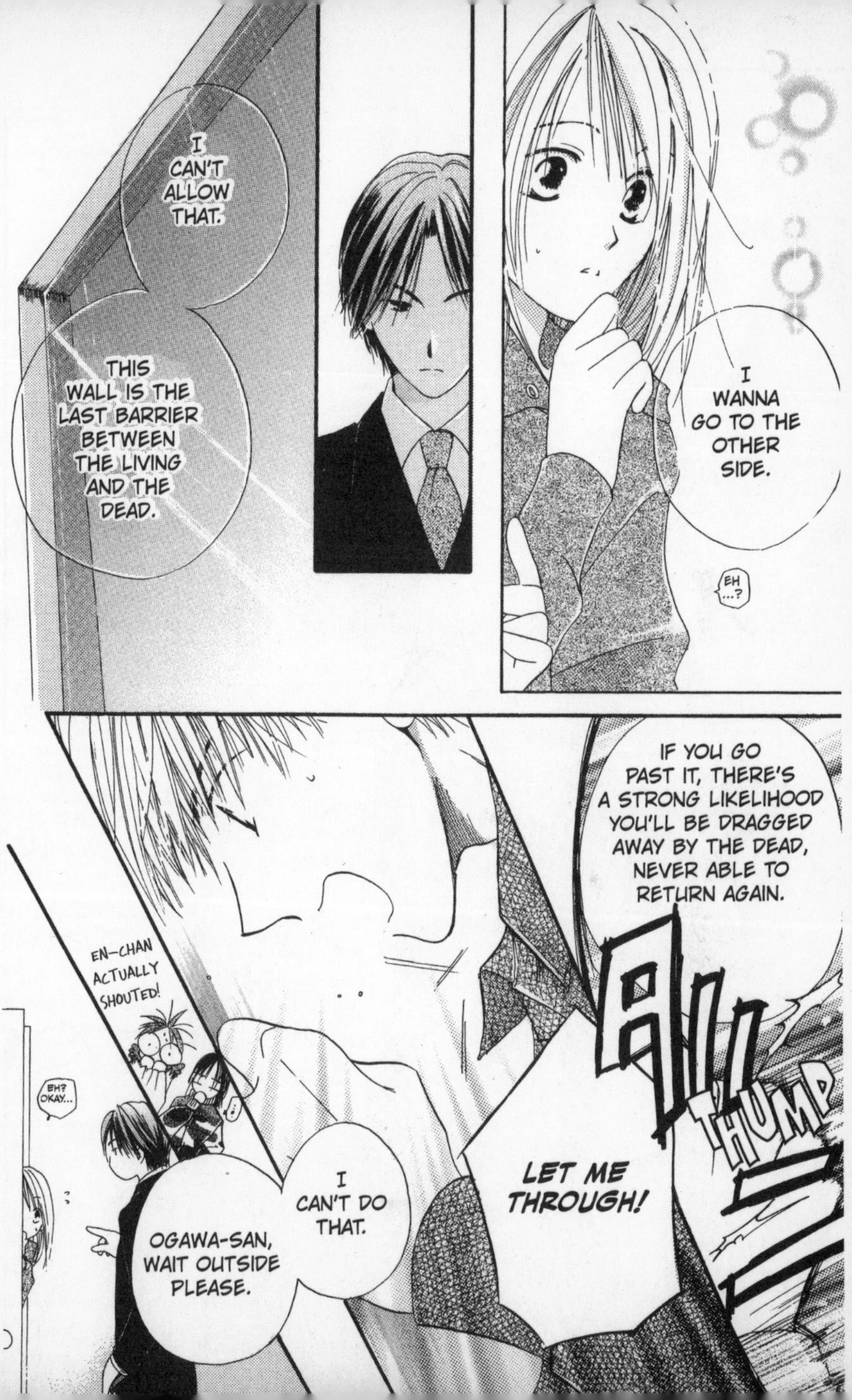
I WANNA GO TO THE OTHER SIDE.
EH ...?
I CAN'T ALLOW THAT.
THIS WALL IS THE LAST BARRIER BETWEEN THE LIVING AND THE DEAD.
IF YOU GO PAST IT, THERE'S A STRONG LIKELIHOOD YOU'LL BE DRAGGED AWAY BY THE DEAD, NEVER ABLE TO RETURN AGAIN.
THUMP
LET ME THROUGH!
I CAN'T DO THAT.
OGAWA-SAN, WAIT OUTSIDE PLEASE.
EN-CHAN ACTUALLY SHOUTED!
EH? OKAY...

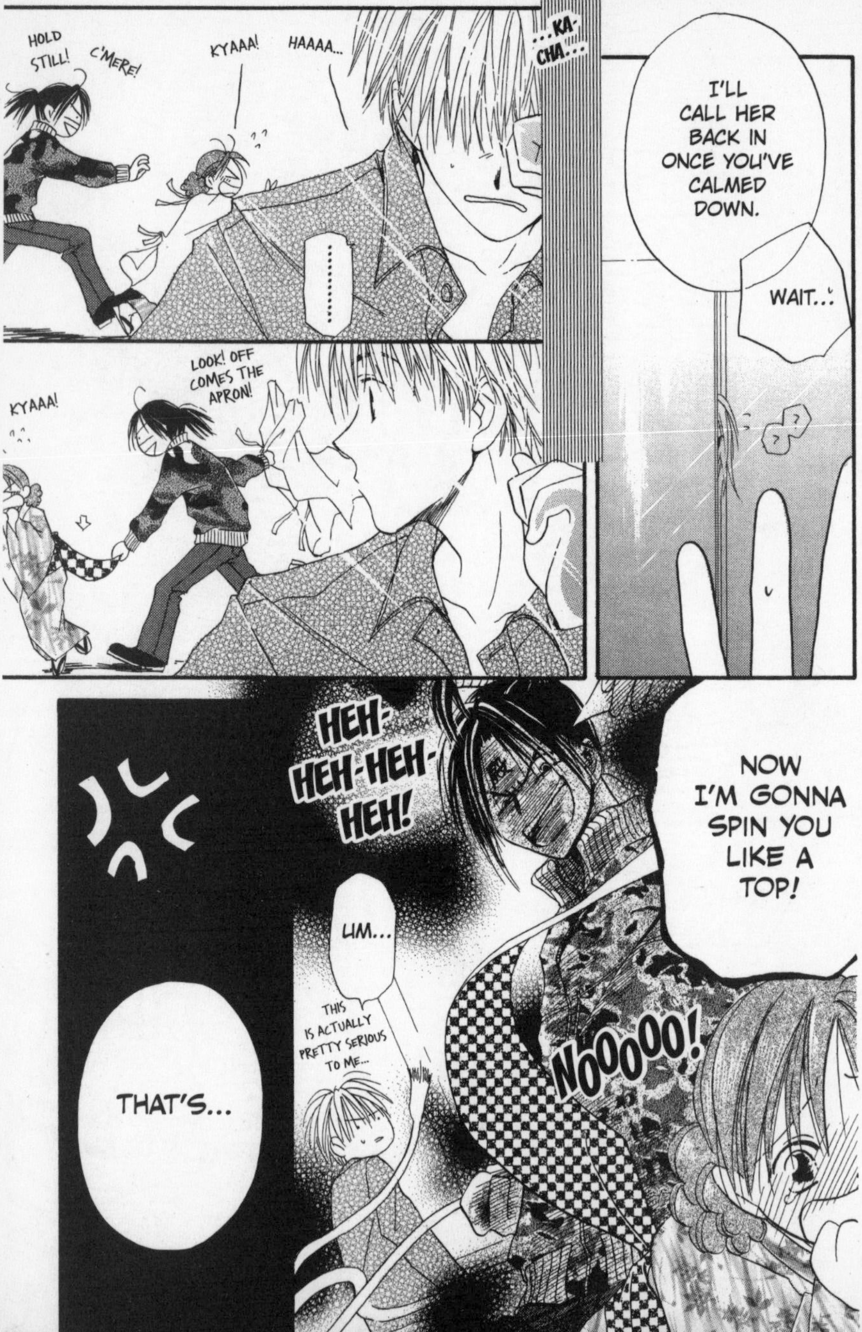
I'LL CALL HER BACK IN ONCE YOU'VE CALMED DOWN.
WAIT...
...KA-CHA...
HAAAA...
KYAAA!
C'MERE!
HOLD STILL!
......
LOOK! OFF COMES THE APRON!
KYAAA!
NOW I'M GONNA SPIN YOU LIKE A TOP!
HEH-HEH-HEH-HEH!
NOOOOO!
UM...
THIS IS ACTUALLY PRETTY SERIOUS TO ME...
THAT'S...

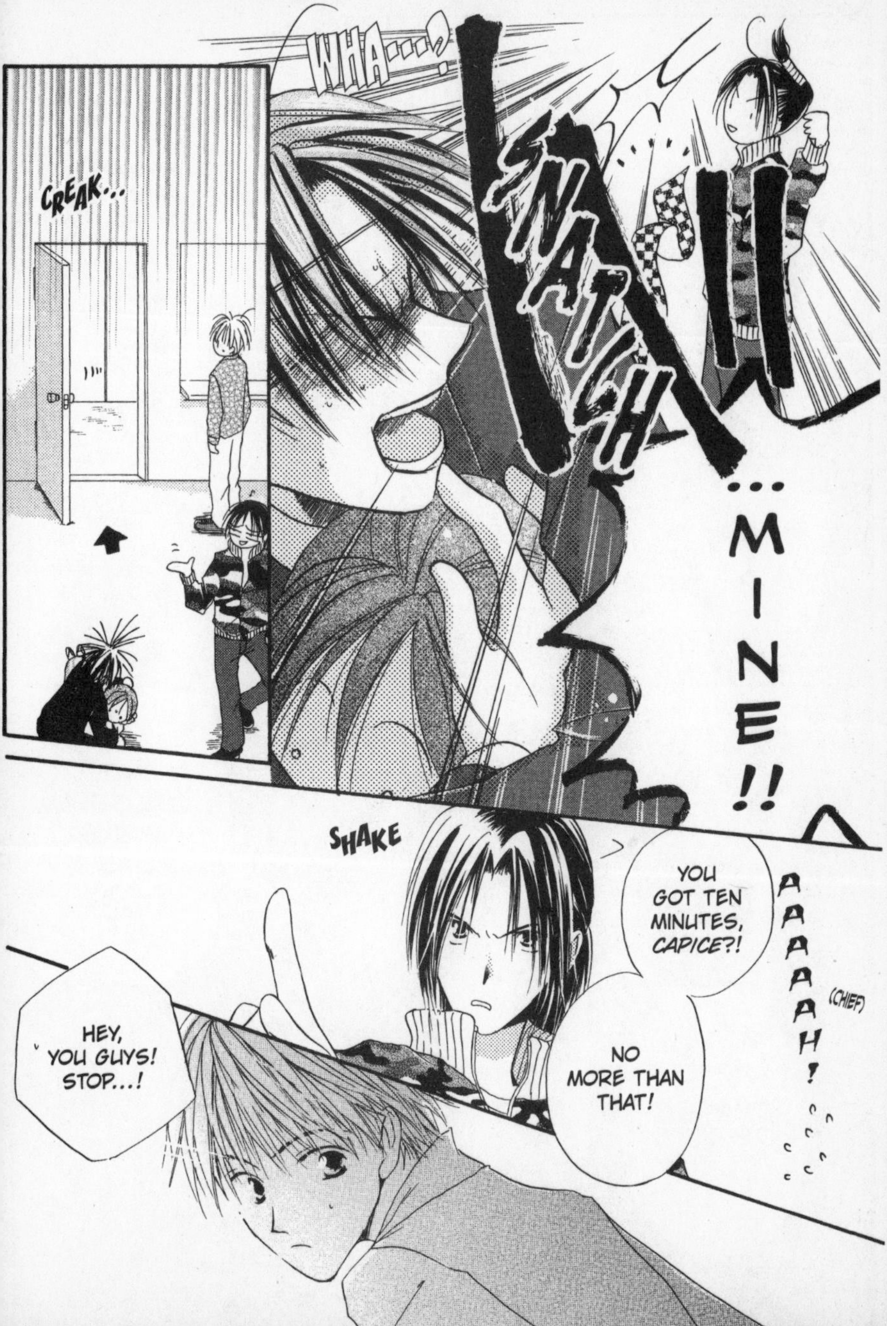
WHA...?
SNATCH
...MINE!!
CREAK...
SHAKE
YOU GOT TEN MINUTES, CAPICE?!
AAAAAH!
(CHIEF)
NO MORE THAN THAT!
HEY, YOU GUYS! STOP...!

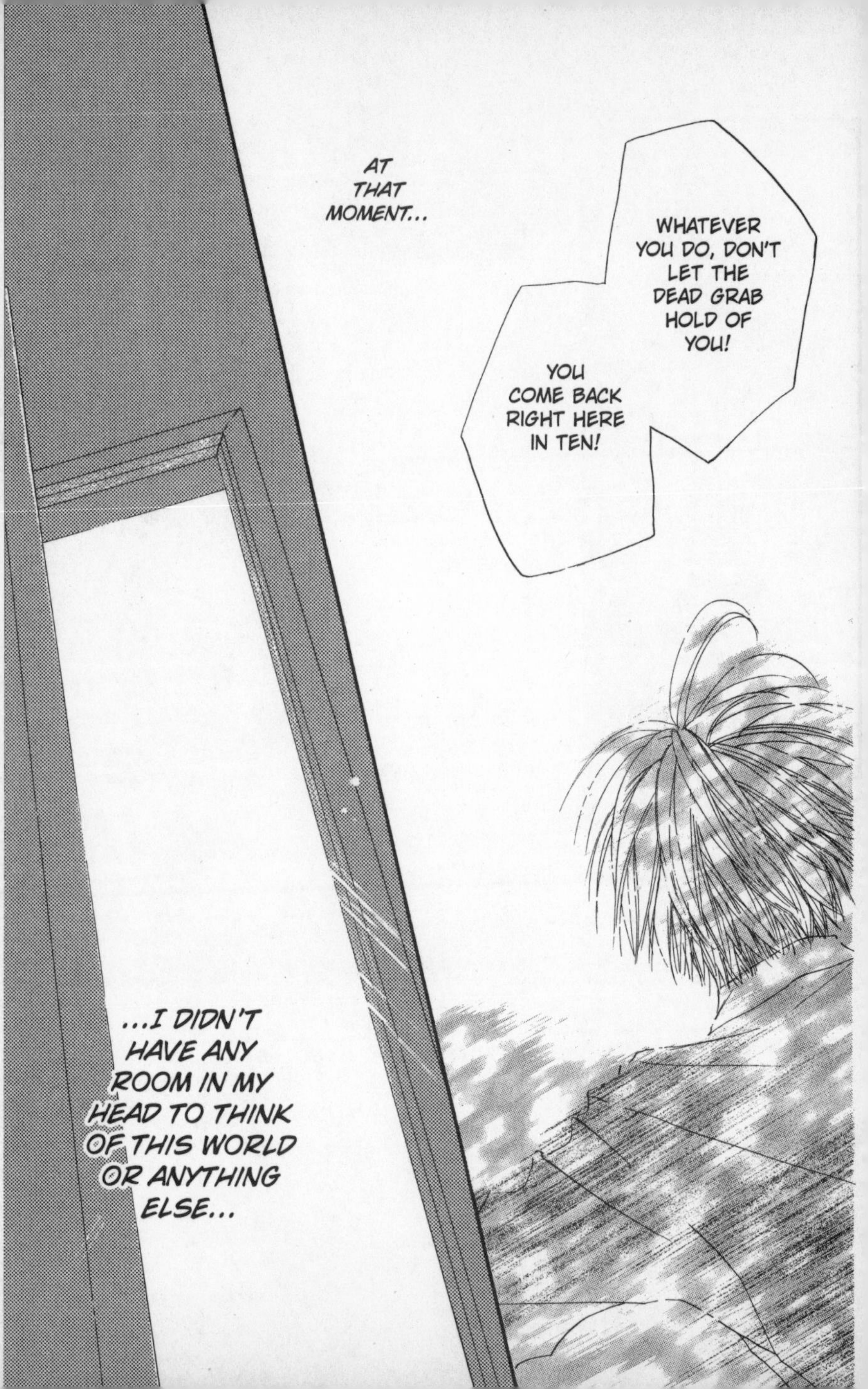
WHATEVER YOU DO, DON'T LET THE DEAD GRAB HOLD OF YOU!
YOU COME BACK RIGHT HERE IN TEN!
AT THAT MOMENT...
...I DIDN'T HAVE ANY ROOM IN MY HEAD TO THINK OF THIS WORLD OR ANYTHING ELSE...

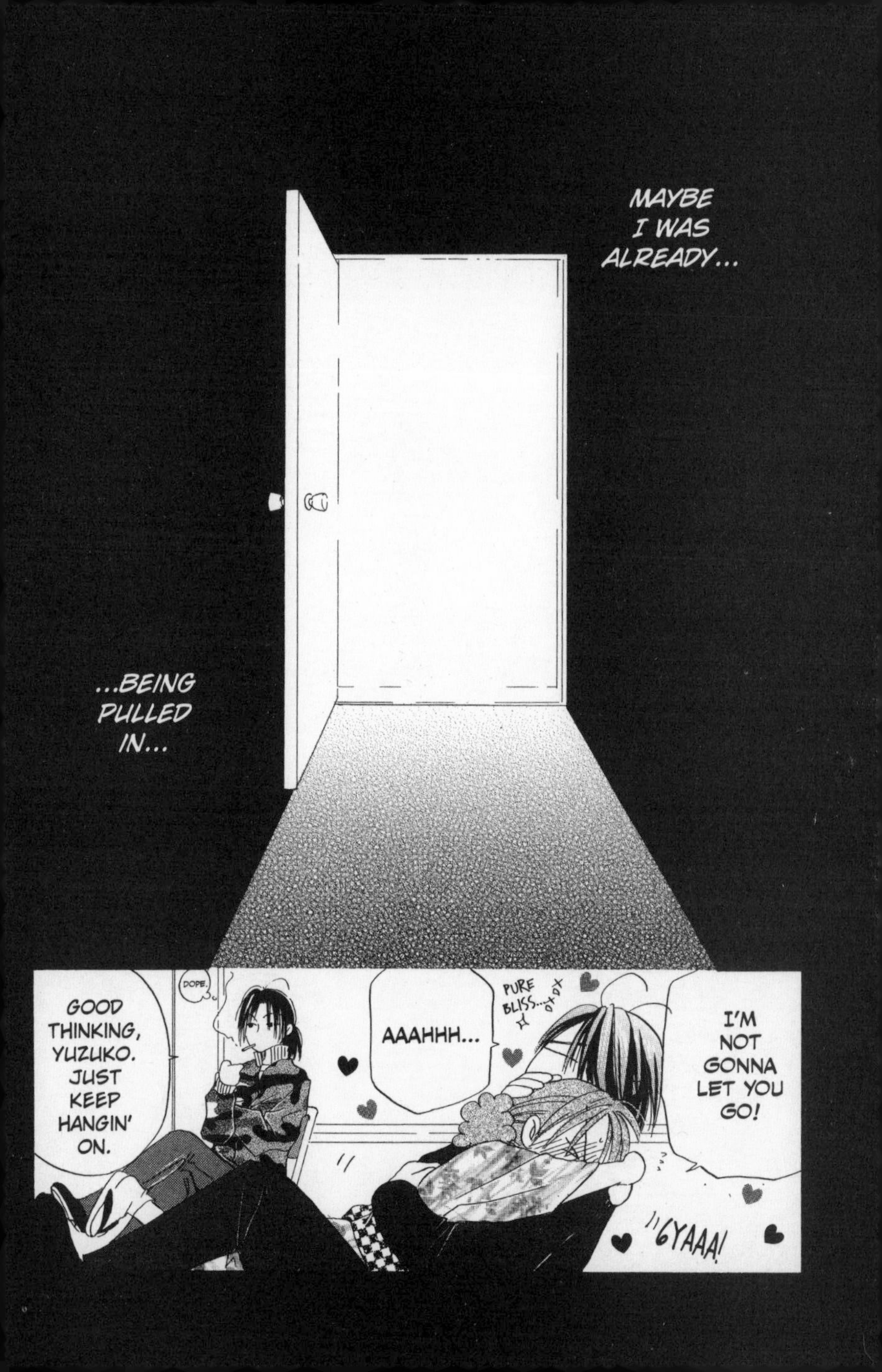
MAYBE I WAS ALREADY...
...BEING PULLED IN...
I'M NOT GONNA LET YOU GO!
GYAAA!
PURE BLISS...
AAAHHH...
DOPE.
GOOD THINKING, YUZUKO. JUST KEEP HANGIN' ON.

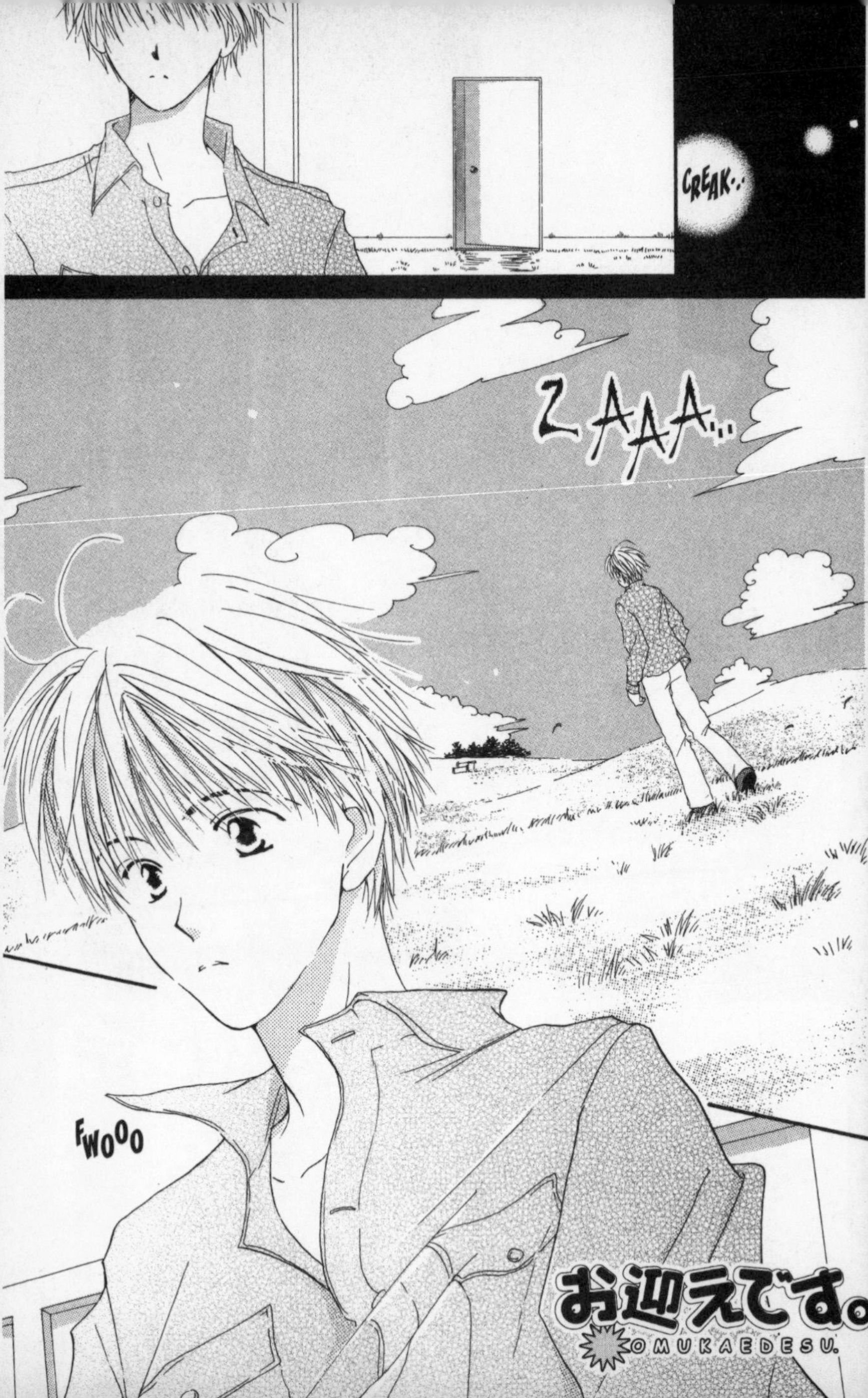
CREAK..
ZAAA...
FWOOO
お迎えです。
OMUKAEDESU.

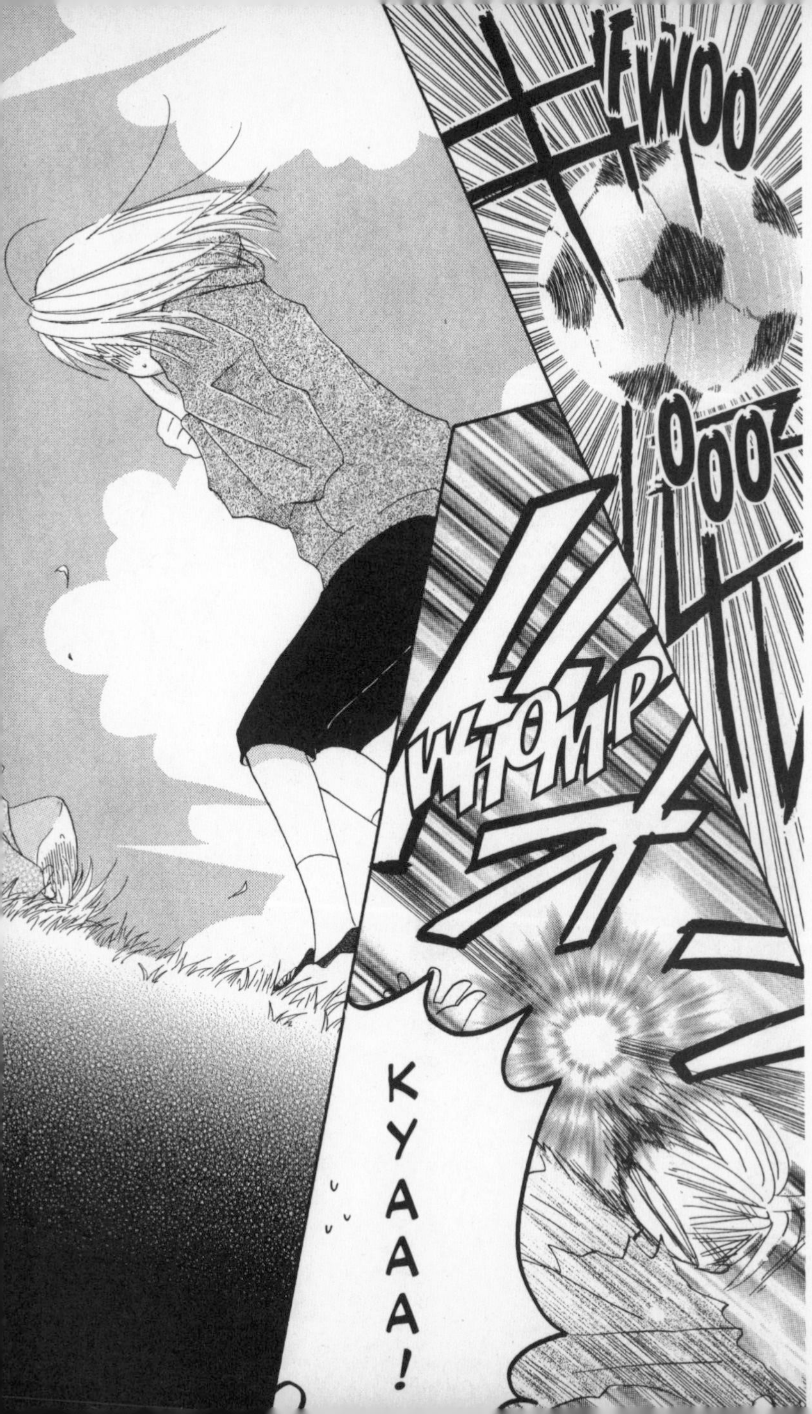
FWOO
OOO
WHOMP
KYAAA!

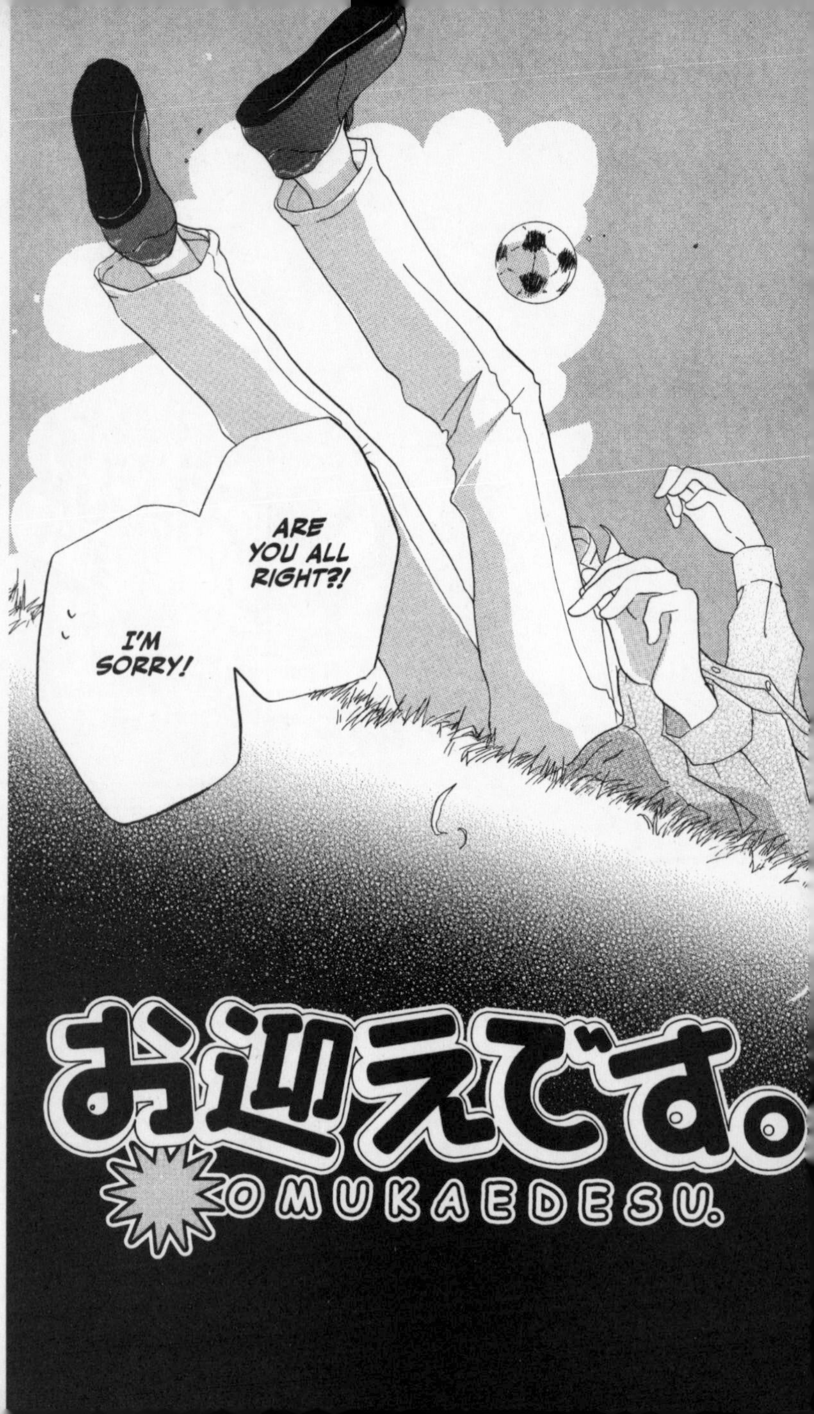
ARE YOU ALL RIGHT?!
I'M SORRY!
お迎えです。
OMUKAEDESU.

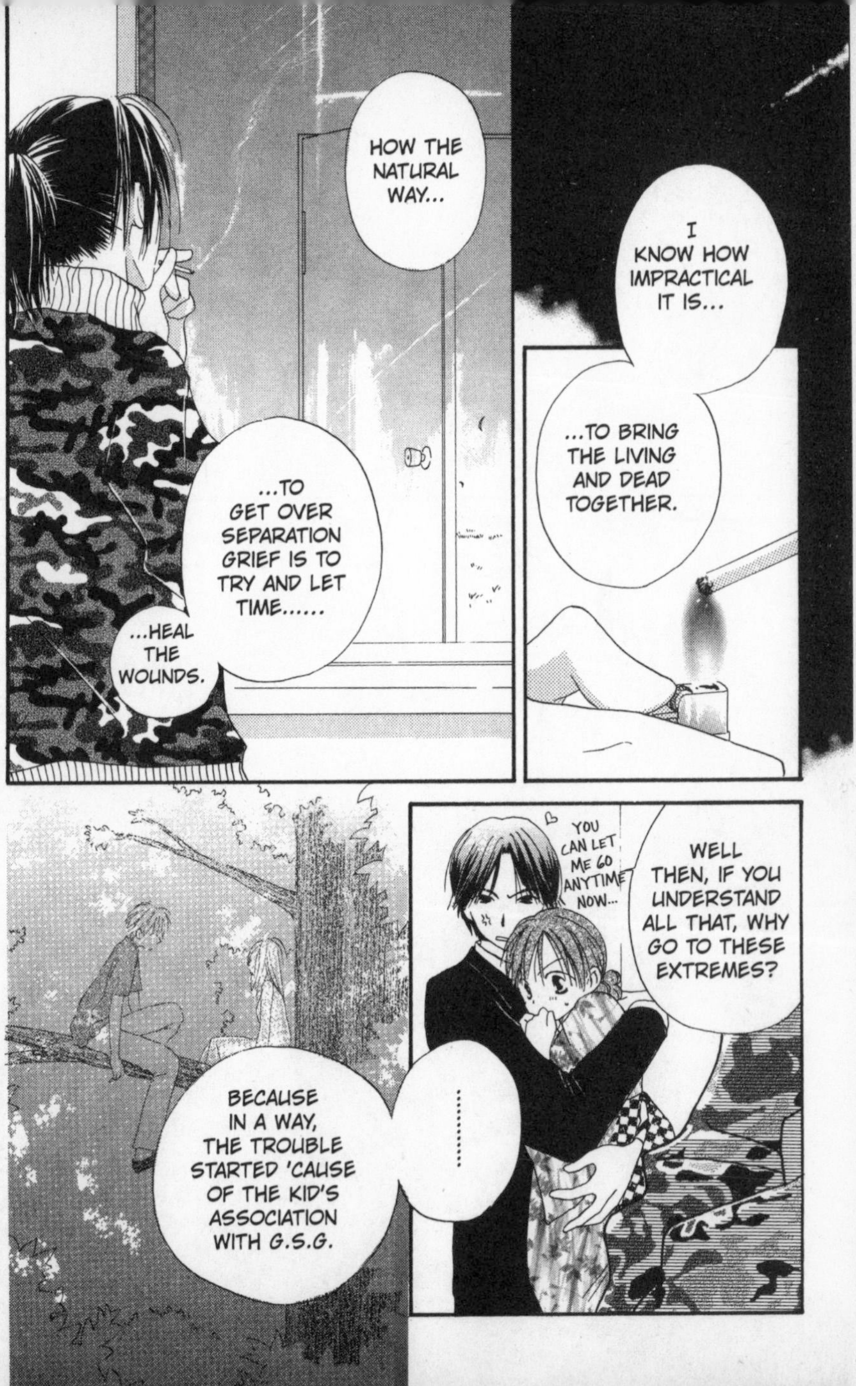
I KNOW HOW IMPRACTICAL IT IS...
...TO BRING THE LIVING AND DEAD TOGETHER.
HOW THE NATURAL WAY...
...TO GET OVER SEPARATION GRIEF IS TO TRY AND LET TIME......
...HEAL THE WOUNDS.
WELL THEN, IF YOU UNDERSTAND ALL THAT, WHY GO TO THESE EXTREMES?
YOU CAN LET ME GO ANYTIME NOW...
......
BECAUSE IN A WAY, THE TROUBLE STARTED 'CAUSE OF THE KID'S ASSOCIATION WITH G.S.G.

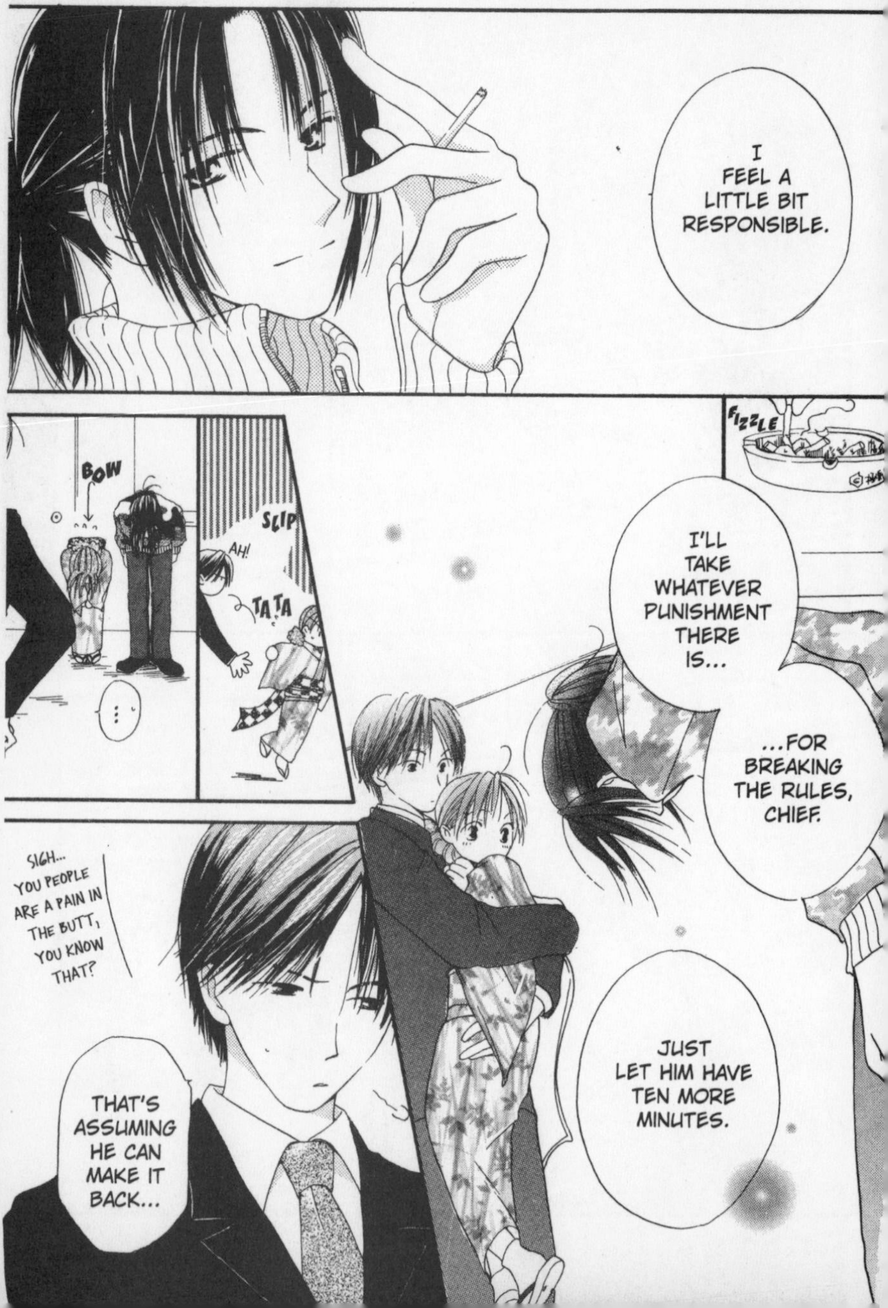
I FEEL A LITTLE BIT RESPONSIBLE.
FIZZLE
I'LL TAKE WHATEVER PUNISHMENT THERE IS...
...FOR BREAKING THE RULES, CHIEF.
SLIP
AH!
TA TA
BOW
...
JUST LET HIM HAVE TEN MORE MINUTES.
SIGH... YOU PEOPLE ARE A PAIN IN THE BUTT, YOU KNOW THAT?
THAT'S ASSUMING HE CAN MAKE IT BACK...

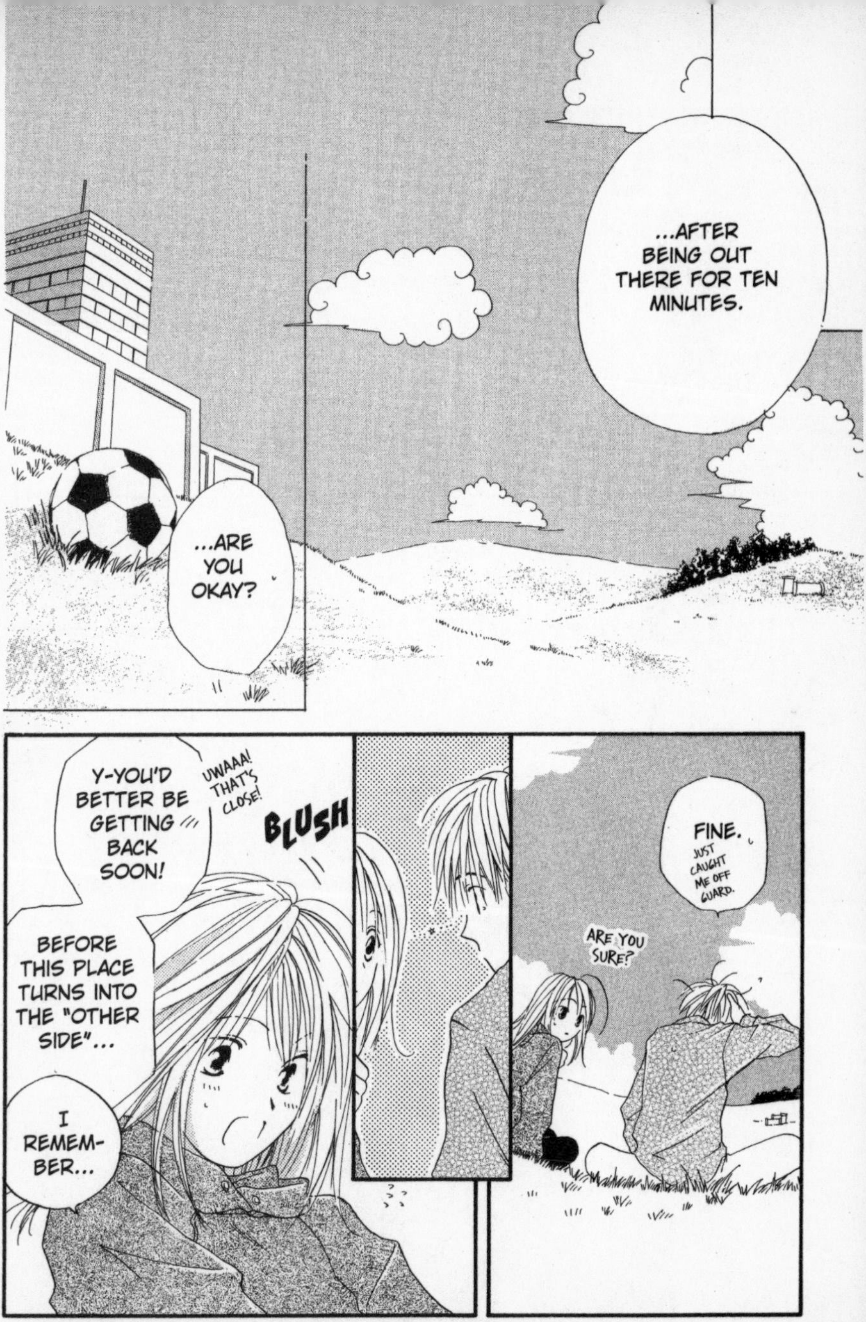
...AFTER BEING OUT THERE FOR TEN MINUTES.
...ARE YOU OKAY?
FINE.
JUST CAUGHT ME OFF GUARD.
ARE YOU SURE?
BLUSH
UWAAA! THAT'S CLOSE!
Y-YOU'D BETTER BE GETTING BACK SOON!
BEFORE THIS PLACE TURNS INTO THE "OTHER SIDE"...
I REMEMBER...

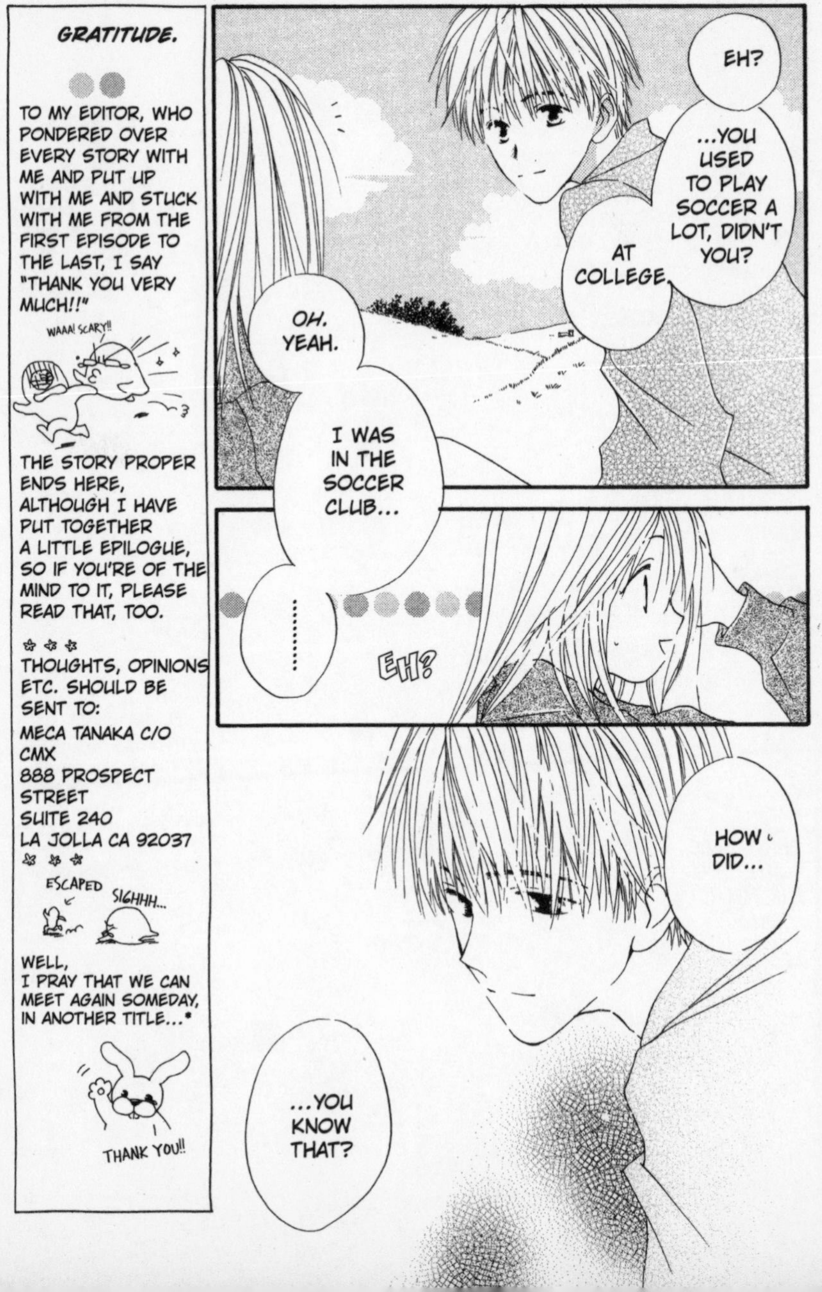
EH?
...YOU USED TO PLAY SOCCER A LOT, DIDN'T YOU?
AT COLLEGE.
OH. YEAH.
I WAS IN THE SOCCER CLUB...
......
EH?
HOW DID...
...YOU KNOW THAT?

GRATITUDE.

TO MY EDITOR, WHO PONDERED OVER EVERY STORY WITH ME AND PUT UP WITH ME AND STUCK WITH ME FROM THE FIRST EPISODE TO THE LAST, I SAY "THANK YOU VERY MUCH!!"

WAAA! SCARY!!

THE STORY PROPER ENDS HERE, ALTHOUGH I HAVE PUT TOGETHER A LITTLE EPILOGUE, SO IF YOU'RE OF THE MIND TO IT, PLEASE READ THAT, TOO.

THOUGHTS, OPINIONS ETC. SHOULD BE SENT TO:

MECA TANAKA C/O
CMX
888 PROSPECT STREET
SUITE 240
LA JOLLA CA 92037

ESCAPED

SIGHHH...

WELL,
I PRAY THAT WE CAN MEET AGAIN SOMEDAY, IN ANOTHER TITLE...*

THANK YOU!!

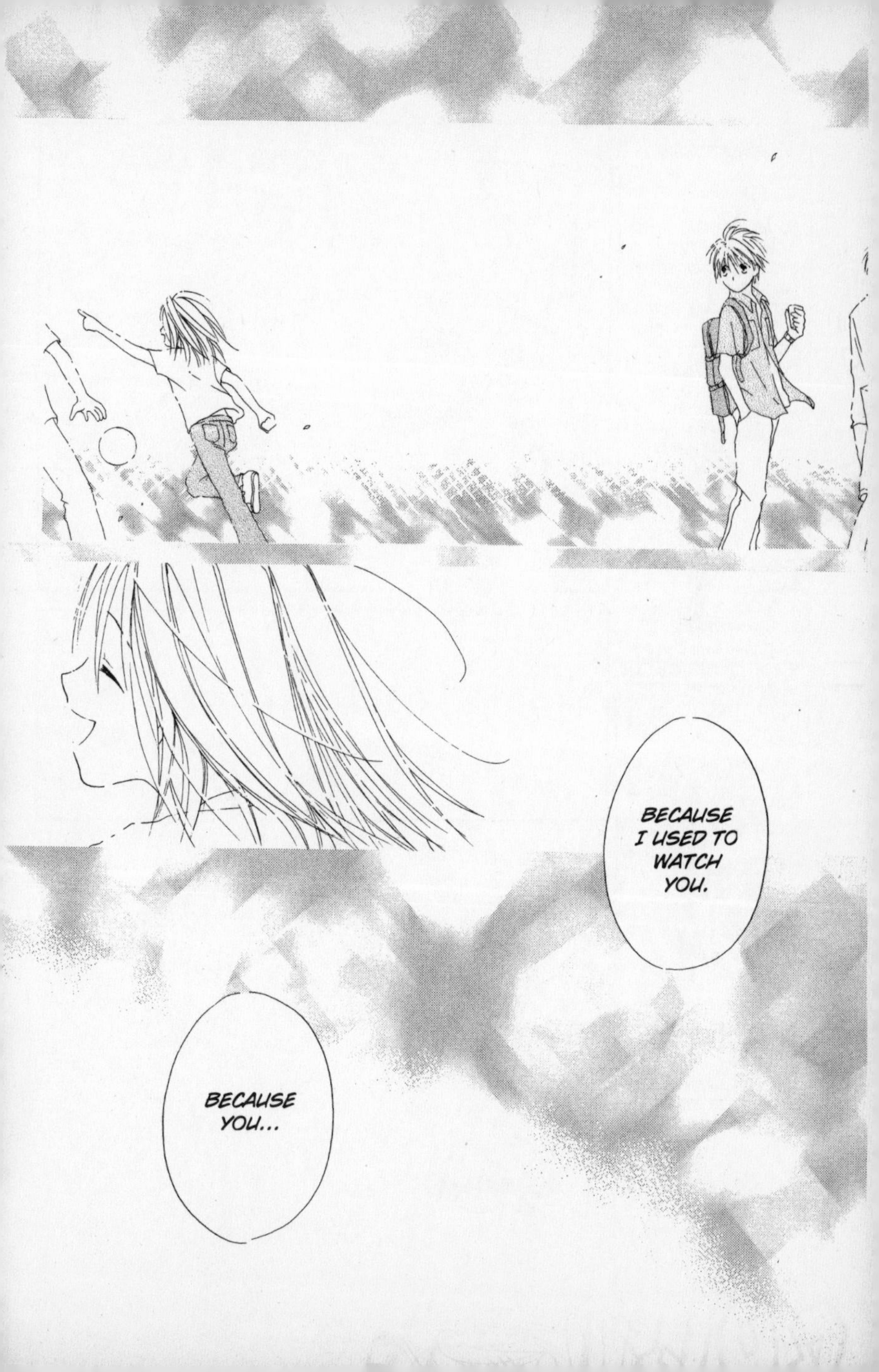
BECAUSE I USED TO WATCH YOU.
BECAUSE YOU...

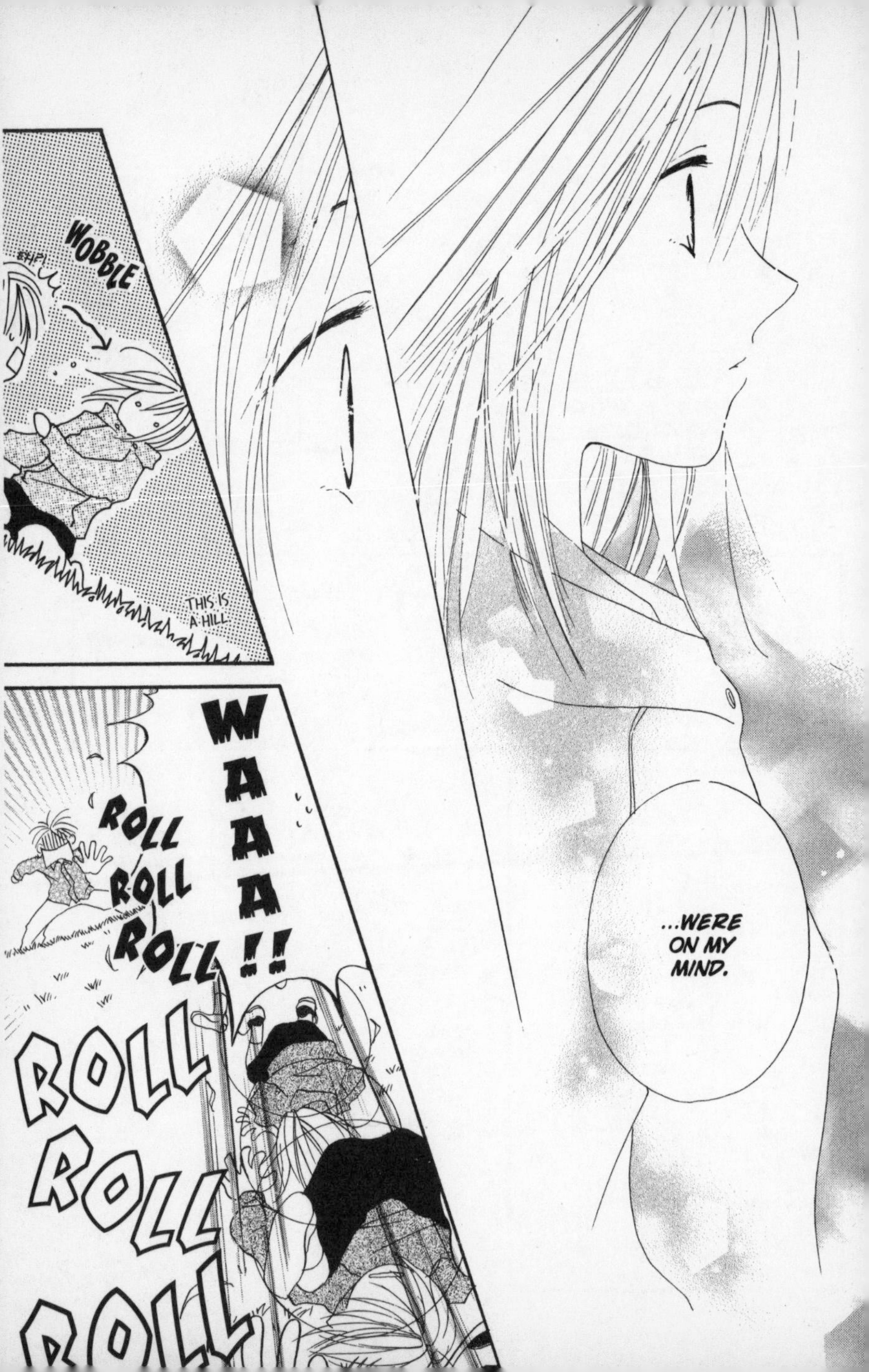
...WERE ON MY MIND.
WOBBLE
EH?!
THIS IS A HILL
WAAAA!!
ROLL ROLL ROLL
ROLL ROLL ROLL

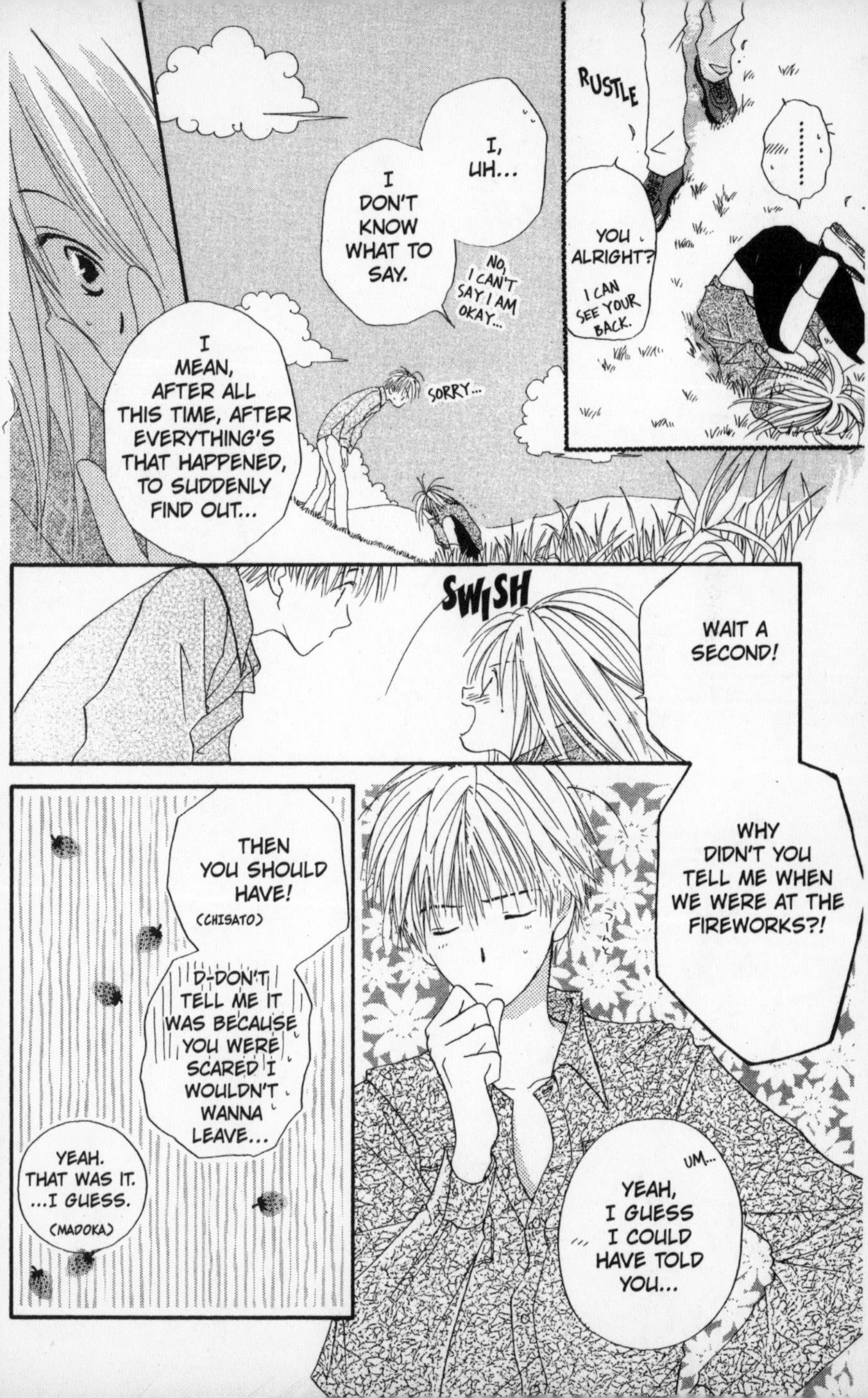
RUSTLE
......
YOU ALRIGHT?
I CAN SEE YOUR BACK.
I, UH... I DON'T KNOW WHAT TO SAY.
NO, I CAN'T SAY I AM OKAY...
SORRY...
I MEAN, AFTER ALL THIS TIME, AFTER EVERYTHING'S THAT HAPPENED, TO SUDDENLY FIND OUT...
SWISH
WAIT A SECOND!
WHY DIDN'T YOU TELL ME WHEN WE WERE AT THE FIREWORKS?!
UM...
YEAH, I GUESS I COULD HAVE TOLD YOU...
THEN YOU SHOULD HAVE! (CHISATO)
D-DON'T TELL ME IT WAS BECAUSE YOU WERE SCARED I WOULDN'T WANNA LEAVE...
YEAH. THAT WAS IT. ...I GUESS. (MADOKA)

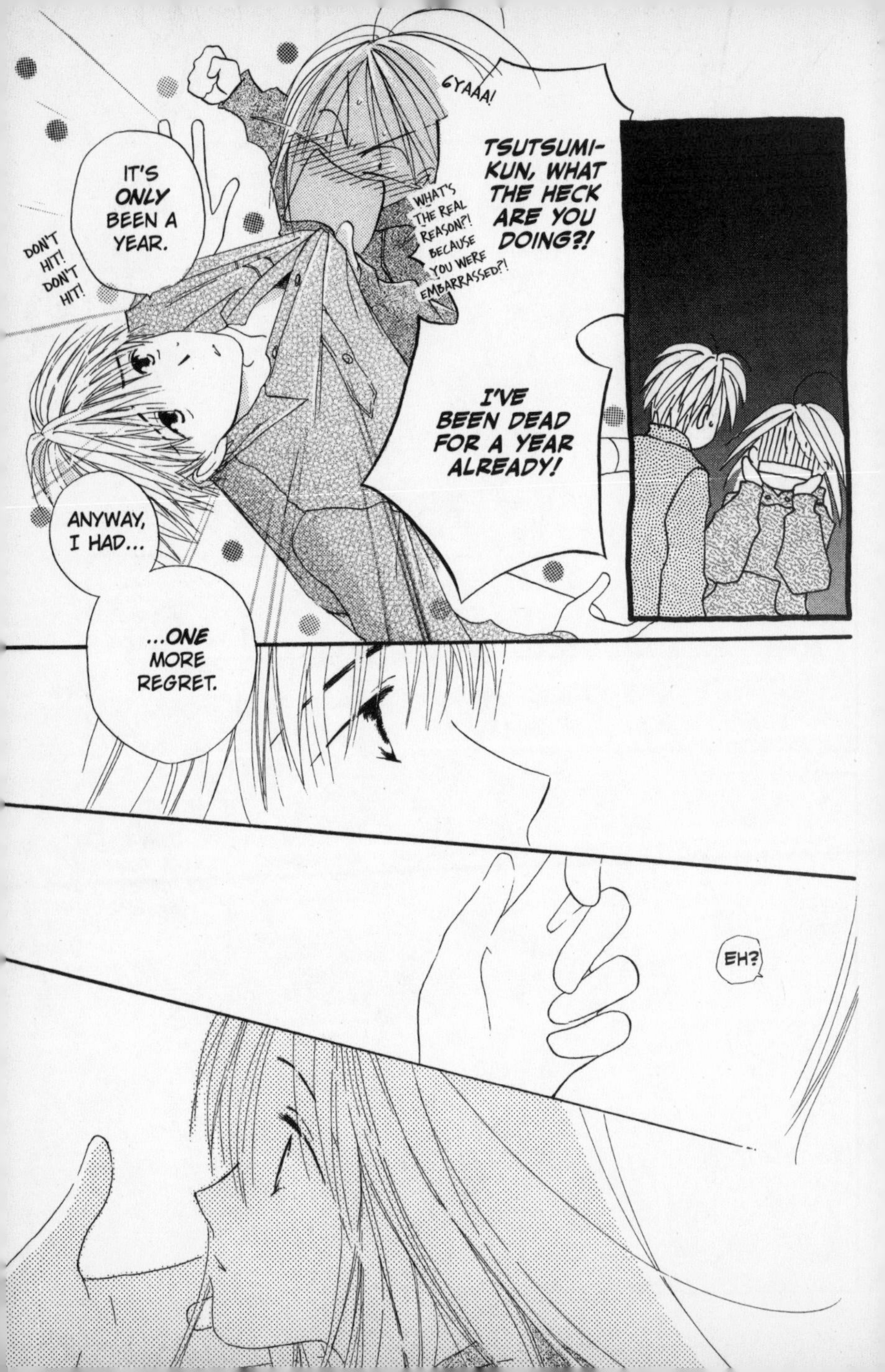
TSUTSUMI-KUN, WHAT THE HECK ARE YOU DOING?!
I'VE BEEN DEAD FOR A YEAR ALREADY!
GYAAA!
WHAT'S THE REAL REASON?! BECAUSE YOU WERE EMBARRASSED?!
IT'S ONLY BEEN A YEAR.
DON'T HIT! DON'T HIT!
ANYWAY, I HAD...
...ONE MORE REGRET.
EH?

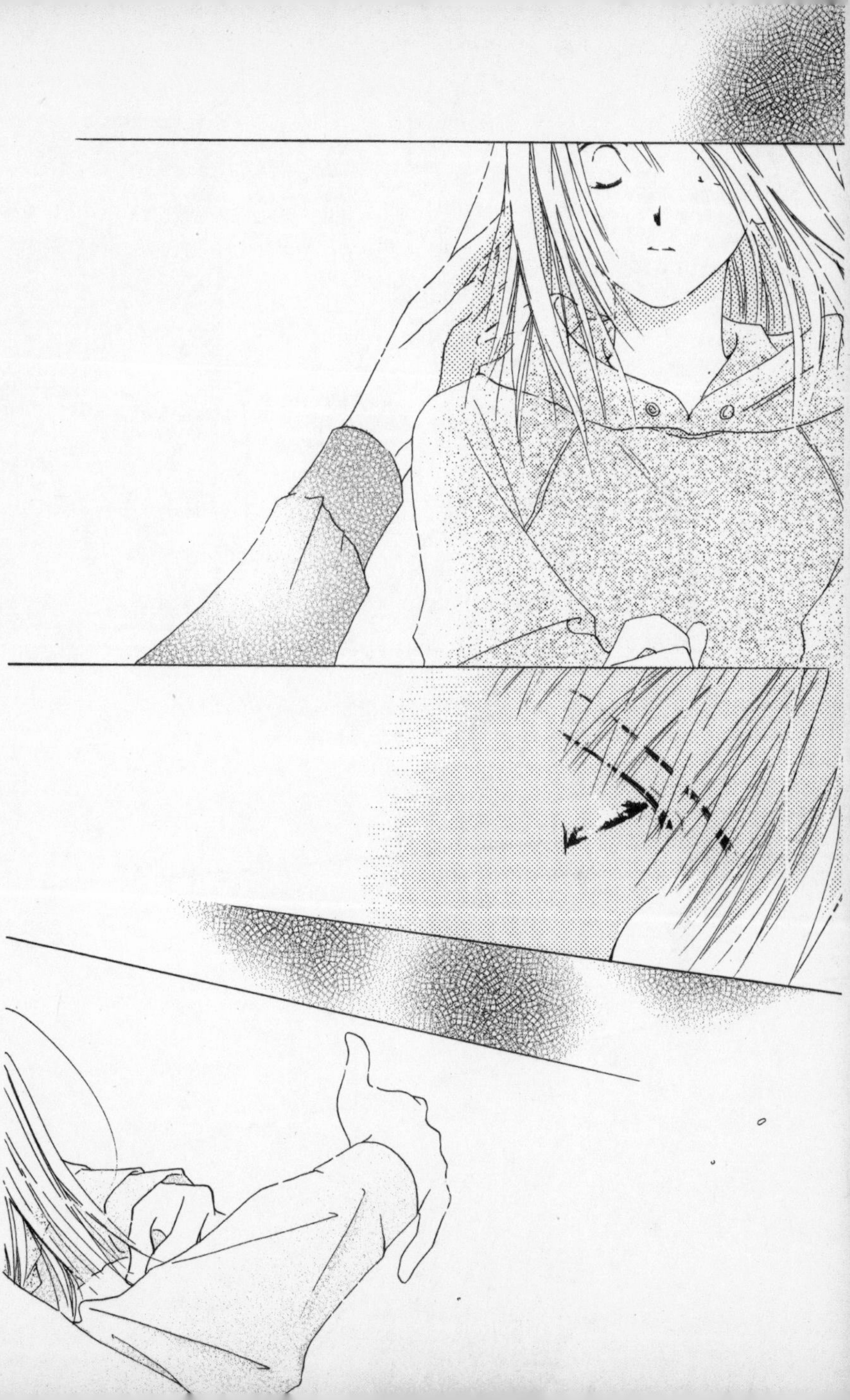

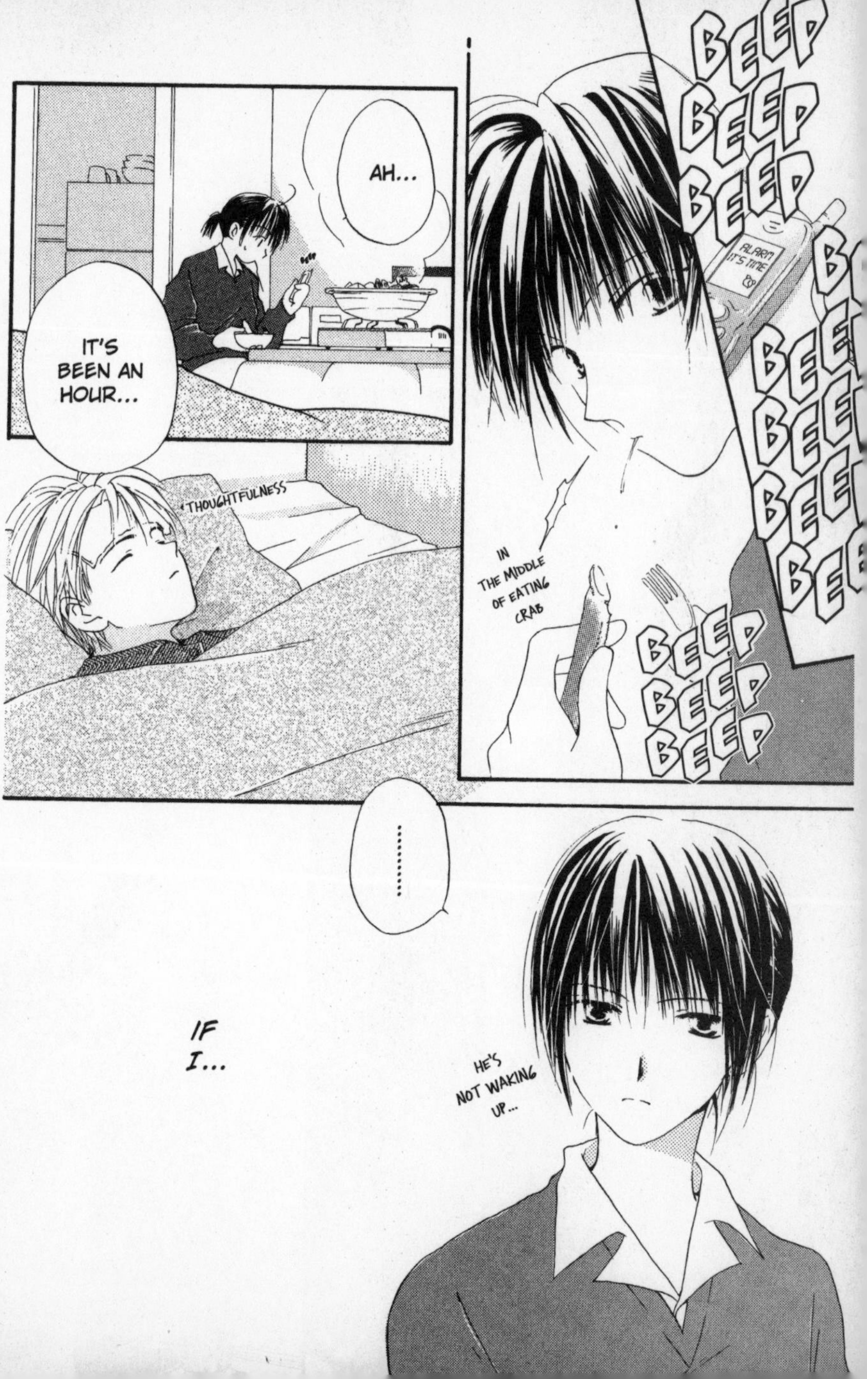
BEEP
BEEP
BEEP
ALARM
IT'S TIME
IN THE MIDDLE OF EATING CRAB
BEEP
BEEP
BEEP
AH...
IT'S BEEN AN HOUR...
THOUGHTFULNESS
......
HE'S NOT WAKING UP...
IF I...

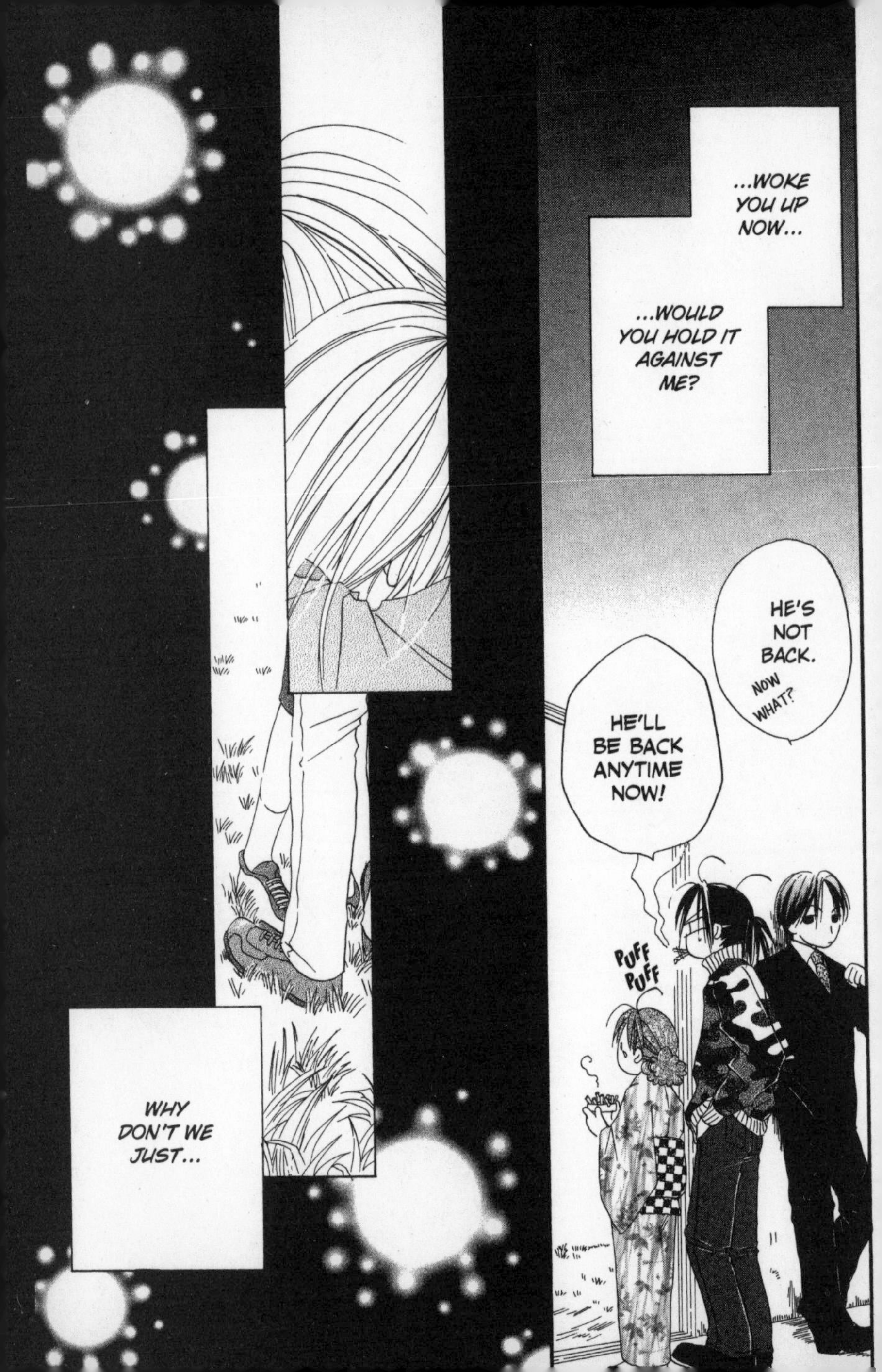
...WOKE YOU UP NOW...
...WOULD YOU HOLD IT AGAINST ME?
HE'S NOT BACK.
NOW WHAT?
HE'LL BE BACK ANYTIME NOW!
PUFF PUFF
WHY DON'T WE JUST...

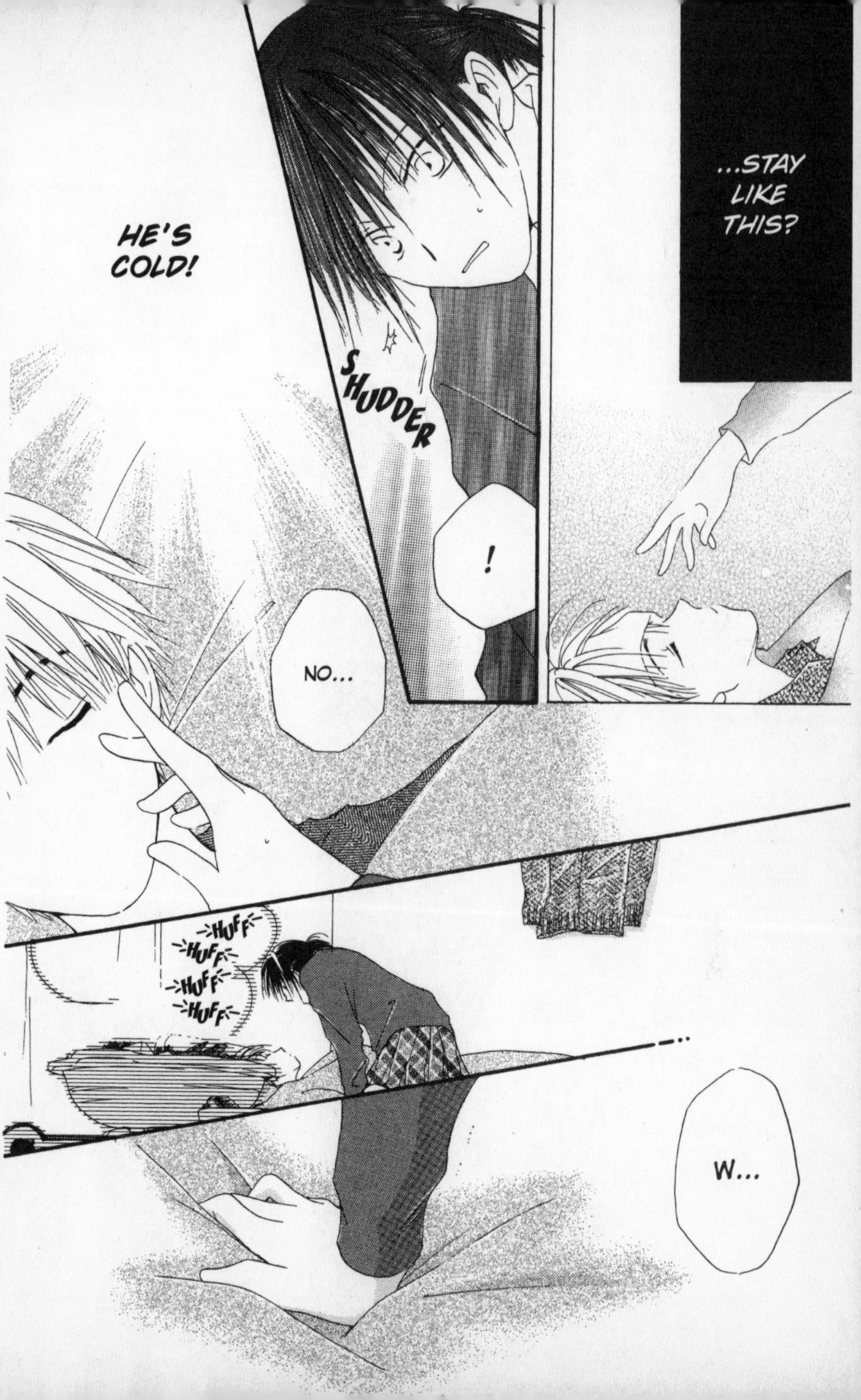
...STAY LIKE THIS?
SHUDDER
!
HE'S COLD!
NO...
HUFF
HUFF
HUFF
HUFF
W...

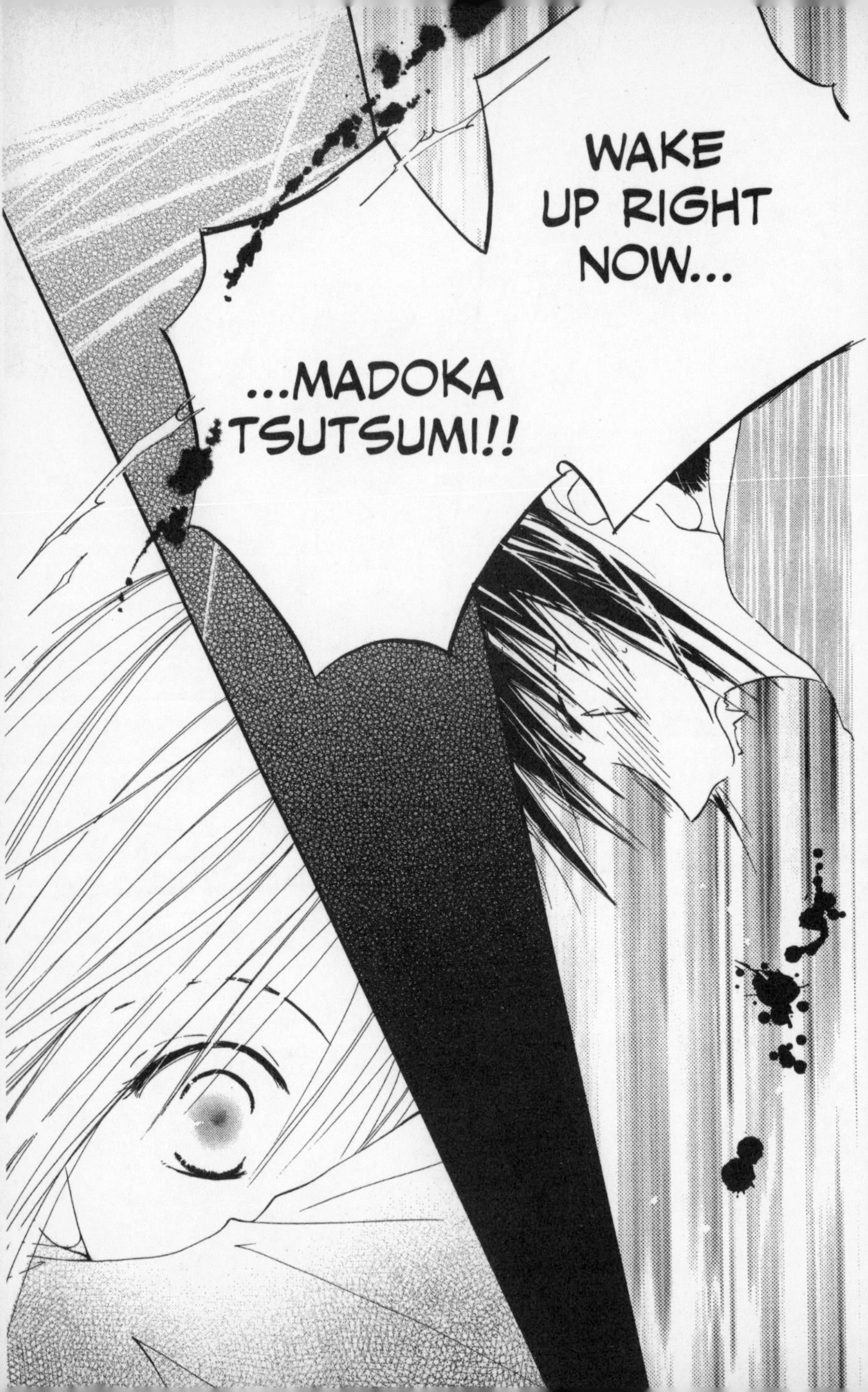
WAKE UP RIGHT NOW...
...MADOKA TSUTSUMI!!

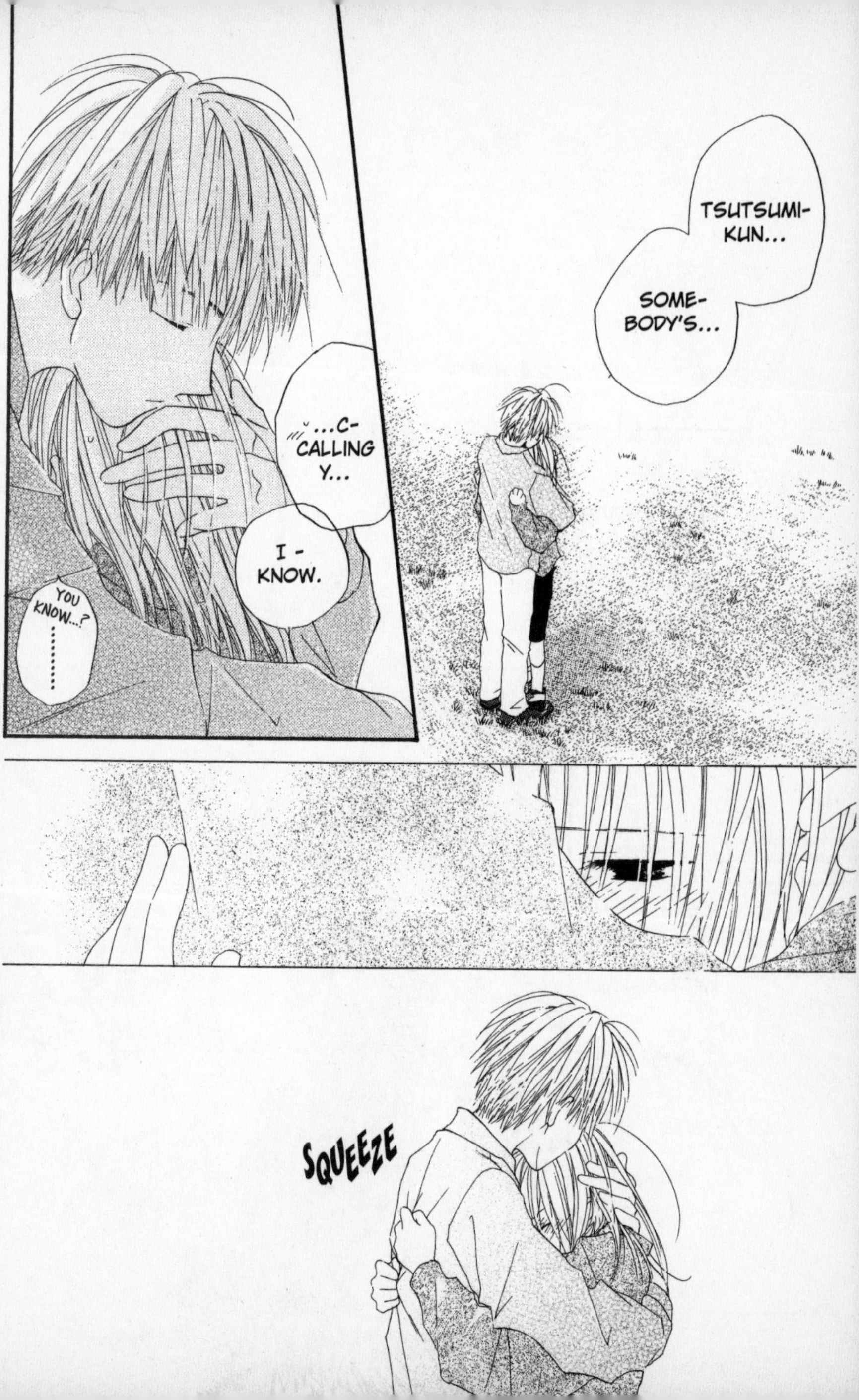
TSUTSUMI-KUN...
SOME-BODY'S...
...C-CALLING Y...
I - KNOW.
YOU KNOW...? ......
SQUEEZE

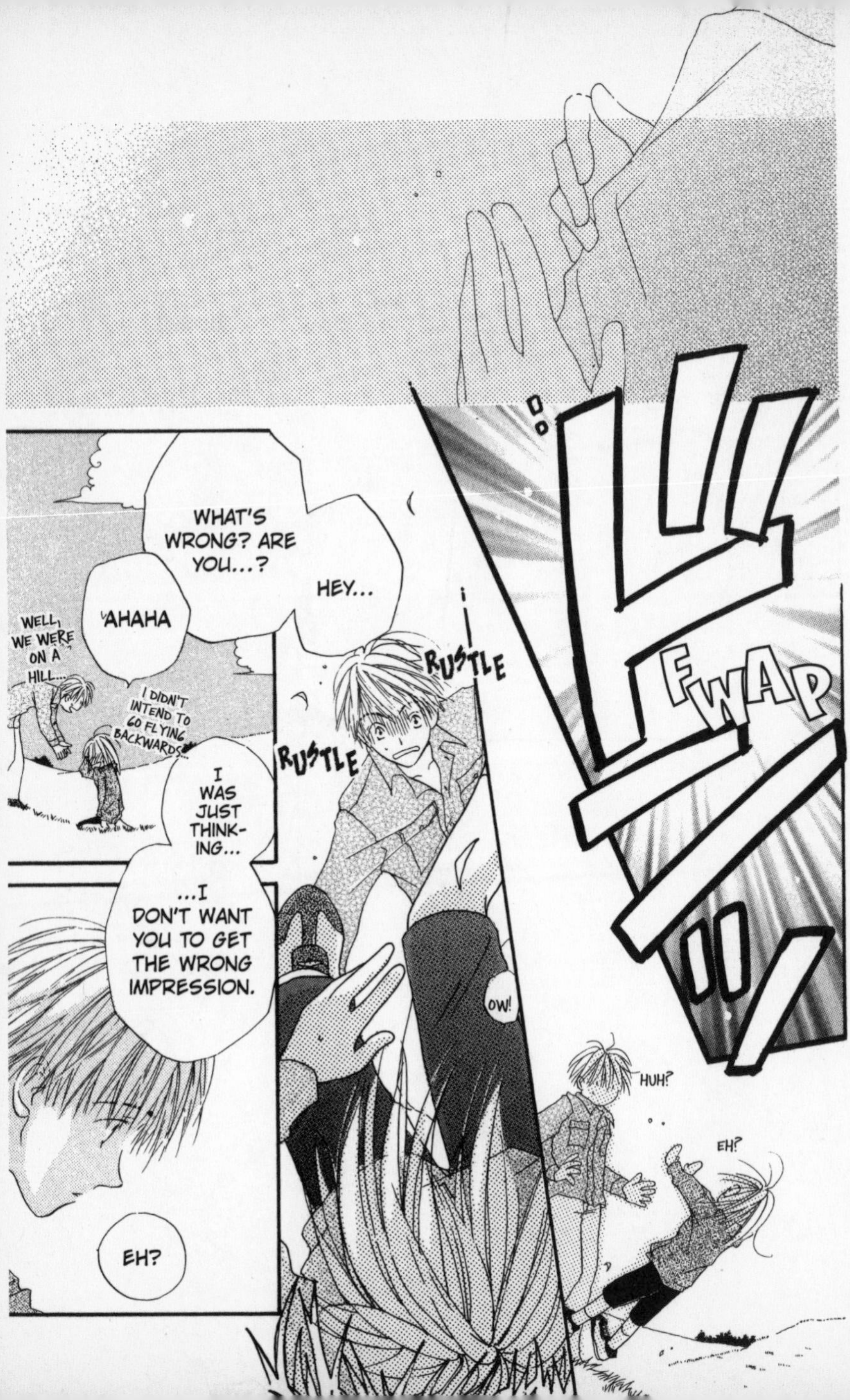
FWAP
HUH?
EH?
HEY...
RUSTLE
RUSTLE
OW!
WHAT'S WRONG? ARE YOU...?
AHAHA
WELL, WE WERE ON A HILL...
I DIDN'T INTEND TO GO FLYING BACKWARDS...
I WAS JUST THINKING...
...I DON'T WANT YOU TO GET THE WRONG IMPRESSION.
EH?

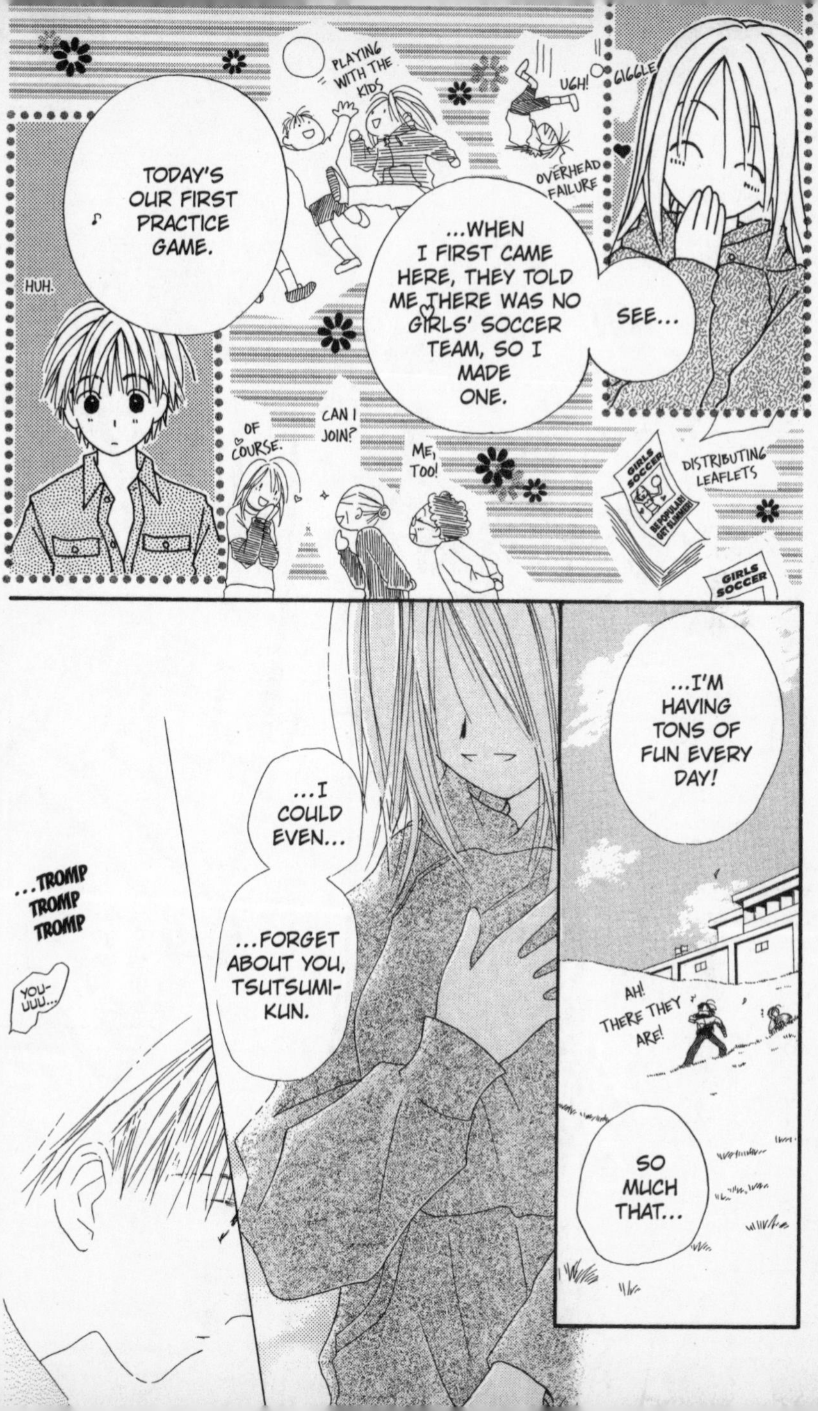
GIGGLE
SEE...
...WHEN I FIRST CAME HERE, THEY TOLD ME THERE WAS NO GIRLS' SOCCER TEAM, SO I MADE ONE.
UGH!
OVERHEAD FAILURE
PLAYING WITH THE KIDS
DISTRIBUTING LEAFLETS
GIRLS SOCCER
BE POPULAR! GET SLIMMER!
GIRLS SOCCER
ME, TOO!
CAN I JOIN?
OF COURSE.
TODAY'S OUR FIRST PRACTICE GAME.
HUH.
...I'M HAVING TONS OF FUN EVERY DAY!
AH! THERE THEY ARE!
SO MUCH THAT...
...I COULD EVEN...
...FORGET ABOUT YOU, TSUTSUMI-KUN.
...TROMP TROMP TROMP
YOU-UUU...

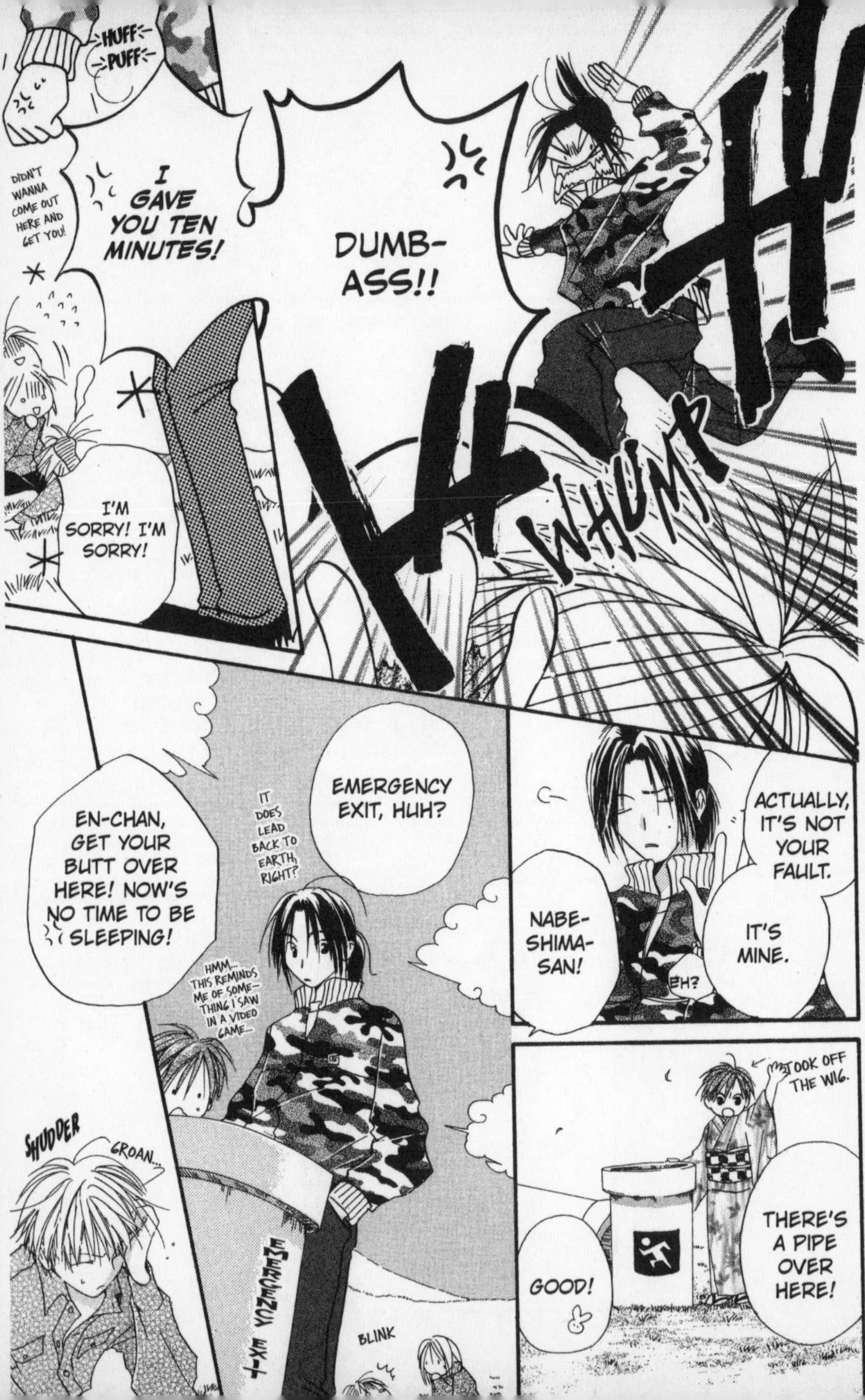
I GAVE YOU TEN MINUTES!
DUMB-ASS!!
WHUMP
HUFF PUFF
DIDN'T WANNA COME OUT HERE AND GET YOU!
I'M SORRY! I'M SORRY!
ACTUALLY, IT'S NOT YOUR FAULT.
IT'S MINE.
EH?
NABE-SHIMA-SAN!
TOOK OFF THE WIG.
THERE'S A PIPE OVER HERE!
GOOD!
EMERGENCY EXIT, HUH?
IT DOES LEAD BACK TO EARTH, RIGHT?
HMM... THIS REMINDS ME OF SOMETHING I SAW IN A VIDEO GAME...
EN-CHAN, GET YOUR BUTT OVER HERE! NOW'S NO TIME TO BE SLEEPING!
SHUDDER
GROAN...
EMERGENCY EXIT
BLINK

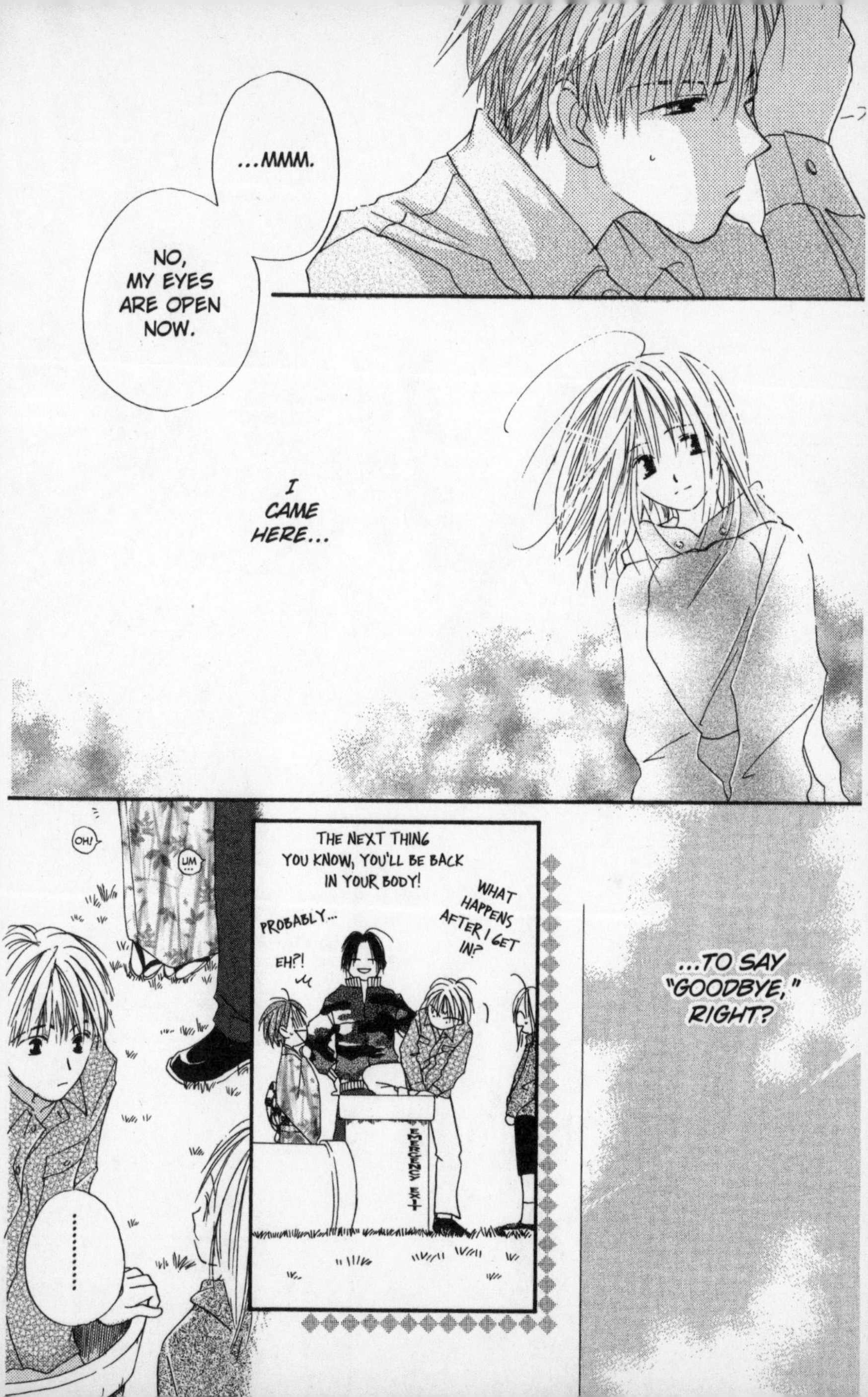
...MMM.
NO, MY EYES ARE OPEN NOW.
I CAME HERE...
...TO SAY "GOODBYE," RIGHT?
THE NEXT THING YOU KNOW, YOU'LL BE BACK IN YOUR BODY!
WHAT HAPPENS AFTER I GET IN?
PROBABLY...
EH?!
EMERGENCY EXIT
OH!
UM...
....

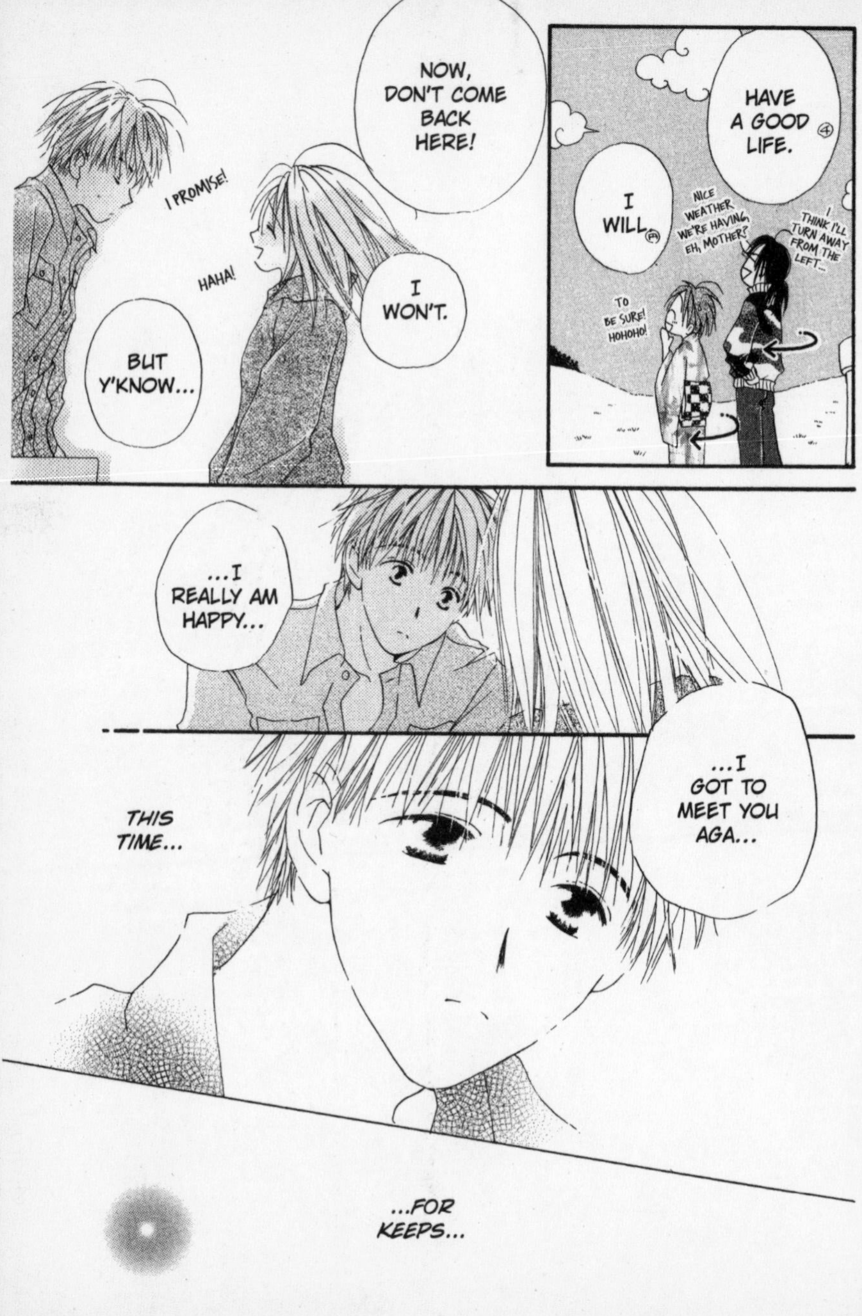
HAVE A GOOD LIFE.
I WILL.
NICE WEATHER WE'RE HAVING, EH, MOTHER?
TO BE SURE! HOHOHO!
I THINK I'LL TURN AWAY FROM THE LEFT...
NOW, DON'T COME BACK HERE!
I WON'T.
I PROMISE!
HAHA!
BUT Y'KNOW...
...I REALLY AM HAPPY...
...I GOT TO MEET YOU AGA...
THIS TIME...
...FOR KEEPS...

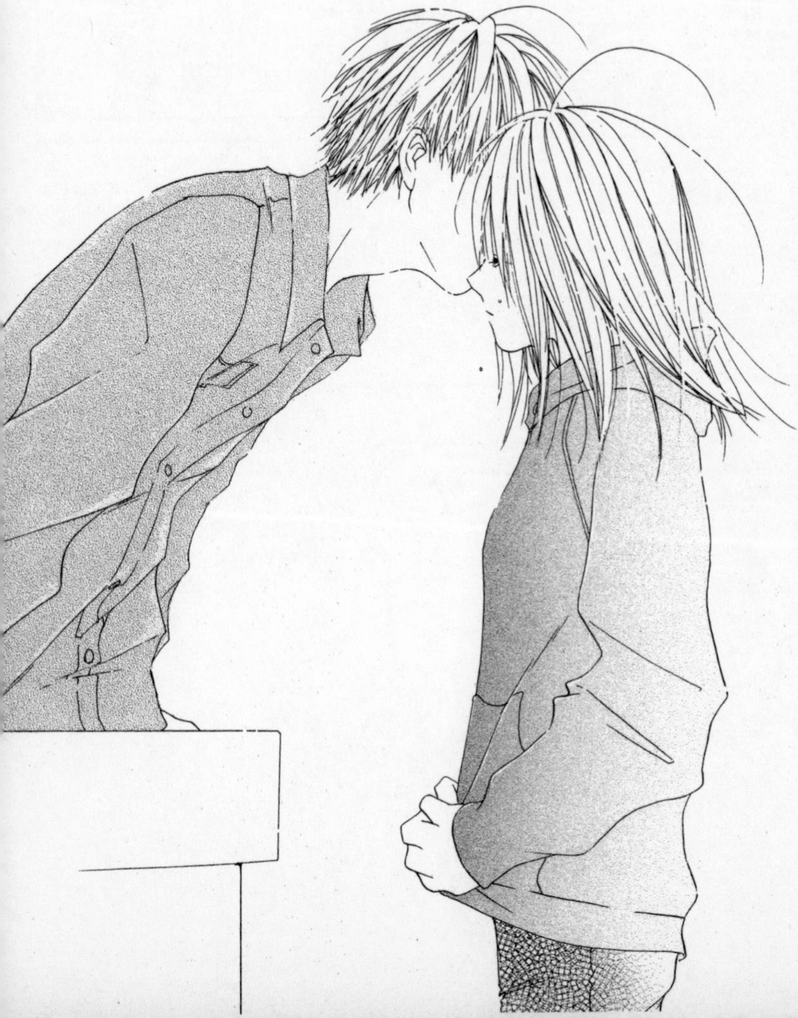

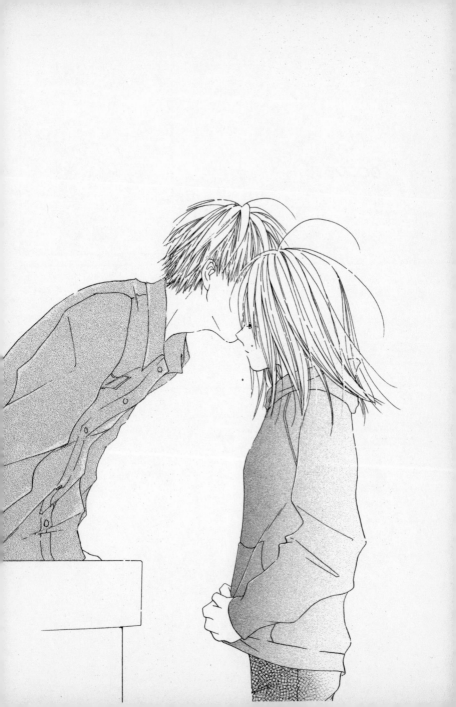

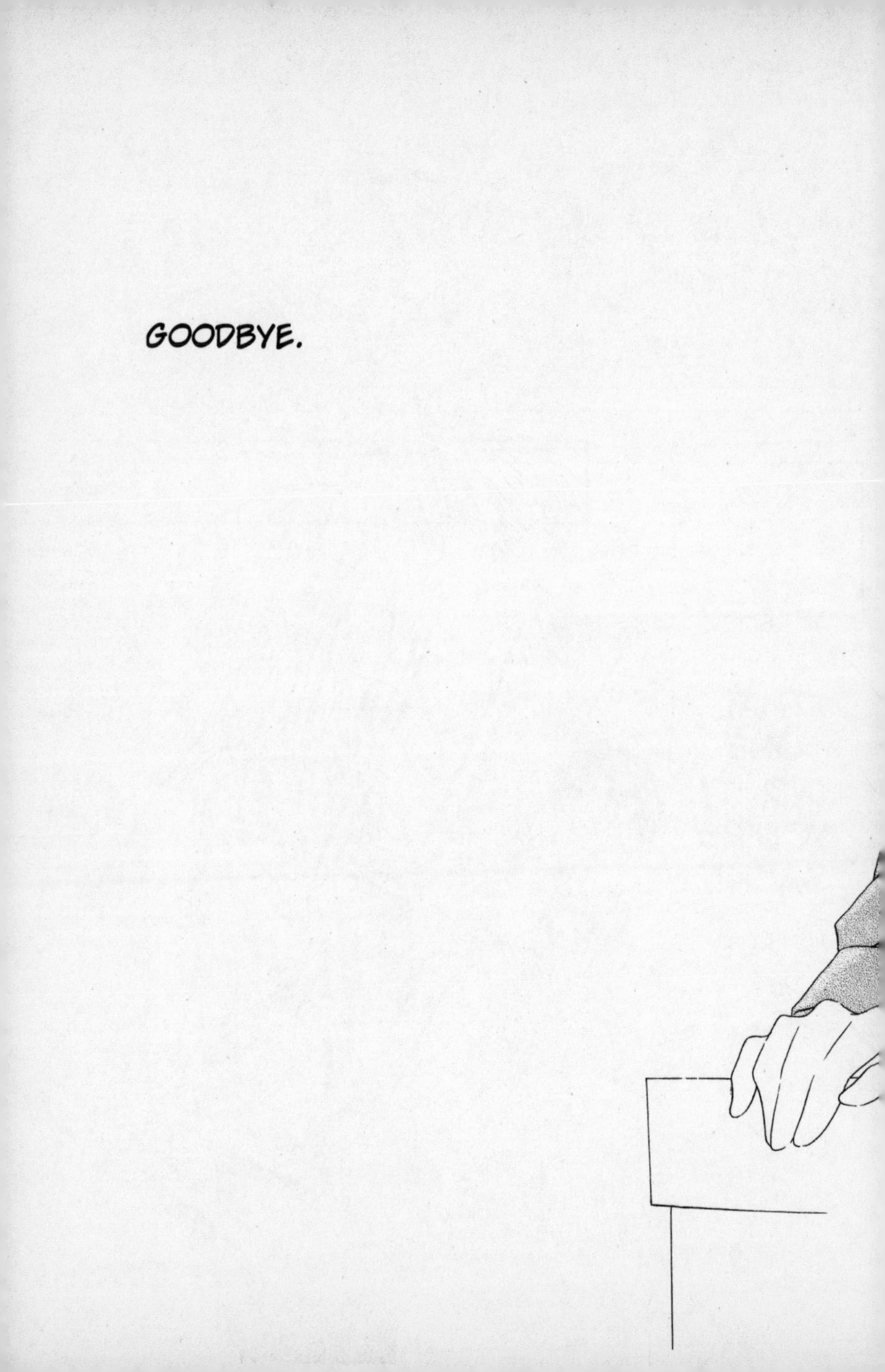
GOODBYE.

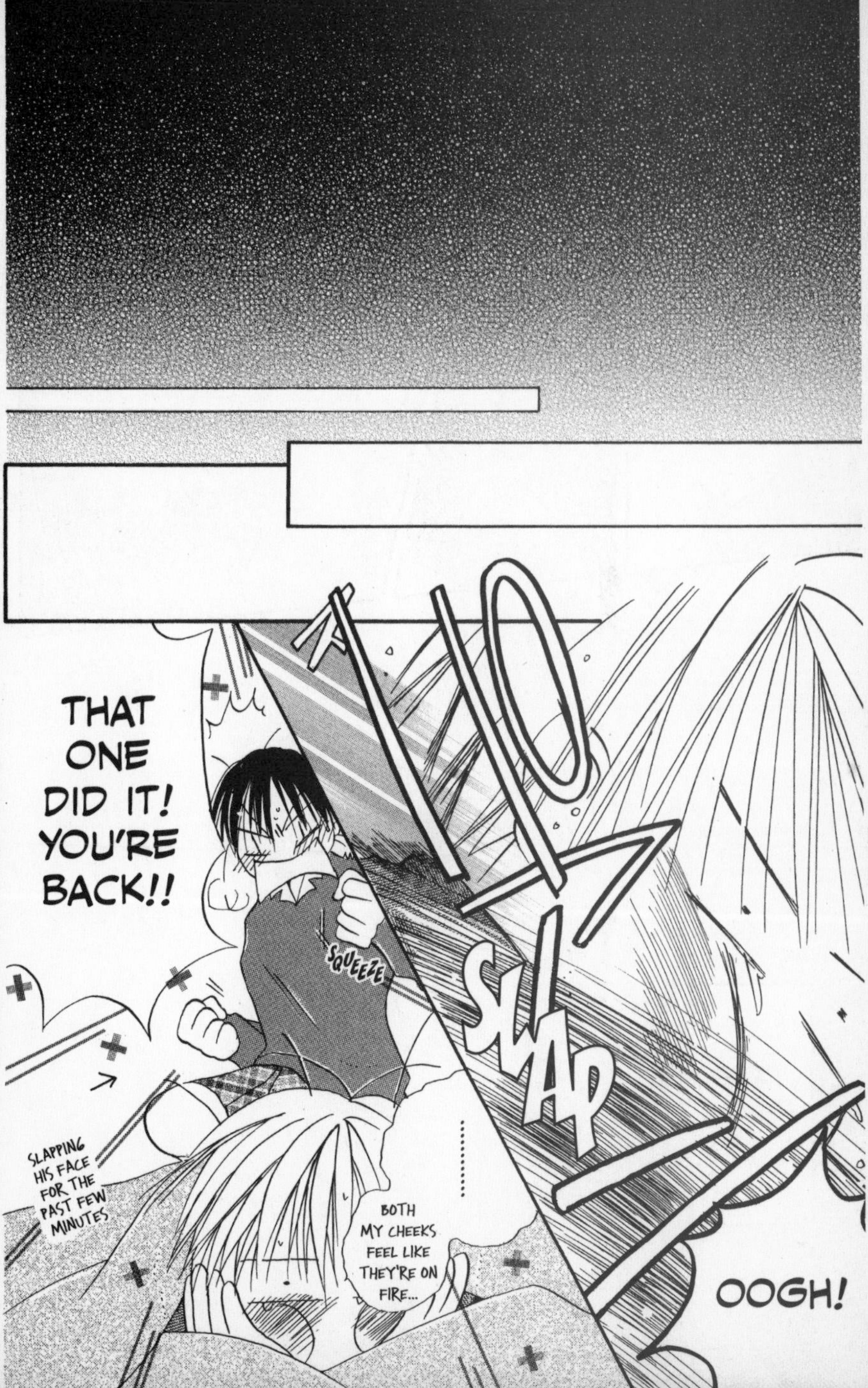
SLAP
THAT ONE DID IT! YOU'RE BACK!!
SQUEEZE
OOGH!
BOTH MY CHEEKS FEEL LIKE THEY'RE ON FIRE...
SLAPPING HIS FACE FOR THE PAST FEW MINUTES

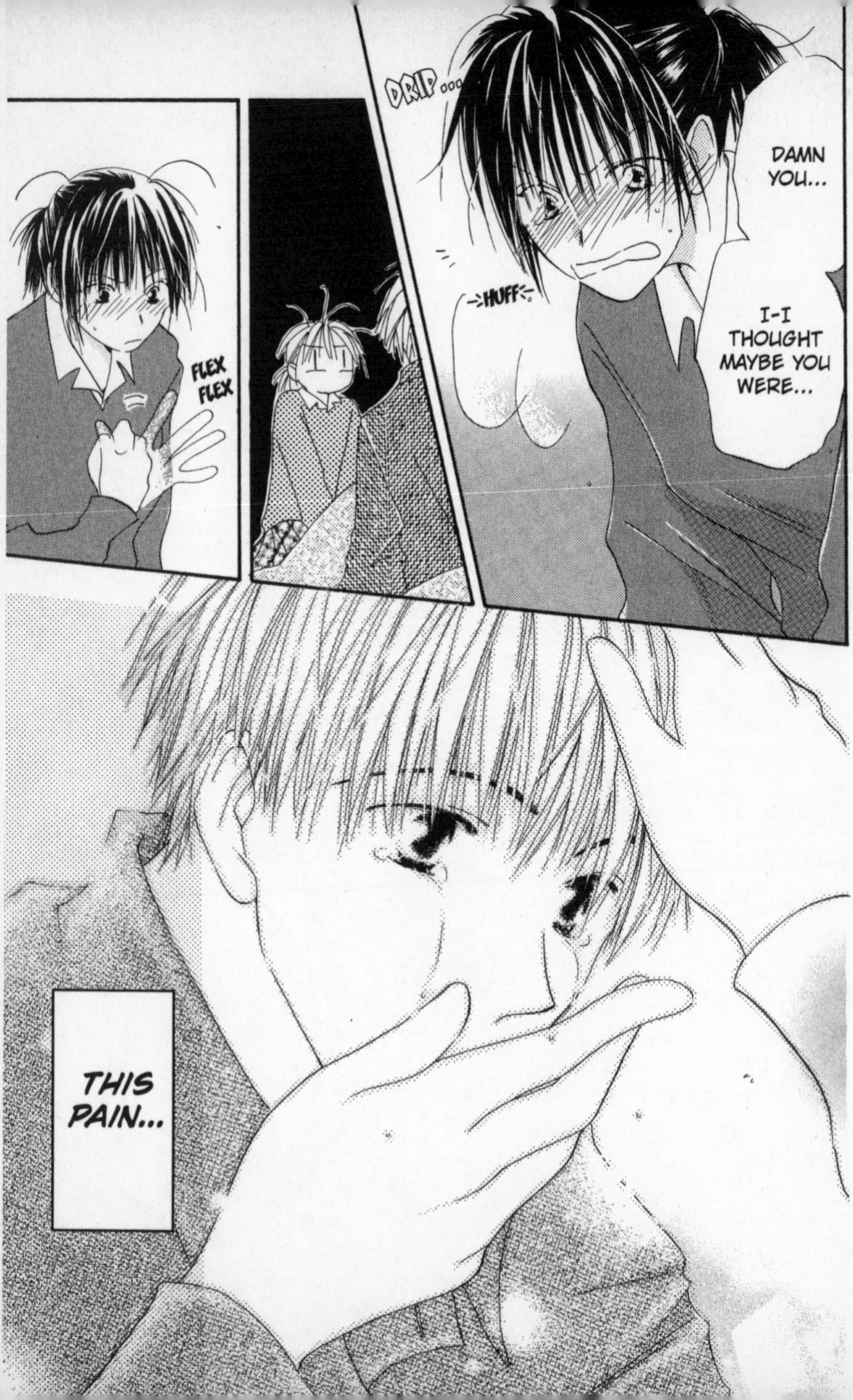
DRIP...
DAMN YOU...
HUFF
I-I THOUGHT MAYBE YOU WERE...
FLEX FLEX
THIS PAIN...

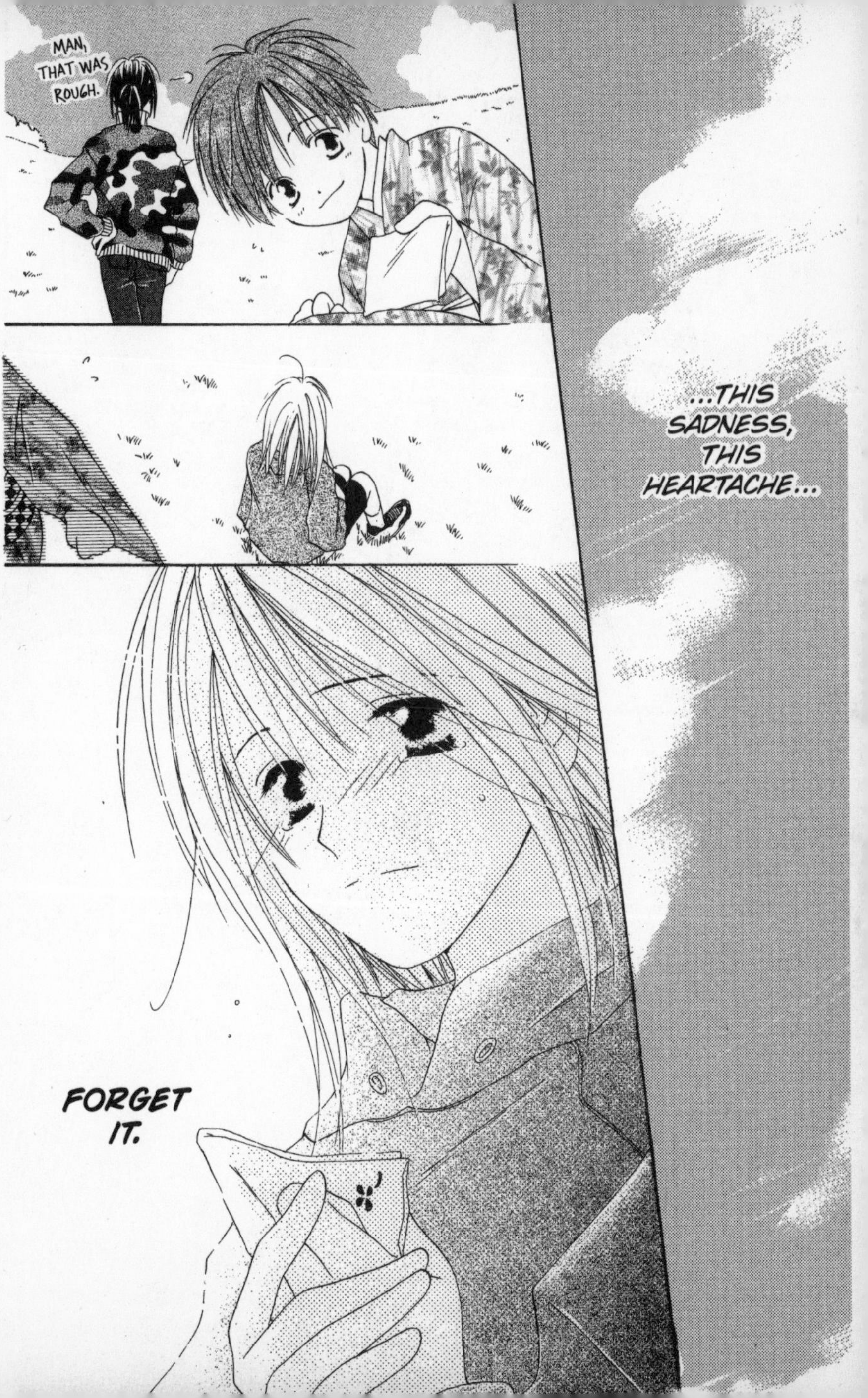
...THIS SADNESS, THIS HEARTACHE...
MAN, THAT WAS ROUGH.
FORGET IT.

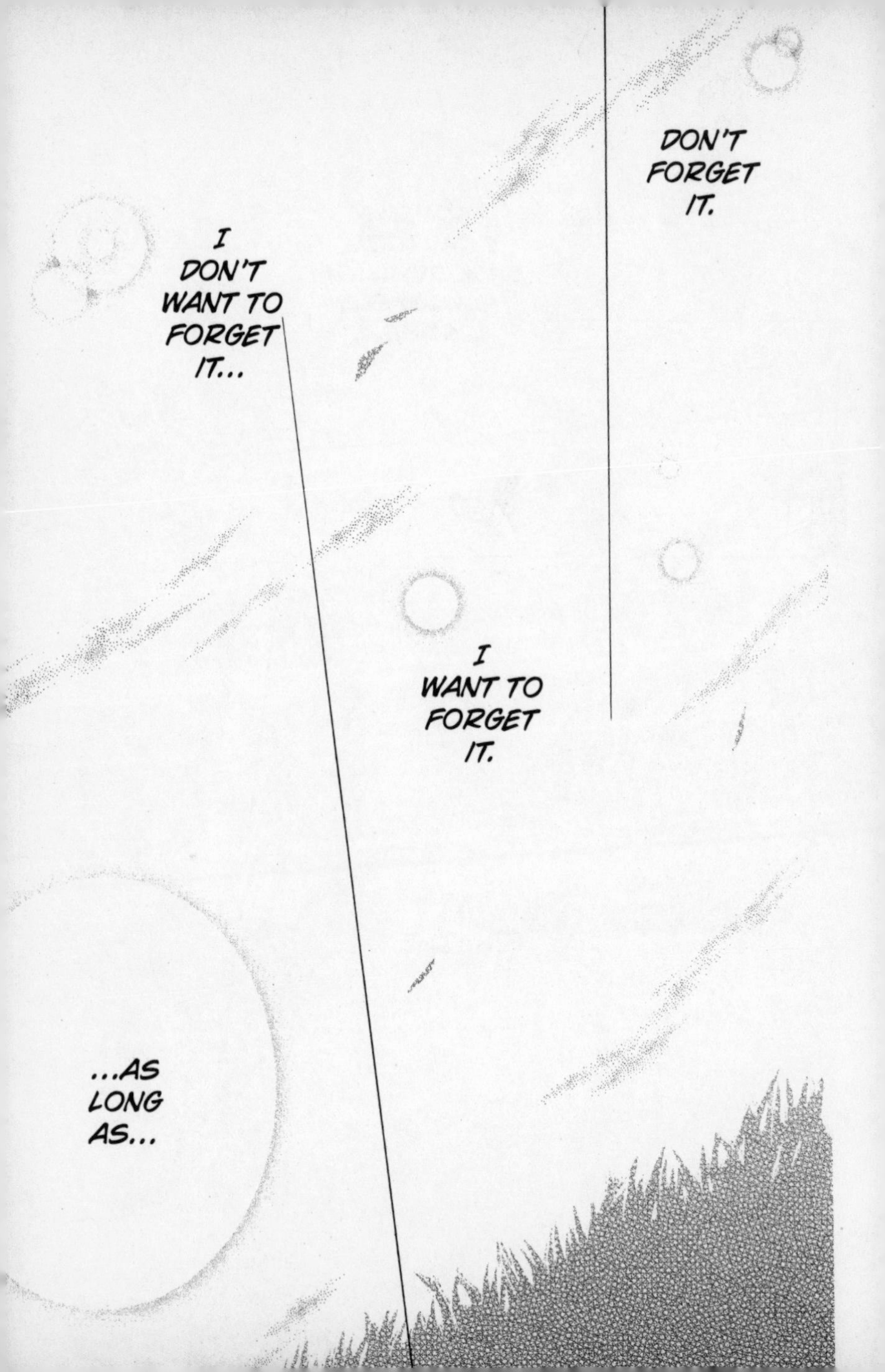
DON'T FORGET IT.
I WANT TO FORGET IT.
I DON'T WANT TO FORGET IT...
...AS LONG AS...

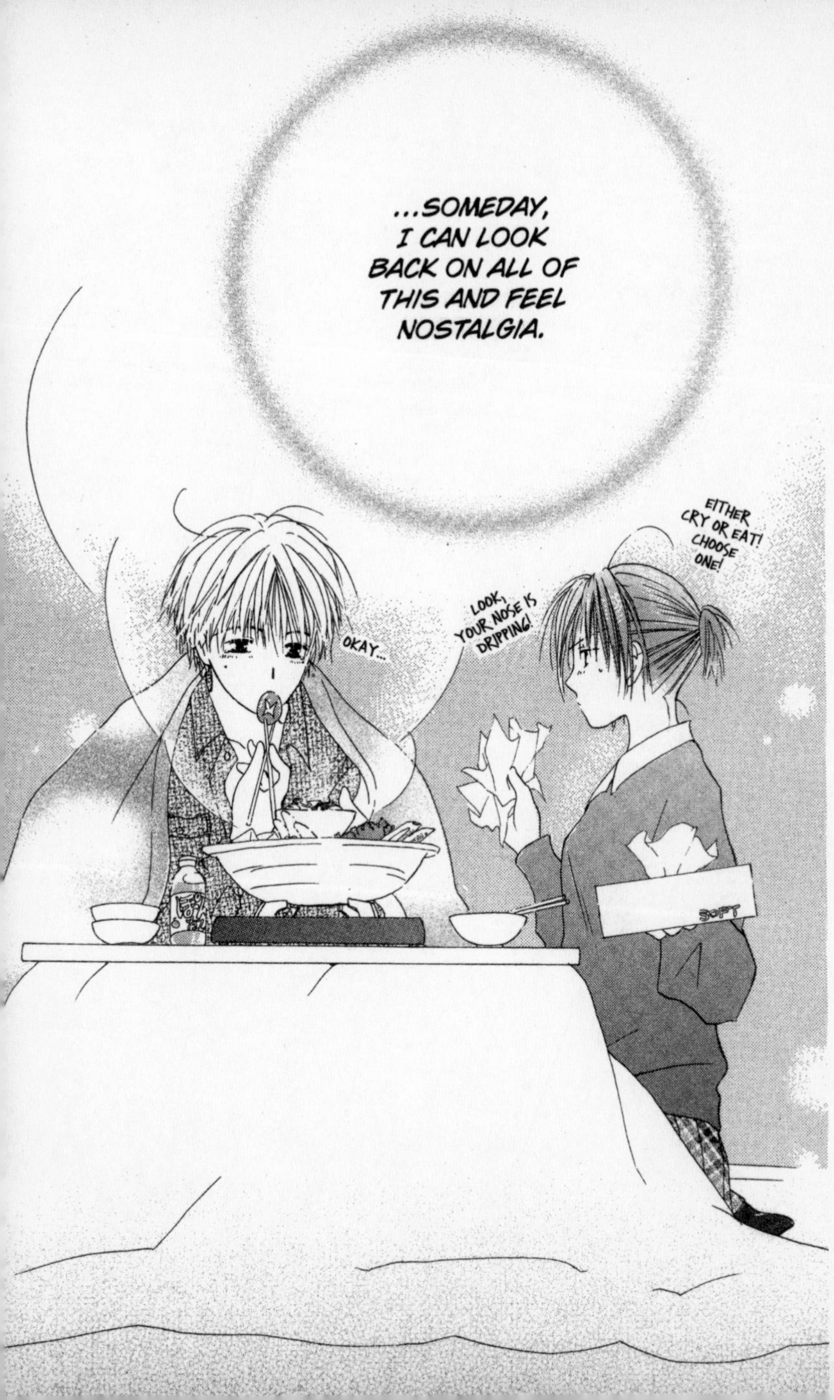
...SOMEDAY, I CAN LOOK BACK ON ALL OF THIS AND FEEL NOSTALGIA.
EITHER CRY OR EAT! CHOOSE ONE!
LOOK, YOUR NOSE IS DRIPPING!
OKAY...
SOFT

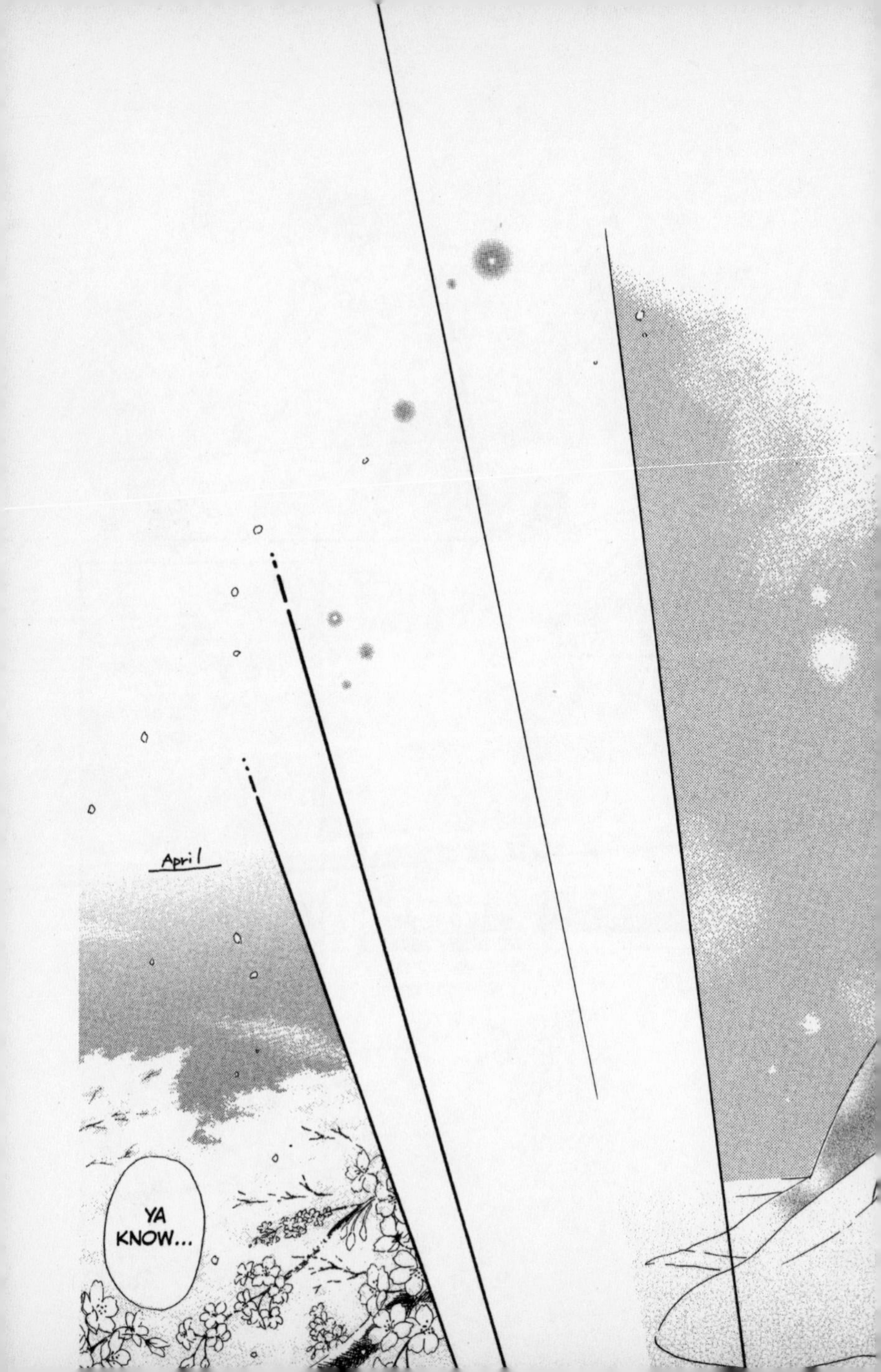
April
YA KNOW...

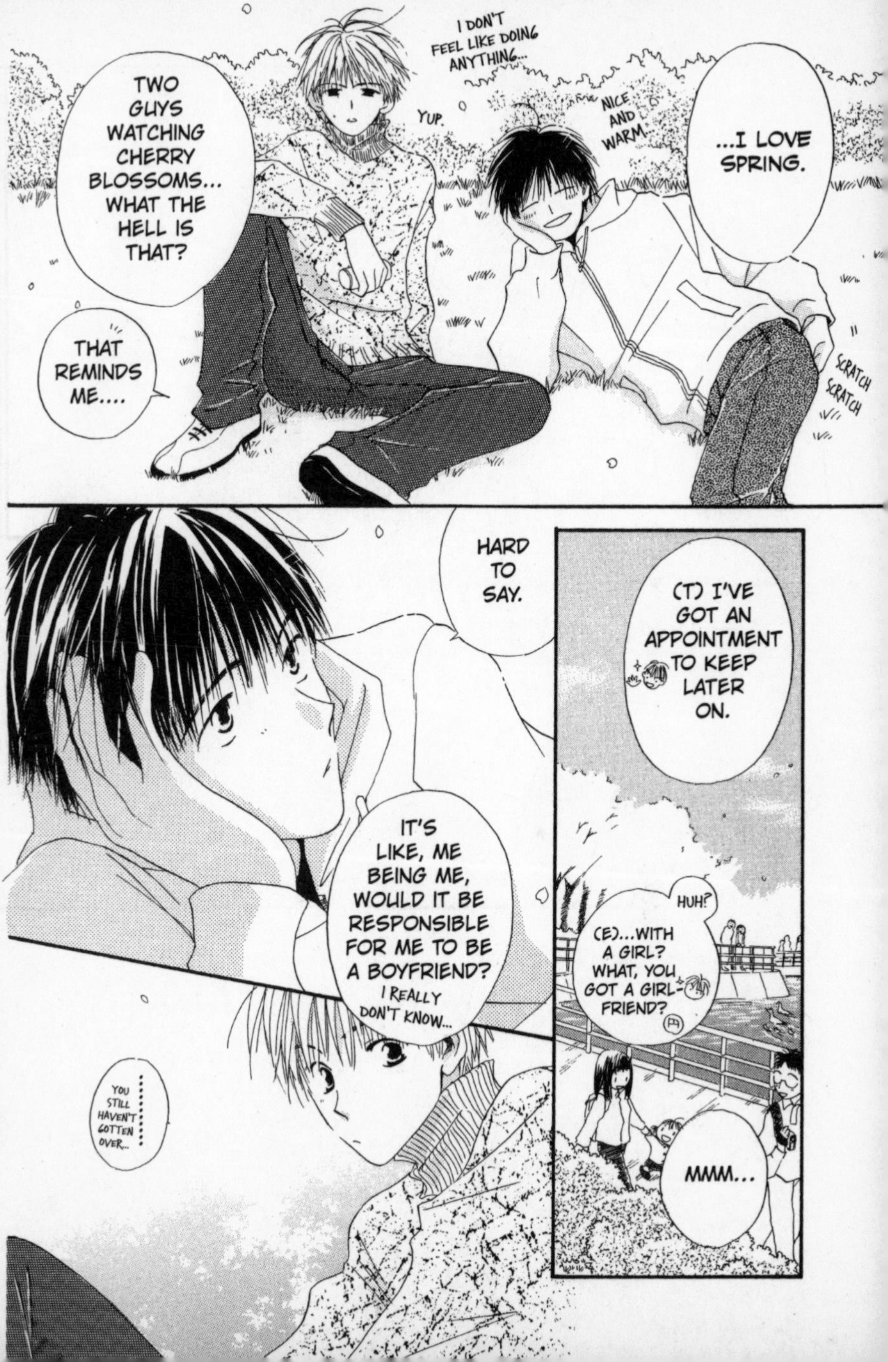
...I LOVE SPRING.
NICE AND WARM.
I DON'T FEEL LIKE DOING ANYTHING...
YUP.
TWO GUYS WATCHING CHERRY BLOSSOMS... WHAT THE HELL IS THAT?
SCRATCH SCRATCH
THAT REMINDS ME....
(T) I'VE GOT AN APPOINTMENT TO KEEP LATER ON.
HUH?
(E)...WITH A GIRL? WHAT, YOU GOT A GIRL-FRIEND?
MMM...
HARD TO SAY.
IT'S LIKE, ME BEING ME, WOULD IT BE RESPONSIBLE FOR ME TO BE A BOYFRIEND?
I REALLY DON'T KNOW...
YOU STILL HAVEN'T GOTTEN OVER...

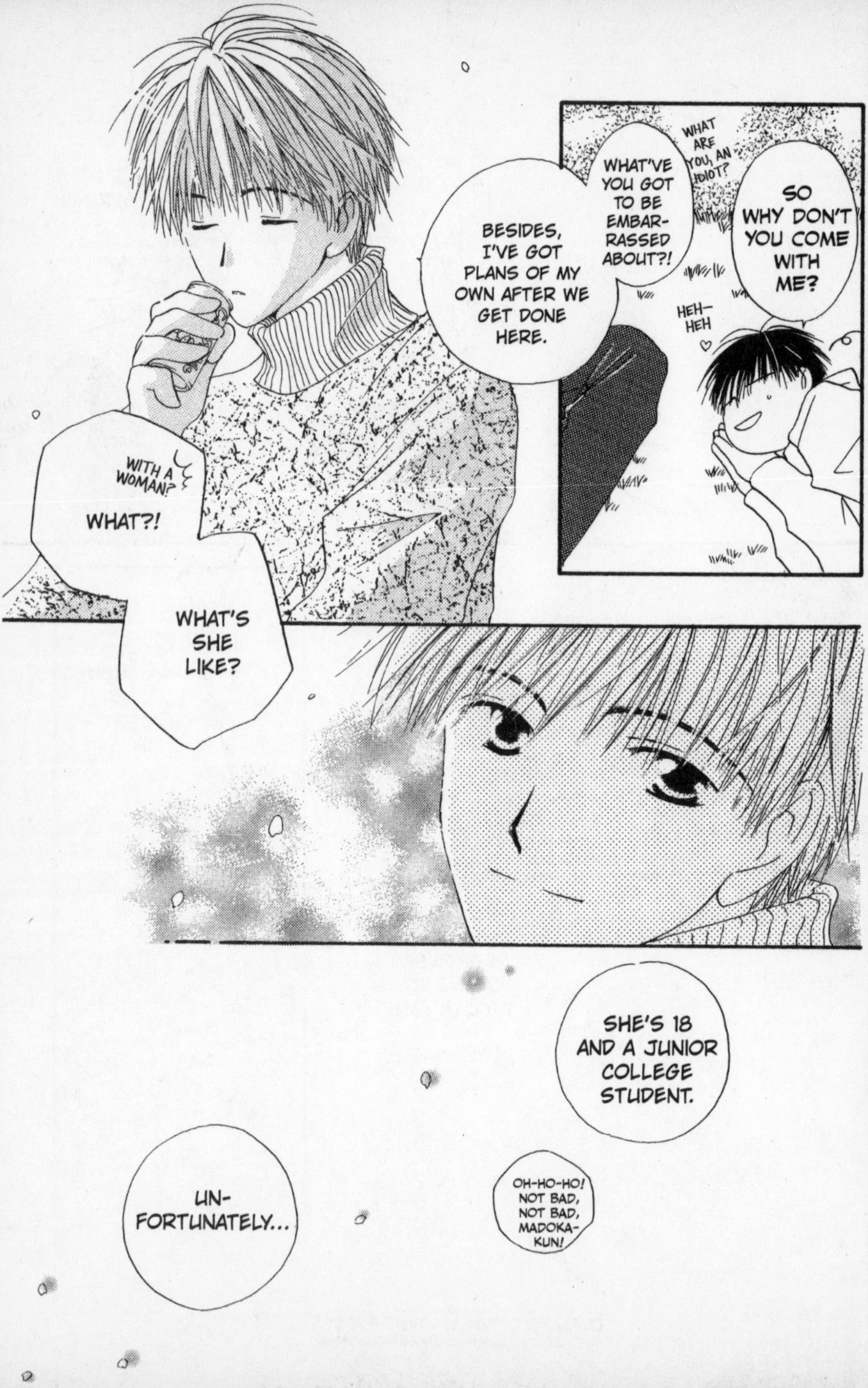
SO WHY DON'T YOU COME WITH ME?
HEH-HEH
WHAT ARE YOU, AN IDIOT?
WHAT'VE YOU GOT TO BE EMBAR-RASSED ABOUT?!
BESIDES, I'VE GOT PLANS OF MY OWN AFTER WE GET DONE HERE.
WITH A WOMAN?
WHAT?!
WHAT'S SHE LIKE?
SHE'S 18 AND A JUNIOR COLLEGE STUDENT.
OH-HO-HO! NOT BAD, NOT BAD, MADOKA-KUN!
UN-FORTUNATELY...

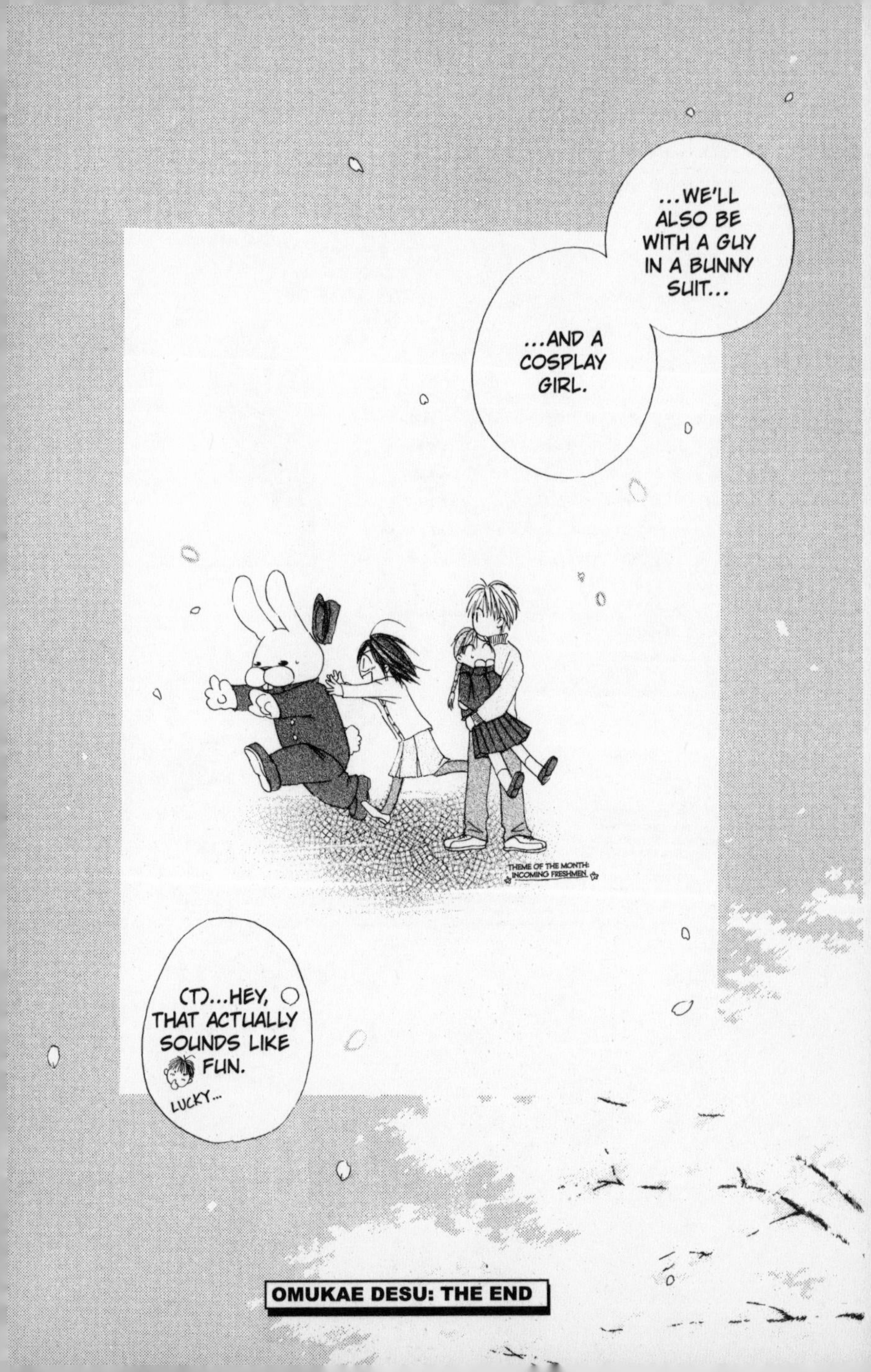
...WE'LL ALSO BE WITH A GUY IN A BUNNY SUIT...
...AND A COSPLAY GIRL.
THEME OF THE MONTH: INCOMING FRESHMEN
(T)...HEY, THAT ACTUALLY SOUNDS LIKE FUN.
LUCKY...
OMUKAE DESU: THE END

...Well.
a lot of time has passed between En-Chan bawling his eyes out and cherry blossom season. Because of this, I tried doing a bonus story that may shed some light on whether something happened in the interim. Those of you with free time, please read the following story, set the night before Valentine's day.♡

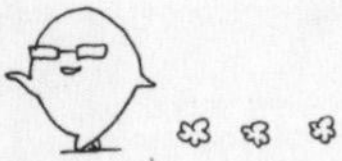

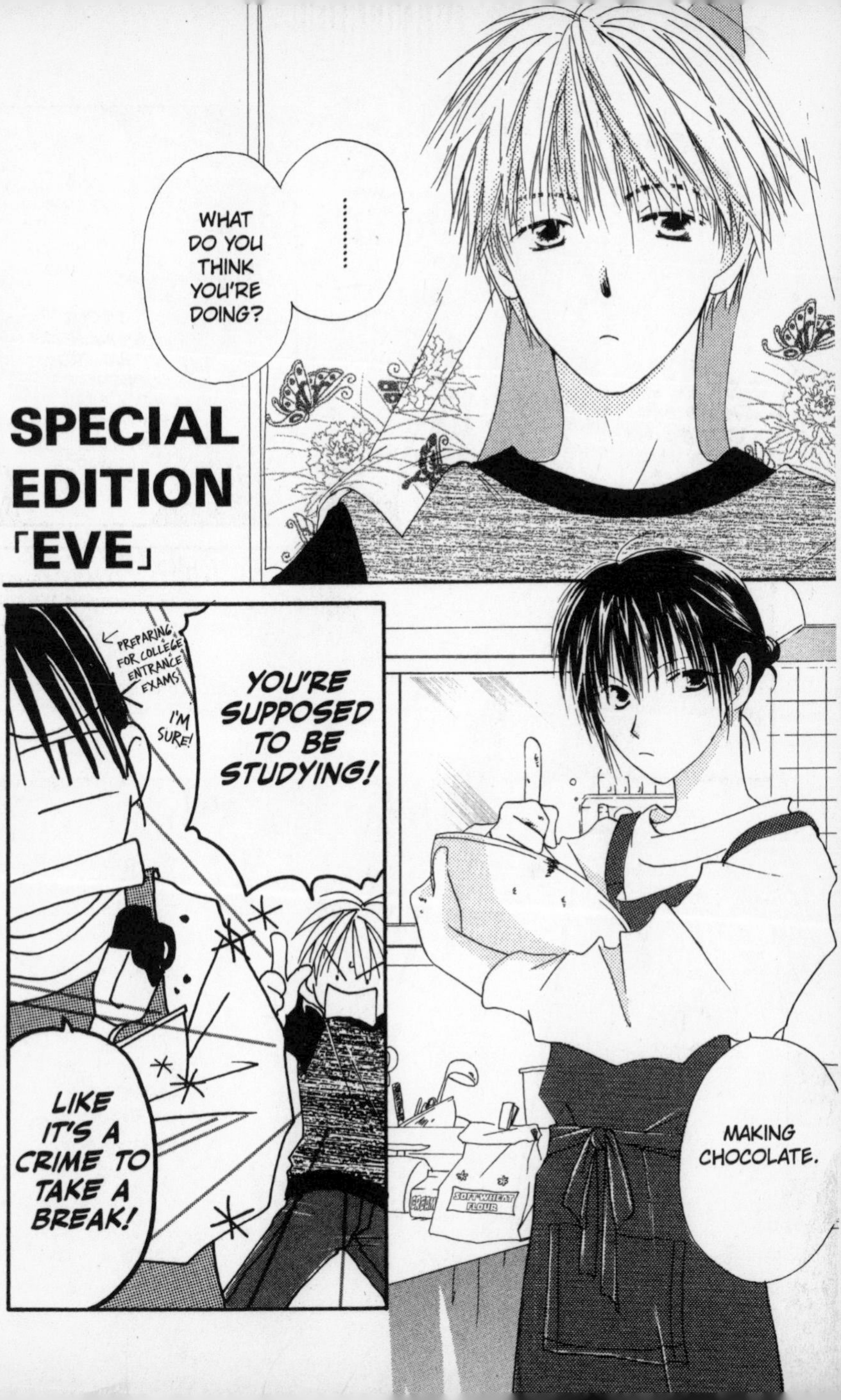

......
WHAT DO YOU THINK YOU'RE DOING?
SPECIAL EDITION 「EVE」
MAKING CHOCOLATE.
YOU'RE SUPPOSED TO BE STUDYING!
PREPARING FOR COLLEGE ENTRANCE EXAMS
I'M SURE!
LIKE IT'S A CRIME TO TAKE A BREAK!

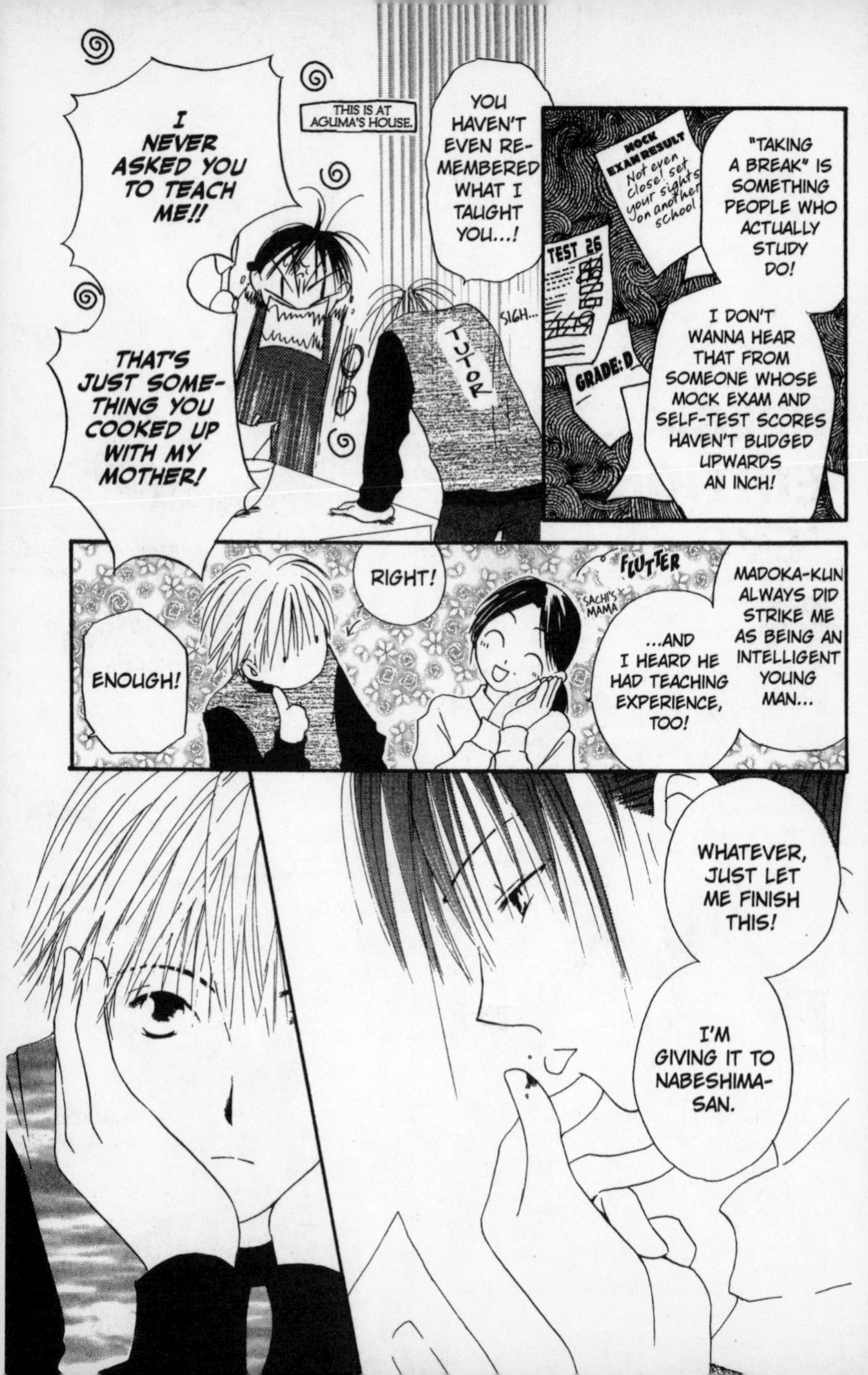
MOCK EXAM RESULT
Not even close! set your sights on another school
TEST 26
GRADE: D
"TAKING A BREAK" IS SOMETHING PEOPLE WHO ACTUALLY STUDY DO!
I DON'T WANNA HEAR THAT FROM SOMEONE WHOSE MOCK EXAM AND SELF-TEST SCORES HAVEN'T BUDGED UPWARDS AN INCH!
THIS IS AT AGUMA'S HOUSE.
YOU HAVEN'T EVEN RE-MEMBERED WHAT I TAUGHT YOU...!
SIGH...
TUTOR
I NEVER ASKED YOU TO TEACH ME!!
THAT'S JUST SOME-THING YOU COOKED UP WITH MY MOTHER!
MADOKA-KUN ALWAYS DID STRIKE ME AS BEING AN INTELLIGENT YOUNG MAN...
FLUTTER
SACHI'S MAMA
...AND I HEARD HE HAD TEACHING EXPERIENCE, TOO!
RIGHT!
ENOUGH!
WHATEVER, JUST LET ME FINISH THIS!
I'M GIVING IT TO NABESHIMA-SAN.

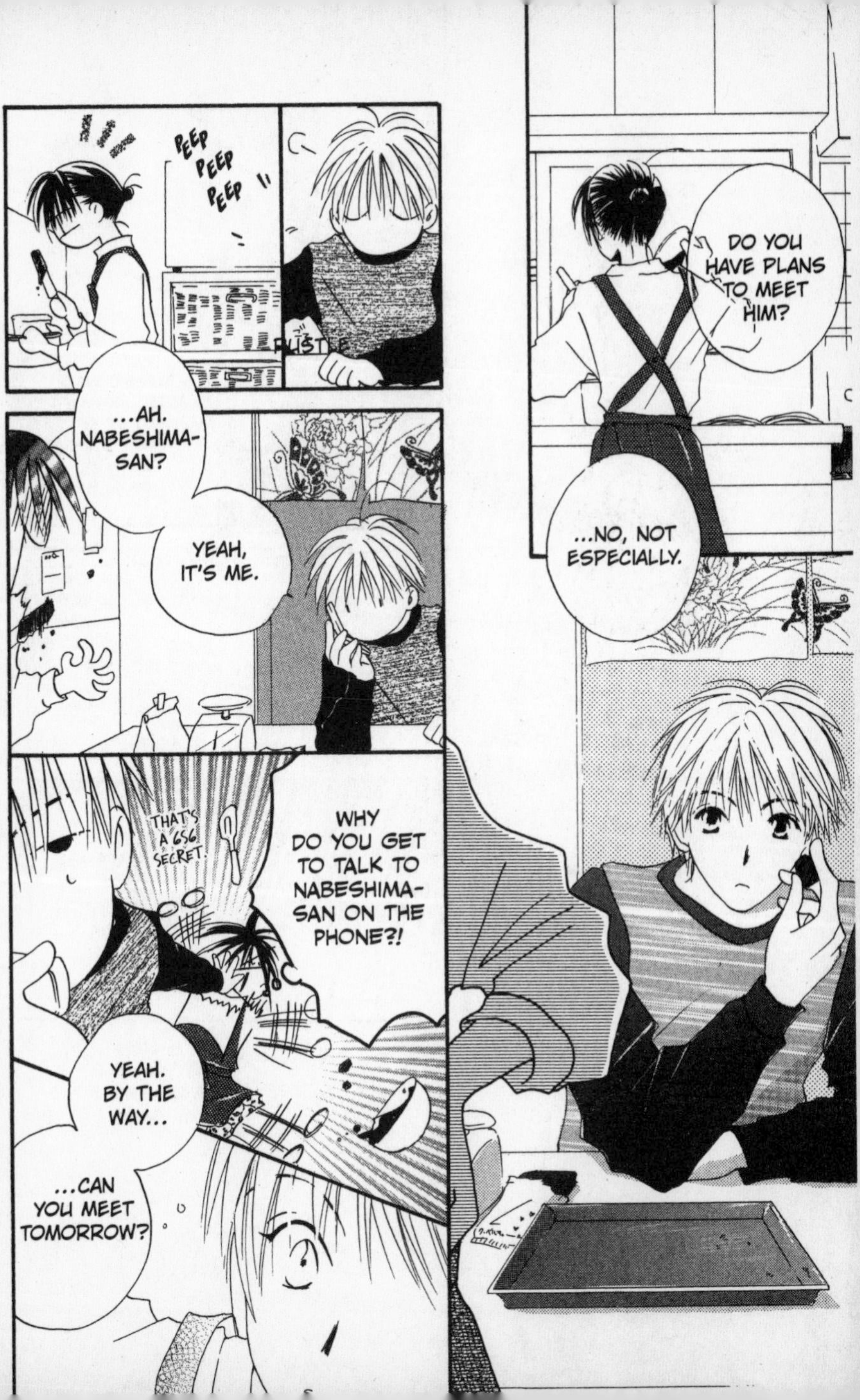
DO YOU HAVE PLANS TO MEET HIM?
...NO, NOT ESPECIALLY.
RUSTLE
PEEP PEEP PEEP
...AH. NABESHIMA-SAN?
YEAH, IT'S ME.
WHY DO YOU GET TO TALK TO NABESHIMA-SAN ON THE PHONE?!
THAT'S A 656 SECRET.
YEAH. BY THE WAY...
...CAN YOU MEET TOMORROW?

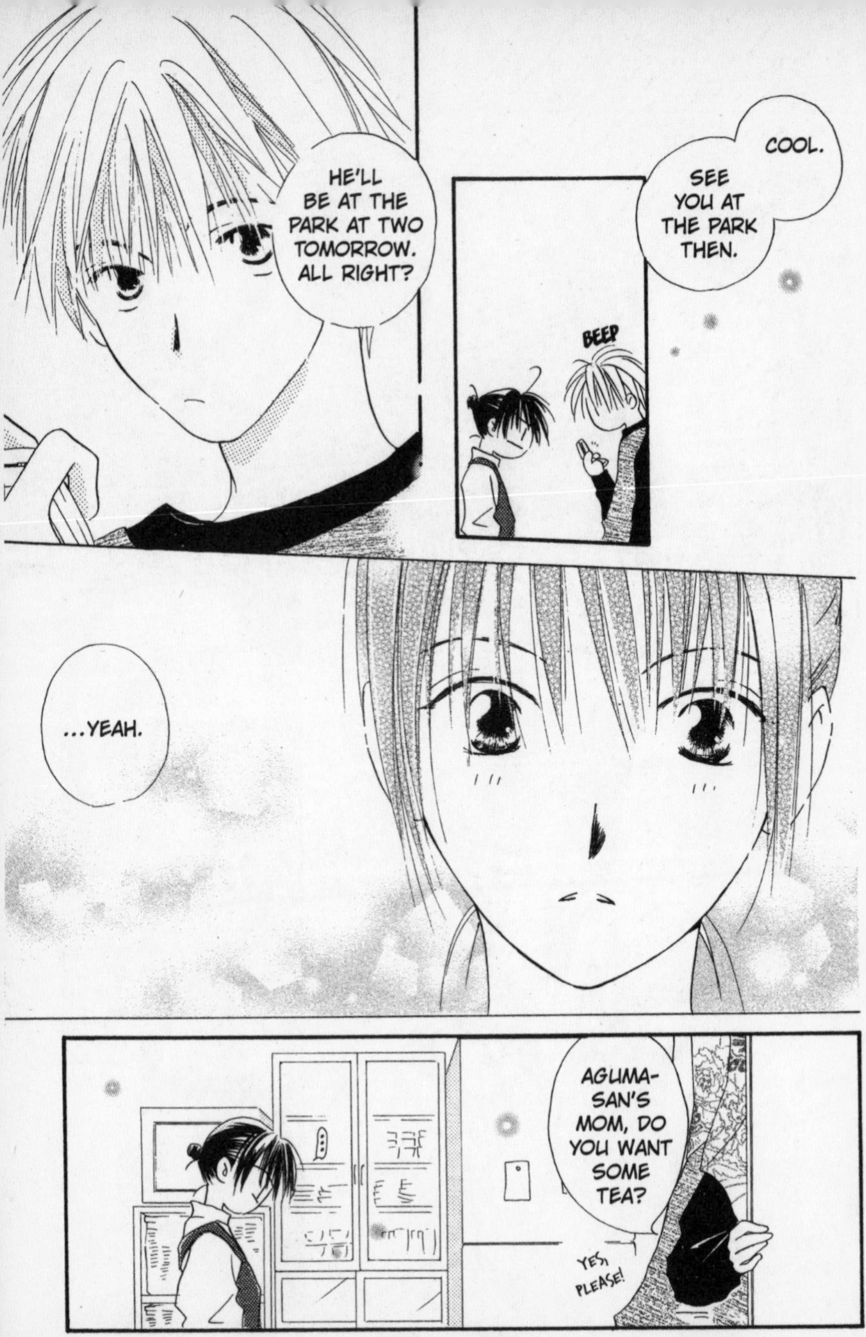
COOL.
SEE YOU AT THE PARK THEN.
BEEP
HE'LL BE AT THE PARK AT TWO TOMORROW. ALL RIGHT?
...YEAH.
AGUMA-SAN'S MOM, DO YOU WANT SOME TEA?
YES, PLEASE!

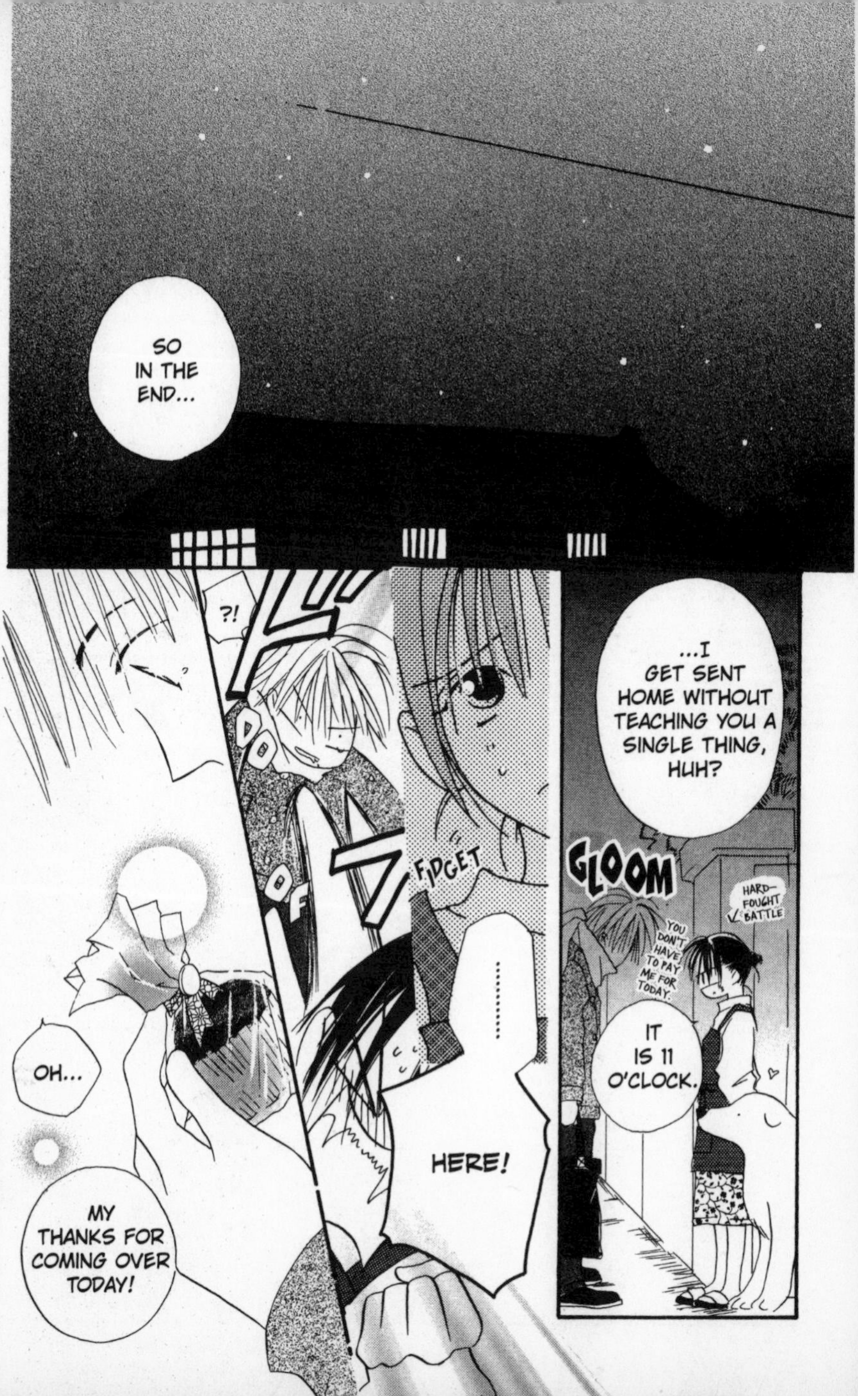
SO IN THE END...
...I GET SENT HOME WITHOUT TEACHING YOU A SINGLE THING, HUH?
GLOOM
HARD-FOUGHT BATTLE
YOU DON'T HAVE TO PAY ME FOR TODAY.
IT IS 11 O'CLOCK.
FIDGET
......
HERE!
?!
OH...
MY THANKS FOR COMING OVER TODAY!

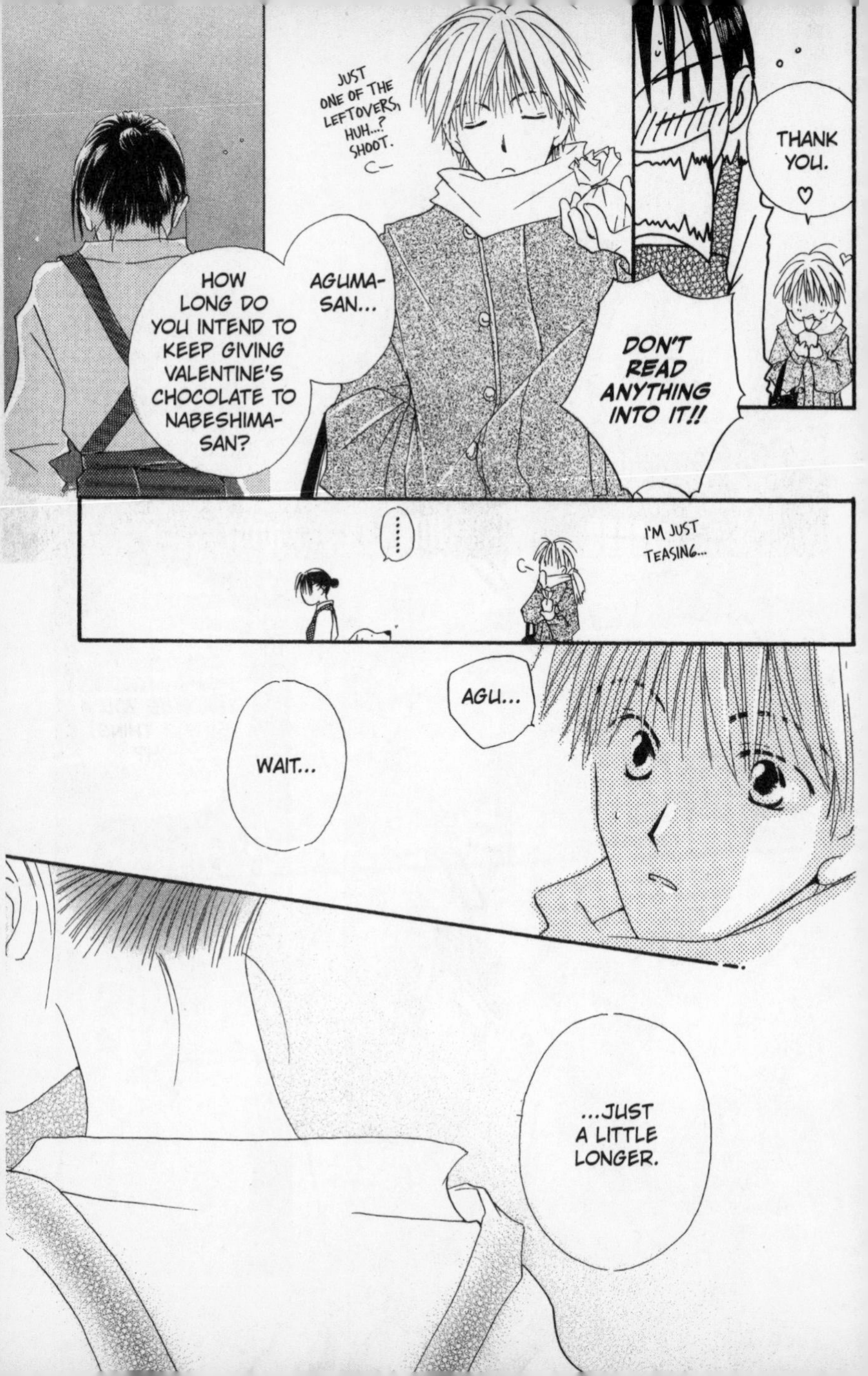
THANK YOU. ♥
DON'T READ ANYTHING INTO IT!!
JUST ONE OF THE LEFTOVERS, HUH...? SHOOT.
AGUMA-SAN...
HOW LONG DO YOU INTEND TO KEEP GIVING VALENTINE'S CHOCOLATE TO NABESHIMA-SAN?
I'M JUST TEASING...
......
AGU...
WAIT...
...JUST A LITTLE LONGER.

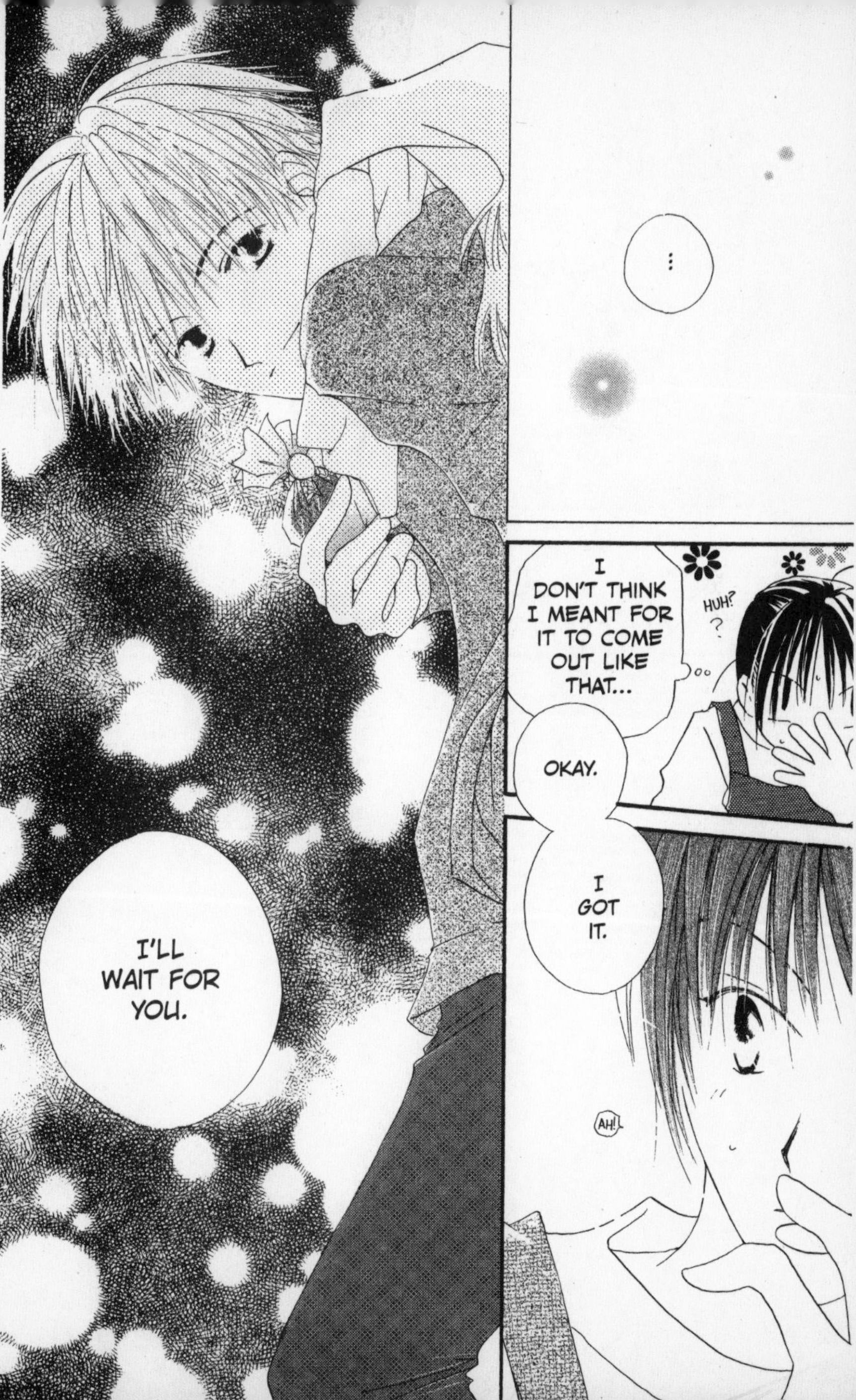
...
I DON'T THINK I MEANT FOR IT TO COME OUT LIKE THAT...
HUH?
OKAY.
I GOT IT.
AH!
I'LL WAIT FOR YOU.

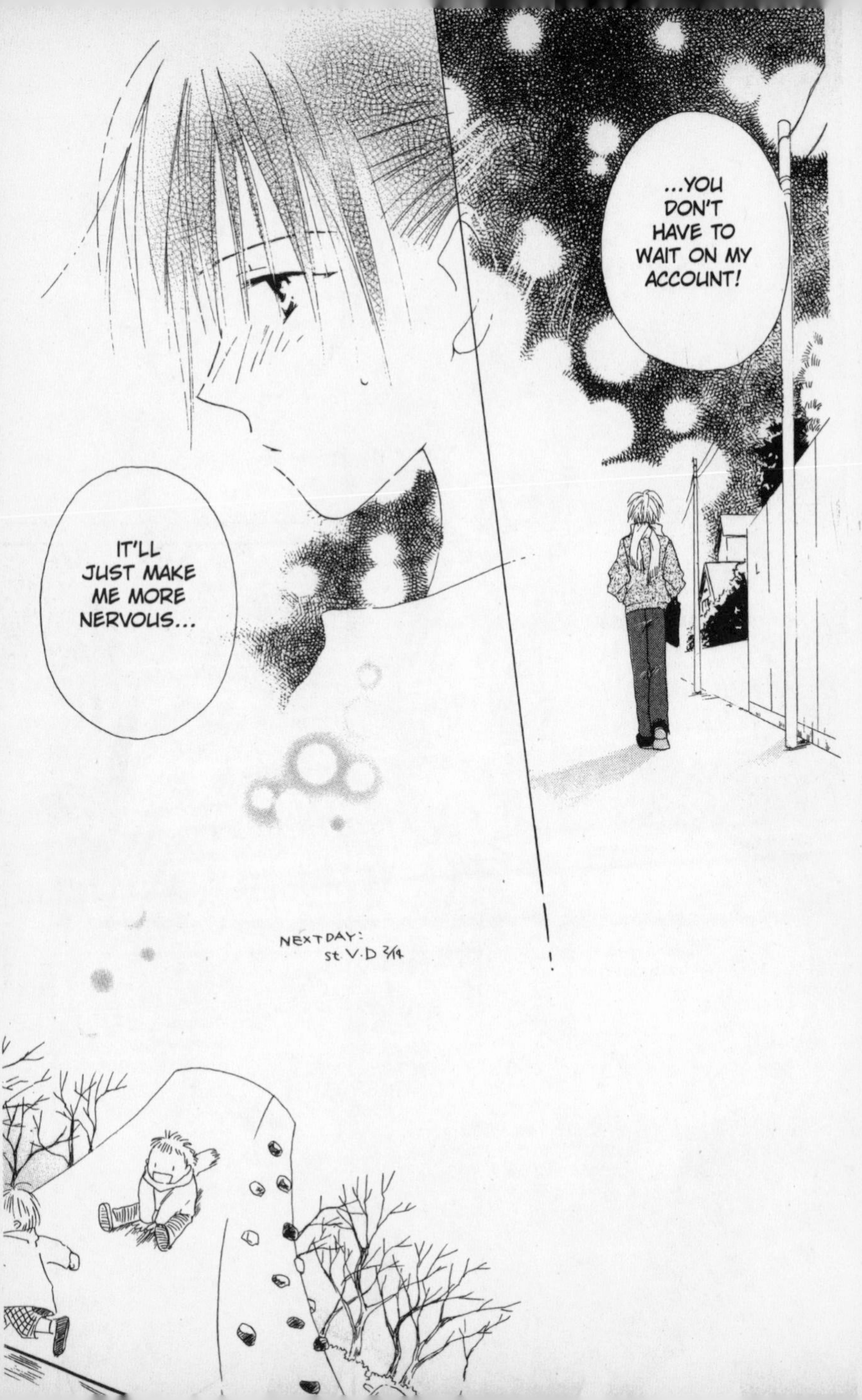
...YOU DON'T HAVE TO WAIT ON MY ACCOUNT!
IT'LL JUST MAKE ME MORE NERVOUS...
NEXT DAY:
St. V.D 2/14

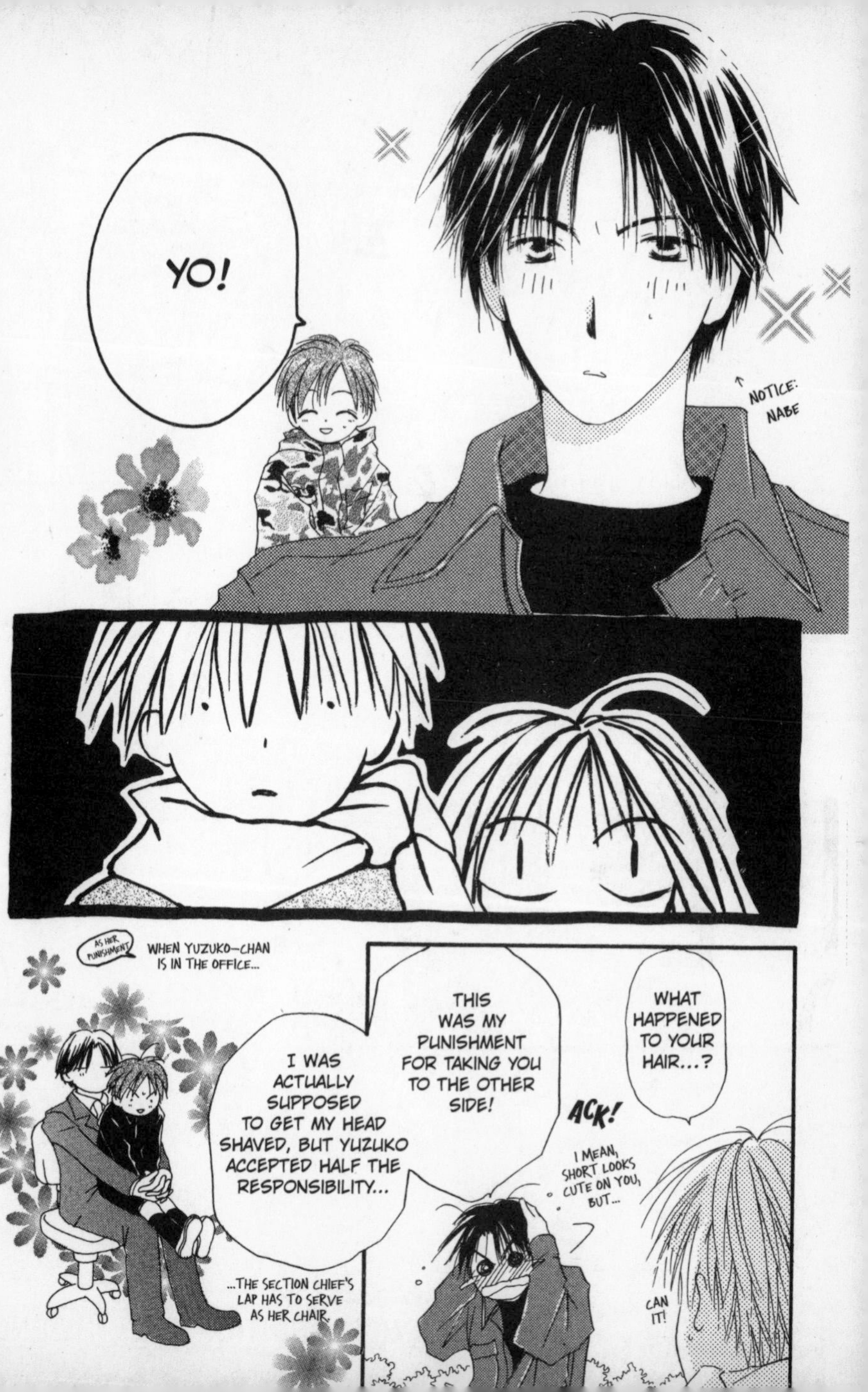
YO!
NOTICE: NABE
WHAT HAPPENED TO YOUR HAIR...?
ACK!
I MEAN, SHORT LOOKS CUTE ON YOU, BUT...
CAN IT!
THIS WAS MY PUNISHMENT FOR TAKING YOU TO THE OTHER SIDE!
I WAS ACTUALLY SUPPOSED TO GET MY HEAD SHAVED, BUT YUZUKO ACCEPTED HALF THE RESPONSIBILITY...
AS HER PUNISHMENT
WHEN YUZUKO-CHAN IS IN THE OFFICE...
...THE SECTION CHIEF'S LAP HAS TO SERVE AS HER CHAIR.

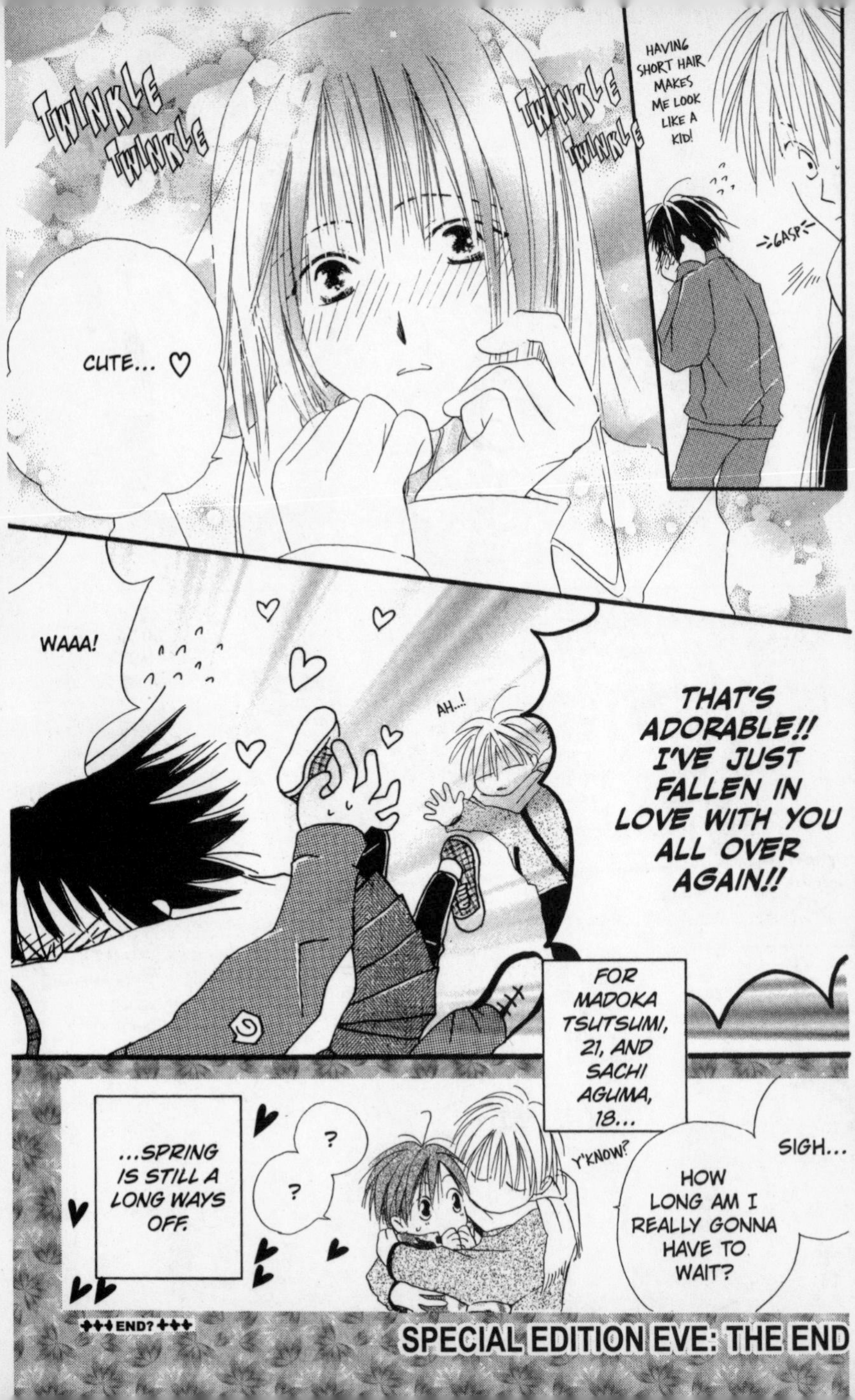
HAVING SHORT HAIR MAKES ME LOOK LIKE A KID!
GASP
TWINKLE TWINKLE
TWINKLE TWINKLE
CUTE... ♡
THAT'S ADORABLE!! I'VE JUST FALLEN IN LOVE WITH YOU ALL OVER AGAIN!!
AH..!
WAAA!
FOR MADOKA TSUTSUMI, 21, AND SACHI AGUMA, 18...
SIGH...
HOW LONG AM I REALLY GONNA HAVE TO WAIT?
Y'KNOW?
?
?
...SPRING IS STILL A LONG WAYS OFF.
END?
SPECIAL EDITION EVE: THE END

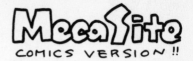

MecaSite
COMICS VERSION!!

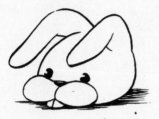

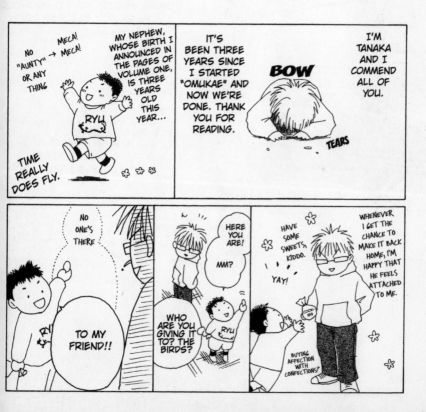

I'M TANAKA AND I COMMEND ALL OF YOU.
BOW
IT'S BEEN THREE YEARS SINCE I STARTED "OMUKAE" AND NOW WE'RE DONE. THANK YOU FOR READING.
TEARS
MY NEPHEW, WHOSE BIRTH I ANNOUNCED IN THE PAGES OF VOLUME ONE, IS THREE YEARS OLD THIS YEAR...
MECA! → MECA!
NO "AUNTY" OR ANY THING
RYU
TIME REALLY DOES FLY.
WHENEVER I GET THE CHANCE TO MAKE IT BACK HOME, I'M HAPPY THAT HE FEELS ATTACHED TO ME.
HAVE SOME SWEETS, KIDDO.
YAY!
COOK-IES
BUYING AFFECTION WITH CONFECTIONS?
HERE YOU ARE!
MM?
WHO ARE YOU GIVING IT TO? THE BIRDS?
RYU
NO ONE'S THERE
TO MY FRIEND!!
RY

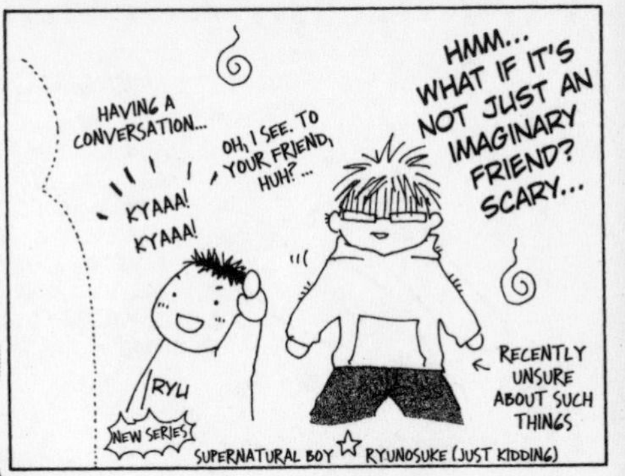
HMM... WHAT IF IT'S NOT JUST AN IMAGINARY FRIEND? SCARY...
OH, I SEE. TO YOUR FRIEND, HUH?...
HAVING A CONVERSATION...
KYAAA! KYAAA!
RECENTLY UNSURE ABOUT SUCH THINGS
RYU
NEW SERIES
SUPERNATURAL BOY ☆ RYUNOSUKE (JUST KIDDING)

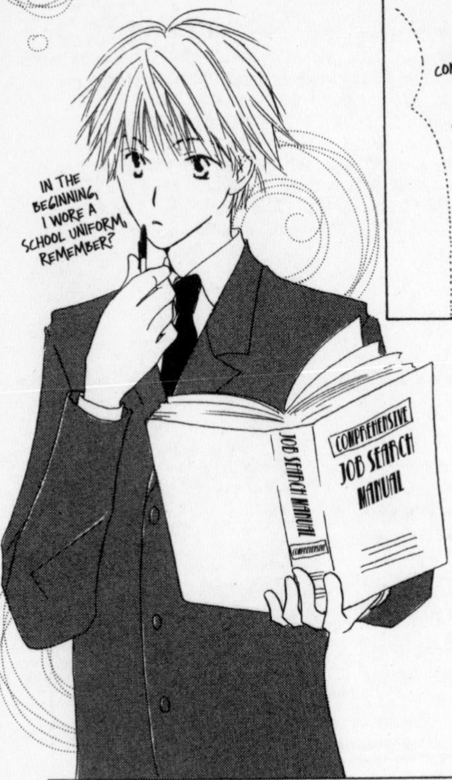
IN THE BEGINNING, I WORE A SCHOOL UNIFORM, REMEMBER?
COMPREHENSIVE JOB SEARCH MANUAL

IN THE SPACE OF THREE YEARS, A SIXTH GRADER BECOMES A THIRD-YEAR JUNIOR HIG SCHOOL SENIOR AND A 17-YEAR-OL GIRL OR BOY BECOMES 20. WOW...

THE CHARACTERS IN OMUKAE ALSO AGED IN REAL-TIME.

AROUND ABOUT NOW, EN-CHAN IS PROBABLY WEARING A SUIT AS HE GOES JOB HUNTING. WHAT KIND OF WORK COULD HE POSSIBLY BE SUITABLE FOR?

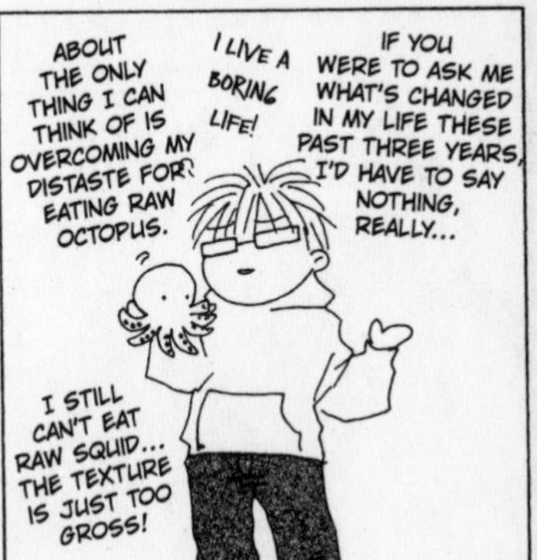
IF YOU WERE TO ASK ME WHAT'S CHANGED IN MY LIFE THESE PAST THREE YEARS, I'D HAVE TO SAY NOTHING, REALLY...
I LIVE A BORING LIFE!
ABOUT THE ONLY THING I CAN THINK OF IS OVERCOMING MY DISTASTE FOR EATING RAW OCTOPUS.
I STILL CAN'T EAT RAW SQUID... THE TEXTURE IS JUST TOO GROSS!

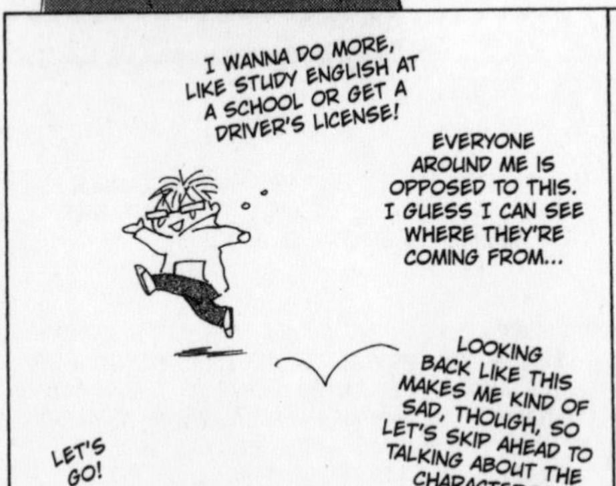
I WANNA DO MORE, LIKE STUDY ENGLISH AT A SCHOOL OR GET A DRIVER'S LICENSE!
EVERYONE AROUND ME IS OPPOSED TO THIS. I GUESS I CAN SEE WHERE THEY'RE COMING FROM...
LOOKING BACK LIKE THIS MAKES ME KIND OF SAD, THOUGH, SO LET'S SKIP AHEAD TO TALKING ABOUT THE CHARACTERS!
LET'S GO!

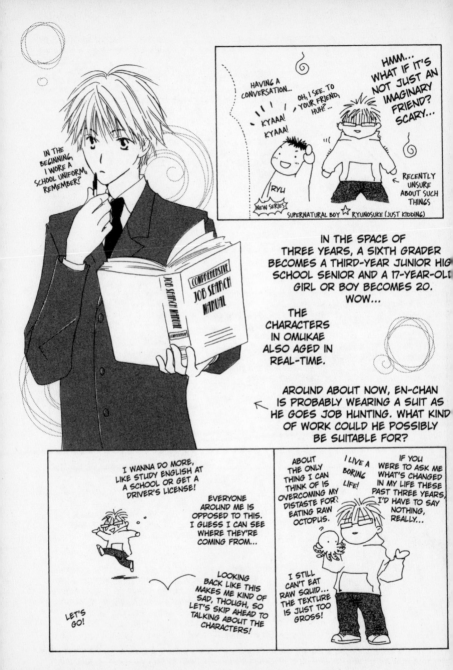

IN THE ORDER OF THEIR POPULARITY, ACCORDING TO LALA MAGAZINE* READER RESPONSE

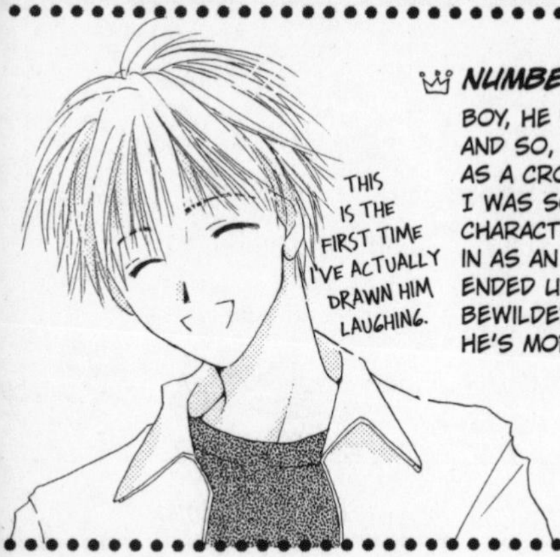
THIS IS THE FIRST TIME I'VE ACTUALLY DRAWN HIM LAUGHING.

NUMBER ONE: MADOKA TSUTSUMI

BOY, HE WAS REALLY POPULAR... AND SO, I'M HAVING HIM GO OUT WITH A SMILE, AS A CROWD-PLEASER. IN THE VERY FIRST STORY, I WAS SO FOCUSED ON THE GUEST GHOST CHARACTER THAT I ALMOST THREW EN-CHAN IN AS AN AFTERTHOUGHT AND THIS IS HOW HE ENDED UP. HE'S THE TYPE THAT LEAVES EVERYONE BEWILDERED AS TO HIS TRUE FEELINGS. I HOPE HE'S MORE OPEN WITH HIS FEELINGS IN THE FUTURE.

NUMBER TWO: SACHI AGUMA

HER POPULARITY REALLY TOOK OFF DURING THE SECOND HALF OF THE SERIES RUN. I'VE EVEN RECEIVED MISSIVES ABOUT HER SAYING: "AT FIRST, I ACTUALLY HATED SACHI..." SHE'S A YOUNG GIRL WHO'S ASSERTIVE TO A FAULT BUT ISN'T USED TO BEING THE ***ASSERTEE***, SO SHE BLOWS HER STACK WHEN SHE GETS TEASED EVEN A LITTLE. SHE SHOULD BE CAREFUL AROUND EN-CHAN, THEN, WHO GETS A KICK OUT OF TEASING HER.

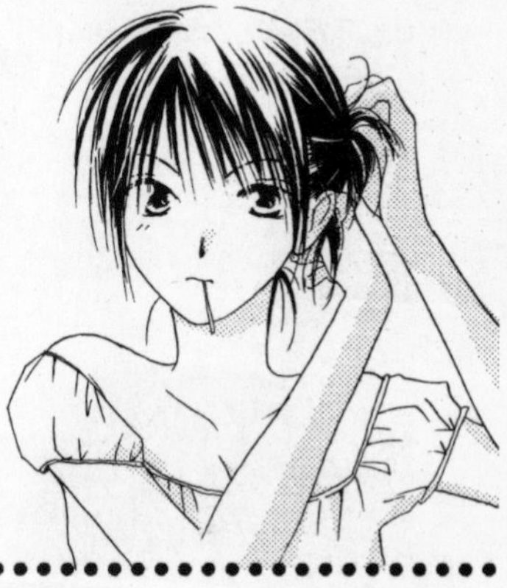

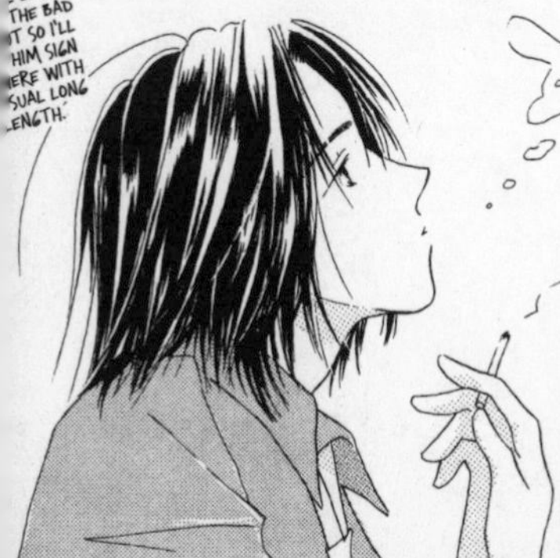
BAD
THE BAD
IT SO I'LL
HIM SIGN
HERE WITH
SUAL LONG
LENGTH."

NUMBER THREE: NABESHIMA

SORRY THAT I CUT HIS HAIR. ACTUALLY, I WANTED TO GIVE HIM A CREWCUT, BUT WHEN I TRIED DRAWING IT...

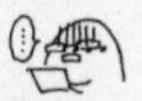

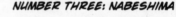

IT DIDN'T LOOK RIGHT AT ALL. SO I TOSSED OFF SOMETHING THAT WAS "EH." I FEEL SORRY FOR NABESHIMA-SAN BECAUSE MOST OF THE LETTERS THAT SAID, "I LOVE NABESHIMA" WERE APPENDED WITH "IN THE BUNNY SUIT"...HE WAS THE CHARACTER WHO CHANGED THE LEAST FROM BEGINNING TO END.

*LALA IS A POPULAR, MONTHLY MAGAZINE IN JAPAN, WHERE OMUKAE DESU WAS FIRST PUBLISHED.)

NUMBER FOUR: YUZUKO

IN HER FIRST APPEARANCE, SHE WAS JUST A BRAT, BUT SOMEWHERE ALONG THE LINE, SHE EVOLVED INTO A MOTHERLY CHARACTER. SHE REALLY IS THE MOST ADULT OF THE BUNCH. SHE GETS APPROACHED SERIOUSLY BY THE SECTION CHIEF, BUT MANAGES TO TURN HIM DOWN WITH A SMILE. I THINK SHE'S SECRETLY IN LOVE WITH NABESHIMA, WHO NOTICES BUT PRETENDS NOT TO...HERE'S MY LAST DEPICTION OF THAT FEELING.

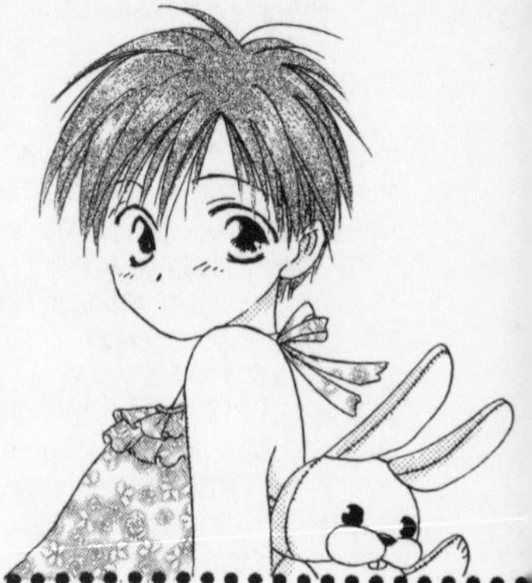

NUMBER FIVE: TSUDA-KUN

YOU KNOW, I NEVER DID THINK OF A FIRST NAME FOR HIM. SORRY. I FELT LIKE I HAD TO USE HIM IN THE CLOSING ACT. ODD, BUT IT'S BEEN A YEAR SINCE "GOODBYE, SHOOTING STAR" AND IT SEEMS LIKE TSUDA-KUN STILL HASN'T MADE HANA-CHAN HIS FULL-FLEDGED GIRLFRIEND... MAYBE SOON?

NUMBER SIX: CHISATO OGAWA

CHISA-CHI ALWAYS PUTS UP A GOOD FIGHT AND IN THE END GAVE EN-CHAN A MUCH-NEEDED PEP TALK. I THOUGHT MAYBE SHE COULD'VE ACTED A LITTLE MORE SELFISHLY BUT AS A DENIZEN OF THE "OTHER SIDE," I GUESS SHE IS SOMEWHAT IMMUNE TO THE WEAKNESSES OF "OUR SIDE."

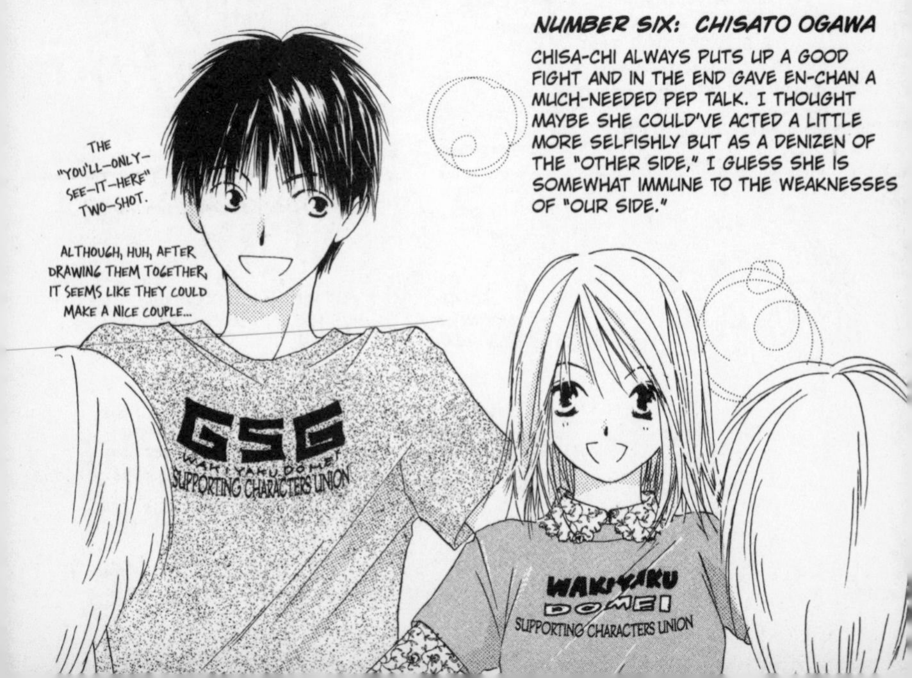
THE "YOU'LL-ONLY-SEE-IT-HERE" TWO-SHOT.
ALTHOUGH, HUH, AFTER DRAWING THEM TOGETHER, IT SEEMS LIKE THEY COULD MAKE A NICE COUPLE...
GSG
WAKIYAKU DOMEI
SUPPORTING CHARACTERS UNION
WAKIYAKU DOMEI
SUPPORTING CHARACTERS UNION

LAST MUTTERINGS.

WHEN I FIRST STARTED WORKING ON "OMUKAE," I WAS STILL A FULL-TIME WORKER. THE PLACE I WORKED AT WAS A SMALL DESIGN FIRM, WHERE EVERYONE WAS FRIENDLY AND MY BOSS WAS SO KIND THAT HE WAS MY GUARANTOR FOR THE APARTMENT I LIVED IN THEN. IT WAS A GREAT PLACE. EVEN WHEN I SELFISHLY TOLD MY BOSS THAT I WAS GOING TO QUIT BECAUSE I WANTED TO DO MANGA, HE GAVE ME HIS BLESSING AND SAID THAT AS MY BOSS, HE DIDN'T WANT TO SEE ME GO, BUT AS MY FRIEND, WOULD CONTINUE TO SUPPORT ME. AND SO, I'VE COMPLETED FIVE VOLUMES OF THIS SERIES. OF COURSE, I NEVER COULD HAVE DONE IT WITHOUT THE SUPPORT AND ENCOURAGEMENT OF ALL OF YOU FANS, BUT I'LL NEVER FORGET THE KINDNESS OF EVERYONE AT MY FORMER COMPANY, WHO LISTENED TO MY SELFISHNESS AND ALLOWED ME TO INDULGE MY PASSION.

I STILL DON'T FEEL LIKE I CAN PUFF MY CHEST OUT WITH PRIDE, BUT AT LEAST I HAVE SOMETHING TO SHOW ALL THE PEOPLE BACKING ME UP. FROM HERE ON IN, I INTEND TO CONTINUE MAKING MANGA, NEVER FORGETTING THAT I DON'T DO IT ALONE, BUT WITH THE SUPPORT OF MANY, MANY PEOPLE.

THANK YOU VERY MUCH FOR BEARING WITH ME.

WITH HARUKA BABA.

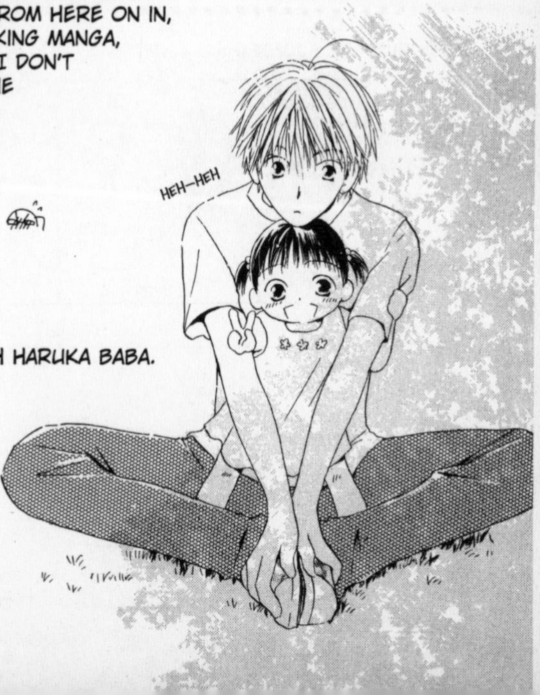
HEH-HEH

THANKS!!

MASTER CHIE YAMAMOTO
MY HOMEPAGE DESIGNER, CHILD*PLANET
MY SUPER-HELPER, KOHATO UCHIDA
MY LOVELY HELPER, HITOMI ADACHI
MY EVIL FRIEND, BISCO NATORI
MY EDITOR, WHO WAS WITH ME THROUGH GOOD TIMES AND BAD
EVERYONE WHO SUPPORTED ME
EVERYONE WHO BOUGHT "OMUKAE DESU."

THANK YOU VERY MUCH!!

(MECA TANAKA)
LOOK OUT FOR MY NEXT SERIES

TSUTSUMI-STYLE JOKES (FINAL EDITION)

READ THIS WAY →

THREE YEARS HAVE PASSED...
UM, SO, DO YOU LIKE ANYONE NOW?
YOU KNOW I DO...
SWISH
HUH?
CAN I JUST CALL YOU YUZUKO?
AH!
HEY!
KYAAA!
NABE'S LEG
IT WAS JUST A JOKE!
JEEZ!
HOW MUCH OF IT?
ALMOST ALL.
"ALMOST?" OKAY, THEN, WHICH PART WAS...?
YOU KNOW WHICH PART...
SWISH
......
YUZUKO FAN

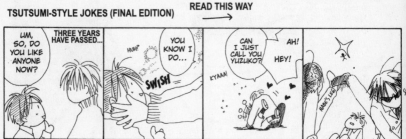

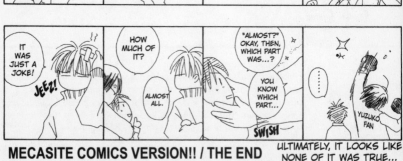

MECASITE COMICS VERSION!! / THE END

ULTIMATELY, IT LOOKS LIKE NONE OF IT WAS TRUE...

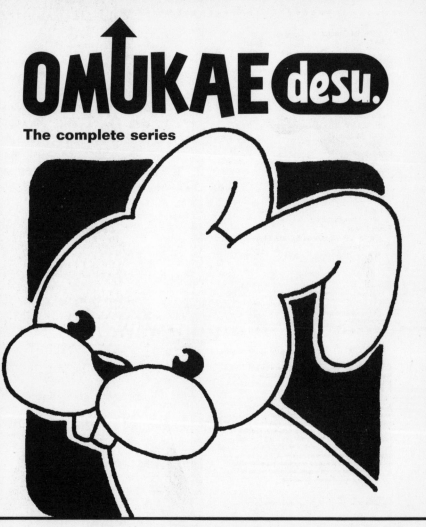